Poe and His Times

Poe and His Times
The Artist and His Milieu

Edited by

Benjamin Franklin Fisher IV

BALTIMORE: THE EDGAR ALLAN POE SOCIETY, INC.

Copyright 1990 by

The Edgar Allan Poe Society, Inc.

ISBN: 0-9616449-2-3

In Memory of

Emma L. Shoener

and

Susanna Tye

CONTENTS

Acknowledgments xi
Key to Recurring References... xii
Introduction xiii
Poe and Washington Allston: Visionary Kin
    Glen A. Omans.. 1
Poe, Locke and Kant
    Joan Dayan 30
Poe and the *Blackwood's* Tale of Sensation
    Bruce I. Weiner... 45
In Search of Truth and Beauty: Allegory in "Berenice"
and "The Domain of Arnheim"
    Liliane Weissberg... 66
"Visionary Wings": Art and Metaphysics in
Edgar Allan Poe's "Hans Pfaall"
    Maurice J. Bennett... 76
Prose Run Mad: An Early Criticism of Poe's *Politian*
    David K. Jackson 88
Poe and the Will
    April Selley 94
The Corpse Within Us
    Steven E. Kagle.. 103
Poe's "Ligeia": Debts to Irving and Emerson
    Jerry A. Herndon.. 113
Emerson, Thoreau, and Poe's "Double Dupin"
    Stanton Garner... 130
Usher's Nervous Fever: The Meaning of Medicine
in Poe's "The Fall of the House of Usher"
    David E. E. Sloane... 146
Poe's Chapters on "Natural Magic"
    Roberta Sharp.. 154
Poe's *Pym*-Esque "A Tale of the Ragged Mountains"
    Richard Kopley.. 167
"Eleonora": Poe and Madness
    Benjamin Franklin Fisher IV 178
"The Raven" and "The Bracelets"
    E. Kate Stewart.. 189
The Raven and the Nightingale
    David H. Hirsch... 194
Theme and Parody in "The Raven"
    Dennis W. Eddings... 209

CONTENTS

Edgar Allan Poe in France: Baudelaire's
Labor of Love
    Gary Wayne Harner 218
Elegy for a "Rebel Soul": Henry Clay Preuss
and the Poe Debate
    J. Gerald Kennedy 226
Elizabeth Oakes Smith on Poe: A Chapter in the
Recovery of His Nineteenth-Century Reputation
    Kent Ljungquist and Cameron Nickels 235
Henry James and the Question of Poe's Maturity
    James W. Gargano 247
In Defense of Beauty: Stedman and the
Recognition of Poe in America, 1880-1910
    Robert J. Scholnick 256
Contributors 277
Index 281

ACKNOWLEDGMENTS

My special gratitude to several persons must be expressed. First, to Brian Reade for gracious permission to reproduce the Beardsley plates that accompany Robert Scholnick's article. Second, to Mary F. and Richard A. Michael for kindness during my proofreading; to Richard Fusco, Robert W. Burns, Angela Dorenkamp, Mike Pettengell, Kelly Cannon, William J. Zimmer, Jr., Kent Ljungquist, Sara E. Selby, Harry M. Bayne, Jonathan C. Tutor, William E. Miller (Editor Emeritus of *The Library Chronicle* of the University of Pennsylvania), and Jeffrey A. Savoye for a variety of helpful contributions; and to Julie A. Fisher for her talents in computer operation and indexing. Finally, to the contributors, whose patience and cooperation have been memorable.

KEY TO RECURRING REFERENCES

Several works to which repeated citations are made, or from which quotations are frequently drawn, will be indicated in these abbreviations throughout this book.

H = The Complete Works of Edgar Allan Poe, ed. James A. Harrison, 17 vols. (New York, 1902; rpt. New York, 1965, 1979).

M = Collected Works of Edgar Allan Poe, ed. Thomas Ollive Mabbott, 3 vols. (Cambridge, Mass., 1969-1978).

O = The Letters of Edgar Allan Poe, ed. John Ward Ostrom, rev. ed. 2 vols. (New York, 1966).

INTRODUCTION

The essays assembled here have considerations of Poe in his milieu as their unifying theme, although the phrase "Poe and his times" may be deceptive if it suggests any severe chronological limitations. Poe, we know, might have lived well through, and beyond, the nineteenth century, and so some of the essays encompass literary movements or themes that are not bounded by the midpoint of the nineteenth century, the time of his death at an early age. In terms of the span of his own literary career, Poe stands as a transition figure who imparted renewed life to many cultural phenomena that had preceded him. Therefore in the following pages we will see him, for example, drawing into his own times the thought of Scottish Commonsense doctrines, as well as much that prefigures it, and turning them into new channels of thought. His like refashioning of Gothic tradition is so well known as to require no lengthy expatiation here. What will be found in the pages to come is, so to speak, "Poe's plenty": visionary poetics, the nineteenth-century critical climate, literary periodicals (with *Blackwood's* notable among them, to be sure), Gothic thrillers (replete with perishing frail beauties, eccentric male hero-villains, and backdrops well suited to such character-types), science and detective fiction, magic, metempsychosis, Transcendentalism, Romantic irony, humor of other types, premature burial, brutal versus laudatory (sometimes downright hagiographic) biographers, Poe and the visual arts, Poe and his revisions—and much more. Although the essays speak for themselves, we might pause over some clearcut significances to be found among them.

A companion volume entitled *Poe and Our Times: Influences and Affinities* (1986) revealed the great impact that Poe's short fiction, in particular, has had in our own century. This bonding should not be astonishing; as stated in the "Introduction" to the tales and sketches in Mabbott's edition of the *Collected Works of Edgar Allan Poe* (*M*2: xv), "Poe's tales are his chief contribution to the literature of the world." A follow-up reminds us, however, that Poe himself showed greater partiality toward the poems, not surprisingly since he came of literary age during a period that was dominated by the great Romantic movement in poetry and was affected by the advent of Tennyson. The present book offers more on Poe as poet, from material encountered in the opening essay, by G. A. Omans, to additional comments on Poe's verse interspersed throughout, and, most emphatically, in three essays that take as their central subject "The Raven," fittingly, no doubt, since it is probably better known the world over than many of Poe's other poems. These critiques of "The Raven" may well serve as correctives to presentations of that poem in Mutlu Konuk Blasing's *American Poetry: The Rhetoric of Its Forms* (1987) and in Donald E. Pease's

Visionary Compacts: American Renaissance Writings in Cultural Context (1987). Eddings's study addresses ironies pervading "The Raven," appropriately (in several senses), given that Mabbott's opinion of its being "a tale in verse" may express a great determining factor in its widespread appeal. Just so, Hirsch's essay gives Poe's poem context among other important Romantic poems, most particularly Keats's "Ode to a Nightingale." Hirsch's bracketing of Keats with Poe, moreover, invites further exploration of that subject. Stewart's examination of how "The Raven" devolves from "The Bracelets," a *Blackwood's* tale by Samuel Warren (whose fiction sustained great popularity in his era, though it has long since fallen into neglect), maintains another parallel of Poe with the British Romantics and reveals the spaciousness of his memory as he drew on a commonplace short story to create great literary art. Albeit brief, Stewart's essay stands as a companion piece to Weiner's, which turns new wine into old bottles (without disastrous consequences), of the *Blackwood's*–Poe links. Weiner's views of Poe and the sensational tale compliment those of David S. Reynolds in *Beneath the American Renaissance: The Subversive Imagination in the Age of Emerson and Melville* (1988). Along with Weiner's, the essays by Weissberg and Dayan provide analytical coverage of Poe's philosophical groundings, which, as they demonstrate, reach back into time and across the cultural sea.

Politian, *Pym*, and *Eureka* also come in for merited attention within these pages. Any effort on behalf of the first named work is refreshing because this dramatic fragment has usually drawn cursory, if any, attention from the majority of Poe's critics. David Jackson's essay bears the stamp of his better than half-a-century's unflagging meticulousness in ferreting out little-known, but illuminating, information that enriches the study of Poe. Sharp and Kopley also shed interesting light on *Pym*, the former by highlighting Poe's sources (for *Pym* and other pieces) in Brewster's *Letters on Natural Magic*, and the latter by juxtaposing the novel to "A Tale of the Ragged Mountains." *Eureka*, with its longer-standing recognition as a signal Poe text, continues to furnish solidity in the foundations of many critiques about its creator, and thus it receives additional warranted attention here. Many of the comments about *Eureka*, as well as those by Hirsch on Keats and Poe and my own on Tennyson and Poe, might profitably be read in tandem with views offered by Leon Chai in *Romantic Foundations of the American Renaissance* (1987).

Poe among his contemporaries furnishes the staple for many of the following essays. In his responses to Transcendentalism, Poe continues to attract attention, as has been attested recently by Eric W. Carlson in *Critical Essays on Poe* (1987). Carlson's placement of Poe within Transcendental camps should be read, however, alongside of contrary views expressed by such critics as Michael J. S. Williams in *A World of Words: Language and Displacement in the Fiction of Edgar Allan Poe* (1988) and Joan Dayan, whose analysis of "Eleonora" as anti-Transcendental tale (indeed as embodying a decided materialistic outlook) concludes *Fables of Mind: An Inquiry into Poe's Fiction* (1987). The essays by Selley and Kagel also speak significantly about such matters. As exemplifications of her ideas, Selley incorporates several of Poe's works that often go begging, and thus she implicitly pushes closer the borders of what might be designated "major" and "minor" Poe (attempted distinctions that grow more treacherous as time's passage occasions revaluation of much in Poe's corpus). Kagel also gives us new perspective on burial themes in Poe's works. Poe-as-ironist often surfaces in these contexts, however, as shown by Garner (on the Dupin tales) and Herndon (who also indicates Poe's keen reactions to Washington Irving's writings). Their essays supplement Clark Griffith's long-acclaimed study of comedy at the expense of Transcendentalism in "Ligeia." Fruitful comparisons to these conceptions of Poe's reactions to Transcendentalist doctrines may be found in Beverly Voloshin's recent treatment of "Ligeia" and "Usher" (*MLS* [1988]), Terry Heller's *The Delights of Terror*, S. L. Varnado's *The Haunted Presence* (both 1987), and Douglas Robinson's *American Apocalypses* (1986)—all featuring a Poe of skeptical mind toward Transcendentalism. We will, no doubt, encounter further controversies in this line of explications.

David Sloane takes as his topic Poe and medicine, an area in which he has demonstrated thorough knowledge, to make what initially seem to be weird and fantastic features in "Usher" ultimately betray firm bases in the actualities of medical lore current in Poe's times. Sloane's study dovetails nicely with work done by David Butler (*AL* [1976]) and George R. Uba (*SAQ* [1986]). Uba found much groundwork for Poe's tale in a review by E. F. Dubois, which treated of hypochondria and hysteria, in the *Foreign Quarterly Review* for 1832. Sloane argues just as persuasively that Poe drew extensively on a well-known home medical book, *The Family Physician* (1834). My own piece on "Eleonora" is an attempt to present revelations about Poe's conscious art and craftsmanship as they bear upon contemporaneous theories about madness and as they touch upon his manipulations of Gothic conventions. My considerations of Poe's tale should be read in conjunction with those by Richard Wilbur and Joan Dayan, as cited in my essay, and G. A. Omans (whose *Poe and Passion: The Development of a Critical Term* [1986] deals with analogous matters). Parallels with Tennyson are inescapable in such delineations of passion and psychic imbalances, although the definitive study of Poe and madness awaits its taker. Similarly, in discussing "Hans Pfaall,"

Maurice Bennett shows how that tale, often held up as a pioneer endeavor into science fiction, may be interpreted plausibly as exemplifying loftier Romantic thought and vision.

Ramifications of Poe and the Poesque also receive deserved attention from several contributors. The ever-compelling Poe-Baudelaire relationship is highlighted in Gary Wayne Harner's assessment of Baudelaire as translator. Ideas on "The Tell-Tale Heart" set forth there should stimulate additional approaches to other translations by the Frenchman. In a different vein, that of evaluating Poe's standing with female authors in his times, Kent Ljungquist and Cameron Nickels broaden our knowledge of Poe's reputation in the hands of one of America's then-prominent literary ladies, Elizabeth Oakes Smith. She was not of the Griswold camp of defamers, as her vigorous championing of Poe indicates. Similar defense of Poe against early detractors is the keynote in J. Gerald Kennedy's equally valuable study of Henry Clay Preuss, now a largely-forgotten poet, whose combats with established American authorship operated along lines much like Poe's own literary battles. The essays by Gargano and Scholnick take us into the closing years of the nineteenth century and on into the beginnings of our own. Drawing on materials from later nineteenth-century literary periodicals to establish James's overriding low esteem for Poe's work, Gargano supplements Adeline Tintner and Burton Pollin on the Poe-Henry James relationship. Scholnick also gives us a meaty chapter in the history of Poe's reputation and image as it extended into the 1890s. *Poe and His Times* thereby comes full circle; as the Omans essay opens this book by connecting Poe the visionary writer with one of the foremost visionary painters in the early nineteenth century, Washington Allston, Scholnick's concluding essay leads us to Aubrey Beardsley's illustrations for the Stedman-Woodberry edition of Poe published by Stone and Kimball in 1894-95. Beardsley's death-invested graphics are but one among numerous testimonials of Poe's appeal to visual artists. In fact, as is borne out in Scholnick's and the remainder of the essays here gathered, the overriding and intertwining principle in *Poe and His Times*, whether it be in terms of Poe's looking outward or of the many eyes that often turned in his direction (and often beheld strange sights, contingent upon whatever was in the beholder's eye), is visionary. The many-sided figure emerging from this book is in reality a Poe of all times, whose literary art manifests inexhaustible riches that engender unceasing fascination.

B. F. F.

POE AND WASHINGTON ALLSTON: VISIONARY KIN

GLEN A. OMANS

An evaluation of Poe within the context of his own culture requires a consideration of his work in relation to that of his contemporaries. The most important American visual artist of Poe's day was the painter-poet Washington Allston (1779-1843). At the time of Allston's death, "his own generation believed [him to be] the greatest [artist] that had appeared in America."[1] The retrospective exhibition of his paintings in Boston in 1839 "gave most of the young writers of Boston and Concord their first serious awareness of the art of painting." Emerson's essay, "Art," according to Richardson, was formulated in the discussion of Allston's paintings in the Transcendentalist Club, and Emerson referred to Allston in his letters and journals between 1837 and 1844.[2] Hawthorne cited Allston as a prominent painter in his short story, "The Artist of the Beautiful." Margaret Fuller "thought with delight that such a man as this had been able to grow up in our bustling, reasonable community."[3]

Yet in spite of Allston's artistic prominence, Poe made only one brief and slighting reference to his work. In his "Autography" series in *Graham's Magazine*, January 1842, a year before Allston died, Poe acknowledged that "the name of 'Washington Allston,' the poet and painter, is one that has been long before the public," but commented that "the most noted" of Allston's paintings "are not to our taste." Poe found Allston's poems "not all of a high order of merit," though he did find the "Spanish Maid" and the "Address to Great Britain" productions "of which Mr. Allston may be proud." And though Poe admired the handwriting of Allston's signature, he concluded "that no man of original genius ever did or could habitually indite it under any circumstances whatever" (*H*15: 253-254).

Poe's offhand and negative response to Allston's work is probably due to Allston's friendship with Poe's enemies, the "Bostonians"— William Ellery Channing, Richard Henry Dana, Bronson Alcott, C. C. Felton, Oliver Wendell Holmes, Longfellow and Emerson—and professional association with Poe's bugaboo, the *North American Review*.[4] Poe's response must also have been based on a limited knowledge of the variety of Allston's painting. Writing before the days of color reproduction, Poe would have had to have seen the actual paintings before he could have realized Allston's artistic intentions. The only painting by Allston that was readily viewable by Poe, living in Philadelphia when his "Autography" series was published, was a large and busy picture on a biblical subject, done in Allston's earlier style, which Poe would not have found beautiful. Nor could Poe have known Allston's *Lectures on Art*, "the first American art treatise,"[5] written in the 1830s but not published until after Poe's death. Had Poe studied the entire body of Allston's work, his interest probably would have heightened and his respect increased, since Allston's work is similar to Poe's in striking and important ways. Both were "exceptionally gifted American artists who, being forced by the lack of an existing style to think out for themselves the meaning and purpose of their art, . . . arrived at fundamental discoveries in advance of current European practice."[6] Both produced major aesthetic statements in which the basic principles are often astonishingly close; consequently, the later paintings of Allston and the poems and stories of Poe, in which these principles are put in practice, can often be seen as attempts to achieve the same goal in the same manner.

If it seems a loss that these men had almost no effective contact with each other during the period from 1829 until 1843, when both were alive and professionally active, it is still useful and important to study them in the light of each other. The aesthetic statements of each help to explain those of the other and these statements taken together do much to clarify and define the intentions of their creative work. This clarification is particularly effective in the case of a series of smaller pictures of idealized, beautiful women that Allston painted toward the end of his career. Art historians who have not carefully studied Allston's *Lectures*, poems, or his novel, *Monaldi*, and who are not fully aware of the aesthetic ideas influencing Allston at the time he created these paintings have frequently misunderstood them. The critical statements of Poe and Allston, and Poe's poetry, especially "To Helen" and "Israfel," help us to interpret these paintings and place them properly in the cultural milieu in which they were produced.

In their essays, Poe and Allston were the first to introduce the principles of German Idealist philosophy into the mainstream of American art.[7] The common source of this philosophy was the distillation of the ideas of Kant, Schelling, and A. W. Schlegel, provided by Samuel Taylor Coleridge in his conversation and writings. Allston and Coleridge became close friends after they met in Rome in December 1805. Allston later noted: "To no other man do I owe so much intellectually as to Mr. Coleridge . . . who has honored me with his friendship for more than five and twenty years."[8] Poe's debt to Coleridge is well known.[9] In particular, Poe almost certainly read Coleridge's essays "On the Principles of Genial Criticism," published in the *Bristol Journal* in 1814 to publicize an exhibition of Allston's paintings and which Allston in turn echoes in his *Lectures*.[10]

The aesthetic theory of Allston and Poe as presented in their critical writings, is based on a dualistic conception of existence: phenomenal reality, perceived by the five senses, and conceptualized by the human reason or understanding; and transcendent ideas, or *noumena*, perceived by what Kant called the mental faculty of *Vernunft*, variously translated in English as "Reason," "Imagination," or "Intuition." Allston and Poe, like other popularizers of German Idealism, Victor Cousin, for example, concentrate on three principal ideas, Beauty, Truth, and Good. Allston, in his *Lectures on Art*, discusses "the three Ideas of Beauty, Truth, and Holiness, which we assume to represent the *perfect* in the physical, intellectual, and moral worlds" (p. 16). "These eternal Ideas," "coeternal forms," or "inborn Ideas" are "indestructible" and "cannot be forgotten" (pp. 32, 46-47). The "idea of beauty, in its highest form" seems to refer to "something beyond and above itself, as if it were but an approximation to a still higher form" (p. 7). Like others, Allston and Poe mixed concepts of transcendental idealism with traditional Christian imagery, often associating that "higher form" with God or some less clearly defined Oversoul, Maker, or Demi-Urgos. Allston notes that the ideas "are but the *forms* . . . through or in which a higher Power manifests to the consciousness the supreme truth of all things real," the "Power that prescribes the form and determines the truth of all Ideas" (pp. 3, 7). Thus, the existence of the ideas is often associated with heaven and a distant, immortal life after death. Allston calls them "angelic Forms," representatives of a "higher life," "descended from heaven" in "high, passionless form, in . . . singleness and purity" (pp. 19, 46-47).[11] The ideas are "the shadowing of that which" the human spirit's "immortal craving will sometimes dream of in the unknown future." They are the guarantee of "a higher love than that of earth, which the soul shall know, when, in a better world, she shall realize the ultimate reunion of Beauty with the coeternal forms of Truth and Holiness" (pp. 32, 84). Poe speaks of the human "sense of the beautiful" as "an important condition of man's immortal nature." It is a sense of "the beauty beyond the grave," "a consequence and an indication of his perennial life . . . . It is a forethought of the loveliness to come" (*H*11: 71-72; 14: 273-274).[12]

The artist's imagination was thought to be the most observable form of *Vernunft*, the faculty by means of which we perceive the ideal. Allston, following Coleridge, considered the imagination to be a much more powerful faculty than reason. Allston speaks of the imagination as "that mysterious tract of the intellect," composed of "those intuitive Powers, which are above, and beyond, both the senses and the understanding." The imagination is "the last high gift of the Creator, that imaginative faculty whereby his exalted creature, made in his image, might mould at will, from his most marvellous world, yet unborn forms . . . having all of truth" except for God's "own divine prerogative,—*the mystery of Life.*" "It is by the agency of this intuitive and assimilating Power . . . that [the artist] is able to separate the essential form from the accidental . . . thus educing . . . an Ideal nature from the germs of the Actual" (pp. 13, 111, 132, 155).[13] Poe noted that the imagination is the "soul" of poetry, and paralleled Coleridge's definition of the imagination in calling it "in man, a lesser degree of the creative power in God." It is the imagination "that spiritualizes the fanciful conception, and lifts it into the *ideal*" (*H*8: 283; 10: 65).[14]

In idealist thought, persons gifted with a strong and active *Vernunft* will be dissatisfied with the limitations and imperfections of phenomena and aspire to the purity and perfection of *noumena*. By virtue of his special perceptive capacity, the artist yearns upward for a vision of ideal Beauty. Describing the "temperament of the Artist," Allston noted that it is "not only as being peculiarly alive to all existing affinities, but as never satisfied with those merely which fall within [its] experience; ever striving, on the contrary . . . to supply the deficiency wherever it is felt." Because of his "fuller conception" and "more extended acquaintance with the higher outward assimilants of Beauty," the artist is brought "nearer to a perfect realization of the preëxisting Idea." "Whether poet or painter," the "natural bias" of his mind makes it "more peculiarly capable of its highest development." He will be particularly aware that "the idea of beauty" refers "to something beyond and above itself . . ." (pp. 7, 127). Poe's description of artistic drive is similar to Allston's in tone and imagery. In the act of creation, says Poe, the artist is inspired by no "mere appreciation of the beauty before us," "by no sublunary sights, or sounds, or sentiments," but by a "wild effort to reach the beauty above," by a "burning thirst for supernal BEAUTY—a beauty which is not afforded the soul by any existing collocation of earth's forms—a beauty which, perhaps, *no possible* combination of these forms would fully produce." The artist "struggles by multiform novelty of combination among the things and thoughts of Time, to anticipate some portion of that loveliness whose very elements, perhaps, appertain solely to Eternity" (*H*11: 72-73; 14: 274).

The key element by means of which the artist achieves a vision of ideal beauty is the symbol, a sense-perceivable, beautiful object that has the power to suggest pure beauty because it partially and imperfectly embodies that idea. To designate the symbol, Allston used the term "objective correlative," a term that T. S. Eliot made popular 120 years later. Notes Allston: "As the condition of its manifestation," an idea must have "its objective correlative, . . . the presence of some outward object, predetermined to correspond to the preëxisting idea in its living power" (p. 16). The idea is called to the artist's consciousness by its "objective correlative" because the object has a "predetermined correspondence or correlation" with the idea (p. xiii). A perceiver, by contemplating the symbol, may achieve, through the agency of his imagination, a momentary insight into the existence and true nature of the ideal. In his *Lectures*, Allston describes physical beauty as "the visible sign of that pure idea, in which so many lofty minds have recognized the type of a far higher love than that of earth" (p. 32). The beauty of a human being "is beauty in its *mixed mode*,—not in its high, passionless form." Nevertheless, it has the power to "carry back the soul to whence it came" (p. 19).

In Poe's "Israfel," the earthly poet is the symbol of and imperfect parallel to the ideal poet and immortal spirit Israfel who dwells in "Heaven." The beauties of earthly existence are "modell'd" after the perfection of the ideal realm. By contemplating the condition of the earthly poet, we can glimpse the true nature of the heavenly singer, pure harmony, ideal beauty, and the function of art. Since the poem creates the experience in which the reader is made aware of these parallels, "Israfel" itself may be said to be a poem-symbol that makes possible the perceptual leap from real to ideal, from descendent to transcendent.

As Poe's poem makes clear, the artist's endeavor is to envision the ideal through its symbols and then re-embody the ideal in a work of art. This task, Allston noted, is "bounded only by the . . . confines of that higher world, where ideal glimpses of angelic forms are sometimes permitted to his sublimated vision" (pp. 109-110).[15] As symbol, the work of art has the capacity to lead other, less perceptive viewers to a vision similar to that originally experienced by the artist. Allston claimed: "Every work of Genius" is "*suggestive*; and only when it excites to or awakens congenial thoughts and emotions, filling the imagination with corresponding images, does it attain its proper end" (p. 101). "Neither is it the privilege of the exclusive few, the refined and cultivated, to feel them deeply. If we look beyond ourselves, even to the promiscuous multitude, the instance will be rare . . . where some transient touch of these purer feelings has not raised the individual to, at least, a momentary exemption from the common thralldom of self" (pp. 17-18).[16] For the perception of the ideal through the agency of a work of art expands the consciousness of the viewer and elevates and excites him in a vision that moves always outward and upward. "Who has never felt," asks Allston, "an expansion of the heart, an elevation of mind, nay, a striving of the whole being to pass its limited bounds? . . . . May it not give us, in a faint shadowing at least, some intimation of the many real, though unknown relations, which everywhere surround and bear upon us?" (p. 104). From experiencing a work of art, then, the viewer "doubtless derives a high degree of pleasure, nay, one of the purest of which his nature is capable . . ." (p. 7).

Poe describes the "effect" of poetry on the reader in the same language Allston uses to describe the effect of a painting on a viewer. Praising Tennyson's "Oenone," Poe says that it "exalts the soul . . . into a conception of pure *beauty*, which in its elevation—its calm and intense rapture— has in it a foreshadowing of the future and spiritual life." In "The Philosophy of Composition," Poe noted that a poem produces in the reader a pleasure "at once the most intense, the most elevating, and the most pure," which is experienced in "the contemplation of the beautiful. When, indeed, men speak of Beauty, they mean, precisely, not a quality, as is supposed, but an effect— . . . that intense and pure elevation of *soul* . . . which is experienced in consequence of contemplating 'the beautiful'." In "The Poetic Principle," he insisted: "*That* pleasure which is at once the most pure, the most elevating, and the most intense, is derived . . . from the contemplation of the Beautiful. In the contemplation of Beauty we alone find it possible to attain that pleasurable elevation or excitement, *of the soul*, which we recognize as the Poetic Sentiment" (*H*11: 255; 14: 197-198, 266, 275).

Allston insisted that the first purpose of any work of art is to elevate and excite the perceiver to an intense and pleasurable vision of the ideal in his "Introductory Discourse" and lecture on "Art" (pp. 20, 81) and in some of his sonnets on the works of art to which he himself responded most enthusiastically. The opening two lines of "Sonnet on the Group of the Three Angels before the Tent of Abraham, by Raffaelle, in the Vatican" are: "O, now I feel as though another sense, / From heaven descending, had informed my soul" (p. 274). In his sonnet, "Art," Allston praised Michelangelo as one who "brought to view / The invisible Idea" (p. 327). In "On the Statue of an Angel, by Bienaimé, in the Possession of J. S. Copley Greene, Esq.," Allston exclaimed:

> Ah, who can look on that celestial face,
> And kindred for it claim with aught on earth?
>   . . . .
>
> That, by a simple movement, thus imparts
> Its own harmonious peace, the while our hearts
> Rise, as by instinct, to the world above (p. 345).[17]

In descriptions of his reactions to other works of art in his lectures and letters, Allston records similar transcendent experiences more explicitly.

He characterizes his first response to the paintings of Titian, Tintoretto, and Veronese: "They addressed themselves, not to the senses merely, as some have supposed, but rather through them to that region . . . of the imagination which is supposed to be under the exclusive dominion of music, and which, by similar excitement, they caused to teem with visions that 'lap the soul in Elysium'."[18] Allston's account of the effect of the Apollo Belvedere assumes that his own reaction was typical of a universal response: "Who that saw it . . . ever thought of it as a man, much less as a statue; but did not feel rather as if the vision before him were of another world,—of one who had just lighted on the earth, and with a step so ethereal, that the next instant he would vault into the air? If I may be permitted to recall the impression which it made on myself, I know not that I could better describe it than as a sudden intellectual flash, filling the whole mind with *light*,—and light in motion" (p. 100). Allston is thus, indeed, a visionary artist, but not in the sense that Nathalia Wright or Abraham A. Davidson use the term, to indicate the dreamer whose imagination is freed from restrictions of physical reality.[19] Rather, Allston is a visionary in that he believes in the power of art to produce visions of a transcendent ideality beyond phenomena, and himself paints pictures intended to have this effect on the viewer. Certainly this is how his contemporaries interpreted his aims. Reviewing his 1839 exhibition in Boston, Margaret Fuller exclaimed: "The calm and meditative ease of these pictures, the ideal beauty that shone *through* rather than in them, . . . were . . . unlike anything else I saw. Mr. Allston aims at the Ideal."[20] Horatio Greenough called Allston "the head, and chief, the Adam of American Idealists."[21] Jared B. Flagg portrays Allston as "a man in whom ideality and intellect pushed imagination into realms of the unseen that he might materialize visions of beauty to entertain, purity, and uplift his fellowmen" (p. 424).

Both Poe and Allston prefer a beautiful woman as the symbol most conducive to elevating the imagination to a perception of ideal beauty. At the end of a long list of "elements which induce in the Poet . . . the true poetical effect," Poe stresses that he "feels it in the beauty of woman—in the grace of her step—in the lustre of her eye . . . but above all—ah, far above all—he kneels to it—he worships it in the faith, in the purity, in the strength, in the altogether divine majesty—of her *love*" ($H$14: 290-291). Allston observes that when one looks at "a beautiful woman," there can "be but one feeling: that nothing visible was ever so framed to banish from the soul every ignoble thought, and imbue it . . . with primeval innocence." Woman's beauty "is the embodied harmony of the true poet; his visible Muse; the guardian angel of his better nature; the inspiring sibyl of his best affections, drawing him to her with a purifying charm, from the selfishness of the world, from poverty and neglect, from the low and base, nay, from his own frailty or vices:—for he cannot approach her with unhallowed thoughts, whom the unlettered and ignorant look up to with awe, as to one of a race above them . . ." (pp. 19, 28). The woman, however, must be seen as symbol rather than as human being—not as a lover but as a revelation in material form of ideal beauty. Allston emphasizes the difficulty of so seeing: "Could we look, indeed, at the human form in its simple, unallied physical structure, . . . and forget, or rather not feel, that it is other than a form" (p. 19). Only when and if woman is contemplated as symbol will the experience bring with it the dispassionate pleasure and elevation, the "purifying charm," that Allston and Poe insist upon as characteristic of ideal vision. Poe stresses that the "manifestation" of "the Human Aspiration for Supernal Beauty" is "always found in *an elevating excitement of the Soul*—quite independent of that passion which is the intoxication of the heart—. . . For, in regard to Passion, alas! its tendency is to degrade rather than to elevate the Soul" (*H*14: 290). That the experience of woman's beauty when she is seen as form rather than flesh can be genuinely visionary is recorded in an account of a dream vision that Allston confided to Richard H. Dana, Jr.:

> While I was in Florence I saw in a dream a female whom I may call perfectly beautiful. In form, feature, expression, and dress she was more perfect than anything that my highest imagination had ever conceived. Nothing in ancient or modern art is an approach to it, and if I could have painted her with half her effect I should have painted the most beautiful object in the art. For several days afterward I was in a state of quiet, ethereal exaltation; I felt in whatever I was about that something peculiar had occurred to me, and could hardly realize that I was to act and be treated like other people. The vision . . . haunted me for months. (Flagg, pp. 364-365)

Poe's "To Helen" intends to give the reader the experience that Allston had in his dream, a successful vision of ideal beauty. The symbol which is the basis of the entire poem is a beautiful woman: "Helen, thy beauty is to me, / like those Nicéan barks of yore." Poe's biographers suggest that Helen may be a composite of three real women whom Poe idealized: his own mother, his foster mother, Frances Allan, and Jane Stith Stanard, whom Poe referred to as "the first purely ideal love of my soul."[22] Here we see Poe moving from the specific to the level of *noumenal* abstraction. Meditating on the natural beauty of these women, Poe fuses them into the figure of Helen, symbolic of feminine beauty transcendent of time and space. Helen in turn evokes the beauty of Greek sculpture—of hyacinth hair and classic face—and the "grandeur that was Rome." Helen is presented in artistic terms. She is an art symbol, rather than a natural symbol. She is "statue-like," representing the triumph of beauty through art. Ultimately, she suggests the "Holy-Land," another symbol that adds the feeling of ultimate peace and reassurance of religious belief to the pleasure of aesthetic contemplation. The "brilliant window-niche" in which she stands suggests the light that Allston experienced in his vision of the Apollo Belvedere, as well as the sense of security and protection that reaching the "Holy-Land" provides. Helen is also associated with Psyche, symbol of the human soul and spiritual immortality. Another major symbol in the poem is that of the voyage. Helen's beauty transports the poet from the descendent world, the world of "desperate seas" that is chaotic and fatiguing, to "his own native shore," the calm stasis of the ideal. Space is obliterated, and time is fused into eternity. The eras of Greece, Rome, Poe's nineteenth century, and the reader's present coalesce into one transcendent and eternally recreatable experience of beauty. The "Nicéan bark" is the vehicle, a symbol of the imagination which makes possible the poet's and the reader's journey to the universal world of pure beauty.

The form of the poem is also symbolic because it reinforces the concept of order and proportion. Each of the three stanzas has five lines, and in each stanza the last line is shortened. Stanzas one and two begin in images of flux and turbulence and end in calm and stasis; the images of the last stanza suggest no movement. The shortened final line brings all to a close. Thus, both the arrangement of ideas in the poem and its physical architecture second the major symbols, to translate the reader from the turbulence of reality to a vision of the *noumenal*. Yet the voyage was initiated by and could not have occurred without the material existence of feminine beauty.

Allston's paintings which closely approximate the symbolism of Poe's "To Helen" are those in the series of solitary human figures in which the subject, usually a woman, is isolated and idealized. The apparent intention of each painting is to stimulate an aesthetic experience, a vision of ideal beauty, rather than portray the likeness of a real person. The series includes five paintings of a woman presented half-length and close to the picture plane—"The Valentine" (1809-1811, no. 22, p. 44), "Beatrice" (ca. 1816-1819, no. 53, p. 117), "A Roman Lady Reading" (ca. 1831, fig. 51, p. 140), "Rosalie" (1835, no. 67, p. 199), and "Amy Robsart" (1840, fig. 55, p. 143).[23] The series also includes seven paintings of a full-length, seated figure, set somewhat back from the picture plane in a landscape background. Five of these paintings are of a woman—"Contemplation" (ca. 1817-1818, no. 38, p.

190), "Una in a Wood" (ca. 1831, fig. 53, p. 141), "A Tuscan Girl" (1831, fig. 52, p. 140), "The Spanish Girl in Reverie" (1831, no. 63, p. 125), and "Evening Hymn" (1835, no. 66, p. 128)—and two are of a beautiful, androgynous youth, both entitled "Italian Shepherd Boy" (1819, no. 50, p. 195) and (ca. 1819, no. 51, p. 195).[24]

"The Valentine" and "Contemplation" were painted in England. All the others were painted after Allston's return to the United States in 1818 and are characteristic of the change that occurred in the nature of his art once he re-established residence in his native country. He gave up dramatic, large-scale paintings on biblical subjects, a type popular in Europe, and turned instead to painting smaller canvases of tranquil and meditative subjects, a type of painting that included landscapes and pictures on literary subjects, but that is most clearly represented by his paintings of single figures. His intention, to paint "the inner mind rather than outward experience,"[25] fostered by his friendships in England with Coleridge and Wordsworth, was probably reinforced by his renewed association in America with William Ellery Channing, and new acquaintanceships with Emerson and Hawthorne,[26] whose own work was contemplative, idealistic, and symbolic. Six of his single-figure paintings were done after 1830, four of them in 1831-1832, when Allston began to write his *Lectures on Art*,[27] so these paintings can be considered directly in the context of the *Lectures*. The influence of German Idealism was also strongest in the United States at this time because of the popularity of the writings of Coleridge, Carlyle, and Victor Cousin.[28]

All twelve of Allston's paintings of single figures share several characteristics that indicate his intention to "*realize* the Idea of a *perfect* Human Form" in a work of art (pp. 117, 126-127). All the figures are as beautiful as Allston can make them, not only in the rendition of facial features but also in painterly technique. "He is very beautiful, this boy," Margaret Fuller wrote of the second, larger painting of the "Italian Shepherd Boy." "The Beautiful is Mr. Allston's dominion. There he rules as a Genius."[29] "Rosalie" illustrates Richardson's observation that in Allston's later pictures "the glazes grow deeper and more glowing, the lights more luminous, and the shadows more filled with color."[30] All twelve figures are portrayed in a state of reverie or meditation. The titles of two paintings—"Contemplation" and "The Spanish Girl in Reverie"—insist on this state. It is conveyed most consistently by the lack of eye contact between the subject of the painting and the viewer. In seven paintings the subject's gaze is averted downward—"The Valentine," "Beatrice," "A Roman Lady Reading," "Contemplation," "A Tuscan Girl," and both versions of the "Italian Shepherd Boy." In "The Valentine," the woman is reading a letter and in "A Roman Lady Reading" and "Contemplation," a book. This averted gaze enables viewers to move closer, emotionally, to the figure because apparently unobserved, unchallenged. We are free to contemplate the figure in contemplation. In four paintings—"Rosalie," "The Spanish Girl in Reverie," "Una in a Wood," and "Evening Hymn"—the woman's eyes are directed away from the viewer but up and out of the painting toward distant space. Allston seems to insist on this mannerism, as if a direct exchange of eye contact between subject and viewer would disturb the mood of reverie. The effect of the distant gaze, though, differs from that of the downward glance. It suggests the experience of visionary transcendence, the moment of otherworldly "expansion of the heart" and "elevation of mind, nay, a striving of the whole being to pass its limited bounds" that Allston found characterized a perception of the ideal (p. 104). This is the "divine afflatus"[31] that Allston sought to suggest by the same elevated gaze in his portrait of "Samuel Taylor Coleridge" (1814, no. 32, p. 70) and his painting "Uriel in the Sun" (1817, no. 41, p. 78).

The meditative or visionary mood of these paintings is further enhanced by the two types of settings Allston has given them. In "The Valentine," "Beatrice," "A Roman Lady Reading," and "Rosalie," the woman is posed before an "austere and compressed architectural setting" that closes off the background, pushes the figure toward the picture plane so that it literally fills the canvas, and arrests the viewer's gaze and directs our full attention to the subject's face.[32] Since the woman's own glance is averted, and since the bare and shadowy background offers no distraction, our sense of intimacy and concentration is encouraged and we are drawn into her aura of gentle beauty. In the other eight paintings, the subject is set farther back (but never very far) from the picture plane in an outdoor setting, more space surrounds the figure, and there is always an opening, through dark trees or past mountains, to the infinite space of the warmly lighted sky. This opening suggests the possibility of escape from the turbulence of reality to the calm stasis of the ethereal ideal, symbolized by the figure's beautiful face, a transfer also suggested by the figure's elevated line of sight. "The Spanish Girl" is surrounded by more space than any of the other outdoor figures. The gesture of her right hand directs our attention to the rock on which she sits, but the background opens up past steep mountains to the sky. The outline of her figure is repeated in the shape of the mountains in the middle ground and in the distance. The movement from her right hand in the foreground to the mountains and beyond to the distant sky suggests the voyage from descendent to transcendent in Poe's "To Helen." Like effect is produced by the composition of "Evening Hymn," which invites our examination of the picture to travel from the earth in the foreground, past the woman's face to the art symbolism of the temple in the middle ground, to the open sky of the background.

The style of clothing of the figures in these paintings seems consciously generalized, vaguely archaic, yet timeless, suggestive of the images in "To Helen" that attempt to fuse various historical periods into one eternity. Certainly the clothing, and, at times, the title ("A Roman Lady Reading," "A Tuscan Girl," "The Spanish Girl in Reverie") dissociate the figures from contemporary references and from any specifically American milieu. Usually, the woman or young man in the painting is subtly elevated so that the viewer is made to look up at the figure. The composition of all the half-length figures is a monolithic triangle, and the upper torso of most of the full-length figures has the same form. The pose, though, is always graceful, almost languid, and the figure is softly-molded, so the monumental effect is softened. Since Allston remarks in his lecture on "Composition" that lines in a painting "hold the relation to Painting that versification does to Poetry" (p. 151), we are invited to compare the effect of Allston's composition to that of the architectural form of "To Helen," both of which reinforce the association between static form and the ideal. By such devices, Allston makes the beauty of these figures seem as otherworldly, elevated, archetypal, and eternal as Poe's Helen.

In seven paintings—"The Valentine," "Beatrice," "A Roman Lady Reading," "Rosalie," "The Spanish Girl," "Evening Hymn," and "Amy Robsart"—Allston rather showily adorns his women with lace, pearl fillets, and gold—gold neck chains, pendants, earrings, rings, bracelets, brooches, embroidered hems, and hair nets—often strongly reinforced by the gold of the picture frame. This apparently deliberately-repeated motif (one finds it again in the showy stick-pin that attracts the viewer's attention in Allston's "Self-Portrait," 1805, no. 15, p. 40), this emphasis on decorative artifice may be intended to suggest the artist as artificer, as artisan of beautiful, highly crafted, precious objects, as icon-maker, to further accentuate the difference between Allston's intention to idealize his human subjects and the contrary artistic principle of copying nature as exactly as possible. This typically Symbolist concept was to be emphasized later in the nineteenth century by some of the foremost Symbolist writers—Baudelaire in his essays on *"Le Dandy"* and *"Maquillage,"* Yeats in "Sailing to Byzantium," and Joyce in *A Portrait of the Artist as a Young Man.*

Most significantly, perhaps, the face, hands, and often the throat and shoulders, revealed by a gently-scooped neckline, of each figure in all twelve of these paintings are bathed in a soft but strong light that the figure's translucent skin seems to radiate back again. Because

Allston always poses his figures against a shadowy background and often dresses them in a dark costume, this radiance spotlights the facial beauty of the subject in each painting. This golden light, recalling that which Allston experienced in his vision of the Apollo Belvedere, suggests illumination, lucidity, and vision. Barbara Novak points out that nineteenth-century American landscape painters, especially the luminists, associated light with spirit. Light is "the alchemistic medium by which the . . . artist turns matter into spirit."[33] Since Allston anticipated the luminists in his own landscapes, most notably his "Moonlit Landscape" (1819, no. 54, p. 113), he may have consciously used light in his figure paintings to achieve this spiritualizing effect. This was clearly his intention in two paintings of "angelic" subjects, "Uriel in the Sun" and "Jacob's Dream" (1817, no. 39, p. 190), both of which he flooded with light; the fact that he emphasized this mysterious radiance in all twelve of his single-figure paintings suggests a consistency in symbolism. In two of these paintings, "The Spanish Girl" and "Evening Hymn," he also included a pool of still water, another standard symbol of nineteenth-century American landscape paintings. As Novak notes, the "pool of silence" accumulated several associations—contemplation, calm, "a spirit untroubled in its depths," a refuge which could bathe and restore the spirit—and could be used as a "compositional device marrying sky and ground by bringing the balm of light down to earth on which the traveler stands" (pp. 40-41, 123).

Four of Allston's idealizations of beautiful women are based on earlier literal representations of his first wife. "The Valentine" closely resembles in composition, pose, and mood, Allston's small oil portrait of Ann Channing (no. 21, p. 183), which he painted between 1809 and 1811. The heads of "The Spanish Girl," "Rosalie," and the woman in "Evening Hymn" are almost exact reproductions of a lovely "Life Study of Ann Channing" (ca. 1812-1815, no. 87, p. 227); the angle of the neck, pose of the head, line of sight, and hair style are identical in all four paintings. However, Allston has blurred, generalized, idealized the realistic features of his wife's face to move away from literal portraiture to symbolic painting. "The Valentine" makes no specific reference to Ann. The details of the woman's hair, face, dress, and hands are blurred to the extent that her left hand seems more like a mitten. Some critics conjecture that "The Valentine" may have been inspired by Ann's sister, so Gerdts suggests that "Allston may have combined several images" of Ann and her sister in the painting (p. 60), a process that duplicates Poe's fusion of his memories of his mother, his foster mother, and Jane Stith Stanard into the symbol Helen. In "The Spanish Girl," "Rosalie," and "Evening Hymn," though the face more closely resembles that of the original life study than it does in "The Valentine," the expression of the eyes and mouth is depersonalized. Also, in these paintings Allston moves the woman's image, seen very close up in the "Life Study," farther away from the viewer, to distance her from us. In "Rosalie" the distance is achieved primarily through elevation; in "The Spanish Girl" and "Evening Hymn" the figure is moved back from the picture plane. Novak observes that the effect of the golden light in luminist landscapes is to dissolve form and so to "assist spiritual transmutation" (p. 41), and certainly the light that bathes these four paintings based on Ann Channing, as well as the rest of his single-figure paintings, has much the same effect. Allston complained of paintings of "beautiful faces, without an atom of meaning," which fail to move the viewer because "they have beauty, and *nothing else*. But let another artist, some man of genius, copy the same faces, and . . . breathe into them souls: from that moment the passers-by would see as if with other eyes" (p. 25). By removing all accidental features of the natural woman and all evidence of personal relationship with her from the paintings based on figure studies of his first wife, Allston attempts to add "soul" to a beautiful face and so convert that face into pure form, symbolic of ideal beauty. For the human figure in its most perfect guise is the only "safe ground" and "starting point from whence to ascend to a true Ideal" (p. 130).

Still, the subject matter of several of these idealized figure paintings seems to be human love, a definitely non-ethereal emotion. The woman in "The Valentine" is reading a love letter. Allston wrote to his friend William Collins in 1821 that "Beatrice" was a portrayal of "Dante's Beatrice."[34] Margaret Fuller observed: "The painter merely having in mind how the great Dante loved a certain lady called Beatrice, embodied here his own ideal of a poet's love."[35] The poems Allston wrote to accompany "The Spanish Maid in Reverie" and "Rosalie" indicate that love is at least one of the emotions expressed by the women in these paintings. Thus, Allston's love of his first wife, and his admiration of her delicate beauty, apparently, are the original impulses behind all the pictures of solitary, beautiful women he would paint, beginning with "The Valentine" done shortly before or after her death.[36] So Allston, like Poe, finds the love of a beautiful woman to be the strongest inspiration for art. Flagg notes, however, that "the effect of [Ann's] early death was disastrous and irreparable." Allston was plunged into such grief that he was reported to be insane.[37] Such intense emotion is far from the *"elevating excitement of the soul*—quite independent of . . . the intoxication of the heart" (*H*14: 290) that Poe described as the experience of ideal beauty. Some act of distancing must distill the love from the real present, must purge away the sadness and sense of loss, and allow the image of pure beauty to emerge in order to realize the effect Allston described in his lecture on "Form," that when one looks upon a beautiful face, one "feels himself carried, as it were, out of this present world . . ." (p. 128). To achieve the aesthetic distance needed to convert experience into art, Allston insists on the act of meditation in "Contemplation."

When Allston painted "Contemplation," the influence of Wordsworth, to whom Coleridge had introduced him, was strongest. Johns carefully traces the importance of Wordsworth's poems about isolated women as models for Allston's figure paintings (pp. 123-124, 126). These poems, particularly "She Was a Phantom of Delight," "To a Highland Girl," "The Solitary Reaper," and the Lucy poems, are based on recollection of emotion in tranquility. The Lucy poems—"Strange Fits of Passion Have I Known," "She Dwelt Among the Untrodden Ways," and "Three Years She Grew"—are most relevant to Allston's "Contemplation," because when he painted it his wife had been dead for two years. What the painting may be "about," then, is the process of "Contemplation" or recollection of emotion in moments of tranquility that Allston would have to have experienced in order to convert his memories of Ann into an idealization purged of personal, emotional associations.

Allston's comments about the process of recollection in his letters, poems, and novel, *Monaldi*, indicate that he considered memory an important part of the creative process. Memory is associated particularly with love; it is a strong love in the past that memory most often recalls for Allston. An obvious persona for Allston, Monaldi recalls his childhood love for his sister and realizes how important a support that love has been for him in his years as a student.[38] Almost the identical recollection is the basis of Allston's poem, "To My Sister":

> Yet, haply, not to all
> That once have lived doth wayward Memory close
> Her book of life,—or rather, book of love;
> For there, as quickened by some breath above,
> The pure affections must for aye repose.

Such recollections can serve as the original germ of works of art:

> And how the rudest toys by childhood wrought—
> The symbols of its love,—there live and grow
> To classic forms, on which no after thought,
> No learned toil, can with its skill bestow
>   A truer touch of Art . . . . (p. 322)

Monaldi is an artist of inner vision who relies on memory for the matter of his art:

> To common observers the external world seemed to lie only "like a load upon his weary eye;" but to them it appeared so because he delighted to shut it out, and to combine and give another life to the images it had left in his memory; as if he would sleep to the real and be awake only to a world of shadows . . . . He had looked at nature with the eye of a lover; none of her minutest beauties had escaped him, and all that were stirring to a sensitive heart and a romantic imagination were treasured up in his memory, as themes of delightful musing in her absence; and they came to him in those moments with that never-failing freshness and life which love can best give to the absent. (pp. 23-25)

Recollection serves as a distillation that eliminates all accidentals of an experience and allows the ideal elements to float free. Allston mused: "I seldom step into the ideal world but I find myself going back to the age of first impressions. The germs of our best thoughts are certainly often to be found there." He concluded that memory is where "the poetry of life may be said to have its birth; where the real ends and the ideal begins" (Flagg, pp. 35-36).

If, however, the memory of love recollected in a state of mental tranquility may be the source of Allston's choice of a beautiful woman as symbol of ideal beauty, the poems he wrote to accompany the pictures "A Tuscan Girl," "The Spanish Girl in Reverie," and "Rosalie" indicate that his intention was to provoke a much higher "effect" in his viewers than the experience of chaste love. The poems "The Spanish Maid" and "The Tuscan Girl," both of which clearly refer to the paintings whose titles they approximate, were published in the *North American Review*, October 1831. The poem "Rosalie" is painted directly on the bottom of the frame of the picture in an interesting anticipation of a technique that was to become stock-in-trade for Dante Gabriel Rossetti in his larger-than-life idealized paintings of women and an early instance of the fusion of art forms that became a favorite device of nineteenth-century Symbolist poets. Allston consciously combines painting and poetry to create a doubly-suggestive art symbol; we are clearly intended to consider poem and picture together. When Anna Jameson asked Allston whether the picture or the poem first took shape in his mind, he answered that he could not say; the poem grew along with the painting (Richardson, p. 157).

The poems in each case give us specific clues as to how we might "read" the emotion portrayed on the face in the painting. Gerdts finds the expression of "The Spanish Girl" "wistful" and Mandeles and Johns find it "melancholy."[38] The poem, though, indicates that the mood is, rather, one of hopeful anticipation. For the poem describes a moment in which two long-separated lovers are about to be reunited, but are not yet quite sure that the sight they have of each other is not an illusion. The poem predicts their approaching state as one of "bliss" (1.55, p. 335). Though "The Tuscan Girl" is first described as feeling both "pleasant" and "sad" (1.1, p. 336) as she experiences the transitional state between girlhood and maturity, she is actually much more emotionally buoyant: "She cannot call it gladness or delight; / And yet there seems a richer, lovelier light/ On e'en the humblest thing that lives" (ll. 19-21). By the fifth stanza, she is described as capable of transcendent experience, using a bird as symbol and starting point:

> She hears the bird without a wish to snare,
> But rather on the azure air
> To mount, and with it wander there
> To some untrodden land. (ll. 29-32)

The concluding lines depict her in a truly visionary state:

> Thy heart may still in Earth rejoice
> And all its beauty love,
> But no, not all this fair, enchanting Earth,
> With all its spells, can give the rapture birth
> That waits thy conscious soul above.

This mixture of sadness and rapture associated with transcendent vision is the same as that experienced in "Rosalie"—where these emotions are directly associated with aesthetic perception. This poem, and the painting as the poem describes it, parallel closely the ideas and tone of Poe's "Israfel," first published in *Poems* (1831), which Allston could have read. Both "Rosalie" and "Israfel" treat the nature of idealist art in terms of the human experience of music. Rosalie pleads:

> O, pour upon my soul again
> That sad, unearthly strain,
> That seems from other worlds to plain;
> Thus falling, falling from afar,
> As if some melancholy star
> Had mingled with her light her sighs,
> And dropped them from the skies!

> No,—never came from aught below
> This melody of woe.
>   . . .
>
> For all I see around me wears
> The hue of other spheres.
>   (ll. 1-9, 15-16)

Many critics regard "Rosalie" as a love poem, but only in the last four lines is there a reference to love and even that is not explicit. For "the strain of him who stole / In music to her soul" refers primarily to the poet-artist-musician who plays the "unearthly strain" that is the subject of the poem and only secondarily suggests Rosalie's lover. In the poem, the "soul" is the receptive faculty of the aesthetic experience (the word is repeated in the first and last lines), as it is in Poe's aesthetic theory, and music is the most effective art medium for inducing that experience. As Poe noted: "It is in Music, perhaps, that the soul most nearly attains that end upon which we have commented—the creation of supernal beauty. It may be, indeed, that this august aim is here even partially or imperfectly attained, *in fact*" (*H*11: 74-75; 14: 274-275). Moreover, both "Rosalie" and "Israfel" describe a dualistic concept in which descendent, human art is but an imperfect approximation of the perfect music of a transcendent, heavenly state. In both poems, this dualism is realized by the earthly, imperfect perceiver who is made dissatisfied by his or her inability to match the perfect, heavenly ideal. The poet-narrator in "Israfel" complains admiringly:

> In Heaven a spirit doth dwell
>   "Whose heart-strings are a lute;"
> None sing so wildly well
> As the angel Israfel . . . .
>
> Yes, Heaven is thine; but this
>   Is a world of sweets and sours;
>   Our flowers are merely—flowers,
> And the shadow of thy perfect bliss
> Is the sunshine of ours. (ll. 1-4, 40-44)

In realizing their own imperfections and the distance that separates them from the ideal, both Rosalie and the poet-narrator experience a sense of frustration that translates into a melancholy mood:

> If I would dwell
> Where Israfel
>   Hath dwelt, and he where I,

> He might not sing so wildly well
> A mortal melody,
> While a bolder note than this might swell
> From my lyre within the sky. (ll. 45-51)

The experience of the heavenly strain, however, is so sweet, so enchanting, that the poet-narrator, and Rosalie, experience a "sadness . . . / So like angelic bliss," a something "blent of smiles and tears" (ll. 17, 20-21). Allston signals through the poem that the expression of the woman in the painting may bear something of melancholy, but it is a melancholy equally mixed with joy.

Both Allston and Poe explain the basis of this sad bliss in their prose writings. Poe insists that "the contemplation of the beautiful" brings a "pleasure which is at once the most intense, the most elevating, and the most pure." But this pleasure is always tinged with sadness because of our realization, simultaneous with and as a result of our vision of ideal beauty, that this ideal can never be fully realized by the human, finite, limited consciousness:

> When by Poetry—or when by Music, the most entrancing of the Poetic moods—we find ourselves melted into tears—we weep them . . . through a certain, petulant, impatient sorrow at our inability to grasp, *now*, wholly, here on earth, at once and forever, those divine and rapturous joys, of which, *through* the poem, or *through* the music, we attain to but brief and indeterminate glimpses.

Thus, concludes Poe, the "effect" of art is "one of a pleasurable sadness" because "this certain taint of sadness is inseparably connected with all the higher manifestations of true Beauty" (*H*14: 197, 274, 279). Allston agrees that the pure ideal can never be achieved by a human artist:

> It may well be doubted whether any Primary Idea can ever be fully realized by a finite mind . . . . And what true artist was ever satisfied with any idea of beauty of which he is conscious? From this approximated form, however, he doubtless derives a high degree of pleasure, nay, one of the purest of which his nature is capable; yet still is the pleasure modified . . . by an undefined yearning for what he feels can never be realized. And wherefore this craving, but for the archetype of that which called it forth?—When we say not satisfied, we do not mean discontented, but simply not in full fruition. And it is better that it should be so, since one of the happiest elements of our nature is that

which continually impels it towards the indefinite and unattainable. (p. 7)[39]

This "high degree of pleasure, . . . one of the purest of which [our] nature is capable," modified "by an undefined yearning . . . for what can never be realized" and the resulting "sadness . . . / So like angelic bliss" carefully explained by Poe and Allston seems precisely the experience recorded in "Israfel" and "Rosalie."

"Rosalie" is, then, both a love poem and a poem about aesthetic experience. Allston's poem, "Song," may provide a key link here. "Song" is a love poem, but it describes the experience of ideal love as much the same melancholy bliss of the experience of ideal beauty described in the poem "Rosalie." The speaker in "Song," in trying to explain to his bride why he weeps, affirms "it is not grief that brings the tear." Rather, he says:

> When I hear that tone of love,—
> Unlike all earthly sound,—
> It seems like music from above,
> That lifts me from the ground.
>
> And yet I know that I'm of earth,
> Where all that live must die:
> And these my tears but owe their birth
> To bliss for earth too high.

Here is the same transcendent "music from above" as in "Rosalie" and "Israfel" that causes blissful tears in one "of earth," tears in the realization of the distance between the physical real and the *noumenal* ideal, but bliss in the elevation and pure excitement of the perception of the ideal.[40] In both "Rosalie" and "Song" the music is a love song. Apparently, in Allston's mind the memory of the love of a beautiful woman causes the emotional response (pure, elevating excitement that is both blissful and melancholy) that most closely approximates the aesthetic experience of ideal beauty. The link between the two is the beautiful woman, the beloved object of the original experience of love and the source of the memory, who becomes, as well, the material symbol that makes possible the imperfect, momentary, but nevertheless genuine intuition of ideal beauty. That Poe's concept is much like Allston's is indicated by Poe's conclusion that "melancholy is . . . the most legitimate of all the poetical tones" because "Beauty . . . in its supreme development, invariably excites the sensitive soul to tears . . . . The death, then, of a beautiful woman is, unquestionably, the most poetical topic in the world" (*H*14: 198, 201).

This link between the love of a beautiful woman and the aesthetic experience of a work of art that in turn may inspire an artist to create his own work of art is the basis of a key scene in *Monaldi*; Monaldi first sees and falls in love with Rosalia (cf. "Rosalie") while he is viewing for the first time a madonna by Raphael, an artistic idealization of an adored, elevated, beautiful woman. Looking from the painting through a half-open door at the end of the picture gallery in her home, Monaldi initially sees only the "general loveliness" of Rosalia's form, "and he gazed on it as on a more beautiful picture." As described, Rosalia closely resembles most of the women in Allston's paintings: she is reading, head down, with a "half-averted face," a "pearly forehead, gleaming through clusters of black" hair, "half-closed eyelids," "tremulously-parted lips," and "an almost visible soul that seemed to rush from them upon the page before her." Monaldi's first sight of Rosalia is called a "beautiful vision," and so recalls Allston's own dream of a beautiful woman that left him "in a state of quiet, ethereal exaltation." After a long moment of contemplation, Monaldi looks back again at the Raphael madonna. Still thinking of Rosalia's beauty while studying the painting, he muses: "that ineffable look of love! yet so pure and passionless—so like what we may believe of the love of angels. It seems as if I had never before known the power of . . . art." The effect of Monaldi's falling in love with Rosalia is to enrich his own painting: "His art was now as much indebted to the living presence as a little before it had suffered from it." Monaldi has learned to use the beautiful symbol to stimulate a perception of ideal beauty, whereas before he had had to ignore the symbol as a distracting reality while trying to paint ideal beauty as a total abstraction. He has learned to do what Allston describes Michelangelo as doing in his sonnet "Art." "Life to life responding," Monaldi brings "to view / The invisible Idea." Thus, in spite of his passionate attachment to Rosalia, Monaldi's paintings continue to unite "innocence with pleasure" (pp. 77-81).

This association in the poems "Rosalie" and "Song" and in *Monaldi* between the actual love of a particular woman, the translation of that love into a work of art embodying as its main symbol the image of that woman idealized and universalized, and the experience through this work of art of elevating excitement tinged with melancholy strongly suggests that all of Allston's single-figure paintings, which seem more or less based on his love of his first wife and in which the figure is generalized by a number of techniques, aim finally at such an aesthetic experience. As described by Allston's and Poe's essays, the perceiver's "soul" in this experience transcends physical sensation and moves toward a perception of transcendent beauty. This formulation of Allston's aims helps us to interpret the expression of his other paintings of beautiful women with greater precision. Art critics tend to see these paintings as only melancholy, a singularity which detracts from their suggestiveness of the bitter-sweet nature of aesthetic experience. For example, both Gerdts (p. 97) and Mandeles (p. 143) find the expression of the woman in "Contemplation" melancholy, but the title insists that the painting portrays the act of contemplation. Any emotion suggested by the work is emotion recollected in Wordsworthian tranquility. "A Roman Lady Reading" would seem to be in a state of concentration. There is no hint of sadness in "The Valentine" or "Beatrice." Judging from the implied subject matter of each painting, one would assume that the similar expression of both women is a look of love. The figures in both paintings of the "Italian Shepherd Boy" seem intent on the creation of song, given the rather intense stare of their one visible eye. Mandeles convincingly identifies the primary tone of "Evening Hymn" as melancholy and shows how its iconography, particularly the shadows, the evening setting, the woman's black dress, and the pool in the background in which the ruins are reflected, refers to the long tradition of melancholy in western art and literature (p. 142-145). But certainly the picture evokes more than a sad response; Margaret Fuller and Oliver Wendell Holmes discerned an uplifting spirituality in the painting.[41] The ruins in the middle ground, highlighted by the setting sun, are quite intact, hardly "ruins" at all. They recall the positive imagery of Poe's "glory that was Greece" and "grandeur that was Rome." The face and hands of the woman are bathed in golden light, and her gaze is elevated above the horizon. Certainly the melancholy of the picture is tempered, perhaps dominated by a positive calm, if not the bliss which the poem "Rosalie" insists is also part of the experience of the symbolic connection between the real and the ideal.

In "Amy Robsart," painted three years before Allston died, the symbolism is unequivocally positive. Amy Robsart is the heroine of Walter Scott's novel, *Kenilworth* (1821). Allston, however, has made significant changes from the characteristics of his earlier figures of women so that there is no hint of her tragedy. Her direct gaze, for the first time in any of Allston's twelve paintings of solitary figures, fixes that of the viewer confidently, even aggressively. She is seated in full sunlight; her hair is bright gold and not in shadow. Her jaunty plume gives her a bit of *panache*, her fur collar a touch of *luxe*. Behind her, the background opens full into the blue sky of the ideal. This last of Allston's pictures in which the subject is beauty itself is in no way melancholy. The mood is more calm, reassuring, and confident of the possibilities of ideal vision than ever before.

Unfortunately, Poe probably never saw nor even read about any of these paintings before he published his "Autography" notice of Allston. "The Valentine," "Beatrice," the "Italian Shepherd Boy," "A Roman

Lady Reading," "The Spanish Girl," "Rosalie," and "Evening Hymn" were first shown to the public at Allston's exhibition of forty-seven paintings at Harding's Gallery, Boston, from 1 April to 10 July 1839. Poe was living in poverty in Philadelphia at the time; it is improbable that he had the money or the time for a trip to Boston. Margaret Fuller selected these pictures for enthusiastic praise in her review of the exhibition published in the first number of the *Dial*. Though Poe published an article on "Sarah Margaret Fuller" in *Godey's Lady's Book*, August 1846, in which he admired her contributions to the *Dial* (*H*15: 73-83), he seems not to have read her "Record of Impressions" of Allston's exhibition. Since Fuller understood Allston's aesthetic aims in these idealized paintings well and expressed them accurately in her review, one assumes that if Poe had read that account, he would have expressed a more favorable opinion of Allston's paintings. Neither does Poe seem to have read Oliver Wendell Holmes's review of the exhibition. Since Holmes gave two pages to a discussion of "the various representations of tranquil female beauty," citing "The Valentine," "Beatrice," "A Roman Lady," "The Spanish Girl," "Rosalie," and "Evening Hymn" as examples, and discussed Allston's friendship with Coleridge,[42] the review would likely have attracted Poe's attention had he seen it.

One of the "most noted" of Allston's paintings to which Poe is probably referring in his notice is "The Dead Man Restored to Life by Touching the Bones of the Prophet Elisha." This huge "work that, more than any other single picture, established Allston's position of prominence on both sides of the Atlantic" was acquired by the Pennsylvania Academy of Fine Arts in 1816 and has hung there ever since.[43] Poe could have seen it at the Academy, then located on Chestnut Street within easy walking distance of his home, during his residence in Philadelphia from 1838 until 1844, during which time he was editing *Graham's Magazine*. "The Dead Man Restored" was, in fact, the only painting by Allston exhibited at the Academy between 1838 and January 1842, the date of Poe's notice of Allston.[44] Another of Allston's "most noted" paintings was "Belshazzar's Feast," which, because Allston could not complete it even though a group of subscribers raised $10,000 to enable him to continue working on it, became a *cause célèbre*. Though Poe could not have seen it (Allston kept it hidden even from visitors to his studio), Poe could have known of it through any of the accounts in the newspapers, for "the American press kept a watchful eye on the progress of Allston's picture" (Gerdts, pp. 126-130). Neither of these huge, complex, narrative paintings based on biblical texts could have been to Poe's taste. Yet they may have been the only paintings by Allston that Poe had a strong impression of, let alone had ever seen. This possibility makes Poe's negative comments on Allston's art seem glib and hasty.

Since Allston's poem, "The Spanish Maid," which Poe admires in his notice, was written after publication of Allston's first volume of poems, *The Sylphs of the Seasons, and Other Poems*, in 1813, and not published in an exclusive collection of Allston's poems until after Poe's death, Poe probably read this poem in Rufus Griswold's *The Poets and Poetry of America* (Philadelphia, 1842). Griswold dedicated his volume to Allston and included in it seven of Allston's poems, including the two Poe mentions in his notice as well as "The Tuscan Girl" and "Rosalie." As Poe astutely observed, Allston's "poems are not all of a high order of merit." Poe is generous in praising "The Spanish Maid" and the "Address to Great Britain" (Allston's title was "America to Great Britain"); but one would have expected Poe to take notice of "Rosalie" as well. Poe reviewed Griswold's 1842 edition of *Poets and Poetry of America* in *Graham's Magazine*, June 1842, as "the best collection of the American poets that has yet been made." But he complained that Griswold had "unduly favored the writers of New England" (only three of Poe's poems were included—"The Coliseum," "The Haunted Palace," and "The Sleeper"), and he did not refer to Allston at all (*H*11: 124-125). *Monaldi* was published in 1841, but there is no indication that Poe read it. As already noted, Poe could not have seen Allston's *Lectures on Art*, the work that undoubtedly would have alerted him to the unanimity of aim and technique in Allston's work and his own. Poe knew only Allston's poetry, the quality of which was more likely to arouse Poe's contempt than his recognition.

Allston seems to have remained unaware of Poe's aesthetic kinship. The volumes of poetry Poe published during Allston's lifetime—*Tamerlane and Other Poems* (1827), *Al Aaraaf, Tamerlane, and Minor Poems* (1829), and *Poems* (1831)—attracted little critical attention. After his return to the United States, Allston seldom left the Boston area; Poe's mature poetry and tales appeared in Baltimore, Philadelphia, and New York periodicals. Richardson, Wright, and Johns all claim that Allston's *Lectures on Art* were written in the 1830s,[45] but Wright and Johns seem to merely echo Richardson (pp. 4, 135), whose observation that Allston read his lectures to Longfellow and Felton during the winter of 1842-1843 suggests a later date of composition. One is tempted to claim that Allston wrote his *Lectures* after reading Poe's aesthetic essays, since the language in key passages is sometimes close enough to suggest influence. The only statements of Poe's mature aesthetic position that Allston could have read before his death, however, were Poe's review of Longfellow's *Ballads and Other Poems*, and his review of Hawthorne's *Twice-Told Tales*, both published in April 1842, in *Graham's Magazine.* "The Philosophy of Composition" and "The Poetic Principle" were yet to come.

This ignorance of each other's work on the part of two of the most seminal aestheticians in America in the nineteenth century seems a waste. Allston's career was well established before Poe emerged on the American literary scene, but Poe could have used the support of Allston's influential friends. Or would an awareness of Allston's aesthetic position have caused Poe to consider him another Frogpondian to be attacked? In any case, the history of western culture indicates that it did not matter in the long run. Allston, the first American Symbolist painter, and Poe, the first American Symbolist poet, together in practice and in theory, began a tradition that is still alive.

NOTES

[1] Edgar Preston Richardson, *Washington Allston: A Study of the Romantic Artist in America* (New York, 1948), p. 154.

[2] Richardson, pp. 155, 180. See letter dated 11 July 1843 in *Letters of Ralph Waldo Emerson*, ed. Ralph L. Rusk, 6 vols. (New York, 1939), 3: 182. See also journal entries for 6 October 1837, 12 March 1844, and 8 May 1844 in *Journals of Ralph Waldo Emerson*, eds. Edward Waldo Emerson and Waldo Emerson Forbes, 10 vols. (Boston, 1909-14), 4: 311; 6: 501, 512.

[3] Margaret Fuller, "A Record of Impressions, Produced by the Exhibition of Mr. Allston's Pictures in the Summer of 1839," *Dial*, 1(1840), 74.

[4] For examples of Poe's battles with the "Frogpondians," see *H* 11: 67-69, 253-254; 12: 5-6, 41-106; 13: 1-13, 129; 14: 271.. See also Sidney P. Moss, *Poe's Literary Battles: The Critic in the Context of His Literary Milieu* (Durham, N.C., 1963), pp. 132-89. Holmes reviewed Allston's exhibition of 1839 in the *North American Review*, 50(1840), 358-381.

[5] Washington Allston, *Lectures on Art and Poems (1850) and Monaldi (1841)*, "Introduction" by Nathalia Wright (Gainesville, 1967), p. xiii. All further references to this work appear in parentheses in the text.

[6] Richardson, p. 87.

[7] Wright, "Introduction," *Lectures on Art and Poems*, p. xiii, is the only person in addition to myself to claim that Allston's *Lectures* are "based on the German Idealist philosophy," but she does not discuss the point. Elizabeth Johns, "Washington Allston's Later Career: Art About the Making of Art," *Arts Magazine*, 54(1979), 122-129, gives a detailed account of the

influence of Coleridge's and Wordsworth's poetry on Allston's paintings, but does not discuss either Coleridge's critical writings or Allston's *Lectures*. Regina Soria, "Washington Allston's *Lectures on Art*: The First American Art Treatise," *JAAC*, 18(1960), 329-344, concentrates on Allston's aesthetic theories but argues that his metaphysics "are not those of the German Idealists" (p. 338). She briefly considers Poe in connection with Allston (pp. 335-336), but does not give a systematic exploration of parallels between either their theories or their works. William H. Gerdts and Theodore E. Stebbins, Jr., *"A Man of Genius": The Art of Washington Allston (1779-1843)* (Boston, 1979), discuss Allston's paintings and drawings in light of his letters and biography but do not consider his *Lectures*, poems, or *Monaldi* in any detail. My study is the first, I believe, to consider a group of Allston's paintings in close connection with his *Lectures on Art*, his poems, and *Monaldi*.

[8] Jared B. Flagg, *The Life and Letters of Washington Allston* (1892; rpt. New York, 1969), p. 64. For further discussion of Coleridge's impact on Allston's aesthetic theory and artistic practice, see Flagg, pp. 61, 64, 77, 129; Richardson, pp. 1, 25, 75, 77, 101-103, 111, 159; Johns, pp. 123-125, 129.

[9] I have evaluated the nature and extent of Poe's debt to Coleridge in "'Intellect, Taste, and the Moral Sense': Poe's Debt to Immanuel Kant," *SAR* (1980), pp. 136-140.

[10] Samuel Taylor Coleridge, *Biographia Literaria*, ed. J. Shawcross, 2 vols. (Oxford, 1907), 2: 219-246, 304-306. Allston, for example, in his "Introductory Discourse," *Lectures on Art*, p. 64, tells an anecdote similar to one in Coleridge's "Essay Second" of "On the Principles of Genial Criticism" (*Biographia* 2: 224-225), in which a stranger, in conversation with Allston, confuses the difference between the "beautiful" and the "sublime." Poe probably read Coleridge's essays when they were published in Joseph Cottle's *Early Recollections of Samuel Taylor Coleridge* in 1837 (*Biographia* 2: 305).

[11] Pp. 46-47 contain a key passage in Allston's *Lectures* in which he defends the validity of the ideas. He proves their "common source" by means of a Wordsworthian recollection of youth and moral innocence.

[12] Barbara Novak, *Nature and Culture: American Landscape and Painting, 1825-1875* (New York, 1980), pp. 7, 90, discusses the "fusion of esthetic and religious terms" in nineteenth-century aesthetic theory.

[13] Cf. other statements Allston makes about the imagination, pp. 127, 146.

[14]Cf. Coleridge's definition of the imagination as "a repetition in the finite mind of the eternal act of creation in the infinite I AM" (*Biographia* 1: 202).

[15]Novak considers at length the attempt to portray the ideal in landscape painting (see, especially, pp. 25, 72, 74, 83, 89, 106, 118, 130, 265). She notes that in nineteenth-century American art, "all processes—particularly the engines of poetry—move inexorably from the particular to the eternal . . ." (p. 109). For further discussion of the attempt to refine the particularities of natural scenery into symbols of the ideal, see pp. 68, 123, 185, 187-188, 232, 271, 273, 299.

[16]See Novak, pp. 15, 200, on the attempt by American artists to paint "the face of God in the landscape so that the less gifted might recognize and share in that benevolent spirituality."

[17]See also stanza four of "On Greenough's Group of the Angel and Child," *Lectures on Art and Poems*, p. 364.

[18]Flagg, p. 56.

[19]Wright, "Introduction," *Lectures on Art and Poems*, pp. v-vi; Abraham A. Davidson, *The Eccentrics and Other American Visionary Painters* (New York, 1978), pp. 8-10, 12, 15.

[20]Fuller, pp. 74-75.

[21]Flagg, p. 380, quotes this from a letter written by "an unknown American Artist," 23 September 1844. Gerdts, "The Paintings of Washington Allston," *"A Man of Genius": The Art of Washington Allston*, p. 174, n116, identifies the writer as Greenough.

[22]Eric W. Carlson, ed., *Introduction to Poe: A Thematic Reader* (Glenview, Ill., 1967), p. 567.

[23]I refer throughout this discussion to Allston's paintings as they are reproduced in Gerdts's and Stebbins's beautiful catalogue. References to dates of composition of Allston's paintings, numbers of plates and figures, and pages on which they are located in Gerdts and Stebbins appear in parentheses in the text.

[24]Both androgynous figures closely resemble a chalk drawing, "Young Boy Seated on a Stone Block" (no. 83, p. 220) which Allston did much earlier, between 1804 and 1808.

[25]Gerdts, p. 156. For further discussion of this remarkable shift, see Gerdts, pp. 60, 134, 135, 140-141, 143; Richardson, pp. 125, 137; Johns, pp. 122, 126.

[26]Richardson, pp. 136, 174.

[27] Ibid., p. 157; Johns, p. 129.

[28] Omans, "'Intellect, Taste, and the Moral Sense,'" pp. 143-154; "Victor Cousin: Still Another Source of Poe's Aesthetic Theory?" *SAR* (1982), pp. 13-15.

[29] Fuller, pp. 79, 80.

[30] Richardson, p. 149.

[31] Flagg, p. 104.

[32] Gerdts, p. 50.

[33] Novak, pp. 41, 270.

[34] Richardson, p. 139.

[35] Fuller, p. 81.

[36] For a discussion of the possible date of composition of "The Valentine," see Gerdts, p. 60.

[37] Flagg, pp. 82, 109-110.

[38] *Monaldi*, pp. 67-68. *Monaldi* is bound, with separate pagination, with *Lectures on Art and Poems*.

[38] Gerdts, p. 140; Chad Mandeles, "Washington Allston's 'Evening Hymn'," *Arts Magazine*, 54(1980), 145; Johns, p. 129.

[39] Allston insists on human inability to achieve ideal perfection. In his "Introductory Discourse" he says that artists' "apprehension" of beauty may undergo many changes "as their more extended acquaintance with the higher outward assimilants of Beauty brings them . . . nearer to a perfect realization of the preëxisting Idea. By *perfect*, here, we mean only the nearest approximation by man" (p. 30). In his lecture on "Art" he observes: "Where the outward and inward are so united that we cannot separate them, there shall we find the perfection of Art. So complete a union has, perhaps, never been accomplished, and *may* be impossible; it is certain, however, that no approach to excellence can ever be made, if the *idea* of such a union be not constantly looked to by the artist as his ultimate aim" (p. 83).

[40] This emphasis on music as the most effective medium for conveying transcendent experience in "Rosalie" and "Song," and in Allston's description of the effect of the paintings of the Venetian school that "addressed themselves, not to the senses merely, . . . but rather through them to that region . . . of the imagination which is supposed to be under the exclusive dominion of music"

(Flagg, p. 56) is another point of resemblance between Allston and Poe. ("It *may* be" "in Music" that the experience of "supernal Beauty" is "now and then attained *in fact*.") It may account for the fact that three of the figures in Allston's idealized figure paintings are playing musical instruments. In both versions of the "Italian Shepherd Boy" the youth holds a flute and the woman in "Evening Hymn" strums a lute. The pose of the woman and the position of the fingers of her right hand are exactly that of the young man in "Lover Playing a Lute" (ca. 1830s, no. 70, p. 201). In "Girl in Persian Costume" (ca. 1832, no. 65, p. 198), a single woman in a landscape is again playing a lute. All five paintings, which have several characteristics in common, seem to associate playing or listening to music with artistic inspiration and aesthetic perception.

[41] Oliver Wendell Holmes, "Exhibition of Pictures Painted by Washington Allston at Harding's Gallery, School Street," *North American Review*, 50(1840), 378; Fuller, p. 79.

[42] Holmes, pp. 368-369, 375, 377-378.

[43] Gerdts, pp. 118-119, 65; Richardson, p. 106.

[44] Anna Wells Rutledge, *Cumulative Record of Exhibition Catalogues: The Pennsylvania Academy of Fine Arts, 1807-1870* (Philadelphia, 1955), p. 15. My thanks to Kathleen Foster, Curator, Pennsylvania Academy, for her help in using this source.

[45] Richardson, p. 157; Wright, "Introduction," *Lectures on Art and Poems*, p. xiii; Johns, p. 129.

POE, LOCKE AND KANT

JOAN DAYAN

> "'Tis true, on Words is still our
> whole debate,
> Disputes of *Me* or *Te*, of *aut* or *at*,
> To sound or sink in *cano*, O or A,
> Or give up Cicero to C or K."
> —Pope, *The Dunciad*

In the battle between the praised "philosopher proper—one whose frenzy takes a very determinate turn" (*H*16: 293) and the damned and despised litterateur of Boston (the "mystics for mysticism's sake"), Poe plays out to excess the faults he condemns. This parodic bent—a plea for the plain style couched in layers of hyperbole—has cost him the careful reading he deserves as scientist of method in a society sunk in feeling. Poe's critics forget that the antic disposition manifested in his satirical account, "How to Write a Blackwood Article," is reduplicated in the *cant* of those tales sometimes judged as serious expressions of his "poetic principle." In "How to Write a Blackwood Article" Poe delights in exposing his own scraps of learning as well as those he mocks: "it was all low—very! No profundity, no reading, no metaphysics—nothing which the learned call spirituality, and which the unlearned stigmatise as cant. [Dr. M. says I ought to spell 'cant' with a capital K—but I know better]" (*M*2: 338). And he playfully directs the composition of the proper tale: "The tone metaphysical is also a good one. If you know any big words this is your chance for them . . . . Say something about objectivity and subjectivity. Be sure and abuse a man called Locke . . . . A little reading of the 'Dial' will carry you a great way . . . . Put in something about the Supernal Oneness. Don't say a syllable about the Infernal Twoness" (*M*2: 341). Here, Poe mimes the pretensions of the Orphicists (and perhaps even his own call for "Supernal Beauty"), advises one to dive deep for the inexpressible (signified by a descent into the pages of the "Dial," chief journal of the Transcendentalists), and warns against the clarities of a man named Locke.

Now this Locke figures in some of Poe's most phantasmal thrillers. What we learn in re-reading the so-called "Gothic" tales is that Poe *uses* fiction to address philosophical and linguistic issues.[1] His own fight against vague, high-sounding language grounds itself in Locke's *Essay Concerning Human Understanding*. Melville would later tacitly acknowledge the import of Poe's conjunction of cant/Kant, joining of the jargon of ineffables to the Kantian idealism translated into the peculiar Transcendentalism of nineteenth-century America.[2] As Poe blasts through all idealisms with a wildly canting overflow of words, Melville overworks the language of *Pierre* in confrontation with the Transcendental optimism of the apostles of thought (the "speculative nut crackers"). Melville like Poe gives "cant" as surrogate for "Kant": in Book 19 of *Pierre*, Melville describes the inhabitants of "The Church of the Apostles," who compensate for "physical forlornness, by resolutely revelling in the region of blissful ideals." Playing on Poe's accord between jargon and idealism, he continues:

> Often groping in vain in their pockets, they cannot but give in to the Descartian vortices; while the abundance of leisure in their attics (physical and figurative), unite with the leisure in their stomachs, to fit them in an eminent degree for that undivided attention indispensable to the proper digesting of the sublimated Categories of Kant (can't) is the one great palpable fact in their pervadingly impalpable lives.[3]

In this essay I will consider Poe's fiction as a discourse on method. When Poe is most dogmatic, he is most oblique: his most obviously supernatural tales are more accurately a criticism of a repressive culture. Against those who "prefer having it understood that they compose by a species of fine frenzy—an ecstatic intuition" (*H*14: 194), Poe takes great pains to establish himself as nay-sayer fallen from the eighteenth-century empyrean, confronting a literary establishment that took little notice of him. As critic, he sets forth a program of literary purification with the intent to detach "criticism" from its attachment to "Orphicism, or Dialism, or Emersonianism, or any other pregnant compound indicative of confusion worse confounded" (*H*11: 6-7). He mocks the orphic talkers who blur the bounds of sense and thus render language imprecise: "we earnestly ask if *bread-and-butter* be the vast IDEA in question . . . for we have often observed that when a SEER has to speak of so usual a thing as bread-and-butter, he can never be induced to mention it outright" (*H*11: 253). Or again, "What is worth thinking is distinctly thought: what is distinctly thought, can and should be distinctly expressed, or should not be expressed at all" (*H*12: 6). Reacting against his contemporaries' abuse of words, Poe conducts his attack as did Locke on the level of language.

Procedural strategies culled from those eighteenth-century satirists who made the most of Lockean assumptions give Poe the conjoint humor and awe through which he invents his new mode of instruction. Arguing for all "that seems akin to the conservatism of half a century ago," he laments that those "justifiable *decora* of composition . . .

which in the time of Pope were considered as *prima facie* and indispensable indications of genius" are now regarded suspiciously (In "The American Scholar," for example, Emerson pitted "the style of Pope, Johnson, of Gibbon" against Romantic genius, as "cold and pedantic" to "blood-warm.").[4] Poe's "genius" is not irreconcilable with "artistic skill." Aware that "the finest quality of Thought is its self-cognizance" (*H*16: 204), he fights for a language of "Common Sense," what he calls "*ordinary* language" (*H*11: 252).

What then of the lapses in Poe's fiction, the wordy raptures of his tortured narrators, their obvious recourse to abstraction and vague phraseology? If we seek out the method in these tales, we find that the most bathetic exempla compose his strategy, a devious undoing of the vagaries of mysticism and inflated rhetoric. In his most "Gothic" tales Poe is trying to kill off, or as he puts it, "use up" the language of his contemporaries, the blustering *afflatus* of the Frogpondians (his name for the Boston Transcendentalists).[5] If Poe mimes canting so well that the reader believes these ethereal approximations to be the writer's own, this technique simply proves his talent in converting the language of idealism into a cause for madness and source of vulgarity.

Against what he calls in *Eureka* "the monomaniac grasping at the infinite" (*H*16: 292), Poe will create a narrator well-honed in the art of canting, a monomaniac who pursues the absolute in the form of a melancholy, erudite lady. The common setting for these narratives is Locke's "*dark room*." A worm rising from the depths of "the one drawer of a cabinet,"[6] the ruminating, though restricted mind, ever remains in that "closet shut from light, with only some little openings left, to let in external visible resemblances, or ideas of things without" (2.11.7, 211-212). These narrow, circumscribed settings, whether chambers or oblong boxes are spatial images of mind; and Poe's preoccupation with premature burial and the sudden awakening inside the crib of confinement is an allegory for that delimitation of mentality apparent everywhere in Locke's epistemology.

Locke's madman, like Poe's monomaniac, is quite normal except for one obsession—an obsession manifested for both Poe and Locke in terms of false ideas caused by obscure and undefined words. As Locke describes the madman:

> Hence it comes to pass that a man who is very sober and of right understanding in all other things, may in one particular be as frantic as any in Bedlam; if either by any sudden very strong impression, or long fixing his fancy upon one sort of thoughts, incoherent ideas, have been cemented together so powerfully, as to remain united. (2.11.11, 209-210)

The Poeian monomaniac dramatizes the dangers implicit in "the exquisite jargon" Locke warned against. If "the demands of truth are severe" ($H$11: 70), as Poe writes in a passage oddly reminiscent of Locke's elevation of *"judgement"* above *"wit,"* of "the severe rules of truth and good reason" over delusion (2.11.2, 203-204), then these romantic ladies must first suffer under the scrutiny of a discerning judgment in confrontation with wit. What separates attacks what combines, and in the oscillation between restraint and expansion of mind (or reason and fancy), Poe constructs his plot in the shadow of Locke's attack on sublime conceits and exalted strains—against "all the artificial and figurative application of words eloquence hath invented" (3.10.32, 146).

Poe gives us a clue to the characterization of most of his narrators when he argues in his review of Longfellow's "Ballads and Other Poems," against the sin of decking truth in "gay robes." To do so, he writes, is "to render her a harlot. It is but making her a flaunting paradox to wreathe her in gems and flowers." He then verifies his words by giving the reader the kind of style that can house such a primary, plain and strict content:

> —we feel the necessity, in enforcing this *truth*, of descending from metaphor. Let us then be simple and distinct. To convey 'the true' we are required to dismiss from the attention all inessentials. We must be perspicuous, precise, terse. We need concentration rather than expansion of mind. We must be calm, unimpassioned, unexcited—in a word, we must be in that peculiar mood which, as nearly as possible, is the exact converse of the poetical. ($H$11: 70)

We recognize the technique of Poe's rational talkers who insist that they will be precise, that they are calm: "Hearken! and observe how stealthily—how calmly I can tell you the whole story" ($M$3: 792); and the killer of cat and wife assures, "My immediate purpose is to place before the world, plainly, succinctly, and without comment, a series of mere household events" ($M$3: 849). We could of course go on; the oddest and most exaggerated tales always begin with claims for plain discourse.

The narrating "I" who reasons, distinguishes and discerns, who can break down wholes into parts, is a fanatic—and such a clarifying, determining tendency is only one stage, the most obvious, in a progression of extremes. Dismissing any mere happiness as deception, this character makes the myrtles (or his spouse) wither under Locke's "labor of thought." Yet in the course of the tale, Poe allows this same harsh raconteur to use (perhaps unwittingly) the very implements of deceit, the arts that "dupe and play the wag with the senses," to recall Swift's "Digression on Madness." As acolyte of the beautiful lady of mystic knowledge, this analyst becomes prone to the vision and fancy, the prophetic dreams and sortilege, that once seemed so alien to his personality. Contrary to "separating carefully, one from another, ideas wherein can be found the least difference, thereby to avoid being misled by similitude, and by affinity to take one thing for another," the narrator finds himself caught in scenes of collapsing identities and confounded likeness (2.11.2, 203). He sees Berenice's teeth here, there and everywhere, and finds the first Morella reproduced in the simulacrum of his own imaginings. Ligeia, whose existence is composed of "a circle of analogies," returns to deny difference and to reaffirm her identity not only with her rival Rowena but with the narrator himself.

Through a witty juxtaposition or mixing up of wit and judgment, Poe effects the conversion that is itself underlying the interaction between self and object in each tale. As the narrator sinks into the object of his scrutiny (a disease that overtakes him as he talks), his powers of concentration falter, his mind digresses, rendered impotent by the very dissipation his "beloved" undergoes. Indeed, as she fades into a kind of neutral gray of non-being (in Lockean terms, left only with those original or primary qualities of body), his language assumes all the superfluities and colorful harangues appropriate to "rhetoric, that powerful instrument of error and deceit" (3.10.34, 146).

Poe's deflation of illusory ideals and exposure of imprecise language (the two cannot be separated: a murky ideal produces murky language) becomes certain in these dialogues between the observing, willful narrator and an apparently passive external and female object. The narrator of these tales does finally "cant it," meaning that he places his story in the special phraseology of romantic love and of the Transcendental "cuttlefishes of profundity." And Poe's male narrators are indeed haunted, possessed by those active spirits of secret knowledge; but this filling is in truth an emptying—a destructive influx of a language (note the *"filling up"* of "How to Write a Blackwood Article," *M*2: 343), corrupt and gone to seed. We might be tempted to say that language has driven the narrator crazy—that the superfluities of spirit (in its worse manifestations) have taken over his mind and overturned his reason. "Cant" also means, according to the OED, "a sudden movement which tends to or results in, tilting or turning over." The lady's cant (though presented to us indirectly through the narrator's recanting) leads to the violent revolution in the minds of Poe's most wordy narrators.

Poe is preoccupied with correct language; therefore each narrator makes the same mistakes. Guilty of the same kind of redundancies, haunted by the same spirits, he always digresses in the same way. For Poe these digressions do not merely mark a surprising ghost story but the overreaching of dead utterances. This radical reuse of Romantic ideals of beauty or wisdom privileges Poe's anti-idealist propensities in a radical reinterpretation of Gothic haunting. Although these hauntings invite us to seek a mysterious or elevated first cause, their presentation leaves us with no more than material disintegration—a collapse that the diction enacts. What the narrator most often beholds with horror are similes, syllables, types and expressions. A citation from Swift's "Mechanical Operation of the Spirit" will prepare us for Poe's own critical fictions on the Canter's Art:

> I shall now Discourse briefly, by what kind of Practices the Voice is best governed, towards the Composition and Improvement of the *Spirit*: for, without a competent Skill in turning and toning each Word, and Syllable, and Letter, to their due Cadence, the whole Operation is incompleat . . . . For, it is to be understood, that in the Language of the Spirit, Cant and Droning supply the place of Sense and Reason, in the Language of Men: Because, in spiritual Harangues, the Disposition of the Words according to the Art of Grammar, hath not the least Use, but the Skill and Influence wholly lie in the Choice and Cadence of the Syllables . . . .[7]

Poe takes Swift's instructions for how to "draw sighs from the multitudes"—"The Force, or Energy" of the utterance found "wholly in dwelling, and dilating upon Syllables and Letters"—to enact the plight of his own narrators whose hearts are pierced by the "forcible Effects" of "a single Vowel" (p. 279). The language of awe becomes the language of damnation. This is the world of the unregenerate who damned to repeat the torment, has gone mad in the attempt to say—to name the unnameable. Reading the physical world as if it were a visual language, he shudders before the effects of utterance. The prisoner in "The Pit and the Pendulum" perceives the black-robed judges' lips as they "writhe with a deadly locution" (*M*2: 681). William Wilson is struck by the "character, the tone, *the key*, of those few, simple, and familiar, yet *whispered* syllables" that strike his soul "with the shock of a galvanic battery" (*M*2: 439).

As readers we must not forget that in Poe's world, consecration (the fetishistic regard of the lady), becomes through the narration equivalent to magic incantation. The OED places the first use of the word "cant" in the Latin "*cant-us*, singing, song, chant," and in *The*

Spectator Steele traces the word to "one Andrew Cant . . . a Presbyterian Minister in some Illiterate part of *Scotland*": "Since *Mas. Cant's* time, it [cant] has been understood in a larger Sense, and signifies all sudden Exclamations, Whinings, Unusual Tones, and in fine all Praying and Preaching like the unlearned of the Presbyterians . . . ."[8] In "Ligeia" and "Morella" the narrator's canting, joins the sirenic cadences of the lady. In fact, in these tales of mystery, his sing-song disquisitions and monotonous intonings are ironically mirrored in the mystic ladies' own sonorities. Through the curious colloquy between subject and object, the narrator seems to imbibe a certain talent for muttering obscure, equivocal and unsteady terms, just as he forever sits in libraries filled with the inherited words of metempsychosis and Rosicrucian demonology. Morella and especially Ligeia are mediums for a certain kind of magical, murderous cant.

Morella utters "some low, singular words," and the hearer shudders "at those too unearthly tones" (*M*2: 230). Ligeia too is cast in the role of orator imprinting inscrutable *notae*, "wild words" on his brain. Significantly, it is, he insists, not just the "almost magical melody, modulation, distinctness and placidity of her very low voice—" that he remembers with greatest awe, but "her manner of utterance" (*M*2: 315). And since we never hear Ligeia speak, except through the transmission or revision of the monomaniac, the manner of his speech can tell us more about the wonders of this utterance—and its negative attributes—than what he says. "Ligeia" is the feminine of the Homeric Greek adjective *ligys*, meaning canorous, high-sounding or shrill. Ligeia, then, is a siren; no mere singer, she is a sorceress who enthralls men with her spells.[9] Poe apostrophizes this Ligeia in "Al Aaraaf":

> Ligeia! Ligeia!
>   My beautiful one!
> Whose harshest idea
>   Will to melody run . . .
>
>   . . .
>
> Ligeia! wherever
>   Thy image may be,
> No magic shall sever
>   Thy music from thee.
> Thou hast bound many eyes
>   In a dreamy sleep—
>   (*M*1: 109-110, ll.100-
>   103/112-117)

In the tale "Ligeia" the song of enthrallment contextualizes itself in a jargon synonymous with that cant condemned by both Poe and Locke. That Poe must create a narrator who is indeed seduced by a "name" and destroyed by its vague sounds reminds us of his concern with the abuses of discourse. The bawling and muttering descanters of Steele and Swift add an ironic twist to Poe's choice of the name "Ligeia." As the acolyte of Ligeia moves "onward to the goal of a wisdom too divinely precious not to be forbidden," groping through "the many mysteries of the transcendentalism in which we were immersed," the heroine sickens, her eyes dim, and he laments: "Wanting the radiant lustre of her eyes, letters, lambent and golden, grew duller than Saturnian lead" (*M*2: 316). Give Poe's eighteenth-century bent, it is not surprising that his subtext in this inverse alchemy is Pope's *Dunciad*, where the Goddess Dulness prepares "To hatch a new Saturnian age of Lead" (1,l.25).

The narrator of "Morella" initiates his story by failing to define. He claims a "deep yet most singular affection" for the lady but adds, "my soul from our first meeting, burned with fires it had never before known; but the fires were not of Eros, and bitter and tormenting to my spirit was the gradual conviction that I could in no manner define their unusual meaning, or regulate their vague intensity" (*M*2: 229). Whereas in "Berenice" the narrator opposes the claims of Eros to those of mind, here he leaves the expected antonym unsupplied, suggesting the inadequacy to plague him throughout his "recollection"—a "meaning" that cannot be defined compounded by an "intensity" too "vague" to be moderated. The connection between an indistinct idea, undefinable terms and the disease of a mind enthused by such studied obscurities (the whispered nothings of a mystic Morella) set the stage for this discourse of unintelligibles.

Morella, consequently, is not merely erudite; an interminable talker, she is more accurately a transmitter of empty speculation through that unintelligible cant that brings confusion into her disciple's mind. As Locke explains this necessary "confusion worse confounded": "Besides, there is no such way to gain admittance, or give defence to strange and absurd doctrines, as to guard them round about with legions of obscure, doubtful, and undefined words . . . . For untruth being unacceptable to the mind of man, there is no other defence left for absurdity, but obscurity" (3.10.9, 128). The texts of this woman from Presburg, home of black magic, were "a number of those mystical writings . . . usually considered the mere dross of the early German literature": they become the narrator's own "favorite and constant study." The inexplicable transference of her preferences to his own results in his inability to express anything with certainty. Each assertion is no sooner stated than cast into doubt: "In all this, / if I err not, / my reason had little to do. My convictions, / or I forget myself,

/ were in no manner acted upon by the ideal, nor was any tincture of the mysticism which I read, to be discovered, / unless I am greatly mistaken, / either in my deeds or in my thoughts" (*M*2: 230). His failed attempt to separate the "ideal" from his reason proves the fatal intercourse between his reasoning and his mania (what he knows and what he dreams). In Lockean terms, madness arises, we recall, through the cementing together of ideas not naturally related; they then fill up the mind with—to use the jargon of Swift's Grub Street Hack—"a redundancy of vapours": "and the confusion of two different ideas, which a customary connexion of them in their minds hath to them made in effect but one, fills their heads with false views, and their reasonings with false consequences" (2.33.18, 235). Once deluded into believing his reason intact, the narrator abandons himself to Morella's cant: "persuaded of this, I abandoned myself implicitly to the guidance of my wife, and entered with an unflinching heart into the intricacies of her studies" (230). He describes his "poring over forbidden pages"; he feels " a forbidden spirit enkindling within," and we now read Poe's imitation of the language of vision.

This very literary pastime has an unending, inescapable quality. Morella would "rake up from the ashes of a dead philosophy some low, singular words," whose "strange meaning," the narrator stresses, "burned themselves in upon my memory." Her verbiage becomes his curse, as unnerving and ominous as the old man's evil eye in "The Tell-Tale Heart": "And then, hour after hour, would I linger by her side, and dwell upon the music of her voice—until, at length, its melody was tainted with terror,—and there fell a shadow upon my soul—and I grew pale, and shuddered inwardly at those too unearthly tones" (230). Her music, its melody and tones—mere sounds—cause the stain upon his soul. And with his transformation, the required conversion occurs: "And thus, joy suddenly faded into horror, and the most beautiful became the most hideous as Hinnom became Gehenna."

As in "Berenice," this narrator might wonder with Egaeus, "How it it that from beauty I have derived a type of unloveliness?" Indeed his growing hatred for Morella causes her decay, but what causes his revulsion? Its source can only be the manner of her discourse ("indeed the time had now arrived when the mystery of my wife's manner oppressed me as a spell") and, further, the "character of those disquisitions" she culls from volumes of forgotten lore. As her body fails, his soul sickens. He looks into her eyes and sinks into himself, "giddy with the giddiness of one who gazes downward into some dreary and unfathomable abyss." And the more he gazes, the more fiendish he becomes. In this sage of his augmenting desire and her diminishing life, his increasing will for her death and her apparently passive decline, Morella's death-bed scene becomes a struggle for control through utterance. Overcome by her words, the narrator is reduced to repeating one name, "Morella."

Ligeia, described as the lady of romance, lures her love beyond life into a more-than-human gnosis. The first few pages of the tale, a paean to ideal beauty, develop through the effects of indescribability. The narrator's speechlessness initially turns on the difficult retrieval of a fading, remote past. Through his insistence that he cannot fittingly remember, he wills a poverty of discourse: "I cannot . . . remember how, when, or even precisely where, I first became acquainted with the lady Ligeia" / "my memory is feeble through much suffering" / "I cannot *now* bring these points to mind" / "a recollection flashes upon me that I have *never known* the paternal name of her who was my friend and my betrothed" / "I but indistinctly recall . . .—what wonder that I have utterly forgotten" (*M*2: 310-311). And his "wildly romantic offering on the shrine of the most passionate devotion" is never to ask her last name (311).

The excesses of this language travesty the high-flown style of romantic love. And Poe, whose criticism most often praised that language in accord with nature's intentions, here exaggerates the expression of sacred furor. Although this language might be interpreted as a fit example of what Poe means by exalting the soul "not into passion, but into a conception of pure *beauty*" (as he describes the effect of Tennyson's "Oenone," *H*11: 254), he demonstrates that this ether-like medium exalts—but not without turning the one exalted into a madman. Recall that Poe's argument against Hawthorne's "mysticism" is based on a call for correct allegory: "Where the suggested meaning runs through the obvious one in a *very* profound under-current so as never to interfere with the upper one without our own volition, so as never to show itself unless *called* to the surface, there only, for the proper use of fictitious narrative, is it available at all" (*H*13: 148). If Poe's "surface" or "upper-current" here is evocative of the "spiritual" and "ideal," we can be sure that Poe means something else—the point of this fiction is not what it seems. The deep "under-current" can only be unveiled by stripping away the obvious—those fascinating appearances that delude the reader as well as the narrator.

The moment he announces that "one dear topic . . . on which my memory fails me not," his personification of a spectre and Poe's ridicule of cant is under way. As well as taking the most suggestively "romantic," fanciful and idealistic material for his subject (inexpressible, undying love), he turns it on itself to take his stand along with Locke against "*enthusiasm* . . . founded neither on reason nor divine revelation, but rising from the conceits of a warmed or overweening brain" (4.19.7, 432). "Buried in studies of a nature more than all else adapted to deaden impressions of the outward world, it is by that sweet word alone—by Ligeia—that I bring before mine eyes in fancy the image of her who is no more." The name alone annihilates sense, and reminds us that this narrator's words are the real phantoms that will startle and confound the reader. Divested of materiality, "slender . . . even emaciated," Ligeia "came and departed as a shadow" ($M$2: 310-311). Through a process of a kind of essentialization, she becomes a sound, a shadow, a lone "marble hand" and finally, two uncommonly giant eyes.

Her face is portrayed as a compound of indefinables: "the radiance of an opium dream—an airy and spirit-lifting vision more wildly divine than the phantasies which hovered about the slumbering souls of the daughters of Delos" ($M$2: 311). And Poe's *"intensities"* here seize upon what he called the "tone transcendental": "Hint everything—assert nothing" ($M$2: 342). The details of her portrait, a close analysis of her face alone, read like a monument to varying discursive types of the ideal lady. A collocation of stock formulae, this pile-up of clichés further artifices his lady out of existence. This portrait is a highly textual satire on the cant that betrays a mind befogged. Obsessed by certain terms, the lover cites one of Poe's own favorite quotations: "'There is no exquisite beauty,' says Bacon, Lord Verulam, speaking truly of all the forms and *genera* of beauty, 'without some *strangeness* in the proportion'." He then takes apart Bacon's quotation and amplifies its jargon: "although I perceived that her loveliness was indeed 'exquisite,' and felt that there was much of 'strangeness' pervading it, yet I have tried in vain to detect the irregularity and to trace home my own perception of 'the strange'" ($M$2: 311-312). Unattached to any clear and distinct idea, his words remain insignificant, floating somewhere in a "vortex of *mysticism*" ($H$11: 254).

Poe, however, makes certain that the narrator's plight is embodied in the relations between his own texts. In reusing the popular stuff of Gothic fiction, Poe becomes involved in his own compulsion to repeat. A look at these lineaments of desire reveals a startling sameness in every image of woman presented. In this rhapsody, Ligeia becomes no more than a chimera constructed out of the impossible extremes of a depraved imagination, an extravagance Poe will later write into "The Spectacles," a parody of a nearly blind lover unaware of the cosmeticized hag before him: "The countenance was a surpassingly beautiful one! Those large luminous eyes!—that proud Grecian nose!— those dark luxuriant curls!—" ($M$3: 909). Ligeia is made up of a "lofty and pale forehead"; "skin rivalling the purest ivory"; "raven-black . . . glossy . . . luxuriant and naturally-curling tresses," which evoke "the full force of the Homeric epithet 'hyacinthine!'" Her nose is outlined as perfectly as the "graceful medalions of the Hebrews"; her chin is Greek, its contours traced to the vision of the dreaming Cleomenes. By means of the bizarre image of "harmoniously curved nostrils speaking the free spirit," we are led to that yoking of abstract and concrete so much a part of Poe's scheme: "Here was indeed the triumph of all things heavenly—the magnificent turn of the short upper lip—the soft, voluptuous slumber of the under—the dimples which sported, and the color which spoke—the teeth glancing back, with a brilliancy almost startling, every ray of the holy light which fell upon them" (312). In this description of the "sweet mouth," we recall Berenice's teeth and their strained collocation of heavenly and demonic (a death's head vision captured brilliantly in "The Spectacles": "The magic of a lovely form in woman—the necromancy of female gracefulness," *M*3: 889). In this picture of sporting dimples, speaking colors and teeth glancingly reflecting some unidentified holy light, Poe turns the jargon of spirit round on itself.

When the narrator confronts the memory of Ligeia's eyes, he reveals the heart of his obsession. Her "divine orbs" recall the neo-platonic paradox of a love, glance or smile that simultaneously kills and quickens. In looking into these "star eyes," the narrator sinks from thought to thought. As these eyes shrink and dilate intermittently, the narrator's language alternately expands and contracts. In this ritual of ever-intensifying thought, he says, these eyes were "far larger than the ordinary eyes of our own race"; and further, "They were even fuller than the fullest of the gazelle eyes of the tribe of the valley of Hourjahad." Yet this exalted beauty is held suspect; "—in my heated fancy thus it appeared perhaps—" he writes, answering her excitement (the eyes' peculiar fullness became noticeable *only* "in moments of intense excitement"), with his own. He then turns away from the physical, however, and denies sensationalist trappings in more mystifying verbiage: "The 'strangeness,' however, which I found in the eyes, was of a nature distinct from the formation, or the color, or the brilliancy of the features, and must, after all, be referred to the expression" (313). As the narrator of "Berenice" displaced the concrete gaping mouth and exposed teeth by an indefinite—"a smile of peculiar meaning"—here the narrator escapes into words, reducing the objects of sense to a mere word. Obsessed now by a sign that signifies nothing, he gives vent to his passion: "Ah, word of no meaning! behind whose vast latitude of mere sound we intrench our ignorance of so much of the spiritual. The expression of the eyes of Ligeia! How for long hours have I pondered upon it! How have I . . . struggled to fathom it!" Much more safely entangled in this labyrinth of unintelligibles than in any more sensuous roots, he can ask, as did the narrator of "Berenice" in vague recollection of an unspeakable deed: "What was it—that something more profound than the well of Democritus—which lay within the pupils of my beloved? What *was* it? I was possessed with a passion to discover.

Those eyes! those large, those shining, those divine orbs! they became to me twin stars of Leda, and I to them devoutest of astrologers" (313).

If in *Eureka*, Poe attempts to "periphrase the conception for which we struggle in the word 'Universe,'" here the narrator desires to circumvolve the idea in Ligeia's "expression," "that sentiment such as I felt always aroused within me by her large and luminous orbs" (314). He chooses to extend the range and influence of those eyes through analogy, moving through varying degrees of reference and finding "in the commonest objects of the universe, a circle of analogies to that expression." His mode of *returning in* determines that monomaniac iteration described in "Berenice" as a stubborn "returning in upon the original object as a centre" (*M*2: 212). Unable to define the sentiment aroused by those eyes, he recognizes it "in the survey of a rapidly-growing vine—in the contemplation of a moth, a chrysalis, a stream of running water." "I have felt it," he continues, "in the ocean; in the falling of a meteor. I have felt it in the glances of unusually aged people" (314). The narrator affects the pietistic jargon of an ineffable ideal, circling round what is neither formed nor form. Poe locates both the humor and the horror in this language of unutterables. Later, in "A Tale of the Ragged Mountains," he explicitly connects an "intensity of interest" in certain phenomena and a specific kind of repetition reminiscent of Ligeia's fanatic scrutinizer: "In the quivering of a leaf—in the hue of a blade of grass—in the shape of a trefoil—in the humming of a bee—in the gleaming of a dew-drop—in the breathing of the wind—in the faint odors that came from the forest—there came a whole universe of suggestion—a gay and motley train of rhapsodical and immethodical thought" (*M*3: 943). Such a pursuit (signified by the sequence of "in" circlings) would be categorized by Locke—and by Poe the ironist—as one of those "excursions into the incomprehensible Inane" (2.21.1, 308).

In reading these documents of a mind undone, we should start with Locke's own question: "Let us then suppose the mind to be, as we say, white paper, void of all characters, without any ideas:—How comes it to be furnished?" (2.1.2, 122). At the inception of every telling, Poe's narrator or mind is "the yet empty cabinet which comes to be furnished with ideas and language, the materials about which to exercise its discursive faculty" (1.1.5, 48-49). Poe's tales should be read as varying attempts to enter the mind, to break into the room or repository filled with the dregs of remembrance (or recycled textual conventions) and there to commemorate this palimpsest defiled.

His narrators, like the hypothetical confessor of "How to Write a Blackwood Article," turn mind inside out to make the page inscribed equal to a mind engraved with the traces of sensory impressions. "The sound drives him mad, and, accordingly, pulling out his tablets, he gives a record of his sensations" (*M*2: 340). Here the Lockean exchange between a once blank page or empty cabinet and the world of sensations (a box filled with Berenice's teeth or a tomb filled with Morella's name) introduces the mind's tablet as synonymous with the pages of the Poeian text. Besides opening up his narrator's mind so that the reader can examine the marks on a once white slate, Poe invents a narratorial voice composed of the histrionic cadences of other texts. In dragging out the retranscriptions of invention, demanding that we see each tale or utterance through the layers of an earlier one, its words superimposed upon past words, Poe transcribes a discourse that traps us into suffering from the effects of a ponderous, all-consuming and unforgettable cant of Beauty. While using his narrator to disincarnate the lady (reducing her either to teeth in "Berenice" or to no more than eyes in "Ligeia" or to the syllables of a name in "Morella"), Poe puts his reader in the position of dismantling the prose connected with her.

Beyond this satiric reuse of a Gothic love of tale-telling, combined with the enthusiast's mystifications, however, Poe's best-known narrators are indeed sinners, violators of the reverenced *donnés* of their culture. In a most interesting way they apply the knife to Poe's literary enemies and to "the customary cant of the day" (*H*11: 253). The Romantic artist's annihilation of his lady the better to address the unattainable idea confined in her too fleshly frame turns into an exquisite experiment to test the assumptions of Locke, while affirming Poe's argument against those misusers of language, the mystifiers of Concord.

NOTES

[1] For a study of Poe's critique of romance as revealed most forcefully in *Eureka* and in his tales of women, see Joan Dayan, *Fables of Mind: An Inquiry into Poe's Fiction* (New York, 1987). Since this essay was accepted a few years before publication of *Fables*, some of its ideas are treated in the book.

[2] As Emerson explained: "The Idealism of the present day acquired its name of Transcendental from the use of that term by Immanuel Kant of Konigsberg, who replied to the sceptical philosophy of Locke, which insisted that there was nothing in the intellect which was not previously in the experience of the senses, by showing that there was a very important class of ideas or imperative forms, which did not come by experience, but through which experience was acquired; that these were intuitions of the mind itself; and he denominated them Transcendental forms"—"The Transcendentalist," quoted in O. B. Frothingham, *Transcendental-*

ism in New England (New York, 1956), p. 127. For more on Poe's argument against Emerson, see *Fables of Mind*.

[3] *Pierre, or the Ambiguities*, ed. Harrison Hayford et al. (Evanston, 1971), p. 267.

[4] *The Complete Essays and Other Writings of Ralph Waldo Emerson*, ed. Brooks Atkinson; forew. Tremaine McDowell (New York, 1950), p. 61.

[5] That Poe means "use up" to annihilate is made clear in a letter of 1835: "I had occasion (pardon me) to 'use *up*'—the *N. Y. Mirror*, whose Editor's Norman Leslie did *not* please me—and the *Philadelphia Gazette*, which, being conducted by one of the subeditors of the Knickerbocker, thinks it its duty to abuse all rival magazines" (*O*1: 101).

[6] Locke, *An Essay Concerning Human Understanding* [1689], ed., A. C. Fraser (New York, 1959), 2.2.3, 146. (Hereafter cited within the text.)

[7] Swift, "A Discourse Concerning the Mechanical Operation of the Spirit," *A Tale of a Tub*, ed. A. C. Guthkelch and D. Nichol Smith. 2nd. ed. (London, 1958), pp. 277-278.

[8] Steele, *The Spectator*, No. 147, 18 August 1711, ed. Donald F. Bond (London, 1965), p. 80. Cf. Addison on the "unintelligible Cant" of the spiritualists: "I was once engaged in Discourse with a *Rosicrucian* about the *Great Secret*" (No. 574, 30 July 1714, pp. 561-562).

[9] The Glanville epigraph that recurs throughout "Ligeia," though Mabbott supposes it to be invented by Poe, is of interest in Poe's compound of Glanville's name and his own citation. Glanville's *Sadducismus Triumphatus*—a vindication of the existence of witches and witchcraft in the seventeenth century (1667)—remains in the background as yet another clue to the unravelling of "Ligeia": If Ligeia survives (through her *will*), is it as a witch?

POE AND THE *BLACKWOOD'S* TALE OF SENSATION

BRUCE I. WEINER

Edgar Allan Poe's penchant for Gothic sensationalism remains an obstacle to a serious appreciation of his fiction. Next to Hawthorne and Melville, who tried to transform Gothic romance into tragedy, Poe seems parochial and immature, working the machinery of terror for its own sake and for more than it is worth. His reliance upon Gothic effects has led such notables as Henry James and T. S. Eliot to conclude that, despite a considerable influence upon other writers, Poe's appeal is chiefly to the adolescent mind. To take him "with more than a certain degree of seriousness," wrote James, "is to lack seriousness one's self."[1] Even Allen Tate, who believed that we should take Poe seriously, had to confess that his style "at its typical worst," the "Gothic glooms . . . done up in a glutinous prose," makes for tiresome reading, "unless one gets a clue to the power underlying the flummery." The clue, Tate believed, lies not in the influence of the Gothic novel but in Poe's impoverished sensibility, at once primitive and decadent, exploiting the Gothic to satisfy an appetite for sensation but lacking the perception or moral perspective to relate such sensation to life.[2]

More recent critics have portrayed Poe as a shrewder and more sophisticated manipulator of Gothic effects. G. R. Thompson maintains that Poe's Gothic tales are informed by an intricate irony, which plays the rational off against the supernatural, not, as in Ann Radcliffe's novels, to restore us finally to reason, but, as in the tales of Hoffmann and Tieck, to leave us in uncertainty about the nature of events. In this way, Thompson argues, Poe gives shape to a vision of despair "over the ability of the mind ever to know anything, either about the ultimate reality of the world or the mind itself."[3] In the view of David Ketterer, Poe's vision has even less to do with Gothic horror. He sees Poe as a visionary rather than a skeptic, who attacks our faith in reason and reality in order to confirm a faith in transcendental imagination and who uses "the horror format largely for market considerations."[4] These readings do much to establish Poe as a serious, philosophical writer, but they exaggerate his detachment from Gothicism. Although no mere Gothicist, Poe was captive, I believe, to a Gothic sensibility. I hope to show at least that, in imitating the late Gothic "tale of sensation," popularized by *Blackwood's Edinburgh Magazine*, Poe was neither as shrewd nor as ironic as recent critics suggest, and that his vision in the tales, though it may at times transcend the sensationalism he employs, is largely shaped by it.

I

Poe's debt to the *Blackwood's* tale of sensation has been firmly established. He testifies to a knowledge of *Blackwood's* thrillers, and many of them have been identified as sources of incident and technique in his own tales.[5] Michael Allen has examined at length the influence of the British magazine tradition, especially the brand of journalism that *Blackwood's* introduced, on Poe's theory and practice as author and critic.[6] Yet Poe's exploitation of the kind of Gothic sensationalism *Blackwood's* was known for is vaguely understood. Part of the problem is that we have no specific study of the tales published in the early numbers of *Blackwood's*. They have been classified and described by critics interested in their influence on Poe, but his parodies in "Loss of Breath," "How to Write a Blackwood Article" and "A Predicament" are the most revealing criticism of them we have. These parodies complicate matters, however, since Poe mocks in them the Gothic formula he seems to take seriously elsewhere in his fiction and criticism.

As Michael Allen points out, Poe was writing for magazines imitating by and large a *Blackwood's* format that had revolutionized the magazine marketplace. Combining the serious review-essays of the established *Edinburgh Review* and *Quarterly Review* with light literature and critical controversy, *Blackwood's* sought to attract both the elite audience of the *Reviews* and the growing mass of semi-educated middle-class readers. Allen identifies three kinds of fiction appearing frequently in the early volumes of *Blackwood's*: the tale of sensation, "usually structured around a protagonist isolated in some strange, horrific, or morbid situation which is progressively exploited for effect"; the burlesque of popular literary fashions or philosophical ideas; and the working-class idyll, usually with political and moral overtones. Poe, he suggests, adopted the first two, the tale of sensation to appeal to the popular fiction-reading audience and the burlesque to cultivate the more sophisticated reader.[7] Thus Poe seems to have been shrewdly adapting himself to the magazine marketplace. That he made the tale of sensation, moreover, the subject of some of his burlesques suggests that he was unusually detached from his craft.

To view Poe, however, as a shrewd exploiter of *Blackwood's* sensationalism is to distort the facts of his magazine career. It is to accept the impression fostered by Poe and credited by scholars that tales of sensation were the main feature in *Blackwood's*. Allen gives them equal footing with the burlesques and moral idylls, but Thompson calls them "the mainstay of the fiction of *Blackwood's*."[8] Mabbott claims that Poe's attempt in "The Pit and the Pendulum" to do "a straight story in the Blackwood manner . . . has outlived all the once famous *Tales of Blackwood*" (*M*2: 679). Actually, I count only nine "straight" tales of sensation in *Blackwood's* from its inception in 1817 to 1845 and eleven others that combine the sensational formula with literary burlesque.[9] All but one of these twenty tales appeared before Poe began to publish fiction in 1832. There are other episodes of Gothic sensationalism in reviews of books and long-running serials like Samuel Warren's "Passages from the Diary of a Late Physician," but the tales of sensation are greatly outnumbered by burlesques, moral idylls, and tales of adventure.[10] Nor was the tale of sensation as widely imitated and pirated as Poe and some of his critics suggest. As Allen notes, very few appear in American magazines, especially after 1832, in proportion to other kinds of fiction.[11] More widely imitated and parodied were *Blackwood's* features such as John Wilson's erudite and gossipy editor's column ("Noctes Ambrosianae"), Warren's "Diary of a Late Physician," DeQuincey's "Murder Considered as a Fine Art" (his more famous "Confessions of an Opium Eater" was written for *Blackwood's* but published in the *London Magazine*), and serials on German literature ("Horae Germinicae") and contemporary philosophy ("The Metaphysician").[12]

Blackwood's gained some notoriety with its tales of sensation, but Poe was wrong to suppose that they carried the magazine or could carry one in America. In fact, he was on the defensive from the start in his attempt to publish such fiction. In response to criticism of the too-horrible nature of "Berenice," one of his earliest tales, Poe proposed to his publisher, Thomas W. White of the *Southern Literary Messenger*, that the most celebrated magazines, such as *Blackwood's*, owed their success to fiction of a similar nature:

> You ask me in what does this nature consist? In the ludicrous heightened into the grotesque: the fearful colored into the horrible: the witty exaggerated into the burlesque: the singular wrought out into the strange and mystical. You may say this is all bad taste. I have my doubts about it.[13]

There was no doubt about it, however, among Poe's publishers and friends, who found his burlesques too grotesque or esoteric, his tales of sensation too strange and mystical. Refusing to publish his tales in 1836, Harpers advised him to "lower himself a little to the ordinary comprehension of the generality of readers" (*H*17: 378). This was the advice of his friends as well. Relaying the reasons for Harpers' rejection to Thomas W. White, who was then Poe's employer on the *Messenger*, James Kirke Paulding advised that Poe apply his considerable skills "to more familiar subjects of satire," to the "habits and manners" of Americans and the literary pretensions of England. Another friend, James E. Heath, explained to Poe in 1839, after White refused to publish "The Fall of the House of Usher," that Dickens had given "the final death blow to tales of the wild, improbable, and terrible class" (*H*17: 378, 48). Philip Pendleton Cooke, more appreciative of Poe's genius, still wished in 1846 that he would bring "his singular capacity for vivid and truth-like narrative to bear on subjects nearer ordinary life" and write "a book full of homely doings."[14]

In the face of such blunt and persistent opposition, Poe's exploitation of the *Blackwood's* tale of sensation can hardly be understood as shrewd journalism. He had some savvy as a magazinist, but his publishers and friends more accurately reflect the preference of readers in his day for realistic fiction with satirical, moral, or sentimental overtones.[15] Poe would have done better to have produced an American version of the moral idyll he seems to have ignored in *Blackwood's*. His persistence in the sensational vein, on the other hand, cannot be dismissed simply as bad taste or bad judgment, since he proves in the parodies of *Blackwood's* that he was aware, even scornful, of the shortcomings of the tale of sensation. A taste for the sensational and some bad judgment, no doubt, contributed to Poe's attempt to market fiction that was idiosyncratic and all but outmoded, but it is explained also, I believe, by his interest in the thematic implications of the tale of sensation. Poe shared with the *Blackwood's* writers not simply a vivid treatment of horrible experiences, calculated to shock and excite the reader, but also an interest in philosophical sensationalism, the idea derived from Locke that human knowledge and identity consists primarily in sensations.

II

Margaret Alterton suggested long ago that Poe's interest in philosophy may have been aroused by his reading of the *Blackwood's* tales of sensation.[16] Although not a serious philosophical literature, the tales of sensation do reflect a significant philosophical context in *Blackwood's*. Published in London, the magazine emanated from Edinburgh and was an unofficial organ of the Scottish philosophy of Common Sense or Scottish Realism, as it was often called. Formulated primarily by Thomas Reid in the late eighteenth century, Scottish Realism was still the dominant mode of thought in Britain and America in Poe's day, despite the significant impact of French and German idealism.[17] *Blackwood's* was known for being tolerant of French and German ideas and literature during a time when hostility toward those foreign schools generally prevailed, but it was chiefly inspired by the rational, material, and conservative tenets of the Common Sense school.

In *Blackwood's* and its British and American imitators frequently appear reviews of philosophical works and featured series of philosophical discussion, many of which carry on the debate between the Scottish realists and "philosophers of ideas."[18] The Scots sought to refute the skeptical conclusions that David Hume had drawn from Locke's epistemology and to stem the tide of idealism from abroad. As Ernest Lee Tuveson notes, Locke's revolutionary contribution to philosophy was to assert that "the essences of things are unknowable, that all we can know assuredly is the ideas within our own circle of consciousness."[19] The consequences of Locke's proposition were to make knowledge of the world and of the self uncertain. There is no innate or unmediated knowledge of reality, no fixed ego; knowledge and identity are a function of impressions. The closest approach we make to reality or the essence of things is in our sense impressions or "sensations," which Locke often calls "simple ideas."

Locke steers away from skepticism by dwelling upon the primacy of sensations. He conceives of the mind as a *tabula rasa*, or blank screen upon which our experience of the world is projected in the form of fragmented sensations. The surest knowledge, Locke suggests, is a sort of simple "seeing," the sensations entering the "dark room" of the mind and arranging themselves as "pictures" to be viewed by the understanding. He distrusts the more active powers of mind, its capacity to combine and transform sensations into "complex ideas" that have no source in nature, advising that we return frequently to our sense impressions to keep our bearings, to avoid confusion, obscurity and mental illness. Thus, in initiating the philosophy of ideas, Locke paradoxically establishes himself as the father of empirical science.

The Scottish realists were concerned primarily about the skeptical implications of Locke's epistemology, especially as espoused by Hume, who did not share Locke's confidence in the integrity of sensations or "simple ideas." Because sensations are not facsimiles in the mind of the objects that produced them, as Locke suggests, Hume concluded that reality is unknowable. We know only our own ideas, simple or complex. The Scottish realists argued, however, that the mind does make indisputable contact with the world through the faculty of common sense. Accepting the Lockean notion that knowledge is largely the product of experience, they restored to the mind an innate or intuitive understanding that Locke had denied, calling it Common Sense. The sensations were a major bone of contention for the Scots. The problem with Locke and Hume, according to Reid, was that they confused "sensations" with "ideas," the intuitive powers of mind with the abstract, thus divorcing the mind from reality. Reid argued that sensations are indivisible from the objects producing them; they provide Common Sense with direct evidence of the external world, even though they are not, as Locke suggests, an "express image" of it.[20]

The subtleties of the debate need not concern us here. I suggest that the tale of sensation popularized in fiction a widespread interest in philosophical sensationalism and reflected the bias of Common Sense. Locke made sensations the primary stuff of human consciousness and the Scottish realists continued to draw attention to them well into the nineteenth century. "Sensations are the great things after all," Poe's editor in "How to Write a Blackwood Article" tells an aspiring author: "If you wish to write forcibly, Miss Zenobia, pay minute attention to the sensations" (*M2*: 340). On the one hand, the analysis of sensations in magazine articles was indicative of an interest in human psychology, especially unusual states of mind, sparked by Locke's epistemology. On the other hand, it reflected the distrust of the Common Sense school in anything that did not conform to fact and ordinary experience. In spite of their faith in Common Sense, the Scottish realists had to acknowledge, as did Locke, that the mind was capable of straying far from reality. Like Locke, they recommended that the speculative and imaginative powers of mind be held in check so that the simple sensations or impressions of Common Sense might prevail; otherwise, the mind might lose itself in a labyrinth of its own making.[21]

Blackwood's flirted with the fashionable idealism of French and German writers but was regulated on the whole by Common Sense. The rational and material sobriety of Reid, Dugald Stewart, and Thomas Brown are consistently preferred to the wild and shadowy metaphysics of Kant, Schelling, and Cousin. Pretending to appreciate Kant, for example, DeQuincey ironically demonstrates how unsuited his metaphysics are "in an age which, if ever any *did*, idolatrizes the tangible and material."[22] Another *Blackwood's* writer chastises his countrymen for being too smug in their dismissal of German philosophers, although he considers them safe only when they are "scientific," when facts, speculation, and faith are held in "the well-poised union of which alone makes great scientific men."[23] The same writer concedes that German lyric poetry is "in some points perhaps the best: *but it is not for us* . . . . It is too cloudy, too tearful, too shadowy, for the beef-eater" (p. 157). Even Coleridge is attacked for being too subjective in his *Biographia Literaria*, for following the bad examples of Rousseau and Hume by turning "plain flesh and blood matters of fact . . . into a troop of phantoms."[24]

Blackwood's preferred matters of fact in fiction too, even in tales of terror and the supernatural. As Margaret Alterton has observed,

Blackwood's reviewers liked to distinguish between German and English tales of terror.[25] The Germans depended on wild and supernatural fantasy to frighten their readers. English horror, according to the *Blackwood's* critics, derived from more legitimate sources in nature and real life and was therefore more effective. Reviewing E. T. A. Hoffmann's tales, a *Blackwood's* critic asserts that "the *horrible* is quite as legitimate a field of poetry and romance, as either the pathetic or ludicrous"; but for extended praise he singles out a tale in which the horrible is mixed up with "ordinary human feelings," in which Hoffmann has "married dreams to realities."[26] As late as 1847 a *Blackwood's* reviewer was still holding fast to "that old predilection in favor of *a true story*, whenever it can be had."[27] The influence of Common Sense critics, according to Allen, explains why so little fiction appears in the early volumes of *Blackwood's* and why in later volumes it is "usually presented in the form of essay, historical anecdote, or factual reminiscence."[28]

Although the tales of sensation are exceptions to the rule of decorum even in *Blackwood's*, they too answer to the demands of Common Sense. The circumstances and sensations they relate are far from ordinary or true to life, but they are usually presented as true, factual accounts of scientific interest. Poe exposes the empirical pretense of the tale of sensation in "How to Write a Blackwood Article":

> The first thing requisite is to get yourself into such a scrape as no one ever got into before . . . . But if you . . . cannot conveniently tumble out of a balloon, or be swallowed up in an earthquake, or be stuck fast in a chimney, you will have to be contented with simply imagining some similar misadventure. I should prefer, however, that you have the actual fact to bear you out. Nothing so well assists the fancy, as an experimental knowledge of the matter in hand. "Truth is strange," you know, "stranger than fiction"—besides being more to the purpose. (*M*2: 340)

Mr. Blackwood's advice to Psyche Zenobia betrays the preference of Common Sense for the actual over the imaginative, and the several *Blackwood's* "articles" he recommends to her as models are notable for the "experimental knowledge" they convey. In "The Involuntary Experimentalist," for example, a doctor who has been trapped in a fire offers an account of his sensations as scientific evidence of the temperatures man can endure. Such tales, as Margaret Alterton suggests, may be modeled after case studies of sensations in books of medical jurisprudence.[29] These were intended to help prospective jurors understand medical evidence, but they catered to a taste for the sensational by dwelling upon unusual cases of hanging, burial alive, and "suspended animation." Reviewing one of these books, a *Blackwood's* writer exclaims: "We know of no romances half so interesting as the real 'tales of terror' to be found scattered over these pages."[30] Prefacing an account of the sensations of his hanging, the narrator of "Le Revenant" tells us that his "greatest pleasure, through life, has been the perusal of any extraordinary narratives of fact," especially of calamity and crime, which "have always excited a degree of interest in my mind which cannot be produced by the best invented tale of fiction."[31]

The pretense to truth in the tale of sensation has philosophical as well as medical implications. The case study of sensations actually goes back to Locke, who anticipated modern psychology by tracing irrational or unnatural associations of ideas to past traumatic experiences or "shocks" of sensation.[32] The *Blackwood's* thrillers dramatize such shocks, detailing the sensations of a mind dislodged from reality. Poe clearly demonstrates his awareness of the philosophical consequences of the tale of sensation in his spoofs of *Blackwood's*. The question, for example, of whether sensations are merely ideas or evidence of a direct knowledge of the world and the self is humorously raised in "A Predicament," the tale Miss Zenobia composes for *Blackwood's*. Having protruded her head through an opening in the dial-plate of a church clock, she is decapitated by the "scimitar-like minute hand." As her head drops into the street, she reflects:

> I will candidly confess that my feelings were now of the most singular—nay the most mysterious, the most perplexing and incomprehensible character. My senses were here and there at one and the same moment. With my head I imagined, at one time, that I the head, was the real Signora Psyche Zenobia—at another I felt convinced that myself, the body, was the proper identity. (*M*2: 355-356)

Miss Zenobia further confuses her physical and mental identities when, "to clear [her] ideas on this topic," she tries to take a pinch of snuff. Her predicament spoofs the epistemological and ontological problems raised by the tale of sensation. Is the mind in direct contact with the world through the senses, or does it operate independently of the world? And where does identity reside, in the senses (body) or the sensations (mind)?

One *Blackwood's* reviewer saw the debate about sensations in Scottish metaphysics turning on "the point of juncture between matter and mind."[33] This is the nexus of the tale of sensation. The *Blackwood's* protagonist fascinates us not so much with his horrifying predicament as his account of the sensations it produces. His physical discomfort is usually overshadowed by a tormenting uncertainty about his state of mind or being. His scrape serves primarily to place him in a state bordering between wakefulness and dream, sanity and madness, life and death. Here the connection between his sensations and the external situation producing them fades and his chief terror is of losing hold upon reality. Take "The Man in the Bell," for example, by William Maginn, which appeared in *Blackwood's* in 1821.[34] Caught directly beneath a huge, ringing church bell, the narrator's first fears "were mere matters of fact." He was afraid the bell would fall and crush him, or that the weak floor supporting him would give way and drop him 150 feet to the marble floor below. These fears soon gave way to others "not more unfounded, but more visionary, and of course more tremendous. The roaring of the bell confused my intellect, and my fancy soon began to teem with all sorts of strange and terrifying ideas" (pp. 373-374). The shock of sensations causes delirium, and he is tormented by the prospect of losing his reason utterly and throwing himself in madness from the steeple. Escaping finally, he gradually recovers his senses, though, as Locke might predict, the shock leaves him with a "nervous apprehension" of cathedral bells.

The tale of sensation was the instrument of some pseudo-philosophical probing beyond the limits of ordinary experience and Common Sense. The *Blackwood's* sensationalist was fascinated by unusual states of consciousness and the visionary powers of mind, by the idea of transcending the tie of sensations to the physical world, but he was wary of the consequences. His protagonist had to be shocked into a visionary state, carried against his will (except those who are being burlesqued) to the brink of some transcendence, only to be returned to the safe and sober realm of Common Sense. Thus, the tale of sensation is not only disguised to seem factual and scientific, but also structured to confirm the priority of fact and reason. The protagonist's experience is often cathartic, as if the shock of sensation were administered to purge the irrational and visionary powers of mind. In one tale of sensation, for example, a protagonist who is lost in the catacombs of Paris becomes, like the man in the bell, confused, delirious, fearful of losing his reason, and desirous finally of sleep and insensibility. His sleep carries him instead "from death to life, from the dreams of weakness, and lapses of insanity, to the full use and animation of [his] faculties." He wakes a new man, "fearless and serene."[35] Similarly, in "The Buried Alive," a protagonist who suffers the horrors of premature burial blithely concludes that an hour after being restored he "was in the full possession of all [his] faculties."[36]

The rational propensity of the *Blackwood's* sensationalist sometimes takes the form of Mrs. Radcliffe's "explained" Gothicism. Mysterious events and terrifying visions, apparently the result of supernatural agency, are finally explained as deriving from natural causes. A good example is "Singular Recovery from Death," which appeared in *Blackwood's* in 1821.[37] In the guise of a letter to the editor, the narrator relates "the circumstances of an event which some years ago plunged [him] into unutterable horror." He apologizes for the lack of "those mental powers that might present to others a clear picture of the agonies [he] then endured; but there is often felt to be in the simple truth a power of awakening emotion beyond what belongs to the most skilful fiction" (p. 582). The disclaimer is calculated to give his improbable tale the look of truth, but it is doubly false. He leads us to believe that his sensations and visions were the result of an illness. "The truth is, Mr. Editor, that I had gotten drunk as an owl!" (p. 585). At this point he recapitulates, tracing his sensations to their real causes—the efforts of his friends to sober him up. The narrator offers the second half of the story to establish the scientific validity of the first half—that is, to show how the mind deviates wildly from the truth. "This not only throws an air of probability over that part of the previous narrative . . . but also throws, unless I greatly err, much light on the whole theory and practice of dreaming" (p. 587).

The mock-serious tone of "Singular Recovery from Death" is another feature of the sensationalist's wary exploration of the subjective and irrational. The *Blackwood's* thrillers were sometimes cast as parodies of German romance, mixing sensations with burlesque. Drawn by the wild imagination of Hoffmann and Tieck, the *Blackwood's* sensationalist recoiled ultimately from the idealistic or skeptical implications of their fictions. One example that makes clear the philosophical context of the tale of sensation is "The Sphinx. An Extravaganza Sketched in the Manner of Callot."[38] It parodies E. T. A. Hoffmann's "Der Goldne Topf" ("The Golden Flower Pot"), which first appeared in Hoffmann's initial volume of tales, *Fantasiestücke in Callots Manier* (1814). Hoffmann's tale is a multi-layered allegory about the awakening of poetic sensibility in a young German student named Anselmus. His awakening takes the form of a subtle and disturbing intrusion of the unreal, imaginative, and supernatural into his everyday life, so that neither he nor we can tell where reality leaves off and his visions begin. Hoffmann's visionary theme interests the *Blackwood's* writer only to the extent that it raises questions about the connection between mind and reality.

Anselmus' adventures begin when he collides with an old apple vendor who curses him. In "The Sphinx" a young student named Arnold meets an old woman who sells canes. She offers him a choice between Common Sense and Romantic Idealism. She has "Old-fashioned sticks! Rational sticks! Sticks for sober citizens!" and "Fancy sticks! Poetical sticks! Romantic sticks! Mad sticks! and sticks possessed with a devil" (p. 441)! Arnold cynically chooses one of the latter which is ornamented with the head of a sphinx and for which, the old hag tells him, he will pay a "mad price." The consequence of Arnold's purchase is that he begins to lose hold of himself and his world. He fancies that the Sphinx on his cane is haunting him with the questions "Who are you? and, who am I?"— questions which "would have puzzled Oedipus himself" (p. 446). The Sphinx is ostensibly the cause of Arnold's encounter with a bewitching countess who lives in a castle full of "the romantic splendours of the Middle Ages," an experience that completely disorients him:

> "Either my senses are the sport of dreams, or this world is altogether an enigma . . . I know very well that I live in the nineteenth century, and that I have studied at the University of Kiel. Common sense tells me that there are neither witches, ghosts, nor fairies, and yet I could almost swear that ever since yesterday noon, I have been the sport and victim of supernatural agency." (p. 443)

Taking his bewilderment as a sure sign of "a genius for poetry and romance," Arnold sits down to write a book about his strange experiences, entitling it "Adventures of a Student, a Romance of Real Life, in the Manner of Callot and Hoffmann" (p. 446). His writing, however, only aggravates his confusion about what is real. He begins the book "in the form and language of fiction, but the longer he wrote, the more confirmed was his belief in the truth of his romance" (p. 446). The delusion frightens him with the thought that he is living a "double existence," one in the everyday world and the other in the world of imagination. To overcome this fear "he would often rush into the busy streets of Hamburg, and endeavor to regain, by rough collision with the world and its realities, some portion of common sense and self-possession" (p. 447).

Like his *Blackwood's* counterparts, Arnold's predicament drives him to "the brink of absolute insanity." His final sensations are those of being carried by a "boiling labyrinth of waters" to the brink of a "yawning gulf," from which he cries "an inarticulate shriek of horror"

(p. 452). This scrape, however, is merely the climax of a terrible nightmare, from which Arnold awakes in a sweat.

Hoffmann allows his character no such reprieve. Anselmus inhabits a world in which reality and dreams coalesce, in which he is always uncertain about the truth of his experience. There is a consolation, however. In this permutable state of consciousness, Hoffmann suggests, "the sacred harmony of all beings" and "the deepest secret of nature" are discovered.[39] It is the transcendental vision of the Romantic idealist. For the *Blackwood's* satirist, however, it is all nightmare and insanity. He is compelled to rescue Arnold from the confusion of dream and reality because, as a man of Common Sense, he believes that the visionary powers of mind distort and falsify the truth. There is no imaginative harmony for the *Blackwood's* sensationalist. His fiction represents the world as a duality of matter and mind, reality and dream, truth and fiction, and although he is fascinated by the mind's independence of reality, he avoids skepticism and idealism by bringing his protagonist back into collision with the world and its realities and to the full possession of Common Sense.

III

Horrible predicaments like burial alive and first-person narration of the sensations they produce, physical suffering and mental confusion, nightmarish visions, and an inarticulate shriek at the brink of death or madness—these were Poe's stock and trade. Yet one does not have to read too many *Blackwood's* tales to see how much more effectively Poe managed his Gothic sensationalism. In substance and technique his best thrillers surpass the best in *Blackwood's*. Still, to a great extent, his fiction is informed by the vision of the *Blackwood's* sensationalists. Drawn, as they were, to the idealistic and visionary mode of German and English Romanticism, he too frequently falls back upon the rational and conservative position of Common Sense. Despite his reputation as a Romantic visionary and harbinger of the Symbolist Movement, Poe was profoundly influenced by Common-Sense principles and practice.[40]

His Common Sense speaks loudest in his burlesques of *Blackwood's*. Although these are usually read as spoofs on the kind of sensationalism *Blackwood's* promoted, Poe adopts in them essentially the *Blackwood's* manner of scoffing at Gothic extravagance and German metaphysics. Locke, Kant, Fichte, Schelling, Godwin, and Coleridge are the frequent targets of Poe's satire, just as they are in *Blackwood's*.[41] In the anomalous "Loss of Breath," for example, "A Tale Neither in Nor out of 'Blackwood'" (1835), Common Sense ironically emerges from the narrator's idealistic speculation about the breath he has lost:

> It might have a vapory—it might even have a tangible form. Most philosophers, upon many points of philosophy, are still very unphilosophical. William Godwin, however, says in his "Mandeville," that "invisible things are the only realities," and this all will allow, is a case in point. I would have the judicious reader pause before accusing such asseverations of an undue quantum of absurdity. Anaxagoras, it will be remembered, maintained that snow is black, and this I have since found to be the case.[42] (*M*2: 64)

Satire that displaces idealism and sensationalism with Common Sense is found not only in Poe's early burlesques of *Blackwood's* but in later tales too, such as "Never Bet the Devil Your Head" (1841), "The System of Dr. Tarr and Professor Fether" (1845), and "Some Words With a Mummy" (1845).

Poe was still imitating the tale of sensation as a mature writer too. "The Pit and the Pendulum" (1842), as Mabbott suggests, is unmatched in *Blackwood's* for "straight" sensations. Poe marshals all the elements—the successive tortures of a dark dungeon with bottomless pit, a slowly-descending scimitar, and shrinking, red-hot walls; the flood of sensations and struggle to retain sanity; the shriek of final despair and the cathartic deliverance. Not only does Poe surpass the effects of the *Blackwood's* writers, however; he finds universal significance in his narrator's predicament, turning the tale into "a fable of man's condition."[43] In "The Premature Burial," read by some as a parody of *Blackwood's* sensationalism, Poe mixes sensations and burlesque in the manner of "Singular Recovery from Death" and "The Sphinx." His narrator dupes us initially by documenting several cases of premature burial to convince us of the truth of his own horrible experience of it. The truth, however, turns out to be a fiction; he has only imagined the sensations of premature burial after waking up in cramped quarters aboard a boat. He is brought back to his senses after a horrible shriek of despair and experiences the catharsis of his *Blackwood's* counterparts. The tortures endured "for their very excess wrought in my spirit an inevitable revulsion. My soul acquired tone,—acquired temper . . . I thought upon other subjects than Death . . . . I became a new man and lived a man's life" (*M*3: 969).

Poe also relied heavily upon the "explained" mode of Gothic sensationalism, returning to the ken of rational understanding what the Germans left uncertain. The detective stories and other tales of ratiocination are perhaps his most creative extensions of the explained

Gothic. As late as 1846, Poe was still getting mileage from this kind of sensationalism. In "The Sphinx," Poe's narrator retreats from "the dread reign of the cholera in New York" to his relative's cottage on the Hudson.[44] He has a fanciful and superstitious nature, and he is particularly susceptible to a belief in omens. His relative, on the other hand, "was not at any time affected by unrealities. To the substances of terror he was sufficiently alive, but of its shadows he had no apprehension" ($M$3: 1246). This comment precedes his narration of an incident "so entirely inexplicable" as to make him doubt his own sanity. While his thoughts were wandering one day from his reading of superstitious lore to "the gloom and desolation" of New York, he saw out of the window a hideous monster in the shape of a "Death's Head" climbing a hill. His relative's unsympathetic attitude and failure to confirm a second sighting of the monster further convinces the narrator that he is either seeing an omen of his death or losing his mind. At this point his relative takes over and explains the phenomenon. The narrator had focused on the hill while staring out of the window and magnified a moth passing about a "sixteenth of an inch distant from the pupil of his eye" ($M$3: 1251). Ironically, it was the narrator's attempt to credit his story, his "exceeding minuteness . . . in describing the monster" that enabled his relative to identify it. The narrator's vision illustrates the capriciousness of sensations and the mind's ability to deviate from the "truth" of experience. The narrator sees the omen he has been anticipating. His relative, however, proves it to be merely the distortion of a gloomy mind and restores our blithe, common-sense faith in the transigence of reality.

What about Poe's best tales of terror? It is worth noting perhaps that in "The Sphinx" Poe inverts the situation of "The Fall of the House of Usher."[45] A gloomy, superstitious narrator accepts the invitation of a common-sense relative to escape the desolation and death in New York. In "Usher," a common-sense narrator comes to the aid of a gloomy and superstitious friend who lives in a desolate country and decaying mansion. The circumstances of "Usher" make for more dire consequences. In the midst of terrifying desolation, the narrator is unable to perform the function of the relative in "The Sphinx." Rather than restore Roderick Usher to the full possession of his faculties, the narrator is infected by Usher's gloom and witnesses strange events he cannot explain. In this tale Poe ventures beyond the safeguards of Common Sense. His Gothicism, as G. R. Thompson argues, is ambiguous. We are uncertain whether to attribute the terrifying phenomena reported by the narrator to natural or occult causes. The uncertainty indicates, in Thompson's view, Poe's ironic mockery of the limits of rational understanding and his transcendence to a visionary perspective like that of the German romancers, Tieck and Hoffmann.[46] Poe falls short, however, of the transcendental harmony suggested in tales like "The Golden Flower Pot." Thompson argues that the vision of the German Romantics was itself double, their desire for imaginative harmony checked by their awareness of a disconnected and absurd universe.[47] It is, however, I think, the ambivalence of the sensationalist that checks Poe's transcendence, the brakes of Common Sense applied during the dizzying descent (this is how the sensationalist conceives of transcendence) into skepticism, nightmare, and madness. The obtuse Common Sense of the narrator in "Usher" and the obsessive desire of the narrator in "Ligeia" for concrete experience of his transcendental wife serve to distance us from the visionary Usher and Ligeia even as they draw us near, accentuating the disparity between the mundane and the occult, between reason and imagination. In the visages of Roderick Usher and Ligeia, Poe's narrators confront sphinxes whose mysteries Common Sense cannot explain, but even in these tales the Common Sense Poe assimilated from the *Blackwood's* sensationalists is evident.[48]

Much recent scholarship seeks to rescue Poe from his reputation as a writer of popular horror stories by finding philosophical import in his Gothic tales. The trend has merit but in its wake follow two misconceptions. The first is that Poe's Gothic sensationalism is merely an accoutrement to this themes, a shocking wrapper in which he markets a serious product. The second is that his product is essentially visionary and idealistic (or skeptical in the sense of distrusting reason and the senses). Poe's debt to the *Blackwood's* tale of sensation suggests that his philosophical theme is inherent in his Gothic sensationalism. The tale of sensation provided him a vantage point at the juncture between mind and matter, where he could test the claims of Common Sense and Romantic Imagination and work out his own ambivalence about the relationship between mind and reality. Moreover, like his *Blackwood's* counterparts, Poe seems on the whole to remain under the influence of Common Sense; he is drawn to the visionary transcendence of Romantic Imagination but he can not escape the tyranny of sensations and a penchant for rational understanding and tangible truths.

NOTES

[1] "Baudelaire," *French Poets and Novelists* (New York, 1878), p. 76. See also Eliot's "From Poe to Valéry" (1948), rpt. *The Recognition of Edgar Allan Poe*, ed. Eric W. Carlson (Ann Arbor, 1966), pp. 207-208, 212-213.

[2]"Our Cousin, Mr. Poe" (1949), rpt. *Poe: A Collection of Critical Essays*, ed. Robert Regan (Englewood Cliffs, 1967), pp. 48-49.

[3]*Poe's Fiction: Romantic Irony in the Gothic Tales* (Madison, 1973), p. 104.

[4]*The Rationale of Deception in Poe* (Baton Rouge, 1979), p. xii.

[5]Poe praises the *Blackwood's* tales in his reviews of "Peter Snook" (1836, 1845) and Hawthorne's "Twice-Told Tales" (1842), *H*14: 73-74; 11: 109. Most of the *Blackwood's* sources of Poe's tales are noted in *M*2 and 3.

[6]*Poe and the British Magazine Tradition* (New York, 1969).

[7]*Ibid.*, pp. 20-33. On the American imitation of the *Blackwood's* model, see also Frank L. Mott, *A History of American Magazines, 1741-1850* (New York, 1930), p. 393.

[8]*Poe's Fiction*, p. 73.

[9]The nine straight tales are "Remarkable Preservation from Death," 2(1818); "A Night in the Catacombs," 4(1818); "Adventure in the Northwest Territory," 10(1821); "The Buried Alive," 10(1821); "The Man in the Bell," 10(1821); "The Last Man," 19(1826); "Le Revenant," 21(1827); "The Murderer's Last Night," 25(1829); and "The Iron Shroud," 28(1830); the eleven that mix sensations and burlesque are "Singular Recovery from Death," 10(1821); "The Suicide," 16(1824); "The Metempsychosis," 19(1826); "The Man With the Nose," 20(1826); "The Barber of Gottingen," 20(1826); "Who Can It Be," 22(1827); "The Man With the Mouth," 23(1828); "The Sphinx. An Extravaganza," 24(1828); "Singular Passage in the Life of the Late Henry Harris, D.D.," 29(1831); "The Bracelets," 31(1832) [See E. Kate Stewart's demonstration in the present volume of Poe's debt to this tale by Samuel Warren.]; "The Involuntary Experimentalist," 42(1837).

[10]Even in the banner year, 1821, four tales of sensation compete with nine others of a more realistic kind, mostly of sea adventure. In only one other year, 1826, are there as many as four tales of sensation and three of these are of the burlesque variety.

[11]*Poe and the British Magazine Tradition*, p. 32. As Mott suggests, American magazinists preferred to pirate the less sensational works of Scott, Dickens, Thackeray, Bulwer, Marryat, and Mrs. Hemans. *A History of American Magazines*, pp. 307, 356-363, 398, 504-505, 615-617.

[12]Most of these features are imitated or parodied, for example, in the influential *Knickerbocker Magazine*, and one or more of

them can be found in *The United States Magazine and Democratic Review*, *The New-England Magazine*, and *Graham's Magazine*.

[13]*O* 1: 57-58. In *The Mind of Poe and Other Studies* (Cambridge, Mass., 1933), Killis Campbell argues that Poe sets forth in this passage the four kinds of tales he was writing. I agree with Allen, however, that there are really two kinds indicated, the burlesque, which encompasses the first and third type Poe defines, and the tale of sensation, which encompasses the second and fourth type. *Poe and the Magazine Tradition*, pp. 30-31.

[14]"Edgar A. Poe," *The Recognition of Poe*, p. 26.

[15]On Poe's unsuitability as a magazinist, see William Charvat, *The Profession of Authorship in America, 1800-1870* (Columbus, Oh., 1968), p. 86.

[16]*The Origin of Poe's Critical Theory* (1925; rpt. New York, 1965), p. 99. Alterton, however, is not so much concerned with the philosophical implications of the tale of sensation as she is with identifying it as a source for Poe's theory of unified effect in fiction (p. 30).

[17]The predominance of Common Sense in Poe's America is confirmed by I. Woodbridge Riley, *American Thought from Puritanism to Pragmatism and Beyond* (New York, 1915), pp. 118-139; Merle Curti *The Growth of American Thought*, 3rd. ed. (New York, 1964), pp. 157-158, 228; and William Charvat, *The Origins of American Critical Thought* (1936; rpt. New York, 1968), pp. 27-58.

[18]See for example "The Metaphysician" and "Philosophy of Consciousness" series in *Blackwood's*, 39(1836); 41(1837; 43(1838); 45(1839) respectively; the essays in *The Knickerbocker Magazine* on "Intellectual Philosophy," 7(1836); "The Eclectic," 8(1836); and "The New Philosophy of Mind," 15(1840); Orestes Brownson's essays on "Synthetic Philosophy" in the *Democratic Review*, 11(1842); 12(1843); and the essays in the *North American Review* on "Brown's Philosophy of Mind," 19(1824); "Stewart's Moral Philosophy," 31(1831); "Cousin's Philosophy," 35(1832); "Kant and Philosophy," 49(1839); and "Philosophy of Cousin," 53(1841).

[19]*The Imagination as a Means of Grace: Locke and the Aesthetics of Romanticism* (Berkeley, 1960), p. 25. For my discussion of Locke and the Common Sense reply to his epistemology, I am indebted to Tuveson pp. 16-41, and S. A. Grave's *The Scottish Philosophy of Common Sense* (London, 1960).

[20]Reid's objection to the philosophy of ideas spawned by Locke's *Essay Concerning Human Understanding* (1690) and skeptically extended by Hume is set forth primarily in *An Inquiry*

into the Human Mind (1764), 1: i-viii. See Grave, *The Scottish Philosophy of Common Sense*, pp. 11-24, 53-68, 151-183.

[21] Even Edmund Burke, who seeks to justify an enjoyment in irrational compositions of the mind in his *Inquiry into the Origin of Our Ideas of the Sublime and the Beautiful* (1757, 1758), maintains that such compositions should be modified by good sense and promote a mental well-being (Part IV, vii). Tuveson suggests that Burke's caution is reflected in Monk Lewis's self-parody and Ann Radcliffe's rational explanations of Gothic terror. *Imagination as a Means of Grace*, pp. 170-171. Nathan Drake, a leading apologist for the Gothic, felt compelled to warn that an imagination "left to revel in all its native wildness of combination, and to plunge into all the visionary terrors of supernatural agency, undiverted by the deductions of truth, or the sober realities of existence . . . will too often prove the cause of acute misery, of melancholy, and even of distraction." *Literary Hours of Sketches Critical and Narrative* (Sudbury [England], 1800), p. 52.

[22] *Blackwood's*, 28(1830), 244.

[23] "Traits and Tendencies of German Literature," 50(1841), 156.

[24] 2(1817), 5.

[25] *Origins of Poe's Critical Theory*, pp. 14-16. Alterton overestimates, I think, the extent to which "the English magazines are filled with discussions of the advantages of the terrible in fiction writing" (p. 13).

[26] "The Devil's Elixir," 16(1824), 55, 57. For similar criticism of German romance in *Blackwood's*, all calling for realism in tales of terror and the supernatural, see "Phantasmagoriana," 2(1818); "Some Remarks on the Use of the Preternatural in Works of Fiction," 3(1818); "A Chapter on Goblins," 14(1823) [Poe's familiarity with this article is demonstrated in Benjamin Franklin Fisher IV, "Poe, *Blackwood's*, and 'The Murders in the Rue Morgue'," *AN&Q*, 12(1974), 109-110]; "Gillies German Stories," 20(1826); "Werner's Twenty-Fourth of February," 21(1827), and "The Devil's Doings," 40(1836). Walter Scott takes issue with the wild imagination of German romance, Hoffmann's in particular, in "On the Supernatural in Fictitious Composition," *Foreign Quarterly Review*, 1(1827), 61-98.

[27] "The American Library," 62(1847), 578.

[28] *Poe and the British Magazine Tradition*, p. 81. According to Robert D. Mayo, Gothic tales were especially scarce in the magazines because they violated "the canons of 'truth to life,' and offended a morality in which the appeal to reason, common sense, and decorum was a conspicuous feature": "Gothic Romance in the

Magazines," *PMLA*, 65(1950), 787. The impact of Common Sense on fiction in America is examined at length by Terence Martin in *The Instructed Vision: Scottish Common Sense Philosophy and the Origins of American Fiction* (Bloomington, 1961).

[29] *Origins of Poe's Critical Theory*, pp. 15-16.

[30] "Beck and Dunlop on Medical Jurisprudence," 17(1825), 352. Warren's popular series, "Diary of a Late Physician," and DeQuincey's famous "Confessions of an Opium-Eater," are disguised as actual, instructive accounts of medical experimentation or observation.

[31] *Blackwood's*, 21(1827), 409.

[32] *Essay Concerning Human Understanding*, 2: xxxiii. See Tuveson, *Imagination as a Means of Grace*, pp. 34-36.

[33] "Magalotti on the Scotch School of Metaphysics," 16(1824), 228.

[34] 10(1821), 373-375. In "How to Write a Blackwood Article," Poe's editor suggests that Psyche Zenobia pay special attention to this tale (*M*2: 340).

[35] "A Night in the Catacombs," *Blackwood's*, 4(1818), 23.

[36] *Blackwood's*, 10(1821), 264.

[37] 10(1821), 582-587.

[38] *Blackwood's*, 24(1828), 441-452.

[39] *The Best Tales of Hoffmann*, ed. E. F. Beiler (New York, 1967), p. 70.

[40] Robert D. Jacobs discusses Poe's debt to the aesthetics of Common Sense in *Poe: Journalist and Critic* (Baton Rouge, 1969), pp. 19-60.

[41] *Blackwood's* had no qualms either about satirizing one of its own coterie, Thomas DeQuincey, whose visionary pretensions as the famous Opium-Eater are spoofed in "Confessions of an English Glutton," 12(1822) and "Some Account of Himself. By the Irish Oyster-Eater," 45(1839).

[42] Poe appends the following note to a long passage of sensations he deleted from the final printing of "Loss of Breath" in *The Broadway Journal* (1846): "The general reader will, I dare say, recognise in these sensations of Mr. Lack-O'Breath, much of the absurd *metaphysicianism* of the redoubted Schelling" (*M*2: 78). The deleted analysis of sensations is inspired burlesque of

Blackwood's. Whether Poe excised it because of practical considerations, because the subject of his satire had become unfamiliar, or because, as Alterton argues, he had come to consider "the *Blackwood* method inadequate for effective writing" is uncertain. See *Origins of Poe's Critical Theory*, p. 45.

[43] Sidney P. Moss, "Poe's Apocalyptic Vision," *Papers On Poe: Essays in Honor of John Ward Ostrom*, ed. Richard P. Veler (Springfield, Oh., 1972), p. 47. See also David H. Hirsch, "The Pit and the Apocalypse," *SR*, 76(1968), 632-652. The *"Blackwoods"* features may have had antecedents in William Henry Ireland's Gothic novel, *The Abbess* (1799). See Benjamin Franklin Fisher IV, "Introduction" to the reprint in the Arno Press Gothic Novels series (New York, 1974), pp. xxiii-xxv.

[44] Poe's title may have been suggested by the *Blackwood's* tale, but they have little in common except the sensationalist's interest in the relation between mind and matter.

[45] A different sort of inversion, yet still indicative of Common Sense, occurs between "Usher" and "The System of Dr. Tarr and Professor Fether," and between "Ligeia" and "The Man That Was Used Up." See Benjamin Franklin Fisher IV, "Poe's 'Usher' Tarr and Fethered," *PoeS*, 6(1973), 49; and Thompson, *Poe's Fiction*, pp. 83-85.

[46] *Poe's Fiction*, pp. 75-77, 88-89. Additional perspectives on Poe's hoaxing of Gothic features in "Usher" are illuminated in Benjamin Franklin Fisher IV, "Playful 'Germanism' in 'The Fall of the House of Usher': The Storyteller's Art," *Ruined Eden of the Present: Hawthorne, Melville, and Poe—Critical Essays in Honor of Darrel Abel*, ed. G. R. Thompson and Virgil L. Lokke (West Lafayette, 1981), pp. 355-374.

[47] *Ibid.*, p. 164. Thompson argues that Poe's knowledge of the German Romantics was thorough and first-hand and that they comprise his "basic intellectual, philosophical, and artistic milieu"—*Ibid.*, pp. 12, 19-38. But a strong case can be made, I believe, that Poe's knowledge and, more important, his opinion of German Romanticism was gleaned in large part from the pages of magazines like *Blackwood's*. Poe seems closer to DeQuincey in his treatment of German writers, at once appreciative and skeptical, imitative and satirical. See for example DeQuincey's extended reviews of Lessing and Kant in *Blackwood's*, 20(1826), 21(1827), 21(1827), 28(1830). A good example of *Blackwood's* ambivalence towards the fashion of German literature is "Modern German School of Irony," 38(1835).

[48] Clark Griffith finds the animus of Poe's Gothicism in Coleridge's concept of the imagination. "Poe and the Gothic,' *Papers on Poe*, pp. 21-27. Eighteenth-century Gothic, according to Griffith, is accountable in terms of Locke's epistemology, the sensations of terror usually attributed to causes in the external

world. Poe shifts the locus of terror to the mind; his Gothic tales dramatize an imagination which, in Coleridge's terms, "dissolves, diffuses, and dissipates in order to recreate" (*Biographia Literaria*, ch. 13). In Griffith's view, the terror in "Usher" is evidence of the narrator's creative imagination; his errand to his friend is a "symbolic homecoming," the House and events in the tale a projection of his own psyche. But terror of the mind's own making was anticipated by Locke, considered a legitimate form of entertainment by Edmund Burke as long as it was not over-indulged, and condemned by Common Sense critics. The *Blackwood's* sensationalists, moreover, anticipated the shift to psychological terror that Griffith attributes to Poe. Griffith recognizes himself that there is little of the idealism of Coleridge's harmonizing imagination in Poe's Gothic tales. Indeed, the dominant image in "Usher" is of destruction rather than creation. The narrator remains curiously detached from the nightmare vision of his own psyche, if that's what it is, and his escape at the end recalls the catharsis of the *Blackwood's* tales and anticipates the narrator's warning at the end of "The Premature Burial" that "the imagination of man is no Carathis, to explore with impunity its every caverns. Alas! The grim legion of sepulchral terrors . . . must sleep, or they will devour us—they must be suffered to slumber, or we perish" (*M*3: 969).

IN SEARCH OF TRUTH AND BEAUTY: ALLEGORY IN "BERENICE" AND "THE DOMAIN OF ARNHEIM"

LILIANE WEISSBERG

As studies like those by William Charvat or Robert Jacobs show, early nineteenth-century American criticism was very much influenced by eighteenth-century Scottish Common Sense philosophy.[1] Some of Edgar Allan Poe's dicta on language, his praise of Macaulay's "natural" and simple style, for example, may suggest that he fits very well into this tradition, where according to the criterion of successful communication, any ambiguity had to be rejected in favor of clear statements (*H*10: 156-160). Indeed, Poe quite often speaks against the use of metaphor, and allegory is the literary form against which he argues most consistently. Allegory, moreover, is linked with didactic intentions, and Poe's opposition to it can be seen as part of his general campaign against didacticism in poetry. His opposition to allegory reveals, however, the problematic demands of Enlightenment criticism as well as the tension between Poe's theory and practice. Criticism turning toward didacticism and moral judgment had to accept allegory as a genre while rejecting tropes. Poe's description of allegory as a specific narrative form in turn goes beyond that of a genre, excluding any doublings of meanings and intentions—which practice may seem as uncanny as the doublings of characters in Poe's tales themselves. Obviously, there is a need for Poe to reject allegory despite his use of it. A description of Poe's specific understanding and practice may help not only to clarify the contradictions within his work, but also provide some insights into the nature of allegory itself.

Poe alludes to allegory both in his early criticism, for example in his review of Fouqué's *Undine*, and in later discussions of tales or poems.[2] According to Poe, a tale possesses an upper- and an undercurrent of meaning that exist in subtle balance. The undercurrent may be supportive but not independent of the uppercurrent, so as not to destroy the tale's unity and effect. This is for Poe, however, exactly what allegory does: it attempts to reverse the currents of meaning and mixes realms that should be separated, by making visible what should only be suggested. Allegory's fault, therefore, lies not in what it includes, but in the way it presents another meaning; in its obvious placement of what should be unplaceable.

In his discussion of poetry, Poe modified his concept. In the "Philosophy of Composition," he defines metaphor as a concentrated allegory. This definition reverses Quintilian's definition of allegory as trope, which appeared in most of the rhetorical textbooks of Poe's time, and in Rees's *Cyclopaedia* of 1819, where allegory is characterized as a continued metaphor, a sequence in time.[3] In Poe's discussion of "The Raven," the poem bears a metaphor that is permissible. This metaphor, or other meaning for the bird itself, appears in the last stanza of the poem and changes the meaning of the whole. It provokes, in this specific moment, the desired effect, and produces its unity. The poem, therefore, becomes as poem metaphor,[4] disclosing two ways of reading it that are marked by two different concepts of time. The reading process itself, as a 'realistic' or natural venture, is opposed to the momentary disclosure of meaning. Having read a poem, the reader looks back and understands in a new way what had previously seemed straightforward. This moment of recognition defies time. The double process itself parallels Poe's concept of perspectives discussed for example in *Eureka*, and his design of the tale with its logical sequence and sudden dénouement.[5] Metaphor, understood as this peculiar allegorical moment, therefore does not inhibit, but rather presupposes previous separation. Allegory and metaphor, on the one hand treated critically or rejected by Poe, in fact turn out to be central to his poetic theory.

Poe describes and defines different genres and places them within a hierarchical order. His rejection of allegory, however, appears in his criticism of fiction as well as that of poetry. We may remember at this point, that Poe had described Fouqué's *Undine* as a poem rather than a tale. In that discussion, Poe rejects figurative language in general but does uphold the importance of images. It is after all their mastery of the image which defines Fouqué or Shelley as poets. According to Poe, prose is related to truth and poetry to beauty. Yet he redefines truth and beauty during his career as a critic, stressing different aspects of the terms, and shifting their relative importance within his aesthetic theory.[6] In his later writings, they develop from opposites to more closely related terms. Relating allegory to truth may become a problem. If allegory—"speaking otherwise"—involves truth, truth must always be something else.

Yet just this task of speaking otherwise, searching for knowledge, truth, seems to occupy many of Poe's narrators. His early tale "Berenice" may serve as an example. It can be read, moreover, as a reflection upon allegory and metaphor. From the beginning, the narrator Egaeus seems to be concerned with structuring the world into levels of experience. He describes his life as an "inversion": "The realities of the world affected me as visions, and as visions only, while the wild ideas of the land of dreams became, in turn, not the material of my every-day existence, but in very deed that existence utterly and solely in itself" (*M*2: 210). This is made possible by what Egaeus calls "stagnation." Two concepts of time are introduced: time as a sequence, and a kind of stillness which is related to the descriptions of waste and decay. Egaeus observes that "years rolled away," but that he remained, at "the noon of manhood," still unchanged in his father's mansion, in a stable condition resembling waste itself, a boyhood "loitered away" (*M*2: 210). In the tale, the two concepts of time parallel a contrast of light and its absence, another pattern of opposition. Egaeus belongs to a race of visionaries, but visions and memories merge in the prison of his "gray, hereditary halls" to "shadows" and "aerial forms," dependent on his "sunlight of reason." Even his relationship with Berenice is described in metaphors of contrasting light and shadow. He is "buried in gloom," but Berenice is so much in light that she does not reflect upon "shadows in her path" (*M*2: 209-210).

In Egaeus' world of excluded reality, however, memories and musings and trances appear as borderlines themselves. The shadow on the floor or the typography of a book present images of these borderlines, hieroglyphs, promising some other meaning. Locked in his ancestral library, Egaeus seems to occupy himself with the reading of foreign books, the repetitious pronunciations of names. The written and the spoken word, apparently, are similar in their physical existence, but this physical existence also keeps the secret of another meaning. Texts and recollections have to be deciphered. Egaeus remains a latecomer in regard to the history of language.

In his discourse on mental powers, he relates his "intensity of interest" to the "attentive" in contrast to the "speculative faculty" of the mind. "A morbid irritability of those properties of the mind in metaphysical science termed *attentive*" constitutes what he calls his "monomania," an ambiguous term, hinting not only at an obsession with one thing, one concept of occupation, but also at 'oneness,' a search for identities. For Egaeus, only a metaphysical concept seems adequately to describe his peculiar mental state, and he seems unable to change that state except through a momentary, "startlingly abrupt" recovery (*M*2: 211). Illness and disorder are his terms for his attempts and the consequences to reach beyond the frivolous surface of sound and sight. Berenice and Egaeus, described as opposites before, as figures of light and shadow, appear to be identical in their "disorder," united in their complaint of trances and epilepsy, uncanny doubles, dependent on each other. For Egaeus, Berenice achieves importance neither as beauty nor as fairylike nymph but as a physical object desired in its proceeding of decay. For Berenice, illness brings physical disorder as a "most appalling distortion of her personal identity" (*M*2: 213).

Time, then, is reintroduced as loss. Comparable to the loss of meaning in the repeated presence of the word, the wasted Berenice seems to lose more of her "identity" with every reappearance. The problem of who she is, however, seems related to the loss rather than to the presence of her physical appearance. Poe's phrenological description depicts her as "lifeless," "lustreless," "seemingly pupilless" (*M*2: 215). Berenice promises only absences, and Egaeus' quest is without material goal: it has to be for a truth without presence. Berenice's body does not only offer absences, though; it also offers a fetish. The symmetry and lifeless luster of her teeth—indicators of health and beauty—become noticeable only in their difference from the decaying body and its recollection, in their unchangeability. The description of Egaeus' fascination with Berenice's teeth is, moreover, repeated in their second encounter. Poe placed this second, intimate scene outside the library doors in later versions of the story.[7] There, after being informed by a "servant maiden" that Berenice has died, Egaeus enters Berenice's bed chamber, turning the prospective wedding night into a meeting with death. The teeth no longer stand out in contrast to Berenice's body, but they are still remarkable because of the absence of other, more general features. Berenice is enshrouded; her teeth are visible only through a broken band around her jaw.

Egaeus' fixation on the material presence of Berenice's teeth seems to make him unable to deliver the desired knowledge of her identity; like ruins they remain unchanged while suggesting a former, different being. Although attentive to material presence, Egaeus is liable to lose it in trance of obsession; no answers appear without speculative understanding. Like his experience with books, attentiveness seems to prevent answers and to provoke further disorder. The teeth promise something but deliver blanks. Speaking otherwise offers silence.

Poe excised Egaeus' visit to Berenice's bed chamber in later revisions of his story, because he regarded it as possibly too horrible.[8] Asterisks also close a second scene which takes place outside his library doors, and the starred empty space between two paragraphs seems to hide a deed of which Egaeus himself has only a vague apprehension. Ironically, Poe made Egaeus excise this second scene as he himself has excised the first. That the empty space may indicate a visit to Berenice's tomb is suggested by the remarks of a servant, and in the final versions of Poe's tale this absent scene repeats the earlier absent scene. Poe kept just the first vision of the teeth within his last version of the text. Finally, Egaeus perceives merely broken sentences, comparable to the broken band as well as to the "shattered ivory substances" falling out of a broken box at the end of the story. His own hand bears marks from being "*indented* with the impress of human nails" (*M*2: 218). Thus, not only the teeth, but rather the absence they disguise, their trace, seems to rule over the language and the structure of the text to which Egaeus, sitting in his library, compares life itself. It was "a fearful page," he says, "in the record of my existence, written all over with dim, and hideous, and unintelligible recollections" (*M*2: 217-218).

He might have known that the teeth, however, never offer anything but an incomplete answer to the quest for human identity. This ambiguity is suggested as soon as they are mentioned. "*[Q]ue tous ses dents étaient des idées*," "that all of her teeth were ideas" is Egaeus' version of Mlle. de Sallé's "*[q]ue tous ses pas étaient des sentiments*," "that all of her steps were feelings" (*M*2: 216). The word *identité* contracts *dents* and "*idées*" into one expression; they are united in "identity," yet Egaeus hopes to substitute one for the other. The difference between idea and teeth is not simply a contrast of mind and matter. *Dents* like *idées* merge into the word *identité* by disappearing and appearing in an anamorphic manner. Present and not present, independent and embedded in another context, *dents* itself, as a word, can be read as an image for the fetish that the teeth have become. Matter, it seems, promises the ideas of objects, but prevents their existence. At the end of the story, we learn not only about a woman buried alive, or the desecration of her tomb, but also about the shattered, or rather, scattered, fetish, about the object that can neither speak nor prevent danger.

Broken sentences and scattered objects tell how impossible it is to call anything like an 'idea' into presence. Becoming conscious, or, rather, learning about the limits of consciousness, and investigating language becomes one task. Staged as an immoral violation as well as a senseless theft, we are faced with something that cannot be described. Speaking otherwise has become necessary. The process constitutes language itself, which is, in this sense, bound to be metaphoric. But what Egaeus' "attentive faculty" discovers, is, moreover, a property of the spoken word that distinguishes it from writing and likens it to the effect of a tale: its momentary presence defies time. The spoken word—its meaning—does not endure, it can only be repeated. Although Poe instructs us to reject allegory because it may put *more* into the open than is desired, we know now that we have always to deal with less. Truth apparently is possible only when words cease to denote.

Seven years after "Berenice," Poe published "The Landscape Garden," a little dialogue and manifesto of "true Beauty" (*M*2: 709). Later, he revised and expanded the tale as "The Domain of Arnheim."[9] The description of an ideal garden would seem scarcely to resemble the horrors of Egaeus' family mansion, were it not for the name of Arnheim that links Egaeus' description of Berenice's estate with Ellison's chosen and artfully constructed paradise. Ironically, Egaeus' and Berenice's "gloomy, hereditary halls" are in "The Domain of

Arnheim" converted to a picturesque and ideal castle in the air. Hints about Berenice's past as a "nymph of the shrubberies of Arnheim" turn in the "Landscape Garden" into a vision of beauty and a story which, as Poe claimed, "expresse[d] much of [his] soul."[10] The structures of both stories are similar. If Egaeus searches for identity and true knowledge, Ellison seeks beauty and perfection. In "The Domain of Arnheim," no theft is involved, no immoral action. Ellison inherits his money and realizes his dream of perfect beauty; even the amount of his inheritance seems beyond imagination. The art of landscape gardening has superseded reading and writing. A friend and companion describes Ellison's theory, and, in quoting him, reveals his theory as a collection of quotations: from philosophy and garden books, and finally, as regards the name Arnheim itself, from other novels.[11] Like his product, Ellison's theory cannot be original, but Ellison is less concerned with the originality of the theoretical concept than with its actual realization and representation. The physical existence, material forms fascinate the artist: "the creation of novel moods of purely *physical* loveliness" (*M2*: 706; 3: 1271). Beauty itself has changed its attractions. Unlike Egaeus, who in his disinterest in Berenice's physical perfections seems to leave beauty behind, Ellison holds beauty as the absolute goal. But what is it, that absolute perfection and representation may still suggest?

Ellison seems to be satisfied with the creation of physical beauty alone. His obsession is not only permissible, but required, as is one of his other "principles of Bliss":[12] the company of his bride, who, we are allowed to suppose, may have become his wife during or after the creation of his earthly paradise. "His bride was the loveliest and most devoted of women" we learn at the beginning of the story (*M2*: 704; 3: 1269). The narrator later concludes, that, "above all, it was in the sympathy of a woman, not unwomanly, whose loveliness and love enveloped his existence in the purple atmosphere of Paradise, that Ellison thought to find, *and found*, exemption from the ordinary cares of humanity . . ." (*M3*: 1277; 2: 716). The nameless bride, however, seems as absent as relatives, workers, friends; we only know of the narrator, who serves as a commentator rather than an influence on the genial master, trying to divine his taste as the master attempts to divine beauty. The bride is absent, of course, unless we look for her in the obvious, something which is suggested by Poe's motto to both versions of the tale, "The garden like a lady fair was cut," a motto taken from an allegorical poem often quoted elsewhere, Giles Fletcher's "Christ's Victorie on Earth" (*M2*: 712n). If Egaeus is searching for Berenice's identity through a study of her body, Ellison's landscape, this artfully created nature, can be read in terms of its female properties.

The geographical map in "the Domain of Arnheim" parallels the anatomical description of Berenice. Both can be understood as voyages of experience, and both are pictured in sexual imagery, here with the goal of bliss as "exaltation" (*M*2: 708; 3: 1273). Lying in the open, the landscape, designed by the artist, offers herself to the invader. At the same time, the single authorship of the human creator is as questionable as the completeness of the invasion. Instead of the abyss, as in "Berenice," the traveler envisions here a beautiful castle in the air; this vision, not the entrance into the castle, marks the final radiance, the end of the story. The secret remains.

In Ellison's concept, the terms of reality are excluded, but replaced by the rules of the critic. Again, in search for beauty, the artist is confronted with a problem of truth:

> In landscape alone is the principle of the critic true; and, having felt its truth here, it is but the headlong spirit of generalization which has induced him to pronounce it true throughout *all* the domains of Art. Having, I say *felt* its Truth here. For the feeling is no affectation or chimera. The mathematics afford no more absolute demonstrations, than the *sentiment* of his Art yields to the artist. He not only believes, but positively *knows*, that such and such apparently arbitrary arrangements of matter, or form, constitute, and along constitute, the true Beauty. Yet his reasons have not yet been matured into expression (*M*2: 709; 3: 1273).

Beauty, it seems, is already the product of knowledge; it incorporates the truth of art which in turn can only be felt. In the second version, the narrator will have problems similar to the artist's in describing Ellison's domain of art: "I wish to describe, but I am disheartened by the difficulty of description, and hesitate between detail and generality" (*M*3: 1277). The landscape garden can be traveled through, felt, but cannot really be described. Mlle. de Sallé's "*que tous ses pas étaient des sentiments*" seems to have found a form of realization.

If in "Berenice" Poe poses the problem of representation as the impossibility of matching the word, as sign, with the signified, in "The Domain of Arnheim," he seemingly gives us the full experience of unity, of the absolute presence of beauty. Experience itself, shown as a time-dependent travel, is opposed to the momentary insight and the total vision. It seems to be the presence of the interpreter himself, establishing the description and what there is to be described, that prevents this representation.

If Berenice's teeth have acquired the independence of a living object, Ellison's landscape is something alive as well as something object-like.

In the earlier version of "Berenice" Poe quotes Byron, who confronts the living beauty with the stone ideal. There beauty, apparently, cannot be the property of a passive object; it has to bear the marks of independent life (*M*2: 708). Life, on the other hand, bearing accidentals, lacks perfection, and what Poe demands is life-in-death. Like the letters and signs on the margins of Egaeus' books, the landscape has to tell about matter as well as its secret. Furthermore, like Egaeus' books, the ivory canoe that travels through the Domain is covered with arabesque devices, and glides through the water with the double sharpness of a pen.

The art critic, in the "Domain of Arnheim," is not simply a voyeur, noting the features and trying to decipher them. His insistence on beauty presupposes a certain knowledge inherent in his understanding of matter. he therefore needs the acquaintance with death as well as life. The traveler through the still treasures of Arnheim, through the immense body of nature, envisions the unexpected home after turning several times, reversing the direction. In her interpretation of Poe's landscapes, Marie Bonaparte likened the smooth banks of the river to a vision of death.[13] Sliding along the Styx, optimism and hope rather than the horror of Berenice's body set the mood. The traveler sees beauty as a glimpse, the promise of an order he himself, merely human, cannot perceive: "There might be a class of beings, human once but now to humanity invisible, for whose scrutiny, and for whose refined appreciation of the beautiful, more especially than for our own, had been set in order by God the great landscape-garden of *the whole earth*" (*M*2: 709). Or rather, as Poe corrects himself in a later version of the tale: "death-refined appreciation" (*M*3: 1274). The second, sudden understanding unites the vision of beauty, the moment of fulfillment, with that of death. The privileged artist, Ellison himself, is said to have died at an early age, after having a "brief existence" (*M*2: 703; 3: 1268). His death has made the garden accessible, "causing his domain to be thrown open to certain classes of visitors" (*M*3: 1278). Ellison's garden bears the properties of a testament. The story is told, the garden experienced, after the death of its creator. Again, the narrator arrives too late. Beauty cannot be appreciated by the stripping of the idea from the material object, but by the resignation of one's own material existence. The final moment of effect, the metaphor, promising absolute representation, reflects its danger: the loss of identity, the loss of one's self.

Both "Berenice" and "The Domain of Arnheim" show the demands that language should tell of truth and beauty, demands which it cannot fulfill. Unity, identity, fully represented truth or beauty: Poe refers to a speculative moment of effect, a future metaphor which answers for the past. In establishing this metaphor, however, Poe does not escape time. If the interpreter cannot interpret, he fails because the representation of the true and other meaning of the object always involves the acquisition of a different consciousness and the use of different signs. And here all the attempts of replacement and reconstitution of signs have to establish time, despite the wish to overcome it in and for a moment of final experience. Here, ultimately, we have to reach a paradoxical answer: by rejecting it, Poe has to establish allegory.

NOTES

An earlier version of this paper was presented at the tenth meeting of the Poe Studies Association in Los Angeles, December 1982.

[1] William Charvat, *The Origins of American Critical Thought, 1810-1825* (1936; rpt. New York, 1968), especially pp. 27-59; Robert D. Jacobs, *Poe: Journalist and Critic* (Baton Rouge, 1969).

[2] See Poe, "Undine" (review, 1839), *H*10: 30-39; "Alciphron: A Poem" (review, 1840), *H*10: 60-71; "Twice-Told Tales" (review, 1842), *H*11: 104-113; "Tale-Writing. Nathaniel Hawthorne" (review, 1847), *H*13: 141-155; in regard to Shelley, see for example the Drake/Halleck review (1836), *H*8: 299 ff.

In regard to the development of Poe's model, see Jacobs, especially p. 442; Pasquale Jannaccone, "L´Esthetica di Edgardo Poe," *Nuova Antologia*, [58, ser. 3] 15 July 1895; trans. Peter Mitilineos, "The Aesthetics of Edgar Poe," *PoeS* 7(1974), 1-13; Ulrich Horstmann, *Ansätze zu einer technomorphen Theorie der Dichtung bei Edgar Allan Poe* (Bern and Frankfurt/M, 1975), pp. 96-102; Claude Richard, *Edgar Allan Poe: Journaliste et critique* (Paris, 1978). These studies try to relate Poe's concept of the tale and his understanding of allegory to his concept of imagination and fancy, as well as that of "mysticism." A reading of Poe's fiction as allegory and a discussion of its problems can be found in John Irwin, *American Hieroglyphics* (New Haven and London, 1980), pp. 43-223.

[3] Compare Quintilian, *Institutiones oratoriae*, 8.6. 8-9 with "The Philosophy of Composition" (1846)—*H*14: 208. As an example of a popular textbook, see Hugh Blair, *Lectures on Rhetoric and Belles Lettres*, first published in Scotland in 1783, especially lecture XV, "Metaphor." Poe used Rees's *Cyclopaedia* for several of his stories, for example "The Gold-Bug." The *Encyclopaedia Britannica*, also used by Poe (cf. "A Descent into the Maelstrom"), follows the traditional definition, too; the 1771 and later editions document Quintilian with examples from Kames's *Elements of Criticism* (1762).

[4]Compare Franz H. Link, *Edgar Allan Poe: Ein Dichter zwischen Romantik und Moderne* (Frankfurt/M and Bonn, 1968), p. 71.

[5]Compare for example *Eureka* (1848)—*H*16: 298 ff.—and Poe's early review of Bulwer Lytton's *Night and Morning* (1841)— *H*10: 114-133.

[6]See Margaret Alterton *Origins of Poe's Critical Theory* (1925; rpt. New York, 1965); Margaret Alterton and Hardin Craig, "Introduction," *Edgar Allan Poe: Representative Selections* (New York, 1935), pp. xvi ff.

[7]*M*2: 217n. This scene is included in the 1835, 1839, and 1840 versions of the story. For a discussion of Poe's changes of the tale, see also David E. E. Sloane and Benjamin F. Fisher IV, "Poe's Revisions in 'Berenice': Beyond the Gothic," *ATQ* 24, supplement 2(1974), 19-23.

[8]Poe to White, 30 April 1835, *O*1: 57. Poe published "Berenice" in March in White's *Southern Literary Messenger*. In 1841 Poe thought of renaming his story "The Teeth" for his planned *Phantasy Pieces*.

[9]"The Landscape Garden" first appeared in October 1842 in *Snowden's Ladies' Companion*; "The Domain of Arnheim" was completed in 1846 and published in March 1847 in the *Columbian Lady's and Gentleman's Magazine*—quoted here from *M*3: 1267-1285.

[10]"Berenice"—*M*2: 210. Poe refers to the "Domain" in a letter to Helen Whitman, 18 October 1848—*O*2: 397.

[11]"Arnheim" appears in Walter Scott's *Anne of Geierstein* (1829). Poe's principal source is Andrew Downing's *A Treatise on the Theory and Practice of Landscape Gardening* (1841).

[12]*M*2: 703 ff.; compare "The Domain of Arnheim," *M*3: 1268 ff.

[13]Marie Bonaparte, *Edgar Poe: Sa Vie—Son Oeuvre* (1933; rpt. Paris, 1958), 2: 353 ff.

"VISIONARY WINGS": ART AND METAPHYSICS IN EDGAR ALLAN POE'S "HANS PFAALL"

MAURICE J. BENNETT

"The Unparalleled Adventures of One Hans Pfaall," Poe's fictional account of a voyage to the moon, has been frequently discussed as a pioneering exercise in science fiction. The comedy with which the tale begins and ends, however, has led some to deny it as a "pure" example of the genre or to acknowledge it only as a crude and imperfect example.[1] George Bernard Shaw and William Carlos Williams suggest other evaluative categories when they respectively note that Poe's work always has the universe for background and characteristically turns away from its ostensible subject to reveal the "business" of writing.[2] In these terms, the science and technology that clutter the tale for many readers; the heavy-handed satire of the burghers of Rotterdam; and the fantasy of the moon voyage itself may be profitably considered under the aspect of Poe's overt and extensive interest in metaphysics and in the nature of art. As Joseph Moldenhauer observes, Poe's "critical essays point to the fundamental themes and techniques of his creative productions," although "the recurrent terms of Poe's aesthetic themselves comprise a symbolic structure, grounded in the same attitudes as the symbols, motifs, and patterns of characterization in his poetry and tales."[3] Read in the context of his total *oeuvre*, "Hans Pfaall" is of interest here as neither hoax nor science fiction nor a curiously unsuccessful hybrid of the two, but as a fictionalization of Poe's serious aesthetic and metaphysical preoccupations.

There is general consensus among students of Poe that his characteristic subject may be described as the "dissolution of personality," a "flight from corporeality," or "the disembodiment of man."[4] Its most notable narrative expression is his thematic preoccupation with death. The reader must always remind himself, however, that death and psychic disintegration in Poe are necessary stages in his private eschatology; they are the portals to states of consciousness of which mortal existence can offer only brief intimations. On certain prophetic occasions, the soul abandons the body and "separates itself from its own idiosyncrasy, or individuality, and considers its own being, not as appertaining solely to itself, but as a portion of the universal Ens." Death, though, is the final, "painful metamorphosis" whereby man escapes the distortions of the "*sense of self* which debases, and which keeps us debased" and assumes the generalized, divine perspective of the cosmos (*H*14: 186).[5] The final note to *Eureka* extends what is, in many respects, a traditionally

Christian consolation for the inevitable suffering inherent in the process: "The pain of the consideration that we shall lose our individual identity, ceases at once when we further reflect that the process . . . is neither more nor less than that of the absorption of each individual intelligence, of all other intelligences (that is, of the universe) into its own. That God may be in all, each must become God" (*H*16: 336).

Poe's tales are thus often informed by a covert agenda—the quest for transcendence—covert because frequently denied direct narrative representation. Harold Bloom offers a convenient and lucid paradigm for understanding this typically Romantic project, which he describes as involving two basic stages. In the "Promethean" stage, the questing consciousness rejects conventional modes of being, which necessarily involves the destruction of the purely social self and the rejection of ties with ordinary human community. The ultimate goal, however, is the "Real Man" or "Imagination" stages, where the artist attains an imaginative freedom that establishes a fundamental harmony between the universe and consciousness—an ultimate healing of the apparent breech between subject and object that instigates the most familiar forms of Romantic disquietude.[6]

Both the basic project of transcendence and Bloom's description of its essential aspects are directly relevant to "Hans Pfaall." Despite the endnote's misleading emphasis on a putative verisimilitude based on scientific and technological plausibility, the epigraph suggests a different set of concerns: "With a heart of furious fancies, / Whereof I am Commander, / with a burning spear *and a horse of air*, / To the wilderness I wander," (*H*2: 42). This song, attributed to Tom O'Bedlam, immediately introduces the world of madness, which in Poe is often a metaphor for the hypertrophy of imagination (*H*4: 236; 16: 165-166). And the "heart of furious fancies" invoked here bears a generic relation to the "hearts of maddening fervor" that Poe elsewhere attributed to lovers of the beautiful (*H*11: 255). Thus, however indirectly, the reader is immediately introduced to the realm of Poe's aesthetic metaphysics.

The story itself opens with the rejection of conventional values and habits that comprises the fundamental gesture of Romantic literature and that Bloom identifies as the initial stage of the Romantic Quest. The appearance of the messenger balloon carrying Hans's manuscript is described as "an egregious insult to the good sense of the burghers of Rotterdam" (*H*2: 44), and the detailed description of the Dutch crowd's foolishly inadequate reaction to so exotic an event parodies the *merely* logical, "utilitarian" habit of mind that Poe would definitively discredit in the Prefect G___ of the Dupin stories. The arrival of Hans's tale thus constitutes the advent of a new reality that supercedes traditional epistemologies and customary modes of being. The reporter who establishes the *mise en scène* for Hans's narrative notes its revolutionary effect in recording "phenomena . . . of a nature so completely unexpected—so entirely novel—so utterly at variance with preconceived opinions—as to leave no doubt on my mind that long ere this all Europe is in an uproar, all physics in a ferment, all reason and astronomy together by the ears" (*H*2: 42).

In his narrative proper, after identifying himself to the Rotterdam authorities, Hans explains his motivations for escaping to the moon. In so doing, he presents one of Poe's frequent attacks on the materialism and democratic tendencies of contemporary American culture. He finds his traditionally lucrative trade of bellows mender destroyed when his neighbors' heads are "set agog by politics," and he explains:

> . . . we soon began to feel the effects of liberty, and long speeches, and radicalism, and all that sort of thing. People who were formerly the very best customers in the world, had now not a moment of time to think of us at all. They had as much as they could do to read about the revolutions, and keep up with the march of intellect and the spirit of the age. If a fire wanted fanning, it could readily be fanned with a newspaper; and as the government grew weaker, I have no doubt that leather and iron acquired durability in proportion. (*H*2: 48)

The result of these social changes is Hans's business failure; and the accumulation of social and financial pressures attending the support of his family leads him to consider suicide.

Here, in essence, is the progressive and spiritually debilitating encroachment of material and social concerns that harassed the Romantic sensibility. The German Heine uttered a characteristic lament when he claimed that "the gloomy workaday mood of the modern Puritans spreads itself over all Europe like a gray twilight," and at the beginning of the nineteenth century the opening quatrain of a familiar Wordsworth sonnet complained: "The world is too much with us; late and soon, / Getting and spending, we lay waste our powers: / Little we see in Nature that is ours; / We have given our hearts away, a sordid boon."[7] Poe expresses similar attitudes in "The Colloquy of Monos and Una," where the growth of "huge smoking cities" deformed the landscape and symbolized general developments that separated man from "Beauty," "Nature," "Life" (*H*4: 203-204). The disembodied spirit Monos, "Wearied at heart with anxieties which had their origin in the general turmoil and decay" (*H*4; 206), actually died in order to be "born again" into a transcendent reality from which he can view both past and future from the perspective of the "universal Ens." Monos's description of an unequivocal metaphysical translation offers an illuminating context for Hans's own adventure, which, in removing him to the moon, provides him at least with a metaphorical death to those "anxieties" and that "general turmoil" summarized at the beginning of his tale.

That Hans's personal dilemma should be read in terms of the Romantic artist's general displeasure with an emergent social and political order in which he felt oppressed and marginalized is suggested by Poe's review of Henry F. Chorley's *Conti the Discarded*, published in the *Southern Literary Messenger* just seven months after the original appearance of "Hans Pfaall" in the same journal (June, 1835). "When *shall* the artist assume his proper situation in society—in a society of thinking beings?" he asked: "How long shall he be enslaved? how long shall mind succumb to the grossest materiality? How long shall the veriest vermin of the Earth, who crawl around the altar of Mammon, be more esteemed than they, the gifted ministers of those exalted emotions which link us up with the mysteries of Heaven?" (*H*8: 230). Poe's optimistic reply to his own queries was that change is imminent, and in "Mellonta Tauta" (1849) he imagined a futuristic world where "Investigation has been taken out of the hands of the ground-moles and given, as a task, to the only true thinkers, the men of ardent imagination" (*H*6: 206). Hans, however, refuses to wait for the advent of this utopia and decides to remove himself from intolerable conditions. He immediately identifies the metaphysical nature of his projected moon voyage as he confesses: "It was not, however, that to life itself I had any positive disgust, but that I was harassed beyond endurance by the adventitious miseries attending my situation . . . . I determined to depart, yet live—to leave the world, yet continue to exist—in short, to drop enigmas, I resolved, let what would ensue, to force a passage, if I could, *to the moon*" (*H*2: 60-61).

It is the practical result of this decision—Hans's voyage into space—that encourages the inclusion of Poe's work in the genealogy of science fiction. But on the simplest narrative level, the moon toward which Hans travels, as distinct from the satirical world in which he lands,[8] is not merely the planetary body that circles the Earth, but an extension of his imagination. Once aloft, he projects onto it a conventionally Romantic landscape:

> Fancy revelled in the wild and dreamy regions of the moon. Imagination, feeling herself for once unshackled, roamed at will among the ever-changing wonders of a shadowy and unstable land. Now there were hoary and time-honored

> forests, craggy precipices, and waterfalls tumbling with a loud noise into abysses without a bottom. Then I came suddenly into still noonday solitudes, where no wind of heaven ever intruded, and where vast meadows of poppies, and slender, lily-looking flowers spread themselves out a weary distance, all silent and motionless forever. . . . But fancies such as these were not the sole possessors of my brain. Horrors of a nature most stern and most appalling would too frequently obtrude themselves upon my mind, and shake the innermost depths of my soul with the bare supposition of their possibility. (*H*2:80)

In his sketch of Richard Adams Locke, whose "Moon Hoax," published in the New York *Sun* just weeks after the first appearance of "Hans Pfaall," had effectively precluded the projected continuation of his own tale, Poe noted the "fancy-exciting and reason suppressing" character of the lunar subject (*H*15: 134). And the landscape that Hans imagines is analogous to that which Poe described in the poem "Dream-Land"—like that symbolic topography, this, too, is a "wild weird clime that lieth, sublime, / Out of SPACE—out of TIME" (*H*7: 89). Hans is thus enroute towards the imaginative consciousness that Bloom identifies as the ultimate goal of the Romantic quest.

Hans's moon is also the local manifestation of a heavenly body that reappears constantly and with varying significance in Poe's work, from the early lyric "Al Aaraaf" to the culminating prose poem *Eureka*. The title of the early work derives from a star discovered by Tycho Brahe in 1572, which appeared suddenly, attained an unusual brilliance, and then suddenly disappeared. In the poem, this star is the domain of Nesace, the goddess of Beauty, and it functions primarily as a symbol of a divinely aesthetic existence that is inaccessible to mortals, on whom it bursts as a momentary epiphany. In *Eureka*, the star becomes the original cosmos itself—the unitary, undifferentiated particle that Poe identified as God in His divine quiescence before the creative dispersal that constituted the universe. This immense, effulgent, inconceivable particle represents the ultimate development of Poe's star imagery.

Between "Al Aaraaf" and *Eureka*, the astral symbol recedes from narrative prominence and is embedded in Poe's critical discourse as part of an explanatory trope. As such, it is a recurrent figure in his descriptions of imaginative vision. In the preface to *Poems* (1831), for instance, Poe used it to distinguish between poetic and utilitarian perception as he criticized Coleridge's fundamental procedures in his *Biographia Literaria*: "He goes wrong by reason of his very profundity, and of his error we have a natural type in the contemplation of a star. He who regards it directly and intensely sees, it is true, the star, but it is the star without a ray—while he who surveys it less inquisitively is conscious of all for which the star is useful to us below—its brilliancy and its beauty" (*H*8: xxxiv). Dupin uses nearly identical language in "The Murders in the Rue Morgue" to distinguish between his methods and the inferior investigative techniques of the Parisian police, asserting that "To look at a star by glances—to view it in a side-long way . . . is to behold the star distinctly—is to have the best appreciation of its lustre—a lustre which grows dim just in proportion as we turn our vision fully upon it" (*H*4: 166).

On other occasions, the star represents the unattainable beauty toward which the human soul aspires. In his definitive aesthetic statement, "The Poetic Principle," Poe wrote that the desire for Beauty is the hallmark of man's immortality; significantly, "It is the desire of the moth for the star" (*H*14: 273). He defined the poetic principle as "the human Aspiration for Supernal Beauty," and in seeking for an adequate image to figure the essence of poetry, he differentiated the "elevating excitement of the Soul" from mere passion, metaphysical ecstasy from a mere delirium of the senses. He concluded: "Love, on the contrary—Love—the true, the divine Eros—the Uranian, as distinguished from the Dionaean Venus—is unquestionably the purest and truest of all poetical themes" (*H*14: 290). Uranian Venus is, of course, the evening star; the metaphysical desire it elicits is Poe's definitive conception of poetic vision and transcendental aspiration.

"The Power of Words" (1845), another of Poe's metaphysical fantasies, offers an important exception to the general scheme just outlined. In this brief sketch, the poem as artifact and the image of the star are brought into metaphorical juxtaposition. Two angelic spirits, Oinos and Agathos, casually winging among the galaxies, suddenly espy "the greenest and most terrible star," of which Oinos observes, "Its brilliant flowers look like a fairy dream—but its fierce volcanoes like the passions of a turbulent heart" (*H*6: 143). Suddenly weeping, Agathos responds with a confession: "This wild star—it is now three centuries since with clasped hands, and with streaming eyes, at the feet of my beloved—I spoke it—with a few passionate sentences—into birth. Its brilliant flowers *are* the dearest of all unfulfilled dreams, and its raging volcanoes *are* the passions of the most turbulent and unhallowed of hearts" (*H*6: 143-144). This stellar landscape is similar to that which Hans imagines as existing on the moon, which, as he approaches its surface, appears to be in a state of violent eruption. Not only does such a passage provide a key for determining the symbolic value of those poppies and lilies, chasms and cataracts, that comprise Poe's fictional and poetic landscapes, but it also directly recalls Poe's expressed belief in "the power of words" to capture and to embody in objective form the "fancies" that arise in the mind during the somnolence between waking and sleeping that he identifies as aesthetic consciousness (*H*16: 89). Further, it repeats his description of love for the Uranian Venus as the purest of all poetic themes, the result of which, in "The Poetic Principle," is the poem and here is the symbolically *uttered* star.

It should thus be evident that Hans's journey to the moon constitutes the narrational expansion of at least two major aspects of Poe's astral image: the star as the physical object of imaginative perception and as the spiritual object of metaphysical desire. That it constitutes a third aspect—an aesthetic product of the confluence of the former two—depends upon Hans's identification as the artist. It has already been shown that his very desire to escape an existence delimited by intolerable social and economic pressures expresses Poe's understanding of the contemporary hostility between the artist and the servants of Mammon. But the very details of his adventure go even further in adumbrating the defining characteristics and procedures of the artist-figure as it is explicitly defined by Poe.

Imagination, for instance, is the most readily identifiable element in Hans's personality and the real source of his adventure. Not only does he transform the literal moon into a Poesque symbol, but his sudden perception of the possibility of leaving the Earth is itself primarily an imaginative event. Beleaguered by the agents of social conformity and responsibility—his creditors—Hans stumbles upon a book on speculative astronomy. The volume's distance from purely empirical science is indicated by "the wild and sometimes unintelligible reasonings of the writer," which leave an "indelible impression." Certain passages, in particular, strike his *imagination* (as distinct from his reason) and begin a process in which "vague notions" feed on themselves and become "a farther stimulus to imagination." Hans considers his scientific naivety an advantage, for he wonders "whether those crude ideas which, arising in ill-regulated minds, have all the appearance, may not often in effect possess all the force, the reality, and other inherent properties of instinct or intuition" (*H*2: 50).

The role of intuition in Poe as quintessential imaginative perception is well-known.[9] And Hans's speculation prefigures the hypothesis of the narrator of "Eleonora," with whom Hans's "ill-regulated mind" becomes "madness" and points toward revelation:

> ... the question is not yet settled, whether madness is or is not the loftiest intelligence—whether much that is glorious—whether all that is profound—does not spring from disease of thought—from *moods* of mind exalted at the expense of the general intellect. They who dream by day are cognizant of many things which escape those who

dream only by night. In their gray visions they obtain glimpses of eternity, and thrill, in waking, to find that they have been upon the verge of the great secret. . . . They penetrate, however rudderless and compassless, into the vast ocean of the "light ineffable" and again, like the adventurers of the Nubian geographer, *"agressi sunt mare tenebrarum, quid in eo esset exploraturi."* (*H*4: 236)

Poe returned to this figure of the Nubian discoverer again in his own waking dream, *Eureka*, where he is himself the explorer into the dark reaches of interstellar space in search of the "light ineffable"—but Hans is his first portrait of the metaphysical investigator as cosmic voyager.

From the moment of the original "intuition" inspired by the "wild reasonings" of the speculative astronomer, Hans proceeds precisely according to Poe's famous aesthetic prescriptions: that the artist work with his desired effect constantly in view; that all elements in the artwork conspire to that effect; that "It is only with the *denouement* constantly in view that we can give a plot its indispensable air of consequence, or causation, by making the incidents, and especially the tone at all points, tend to the development of the intention" (*H*13: 153; 14: 193). After the encounter with speculative astronomy, he immediately purchases volumes on mechanics and on *practical* astronomy, which, although it makes perfect narrative sense, also directly refers to Poe's theories on the necessarily *executive* nature of the literary enterprise. Poe insisted on art's derivation from both "constructive ability" and certain strengths of character:

> This ability is based, to be sure, in great part, upon the faculty of analysis, enabling the artist to get a full view of the machinery of his proposed effect, and thus to work it and regulate it at will; but a great deal depends upon properties strictly moral—for example, upon patience, upon concentrativeness, or the power of holding the attention steadily to one purpose, upon self-dependence and contempt for opinion which is opinion and no more—in especial, upon energy or industry. (*H*16: 66-67)

Hans's account of the material he collects for his space balloon and its assembly reads like a culinary recipe, and although it may appear to the casual reader as gratuitous and tedious detail, it provides a direct representation of the self-reliance, industry, and concentration that Poe considered indispensable to artistic creation.

Hans's meticulous detailing of his procedures also points to the artist's skilled manipulation of material reality. "There is no greater mistake," Poe asserted, "than the supposition that a true originality is a mere matter of impulse or inspiration. To originate, is carefully, patiently, and understandingly to combine" (*H*14: 73), and he added that "The pure imagination chooses, *from either beauty or deformity*, only the most combinable things hitherto uncombined" (*H*12: 37). But the artist is impelled to such constructive activity by the inevitable earthly frustration of his desire to merge with the universal Ens. The passage in "The Poetic Principle" where Poe describes man's immortal longing for beauty as the desire of the moth for the star is the most important expression of his conflation of aesthetics and metaphysics, but Poe had written earlier that all poetry originated in a metaphysical longing, "in a thirst for a wilder Beauty than Earth supplies" (*H*11: 256). And he claimed that the soul attempts to quench this thirst by "*novel* combinations, *of those combinations which our predecessors, toiling in the same chase of the same phantom, have already set in order.* We thus clearly deduce the *novelty*, the *originality*, the *invention*, the *imagination*, or lastly the *creation* of BEAUTY, (for the terms as here employed are synonymous) as the essence of all Poesy" (*H*10: 73). The carefully constructed and minutely described balloon that carries Hans to the moon should thus be considered in terms of Poe's conception of art as a vehicle for transcendence. With its cambric muslin, gum of caouthchouc, and the unknown gas contributed by Hans's cousin of Nantz, the entire apparatus, like the poem, is the product of the "collocation of forms" and "novel combinations" that result in an ecstatic experience "to which all other human emotions are vapid and insignificant" (*H*11: 256).

Hans's narrative takes the form of a ship's log book or a journal—beginning on April fool's day (which contributes to the hoax readings of the tale) and ending on 19 April. Poe had used the same narrative structure in "MS. Found in a Bottle" (1833) and would resort to it later in *The Narrative of Arthur Gordon Pym* (1838). This particular form, then, should be associated in Poe with narratives whose fundamental projects involve the translation of the questing spirit to some reality beyond the confines of familiar experience. Hans's very surname links him with the narrators of these other tales. Poe illustrated his concept of "perverseness"—a pre-Freudian version of the "death" instinct—by describing the inexplicable temptation one feels when on the brink of dangerous precipices to leap into the abyss, and there is the familiar passage in *Pym* where the narrator, experiencing precisely this "longing to fall," is rescued only by landing in the arms of his companion, Dirk Peters (*H*3: 230, 6: 149-150).[10] Despite the orthographic deformation, "Hans Pfaall" points to this same perverseness, and the mixed jubilation and fear that Hans experiences in the final *bouleversement* and descent to the moon repeat the mingled horror and ecstasy of the closing phrase of "Ms. Found in a Bottle"—"Going down."

All the major features of "Hans Pfaall" are thus directly attributable to Poe's aesthetic and metaphysical concerns. Even its hoax aspects may be profitably considered under such a rubric.[11] Poe differentiated the tale from the poem by identifying "truth" rather than "beauty" as its primary goal. Consequently, its range of reference was broader, and he included "humor" among its possible strategies for achieving or embodying truth. Finally, however, that Poe was profoundly interested in the kind of aesthetic fable outlined here is indicated by another passage from the review of *Conti the Discarded* cited earlier, in which he identified what was for his readers a new kind of fiction:

> We speak of the *Art Novels*—the Kunstromanen—books written not so much in immediate defence, or illustration, as in personification of individual portions of the Fine Arts—books which, in the guise of Romance, labor to the sole end of reasoning men into admiration of the beautiful, by a tissue of bizarre fiction, partly allegorical, and partly metaphysical. In Germany alone could so mad—or perhaps so profound—an idea have originated. (*H*8: 231)

Not only "Hans Pfaall," but the majority of Poe's best and most familiar fiction proceeds from similar considerations and could be described in the same language that he used for the German art-novel.

Critics have noted that this early tale anticipates the culminating and more intense vision of *Eureka*.[12] Poe himself, in describing the mental and perceptual alterations necessary for the visionary enterprise of his prose poem, writes that "Among the vanishing minutiae of a survey of this kind, would be all exclusively terrestial matters" (*H*16; 187)—an observation that equally describes the actual events of "Hans Pfaall." And Michael Davitt Bell employs Henry James's famous trope of the "balloon of experience" in the definition of romance to claim that Poe's art embraces "romance" as a fundamental "sacrifice of relation" to conventional reality.[13] Within such parameters, then, the cosmic balloon voyage becomes a particularly adequate objective correlative for Poe's ever-present and insistent metaphysical preoccupations.

Unfortunately, Poe has been read so often as an anomaly—whether in terms of an arrested juvenile commitment to horror and grotesquerie or of a proto-sophisticate American anticipation of the French Symbolists—that his participation in the concerns of his contemporaries is frequently ignored.[14] In its basic outline, however, the present tale conforms to such patterns as that exemplified by one of his preferred models, Shelley, in his "Epipsychidion":

> Then from the caverns of my dreamy youth
> I sprang, as one sandalled with plumes of fire,
> And towards the lodestar of my one desire,
> I flitted, like a dizzy moth, whose flight
> Is as a dead leaf's in the owlet light,
> When it would seek in Hesper's setting sphere
> A radiant death, a fiery sepulchre,
> As if it were a lamp of earthly flame. (*H*2: 217-224)[15]

Poe's specific imagery, even his plot, is rediscovered here. Thus, although "Hans Pfaall" is undeniably important among the inaugural efforts of science fiction, it must be regarded also as providing American literature with a native version of the general Romantic quest for the transcendence of common reality. Perhaps the signal aspect of its very "Americanness" is its use of science and technology in the projects of idealism.

NOTES

[1] Jules and Edmond Goncourt early identified Poe as a literary pioneer, and in the 16 July 1856 entry to their *Journal* they wrote: "Après avoir lu Poe. Quelque chose que la critique n'a pas vu, un monde littéraire nouveau, les signes de la littérature du XXe siècle." *Journal: Mémoires de la vie littéraire* (Paris, 1956), 1: 256-257. For more recent and disparate evaluations of Poe's science fiction, see Clark Olney, "Edgar Allan Poe—Science Fiction Pioneer," *GaR*, 12(1958), 416-421; and David Ketterer, *New Worlds for Old: The Apocalyptic Imagination, Science Fiction, and American Literature* (Garden City, 1974), pp. 52, 65-66.

[2] See the essays by Shaw and Williams in *The Recognition of Edgar Allan Poe*, ed. Eric W. Carlson (Ann Arbor, 1966), pp. 99, 139.

[3] Joseph J. Moldenhauer, "Murder as a Fine Art: Basic Connections Between Poe's Aesthetics, Psychology, and Moral Vision," *PMLA*, 83(1968), 285.

[4] These terms are employed by Charles O'Donnell in "From Earth to Ether: Poe's Flight into Space," *PMLA*, 77(1962), 85, 86; however, O'Donnell acknowledges Allen Tate's well-known essays, "Our Cousin Mr. Poe" and "The Angelic Imagination: Poe as God" as his sources, which, in turn, acknowledge the ultimate source for this particular reading of Poe, D. H. Lawrence's *Studies in Classic American Literature* (London, 1923).

[5] For Poe's discussion of death as the means of entrance to a state that confounds man with God, see his letter to James Russell Lowell (2 July 1844), *O*1: 257.

[6]"The Internalization of Quest-Romance," in *Romanticism and Consciousness: Essays in Criticism*, ed. Harold Bloom (New York, 1970), pp. 6-12.

[7]The selection from Heine quoted in Lewis P. Simpson, *The Brazen Face of History: Studies in the Literary Consciousness in America* (Baton Rouge, 1980), p. 187, and Wordsworth in *English Romantic Writers*, ed. David Perkins (New York, 1967), p. 289.

[8]The endnote to "Hans Pfaall" distinguishes between the tale's scientific and technological emphases and the primarily satirical concerns of its precursors in the works of Francis Godwin, Cyrano de Bergerac, and George Tucker. But in the final paragraphs of his own narrative, Hans indirectly reintroduces similar concerns by his description of strange beings and allusions to exotic customs (*H*2: 99-101).

[9]For Poe's use of "imagination" and the intuitive "guess" as synonyms, see *H*6: 205; 14: 187; 16: 197, 296.

[10]In his discussion of *Pym*, Charles O'Donnell describes the protagonist's "longing to fall" as a "death urge" that is actually a "higher life urge" *op. cit.*, 87; and Moldenhauer writes of the closing phrase of "MS. Found in a Bottle": "'Going down' into the aesthetic death state is surely fraught with terrific anxieties and physical torments. But madness and pain are necessary stages of the protagonist's progress toward Unity, just as the poet must suffer frustration and anguish in striving to perfect his poem," op. cit. 296.

[11]See David Ketterer's discussion of Poe's use of the hoax as the formal expression of his metaphysics and epistemology in "Poe's Usage of the Hoax and the Unity of 'Hans Pfaall'," *Criticism*, 13(1971), 377-385. See also Michael Davitt Bell's chapter on Poe in *The Development of American Romance: The Sacrifice of Relation* (Chicago, 1980), pp. 86-125.

[12]See J. O. Bailey, "Sources for Poe's *Arthur Gordon Pym*, 'Hans Pfaall,' and Other Pieces," *PMLA*, 57(1942), 513-535; and Margaret Alterton, *The Origins of Poe's Critical Theory* (1925; rpt. New York, 1965), pp. 134-152.

[13]Bell, pp. 7-10, 39, 87-125, *passim*.

[14]Recent and welcome exceptions to this observation include Michael Davitt Bell's work cited above, Kenneth Dauber, "The Problem of Poe," *GaR*, 32(1978), 645-657, and R. E. Foust, "Aesthetician of Simultaneity: E. A. Poe and Modern Literary Theory," *SoAR*, 46(1981), 17-25.

[15]Perkins, *English Romantic Writers*, p. 1042.

PROSE RUN MAD: AN EARLY CRITICISM OF POE'S *POLITIAN*

DAVID K. JACKSON

In the 17 June 1836 issue of the *Newbern* [North Carolina] *Spectator*, a Whig weekly newspaper, appeared a notice of the May number of the *Southern Literary Messenger* so severe as to provoke Poe to resort to an editorial reply in the July *Messenger*.[1] After reprinting the *Spectator*'s comments, Poe began: "We are at a loss to know who is the editor of the Spectator, but have a shrewd suspicion that he is the identical gentleman who once sent us from Newbern an unfortunate copy of verses. It seems to us that he wishes to be taken notice of, and we will, for the once, oblige him with a few words—with the positive understanding, however, that it will be inconvenient to trouble ourselves hereafter with his opinions." John I. Pasteur and Robert G. Moore were the editors and the publishers of the *Spectator* in 1835 and 1836.[2] Then followed, as a reply to one of them, most likely Moore, Poe's comments on the literary style of Alexander Slidell Mackenzie, whose book *Spain Revisited* Poe had reviewed in the *Messenger* for May,[3] and his reporting the recent receipt of favorable comments on his editorial course from Mackenzie himself, Professor Charles Anthon, Mrs. Lydia Huntley Sigourney, Fitz-Greene Halleck, James Kirke Paulding, and an American writer whose identity he did not disclose.[4] In conclusion Poe wrote: "The Messenger merely expresses its particular opinions in its own particular manner. These opinions no person is bound to adopt. They are open to the comments and censures of even the most diminutive things in creation—of the very Newbern Spectators of the land. If the Editor of this little paper does not behave himself we will positively publish his verses."

So far as Poe was concerned, his reply in the Supplement was an end to the controversy. Not so with Moore, who before had found fault with Poe and who was to continue to criticize him and to demand his resignation. One of the earliest of Moore's criticisms appeared in the *Spectator* for 17 January 1836: a notice of the January 1836 *Messenger*, in which Poe had printed the second installment of his unsuccessful drama *Politian*:[5]

> *Southern Literary Messenger.*—The January number of this popular work has been received, and it is replete with amusing, instructive and interesting matter. So much so, that we consider it one of the best numbers of the Messenger. To analyse its contents, or even give an abstract of them, would exceed the limits at our disposal,

and we shall say, generally, that the work is unsurpassed by any original work of equal pretensions, with which we are acquainted in this country.—In our last notice of the Messenger, we expressed disapprobation of the unnecessary severity of the criticism which it contained: this number is a little more moderate, but yet not sufficiently so for a dignified and unbiassed periodical. Believing Mr. Poe to be the ostensible editor, and having had frequent opportunities of estimating his abilities, both as an author and a critic, we cannot consent to make him an umpire in matters of literary nature. We doubt his capability, and protest against the reception of his fiat. Although the columns of a weekly are not the best place for critical remarks, we will use them, as a substitute for a better, to show partially the grounds of our protest.

In the number of the Messenger before us, Mr. Poe continues his "*Scenes from Politian, an unpublished drama.*" The scenes formerly published caused us to doubt the author's talents, taste and acquirements, and these tend to confirm our first impression.

SCENES FROM AN UNPUBLISHED DRAMA,

By EDGAR A. POE.

I.

ROME. A Hall in a Palace. Alessandra & Castiglione.
"*Castiglione.*
    Oh I'm the *happiest, happiest* man in Rome,
    A few more days, thou know*est*, my Alessandra,
    Will make thee mine. Oh, I am very *happy!*"

If genius dictated these lines, they are the dregs of genius. The scarcity of ideas, manifested by the repetition of words, evinces this.

"*Aless.* Methinks thou has a singular way of showing
    Thy *happiness!*—what ails thee, cousin *of* mine?"

Here we have a couplet that requires no comment to convince even the dull of its being neither poetry nor sensible prose. The two italicised syllables will show the accuracy of Mr. Poe's ear for the harmony and measure of blank verse. The superfluous syllable in "singular," is not the only redundant one in the first line, and the *Scenes* abound throughout with similar irregularities. Nor are violations of rhythm, in these and numerous other instances, the only defects in the construction of the poem. It abounds in violations of the commonest rules of grammar.

"*Cass.* I will drop them.
Aless. Thou *must.*
DiBroglie. Far from it love.
  No branch, they say, of all philosophy
  So *deep* abstruse he has not mastered it, —"
    "If *that* we meet at all, it were as well, &c."

We have neither space nor time to follow the learned critick further to-day, and we shall merely transcribe a short extract as a fair specimen of the whole, italicising freely the incongruities in sense and sound, and the unprecedented instances of tautology.

II.

  The suburbs. Politian alone.
This weakness grows upon me. I am faint.
And much I fear me ill—it will not do
To die ere I have lived!—*Stay—stay* thy hand
O Azrael, yet awhile!—Prince of the Powers
Of Darkness and the Tomb, *O pity me!*
O pity me! let me not perish now,
In the budding of my hopes—*give me to live,*
Give me to live yet!—yet a little while:
'Tis *I who* pray for life—*I who* so late
Demanded but to die!—what sayeth the Count!
              Enter Baldazzar.
  Bal. That knowing no cause of quarrel or of feud
Between the Earl Politian and himself.
He doth decline your cartel.
  Pol. What didst thou say?
What answer was it you brought me, good Baldazzar?
With what excessive fragrance the zephyr comes
Laden from yonder bowers!—a fairer day,
Or one more worthy Italy, methinks
No mortal eyes have seen!—*what* said the Count?
  Bal. That he, Castiglione, not being aware
Of any feud existing, or any cause
Of quarrel between your lordship and himself,
Cannot accept the challenge.
  Pol. It is most true—
All this is very true. When saw you, sir,
When saw you now, Baldazzar, in the frigid
Ungenial Britain which we left so lately,
A heaven so calm as this—so *utterly* free
From the evil taint of clouds?—and he did say?
  Bal. No more, my *lord*, than I have told you SIR,
Having no cause of quarrel.
  Pol. Now this is true—

All very true. Thou art my friend, Baldazzar,
And I have not forgotten it—thou'lt do me
A piece of service? wilt thou go back and say
Unto this man, that I, the Earl of Leicester,
Hold him a villain—thus much, I prithee, say
Unto the Count—it is *exceeding* just
He should have cause for quarrel.
    Bal. My lord!—my friend!— —
    Pol. (*aside.*) 'Tis he—he comes himself! (*aloud*)
        thou reasonest well.
I know what thou wouldst say—not send the message—
Well!—I will think of it—I will not send it.
Now prithee, leave me—hither doth come a person
With whom affairs of a most private nature
I would adjust.
    Bal. I go—to-morrow *we meet
Do* we not?—*at the Vatican.*
    Pol. At the Vatican. (*exit Bal.*)
If that we meet at all, it were as well
That I should *meet* him *in the Vatican—
In the Vatican*—within the holy walls of the *Vatican.*
                    (*Enter Castiglione.*)
    Cas. The Earl of Leicester here!
    Pol. I am the Earl of Leicester, and thou seest,
Dost thou not? that I am here.
    Cas. My lord, some strange,
Some singular, mistake—misunderstanding—
Hath without doubt arisen: thou has been urged
Thereby, in heat of anger, to address
Some words most unaccountable, in writing,
To me, Castiglione, the bearer being
Baldazzar, Duke of Surrey. I am aware
Of nothing which might warrant thee in this thing,
Having given thee no offence. Ha!—am I right?
'Twas a mistake?—undoubtedly—we all
Do err at times.
    Pol. Draw, villain, and prate no more!
    Cas. Ha!—draw?—and villain? *have at thee—
Have at thee then.*
Proud Earl! (*draws.*)
    Pol. (*drawing.*) Thus to th' expiratory tomb,
Untimely sepulchre, I do devote thee
In the name of Lalage!
    Cas. (*dropping his sword and recoiling to the extremity of the stage.*)
Of Lalage!
Hold off—hold off thy hand!—Avaunt I say!
Avaunt—I will not fight thee—*I dare not—dare not.*

>   *Pol.* Thou will not fight with me didst say, Sir Count?
> Shall I be baffled thus?—now this is *well*,
> Exceeding *well*!—thou *darest not* fight with me?
> Didst say *thou darest not*? Ha!
>   *Cas.* I dare not—dare not—
> Hold off thy hand—with that beloved name
> So fresh upon thy lips I will not fight thee—
> I cannot—*dare not.*
>   *Pol.* Now by my halidom
> I do believe thee—Coward! I do believe thee!
> Thou *darest not*!

If this be not prose run mad, we have never seen a performance that deserves to be so characterized, and, in our opinion, the author of such a rhapsody should be *very, very* lenient to the faults of others.

NOTES

[1] Newbern, Craven County, once the state capital and the home of the Royal Governors of North Carolina, is now known as New Bern.

[2] Little is known about these two men. Pasteur was a "Major General of Militia and a vigorous writer" [Stephen F. Miller, *Recollections of Newbern Fifty Years Ago; with an Appendix, including Letters from Judges Gaston, Donnell, Manly and Governor Swain* (Raleigh, N.C., 1874), pp. 45-46]. Moore "was an Irishman who came to Newbern in 1818, and at once established a prosperous school. He was very urbane in manner and persevering in the enforcement of his rules . . . . he had a long and useful career, as a teacher of youth and the editor of a Whig journal, the 'Newbern Spectator,' and . . . he raised quite an interesting family" (Miller, p. 18). He retired from the editorship early in 1837. Local historians in New Bern inform me that on his arrival from Ireland Moore was first a tutor at Clear Springs, a large Craven County plantation owned by Joseph Hutton. The Newbern Academy building is now being restored.

News items about the clergyman and historian Francis Lister Hawks (1798-1866), a native of New Bern, appear in the *Spectator*. Poe reviewed Hawks's *Contributions to the Ecclesiastical History of the United States—Virginia* in the March, 1836, *Messenger*. For Poe's association with Hawks, see Dwight R. Thomas, "Poe in Philadelphia, 1838-1844: A Documentary Record" (Unpublished Ph.D. Dissertation, University of Pennsylvania, 1978, 2: 799.

[3] Alexander Slidell (1802-1848) added his last name "Mackenzie" in 1838, after the publication of his *Spain Revisited*. Poe included Mackenzie in "Autography" (Letter XXXI).

[4]Ralph M. Aderman, ed., *The Letters of James Kirke Paulding* (Madison, 1962), p. 179, assigned the letter to Paulding. Poe's description of his correspondent as "an individual second to no American author in the wide-spread popularity of his writings, and in their universal appreciation by men of letters, both in the United States and England" seems to me to apply to Irving more than Paulding, whom Poe had already quoted by name. Both Paulding and Irving were *Messenger* subscribers.

[5]In 1940 the late Thomas Ollive Mabbott and I were unsuccessful in seeking a file of the *Newbern Spectator*. We believed that we might discover a Poe letter. A microfilm of a file of this weekly is now in the William R. Perkins Library of Duke University.

Moore's criticisms of Poe in the *Spectator* are recorded in Dwight Thomas and David K. Jackson, *The Poe Log: A Documentary Life of Edgar Allan Poe, 1809-1849* (Boston, 1987), p. 189. For an account of Poe's problems with his Southern and Northern critics, see Sidney P. Moss, *Poe's Literary Battles* (Durham, N.C., 1963).

POE AND THE WILL

APRIL SELLEY

The image of the perennially pubescent Poe, once fostered even by serious literary critics, may strongly interest high school students. But more advanced students will probably not appreciate Poe unless his works offer more than "The Legend." Therefore teachers must introduce students to the artistically and psychologically mature and perceptive Poe. In thus helping Poe to come out of the cellar, educators can also show how his work is distinctly American and indeed part of the mainstream of American literature.

I wish to concentrate on Poe's short fiction in which, I think, lies his greatest—and most American—achievement as an artist. My most useful approach to the tales is considering them in the context of free will. Poe's interest in the operation of the will has been noted by Henry Bamford Parkes and more recently by Brian Barbour. Barbour maintains that Poe's nine or ten greatest and most characteristic tales "embody the central value of the self-willing, atomistic, autonomous individual, but they wrench us out of the lenitive atmosphere of American optimism to focus our attention on narrators whose willfulness expresses deep disorder within. We are obliged to see the moral consequences, the dark, hidden possibilities in what we believe."[1]

Thus Poe is concerned with Emerson's concept of self-reliance, although, to be sure, he had serious objections to Emerson's Transcendentalism. But "The Philosophy of Composition" and "The Poetic Principle" suggest that Poe's differences from Emerson were principally aesthetic, applicable to their approaches to poetry alone. Certainly, reading Emerson's "The Poet" and Poe's "The Philosophy of Composition" together allows students to contemplate the characteristics of the American poetic tradition. Yet the subtler differences between the two writers emerge when one reads Poe's tales after Emerson's "Self-Reliance" but before his "Experience." This approach shows the manifold problems implicit in self-reliance and the exertion of human will.

Emerson recognizes some of those difficulties in "Experience"; however, he never understood the major subjects of Poe's fiction: the lure or the significance of the dark, often impishly perverse drives within human beings. Like Hawthorne and Melville, Poe implicitly suggests that Emerson's confidence in the self-reliant, imaginative man is too simplistic, that Emerson does not explore the full implications of the exercise of the will in nineteenth-century American life. Poe presents characters who exercise no personal volition (Zenobia, Lacko'breath, Bedloe, M. Valdemar), as well as those who exercise too much (Templeton, Valdemar's mesmerist, the narrator in "Ligeia"), but both types of characters reveal the same difficulty—they cannot see beyond the self. The stories present an implicit question, then: how can one see what *is* beyond the mind, beyond Emerson's transparent eyeball (which becomes the "vacant eyelike windows" in "The Fall of the House of Usher") or the leaden-hued pane of the narrator's bridal chamber/mind in "Ligeia"?

Poe, of course, can offer no answers. In the satires, clearly, the volitionless protagonists can never reform because they cannot perceive their own inadequacies of understanding. Poe evinces clear contempt for these nonselves so well-wadded with stupidity, yet he refuses simplistically to blame their existence on the protagonists themselves, on God, or on society, although all, especially the last, seem culpable. At the other extreme, Poe's monomaniacal characters can perceive only their obsessions, but Poe cannot wholly censure nineteenth-century American society for producing citizens like Montresor or Roderick Usher, for obviously not all Americans became Montresors or Ushers.

Despite his inability to provide either explanations or alternatives, Poe cannot ignore what I believe he considered the major problem of American democracy. That is: how can the individual will function productively and imaginatively within the limitations imposed by time, space, limited self-knowledge, and the need to tolerate the rights and the operation of the wills of others? These limitations must inevitably inhibit psychological growth in certain individuals, thus producing dead-in-life characters such as Allamistakeo, Oinos, Roderick and Madeline Usher.

Poe's tales that employ what I call the "voice from beyond" are especially interesting to teach in the context of free will. Featuring the dead and dead-in-life, these tales suggest that Poe did not build stories around death only because he was fascinated with ghouls and graveyards, but rather because death provided a metaphor for man's physical and psychological limitations. Moreover, everyone who kills in these stories is trying to deny his own mortal limits; he exerts his will most completely over another by taking another's life. I will explain further when referring to individual tales.

Poe's tales with "posthumous" characters also allow students opportunity to read less familiar works, which they will approach with no preconceptions. These tales can be divided into three groups: the satires; the mesmerism tales and other stories that demonstrate the under-use or self-defeating use of free will; and the conversations narrated from the afterlife. Taken as a whole, they develop two themes: Poe's criticism of the diseased will in the dead-in-life, and his praise of the creative faculty in the "born again"—a higher form of will that makes possible the attainment of man's supreme self in Aidenn (or Paradise).

Poe satirizes those incapable of exercising personal volition in "Loss of Breath," "A Predicament" (and its companion piece, "How to Write a Blackwood Article"), "Some Words with a Mummy" and "The Premature Burial." The protagonists of the first two tales have lost body parts crucial to human life—Zenobia, significantly, her head and Lacko'breath his breath; in the third tale, Allamistakeo has been embalmed for 5,050 years. The narrator of "The Premature Burial" has been interred alive within the illusions that his morbid imagination has contributed to his ill-being. He has escaped life and reality through dreams, visions, fantasies and periods of sleep and catalepsy followed by long intervals of forgetfulness. Poe's point is that in terms of intellect, taste, common sense and personality, these characters are all dead-in-life—what T. S. Eliot would call "hollow men."

Only one of these four protagonists "reforms," thus illustrating Poe's lack of hope for the Philistines and for all obsessed individuals. After having his greatest fear *and* supreme masochistic desire realized,[2] the narrator of "The Premature Burial" is purged of his morbidity and "Night Thoughts." But he changes because he *acts*: he goes out into the sunshine and vows never again to read "bugaboo tales . . . *such as this*" (*M*3: 969). Poe's other satiric characters are merely acted upon. Zenobia (unlike her serious counterpart in "The Pit and the Pendulum," who escapes the blade through his wit) is decapitated by the hand of the clock and finds herself with no one and nothing—especially no motivation—at the end: "Dogless, niggerless, headless, what now remains for the unhappy Signora Psyche Zenobia? Alas—nothing! I have done" (*M*2: 357). Lacko'breath receives his breath again, but this restoration only allows him to speak more of the incomprehensibilities that make up his story as a whole. His marriage is apparently finished, and his functioning at all seems impossible: he has left his glass eyes, false hips, *et cetera* in his wife's bedroom, and much of the rest of him has been dissected by physicians and eaten by cats. He cannot act because he has no body left. And Allamistakeo, after observing the shabbiest accomplishments of the nineteenth century (phony patent medicines and the Bowling Green fountain), experiences psychological defeat: "Never was triumph [over Allamistakeo] more consummate; never was defeat borne with so ill a grace" (*M*3: 1195). Allamistakeo is ready to return to a more comfortable state of being: mummification.

By such means Poe undercuts characters of no volition and consequently less integrity by making their "posthumous" existences a metaphor for death-in-life. Similar undercutting appears in "Shadow," which commences: "Ye who read are still among the living; but I who write shall have long since gone my way into the region of shadows" (*M*2: 188). Dead now, the narrator was no more alive when writing the story. There is little difference between the "vague, and formless, and indefinite" (*M*2: 190) Shadow into which all of the characters dissolve at the end of "Shadow," and the existence of these characters earlier in the tale. The narrator Oinos and his friends have locked themselves into a mausoleum-like room and become intoxicated while keeping vigil over the (presumably still infectious) corpse of their friend who has died of the plague. Ironically, Oinos's name means "wine" and "one,"[3] and through "wine" the friends become "one" volitionless and mindless being. When "Shadow" enters at the end, he is an objective correlative of the friends' physical and mental status. They are finally dead in all senses. This death does not lead to Paradise, as in Poe's posthumous "conversation" tales such as "The Conversation of Eiros and Charmion," but to a limbo of stasis.

The same limbo recurs in "Silence—A Fable." The man on the rock is isolated from nature, from other men and ultimately from himself. He is powerless; he is also surrounded by death: the voice that tells most of the tale is that of a demon (i.e., "the spirit of a dead man"), and the lynx who appears later in the tale is a scavenger.[4] According to Poe, there is no possibility of rebirth for the man on the rock because the only legitimate reason for relinquishing one's will is to enter the afterlife and to become one with the Godhead.

Poe also records the over-exertion of the will that can create a perverse world into which his characters retreat. In both "A Tale of the Ragged Mountains" and "Valdemar," he implicitly condemns mesmerists who manipulate and ultimately control their patients' lives. Although the narrator's initial description in "Ragged Mountains" implies that Bedloe is a vampire and a reincarnation of the mesmerist Dr. Templeton's long-dead friend Oldeb (his eyes resemble those of a "long-interred corpse" [*M*3: 940]), Templeton is ultimately the vampire whose supreme act of will over Bedloe is killing him with a poisonous leech.[5] Templeton proceeds from partial to complete mesmerizing, to killing Bedloe, thus gaining domination by extermination, as many of Poe's other protagonists do.

"Ragged Mountains" and "Valdemar" illustrate that using the will to appropriate power over death has hideous results. M. Valdemar is kept in a mesmeric trance seven months after he should have died. When the mesmerist relinquishes control at the dead man's anguished request, Valdemar's body dissolves into liquid putrefaction because it has been decaying while he has been dead-in-life. Critics are often shocked by this ending, but what happens is, for the first time in the tale, something natural. Corpses do decay. Poe's characters must observe this loathsome process only because the mesmerist has compelled the subject to exist past his time.[6]

"Ragged Mountains" and "Valdemar" contrast with "Mesmeric Revelation," in which another character speaks, or seems to speak, from beyond the dead. Here, however, the mesmerist does not attempt to control his patient's destiny, but only mesmerizes Vankirk to allow him to approach a deathlike state. Never manipulative, the mesmerist listens reverently as Vankirk enters the world beyond and peacefully reconciles and relinquishes his psyche and soul to God, death and the afterlife.

Vankirk is one of Poe's few characters who willingly accepts death. Others, like Ligeia (who is most probably a projection of her "husband's" enormous ego and will), believe that nothing can stop the will in its vigor; therefore they resist death. In contrast to Vankirk, the fisherman in "A Descent into the Maelstrom" refuses to relinquish his will and reason. He does not thwart death by clinging to the water cask; rather, he is spiritually unsuited to becoming "*completely absorbed*" (*M*2: 592; Poe's italics) into the maelstrom, and thus into the Divine and the Eternal. As his account of being inside the maelstrom continues, the reader sees him gradually reenter the world of time and measurement. Significantly, he uses words from geometry and physics that define exact positions and measurements, and that thus divide instead of unify: "a plane parallel with that of the water" (590), "angle of more than forty-five degrees" (590) and "dead level" (591).[7] The fisherman's "raving maniac" (589) brother is absorbed, and enters the world out of space and out of time.[8] But the fisherman, who should have died (he seems to be "a *very* old man" [578; Poe's italics] and "a traveller from the spirit-land" [594], is returned to the mortal world. He is haunted and horrified by the experience of the sublime and ineffable that he could not fully embrace—but has not fully escaped. He now belongs neither on earth nor in Aidenn.

The next group of tales presents characters who have been transported to the "world beyond." Unlike the fisherman, the characters in "Eiros and Charmion," ready to enter the eternal realm, wished while on earth to relinquish their mortal bodies. As the earth exploded, mankind held their "arms rigidly outstretched towards the threatening heavens" (461)—in supplicating despair but also in a wish to embrace what was to come. They were overcome by light, the same which constitutes the luminescence of the rainbow and is a sign of God's presence in "A Descent." The light "[penetrated] all things" (*M*2: 461), uniting them as one being and substance. This penetration and unification heralded the afterlife when all (according to Poe's later works) would merge with God. Indeed, as Stephen Mooney notes,

Eiros and Charmion seem to be two aspects of a single intelligence. They, and the universe, are one.[9]

The individual will seems to be lost in the afterlife, but this loss does not concern Poe's characters in "Eiros and Charmion" or in "The Colloquy of Monos and Una." In the latter, Monos describes in detail how his (and presumably Una's) original body, senses and consciousness decomposed, a necessary transformation before Monos was "born again" in mind and in body. Monos laments the misuse of the will among mortals (of which he, too, seems to have been guilty)—instead of submitting to the guidance of natural laws, man had attempted to control them. Only the gruesome process of death and decay could resolve man's "Cartesian dualism, the separation of the mind from physical reality."[10] Monos and Una are now "redeemed regenerated, blissful, and . . . immortal" (*M*2: 612); their names both mean, significantly, "one." But since "Monos and Una" begins as the principals are born again and traces the process of rebirth backward to the grave, how these "integrated" beings are to function is left unclear.[11]

In "The Power of Words," however, Poe hints about regenerated man's activities in Aidenn. He suggests that whenever man exerts his will in the heavenly spheres, he is actually following the will of the Godhead. One narrator in "The Power of Words," Agathos, explains that on earth and in heaven, the source of all physical motion is thought, and the source of all thought is God. The mental and the material are intrinsically related, especially through words. Even on earth, man can, to an extent, participate in the divine as a writer, bringing art into being through words. In Aidenn, the creative process is carried further—creative regenerated beings can bring planets into existence by means of the Word.

In "The Power of Words" Poe thus establishes the force that unifies the here and the hereafter—the force never explained in "Monos and Una." "The Power of Words" ends by making words the basis of the universe: they are "being" as opposed to "silence," or nothingness. Words are mental activity made matter, thought made substance, word made flesh. Whereas many of Poe's other "voices from beyond" demonstrate that death-in-life leads to death and an unsavory existence afterward, the voices in "The Power of Words" show that the rebirth following death can liberate creative faculties in the deserving reborn. Since creation is unity, however, the reborn person is no longer an individual in the human sense. He is rather, by becoming part of the Godhead, his supreme self, participating in what Coleridge calls "the eternal act of creation in the infinite I AM."

To conclude, it is clear why many of Poe's posthumous voices are actually dead-in-(mortal)-life characters such as Lacko'breath, Zenobia, Allamistakeo, the narrators of "The Premature Burial" and "Shadow," the man on the rock in "Silence," the fisherman in "A Descent" and the mesmerized men and their mesmerists in "Ragged Mountains" and "Valdemar." Poe's obsession with death is also understandable: death initiates the process that allows man to escape space and time, the basic limitations upon human beings. Mortal existence almost compels man to be individualistic, bent upon exercising his will against the limitations forced upon him. Thus the imagination of the creative mortal, instead of asserting itself through the unrestricted creation that is made possible only through union with God, often acts perversely to gain power by means of the will. Because his imagination is restricted on earth, man often turns inward to the darkest recesses of his psyche to discover the imp of the perverse lurking there, urging the will to self-destructive actions. (Poe consistently demonstrates that every destructive act is ultimately self-destructive.) But when man becomes one with his universe, he asserts not his insecure self, but rather the infinite act of creation.

The closest man can come to the infinite act on earth is through words that create art and yet paradoxically prove mortal limitations. Poe never uses the macabre gratuitously, but always to convey this painful paradox. Perhaps one of my students was right: Poe thrived on frustration.[12] The imaginative man must inevitably be frustrated by limitations in the human sphere. Poe's "posthumous" voices show that life on earth is death, and that death—although it must break down through decay all matter and spirit—allows the man of imagination to be born again. These voices also demonstrate that Poe can still be appreciated for his terrifying and cosmic themes. He will no longer terrify and inspire as a boogieman, however, but as an original thinker deeply aware of the philosophical and psychological dangers implicit in the American tradition as it was developing in his time and would continue to develop.

NOTES

[1] Parkes, *The American Experience* (New York, 1947), esp. pp. 196-197. Parkes notes that Poe, Hawthorne and Melville "saw life in terms of a battle between the will of man and his environment" (196). Barbour, "Poe and Tradition," *SLJ*, 10(1978), 52. Barbour also notes that Poe's greatest achievement lies in his fiction: "in his verse Poe is the Romantic anchorite indulging a grievance against an ugly world, but in his greatest tales—'Ligeia,' 'The Fall of the House of Usher,' 'William Wilson,' 'The Pit and the Pendulum,' 'The Tell-Tale Heart,' 'The Black Cat,' 'The

Purloined Letter,' 'The Cask of Amontillado,' perhaps one or two more—he grapples with the inner meaning of the American experience and provides a permanently valuable critique of our tradition. It is the purpose of this paper to show that Poe's tales matter in a way the poetry can not, and to show further that their artistic strength is inseparable from the insight they show into the American experience, the effort to become truly human in America" (49).

[2]See Bruce Ira Weiner, "Poe's Subversion of Verisimilitude," *ATQ*, 24(1974): "One wonders whether his [the narrator's in "The Premature Burial"] retrospective complaint against his destiny accounts for burial or whether he had, at that time, doomed himself . . . by a kind of wish fulfillment. The man seems to want to be buried alive to get the ultimate masochistic thrill" (3).

[3]*The Short Fiction of Edgar Allan Poe*, ed. Stuart and Susan Levine (Indianapolis, 1976), p. 145, n. 1.

[4]Benjamin Franklin Fisher IV, "The Power of Words in Poe's 'Silence'," *Poe at Work: Seven Textual Studies*, ed. Benjamin Franklin Fisher IV (Baltimore, 1978), pp. 56-72. Fisher views the tale as "a dramatized version of the bombardment and disintegration of a psyche" (61). He sees the narrator, the man on the rock, the demon and the lynx as parts of one being: "A tortured human self, one who cannot elude his Demon, or his irrational, destructive side, a part of the self that exists close to the animal potential within all of us (witness the lynx) and just as close to death, implicit in the "shadow of the tomb" (60). The protagonist "has become nothing; that is, he has been so lured from normal, everyday reality that he now exists in a mental-spiritual void, comparable to the desolation pictured by the

[5]G. R. Thompson, *Poe's Fiction: Romantic Irony in the Gothic Tales* (Madison, 1973), pp. 147-152, elaborates upon the implications made by other critics that Templeton is Bedloe's murderer.

[6]J. Gerald Kennedy, "Phantasms of Death in Poe's Fiction" in *The Haunted Dusk: American Supernatural Fiction, 1820-1920*, ed. Howard Kerr, John W. Crowley, and Charles L. Crow (Athens, Ga., 1983), pp. 37-65, notes that "the grotesque final scene betrays the limitation of human efficacy and reaffirms the sovereignty of death. In effect, the illusion of a scientifically insured immortality disintegrates with Valdemar" (62). Amplification of such matters may be found in Kennedy's *Poe, Death, and the Life of Writing* (New Haven, 1987).

[7]Poe's use of mathematical language has been well-noted. An overview is Clarence R. Wylie, Jr., "Mathematical Allusions in Poe," *Scientific Monthly*, 63(1946), 227-235. Recent work on mathematical language focuses on "The Pit and the Pendulum." Alexander Hammond has spoken on "Subverting Interpretation:

The Lesson of Poe's Geometry in 'The Pit and the Pendulum'," MLA Convention, New York, 29 Dec. 1983. Rochie Lawes, "The Dimensions of Terror: Mathematical Imagery in 'The Pit and the Pendulum'," *PoeS*, 16(1983), 5-7, observes that "In the tale mathematical imagery is counterpointed against the dark uncertainties of what Kent Ljungquist calls 'a crucible of painful sensations.' The narrator's facility with both the language and the concepts of mathematics allows him to grapple with the enormity of his danger" (6).

[8] Richard Wilbur, "Introduction," in *Poe* [The Laurel Poetry Series] (New York, 1959): "insanity . . . signifies . . . the ascendency of imagination over intellect, the power subjectively to distort or annihilate the world in favor of reverie or vision" (16).

[9] Stephen L. Mooney, "Poe's Gothic Waste Land," *SR*, 70(1962), 272.

[10] Edward H. Davidson, *Poe: A Critical Study* (Cambridge, Mass., 1957), p. 133.

[11] Kennedy shares my perplexity about Poe's vision of the afterlife. Noting that Poe is "no systematic thinker" about death and the hereafter, he discusses "Monos and Una" and other tales with posthumous speakers: "What seems significant about the cycle of spiritualized dialogues is Poe's inclination to see body and soul as inextricably bonded. Despite the conception of an unearthly, astral form, an odd materialism informs Poe's notion of the spirit world; 'Aidenn' is simply a place where things, substances, are less densely constituted. God is 'unparticled matter,' souls have bodies, and words have a 'physical power.' It is as if, for all of his mystical inclinations, Poe cannot escape an empirical vision of a bounded world. His depiction of an afterlife seems to express a yearning for a realm 'out of space, out of time,' beyond the contingencies of mortal existence. Yet in fact his spirit figures carry with them a good deal of earthly baggage—memories, affections, beliefs, political opinions—and spend much of their time (if one can thus speak of the eternal) reflecting upon personal experiences or explaining celestial phenomena according to mundane scientific principles. In short, Poe's visionary texts (and here I include the monumentally confused *Eureka*) project a false transcendence, a phantasmic existence after death, conceptually embedded in a cosmos of matter and energy, a system that culminates in irreversible dissolution: entropy" (59-60).

[12] My thanks for this observation go to Edward Black, a student in English 41, Fall 1979, at Brown University.

THE CORPSE WITHIN US

STEVEN E. KAGLE

Ironically, the word "fantastic," which means unreal, originates in the Greek *phantastikos*, "able to present to the mind," for even in the empirical philosophy of John Locke, physical reality is only known when it is presented to the mind. The most fantastic elements in literature are often effective precisely because on some level they are the most real. Some of the most terrifying incidents in Poe's works seem to draw their power from a "real" fear of premature burial, "real" not because the writer or his readers are in real danger of being buried alive, but rather, because the fear itself is real. In Poe's stories this fear is especially real because it is tied to a companion fear as vital but not so obvious, the fear of being the agent of a premature burial. Stephen Crane noted that the man who fears he will "find a victim" is wiser than the man who fears he will "find an assassin" because the former realizes that he is not in control of his own actions. The man who fears he will commit a misdeed is announcing his inability to determine his own fate.

The fear of premature burial becomes magnified when the agent of the burial is also the tomb. How terrifying it is to realize that a secret from our past, one we had thought safely dead and buried, was still alive at the time of burial and that, even if it is no longer truly alive, it remains animate as a ghost or hallucination. The connection between the guilt from a buried secret and the theme of premature burial is extremely useful in understanding a number of Poe's most famous works. Just as important is how his treatment of these matters suggests that his ideas were much closer to those of his contemporaries than has usually been recognized. In the very places where the "fantastic" qualities of Poe's writings seem to separate him from his contemporaries, a "reality" links him to them.

This theme of buried guilt or secrets is frequently studied in the writings of Poe's contemporaries, a large percentage of whom openly accepted the moral function of literary art that Poe so often claimed to be improper. In "Compensation," Emerson warned that crime could not be hidden for it altered the natures of both the criminal and his environment: "Commit a crime, and the earth is made of glass. Commit a crime, and it seems as if a coat of snow fell on the ground, such as reveals in the woods the track of every partridge and fox . . . . you cannot wipe out the foot track . . . so as to leave no inlet or clew. Some damning circumstance always transpires."[1] Similarly, Bryant in "Inscription for the Entrance to a Wood" cautioned that God had "yoked to guilt her pale tormentor, misery;" and, therefore, man could only escape suffering if he put off his guilt.

Melville was more explicit about the problem of the corpse within. In *Mardi*, Babbalanja's demon, Azzageddi, warns that all men are "full of ghosts and spirits . . . are as graveyards full of buried dead that start to life before us. And all of our dead sires, verily, are in us . . . . From sire to son, we go on multiplying corpses in ourselves."[2] In *Moby-Dick*, the barrels in the hold of the *Pequod* are filled with the distillation of corpses. Indeed, in the chapter entitled "The Try Works" the ship is described as "laden with fire, and burning a corpse," features which make it seem "the material counterpart of her monomaniac commander's soul."[3] The Parsee's prophecy offers another indication that the *Pequod* is a disguised hearse. Only when its coffin shoots out and is exposed to the world, is any escape possible. This internalization of guilt seems at least partially responsible for Ahab's "monomania." This "insanity" did not come when his leg was bitten off by the whale; rather, it "seized him" only afterward when he was bound in his hammock so that his ravings had no outlet and so were driven inward. Outwardly he seemed sane, but "Ahab, in his hidden self, raved on" (p. 160). It may be more than coincidence that, like the crack in the wall of Usher's house, Ahab bears a mark that may run his whole length.

Rejecting this moral function in "The Poetic Principle," Poe maintained that poetry is concerned with beauty and has little to do with either truth or the "moral sense." This argument is sufficient to suggest that he might have been willing to apply his conclusions to prose fiction as well as to poetry. This extension is further supported by his pronouncements in the "Marginalia" that *"Beauty"* is the "sole object" of the imagination (*H*11: 156). Reviewing Hawthorne's *Twice Told Tales*, Poe pronounced *Truth* to be the "aim of the tale," but even in this work Poe did not admit morality as a concern of prose fiction (*H*11: 109).

Many critics deny Poe's concern with moral questions, claiming that he "does not touch morality" and that his tales of terror are not concerned with either sin, crime or moral law, but with "matters of psychology."[4] Others argue that Poe's tales do have a significant moral purpose, a purpose especially evident when one considers the implications of their use in advancing the theme of internal burial. This fear that one may become the agent of a premature burial or the guilt at having actually done such a deed is every bit as vital to an understanding of Poe's work as is the fear of personal suffering. As the narrator in "The Pit and the Pendulum" suggests, "moral horrors" may be at least as dreadful as "physical agonies." We may shrink as much from the destruction of our souls as we do from threats to our bodies. Thoreau in "Civil Disobedience" warned that man's duty to refuse to be the agent of injustice to another was more compelling than that to eradicate "even the most enormous wrong."

One reason this situation is especially terrifying to many of Poe's characters is that, as I have already suggested, in several instances the agent of the premature burial is, at least symbolically, also the tomb. A secret which had seemed dead and safely buried in the securest of hiding places proves, at least at the time of burial, to have been still alive and active within the character's soul. How terrifying is the suspicion that, even if no longer truly alive, the secret is still animate as a spirit, hallucination or demon dwelling in the fittest place to take possession of the guilty party.

One story in which such a situation seems most obvious is "The Fall of the House of Usher." Madeline Usher is not buried in the family graveyard, where her body might become the prey of grave robbers, but in a crypt within the house, which as described, seems excessively secure: "A portion of the floor and the whole interior of a long archway . . . were carefully sheathed with copper. The door, of massive iron, had been, also, similarly protected" (*H*3: 288). The narrator, who seems less than satisfied with the place and manner Roderick Usher has chosen for his sister's interment, considers it "at best a harmless . . . precaution," and so puts aside his suspicions. However, the reader is less likely to be convinced about Usher's motives (*H*3: 288). The very isolation of the house and its family burial ground seems a defense from the prying eyes of the outside world, as yet unaware of Madeline's death. But some secrets are too dangerous to make the slightest risk of exposure acceptable.

Burial within the walls has its risks, however, for as the narrator reveals, Roderick and his house are doubles, "the stem of the Usher race, all time-honored as it was, had put forth, at no period, any enduring branch," and, therefore, the "House of Usher" had come to stand for "both the family and the family mansion" (*H*3: 275). As the sole surviving Usher, Roderick is the house; therefore, in burying his sister within his walls he is burying her within himself. Moreover, as twins, possessing not only "a striking similitude" but also supernatural "sympathies," Roderick and his sister are doubles. In burying her, he attempts to bury a part of himself. In "The House of Poe," Richard Wilbur, who is only one of many critics to examine Poe's use of the enclosure theme, suggests that "circumscription, in Poe's tales, means the exclusion from consciousness of the so called real world, the world of time, reason and physical fact."[5] Few if any of Poe characters can be said to have managed a successful escape from external reality; how much poorer then are their chances of maintaining their isolation from reality when they attempt to circumscribe it, to carry it within themselves.

Roderick claims that he intends his sister's interment within the crypt to be temporary, but this assertion, too, is suspect. If we were reading Hawthorne and not Poe, would we not expect to be immediately cautioned about the danger to the soul from burying guilty secrets with our hearts and deceiving ourselves with the belief that we will confess in time to be forgiven for our sin? Hawthorne's "Bosom Serpent" gnaws at its victim most effectively from within. Even death offers no release or no sure protection against detection. In *The Scarlet Letter*, a man who kept some "hideous secret buried within him, and which he had done better to confess during his lifetime," is betrayed by his own corpse which, decomposing, gives rise to "ugly weeds."[6]

This principle that a buried secret brings suffering is often disguised in Poe's stories because the stories are most frequently conveyed by a first-person narrator. As Emerson wrote in "Experience": "That which we call sin in others is experiment for us . . . . The act looks very different on the inside and on the outside."[7] The murderers in "The Tell-Tale Heart" and "The Black Cat" deny that they are mad. He in "The Imp of the Perverse" blames his confession of an otherwise unpunishable crime on an external power. In all three stories a corpse, seemingly safely walled up within a house, is revealed to public view.

Montresor, the narrator in "The Cask of Amontillado," also seems to have committed the perfect crime. He has walled his victim alive in the depths of the catacombs where he can never be found. But if the victim were safely sealed, why is this confession, for the story is a confession of the deed, recounted fifty years later when the narrator is so old that he must sense death close to him? Why does he still recollect that "his heart grew sick" or feel the need to rationalize this "sickness" as the result of the dampness of the catacombs? Why does he pray that the bones of his victim will rest in peace? He has asserted that "for half a century no mortal has disturbed them," but is not his confession a sign that some immortal force has done so? Let us remember that the victim was not buried in some external graveyard, but in vaults located deep beneath and within Montresor's own house. D. H. Lawrence even suggested that Montresor is guilty of an attempt to incorporate Fortunato's soul within his own, that "in walling-up his enemy in the vault, Montresor seeks to . . . possess himself of the very being of the vanquished."[8] If so, this incorporation is but another form of internal burial.

"Ligeia," too, includes the theme of interior burial. When the narrator's second wife, the Lady Rowena dies, she is not immediately entombed or even moved; instead, she is wrapped in a shroud and left in the room in which she died, a room which was also her bridal chamber. This room in one of Poe's "castellated abbeys" has been decorated according to the narrator's own morbid fantasies with items associated with tombs. In each of the angles of the room stood a "sarcophagus of black granite from the tombs of the kings over against Luxor." Even the "bridal couch" carved of ebony had a "pall-like canopy" (*H*2: 259-260). From this and a wealth of other details we can see that the narrator has already built a tomb within his house.

Ligeia, the narrator's first wife, has also died and been "entombed," but the narrator makes no mention of where her tomb is. To find that we must first unravel mysteries about her identity. Tracing the origin of Ligeia from her first appearance as a siren in Milton's "Comus" through her depiction as spirit of harmony in Poe's own poem, "Al Aaraaf," Richard Wilbur argues that she is "not a woman, but a mediating spirit embodying the Platonic idea of harmony" and that her function is to keep her husband's "soul untouched by his diseased Earthly environment . . . [so that it might devote] itself to unbroken poetic visions of ultramundane harmony and beauty." Wilbur suggests that Ligeia's resurrection within the corpse of Rowena represents "a Platonic version of the art process in which beauty is imaginatively extricated from the temporal and physical."[9] This interpretation does much to explain some of the narrator's initial comments on Ligeia's background and actions; however, it does nothing to explain why or how such a spirit has died, and Wilbur never discusses that death.

I suggest a modifying of Wilbur's explanation that can provide a consistent explanation of Ligeia's death. There is a particular type of "mediating spirit" who in mythology performs as Ligeia does, and this is a muse. If Ligeia is the narrator's muse, a number of otherwise strange points in his account become clear. Like Ligeia, a muse has a lineage "of remotely ancient date" but no "paternal name." Even today, we speak of an artist's search for inspiration as "courting the muse." Poe's narrator is a scholar/artist who has become so devoted to his studies that he has in his mind married his muse. As a muse, Ligeia can come and depart "as a shadow" entering a closed study without any action that might be noticed by the physical senses. Indeed, the narrator explains that he "never" became "aware of her entrance" until she had touched, inspired, him. Her physical characteristics further delineate her nature. As a muse of the Romantic Period, she has a beauty which is marked by "strangeness" and irregularity rather than the "classical regularity" which was the standard of beauty in the Age of Reason. We can well understand why the narrator, who is associated with Romanticism, should have "met her first and most frequently in some large, old, decaying city near the Rhine" (*H*2: 248).

Seen in this way, Ligeia's death is the death of the muse, the loss of artistic inspiration and power. When Ligeia, using a phrase attributed to Glanvill, declared that "man does not yield himself to the angels, *nor unto death utterly*, save only through the weakness of his feeble will," she is warning her husband that the weak will which is bringing about her death is not hers but his (*H*2: 257). Her statement also indicates that the loss of creative power need not be permanent. She may die, but he will carry her corpse with him.

When the narrator marries the Lady Rowena Trevanion of Tremaine, he takes a bride who is the antithesis of Ligeia. Rowena has not only a maiden name, but one that gives her a place in space and time. Ligeia was dark; Rowena is fair. Ligeia was spiritual; Rowena is physical. Ligeia can be loved only spiritually; Rowena can also be loved physically and may expect such love. Poe gives no other possible explanation for the narrator's marriage to Rowena beyond physical attraction; Ligeia's inspiration had already brought him wealth and some measure of fame. But if Rowena represents for the narrator the desires of sexual attraction, that sexuality also can be a source of anxiety. Thus the narrator comes to "loathe her with a hatred belonging more to demon than to man" and "with what intensity of regret!" to remember "the entombed" Ligeia and to revel in "recollections of her purity" (*H*2: 260). His loathing is intensified by his awareness of the corpse within him and its constant reminder of his failed powers. Only when Rowena has died is her physical threat removed. Only after death can she be loved "purely." The narrator's emotion, the result of sorrow and guilt, is profound; and, in keeping with the Romantic tradition, heightened emotion results in a revival of poetic inspiration, the resurrection of Ligeia.

One might suppose that if the rebirth of Ligeia is a return of the narrator's creativity, this appearance of what had been the corpse within is a very positive event and thus is much different from the reappearance of Madeline Usher. Certain subtle details, however, indicate that this is not the case. When, in the final paragraph, the narrator describes his attempt to reach toward the reviving body of Ligeia, he talks of her "shrinking from my touch." And in the opening paragraph, as he begins to tell his story, he mentions that his "memory is feeble through much suffering" (*H*2: 248, 268). In other words, Ligeia's return may have brought back his creative power, but it did not restore the joy that he had once felt in its operation. He may have regained his art but at an enormous price. Moreover, the corpse of his second wife who is Ligeia's double, has never left his house. Whether, as some critics suggest, she died by his own hand, or whether he merely wished for her death, he knows that he is guilty of a crime. Like Fortunato, this narrator is attempting by telling his tale to re-invert his world, to expiate his guilt by externalizing the hidden corpse, but in each case the attempt is half-hearted; like Claudius' prayers in *Hamlet* such actions cannot gain redemption for the sinner who is not fully repentant.

"The Masque of the Red Death" provides another telling example of Poe's typical inversion of inner and outer reality. Prince Prospero believes that he is safe because he walled the plague outside the "castellated abbey" in which he takes refuge with a select group of his own courtiers. Soon, however, the Red Death appears within the abbey costumed as a corpse. The Prince—welding the bolts of his gates in an attempt to secure himself from what he perceived as the threat from outside the self—had, in actuality, locked the danger inside.

Like Shakespeare's Prospero, Poe's character is punished for a real transgression, dereliction of duty. Both monarchs try to escape their obligations to their subjects, and both try to deny their responsibility for their fate. Poe's Prospero demands of the figure of the Red Death, "who dares insult us with this blasphemous mockery?" How can he call the figure "blasphemous?" Who is "mocked?" The figure might be blasphemous if it were accusing God of being derelict in His obligation to His creations, to those who depended upon His care. If God were, indeed, responsible, Prospero could have absolved himself of guilt. Instead, by his own accusation, he is himself guilty of this blasphemy. Moreover, when Prospero chases the Red Death, he does so because the figure's presence is an accusation against him. The figure has "blasphemed" against Prospero who, in assuming a god-like role, is guilty of the deadly sin of pride.

The theme of the corpse within is also apparent in Poe's poetry, and a good example is "Ulalume." At first glance, this poem seems to have little that relates to the theme of the corpse within; the dead lover is buried in an outdoor tomb which is clearly labeled and so precludes any sense of secret interment or the guilt that such an action symbolizes. But "Ulalume" is a poem with what appears to be a major contradiction.

Accompanied by his soul, the hero of the poem follows the "tremulous light" of a spectral moon in the belief that he can "trust to a gleaming / that cannot but guide us aright," because its beams of hope and beauty are influenced by heaven (ll. 69-70). He finds that instead of offering an escape from his "treacherous" memories, the moon in a greater treachery has led him to Ulalume's tomb. If it was the moon that tempted them toward the tomb, why in the final stanza do the hero and his soul agree that the moon was created "to bar up our way and to ban it / From the secret that lies in these wolds" (ll. 98-99)? One logical solution to this paradox is that the hidden secret is neither the tomb of Ulalume nor the body it contains.

Few critics have even tried to address this problem. Most seem content either to see it and the related problems of the poem as either further evidence of their beliefs that Poe is a poor poet (an excuse to consider the poem merely a semi-autobiographical contemplation of the poet), or as an opportunity to concern themselves solely with identifying details such as the origin of "Auber" and "Weir." One of the few who do otherwise is James E. Miller, who correctly notes that words such as "the secret" and "the thing" are "hardly terms to describe a beloved."[10]

Unfortunately, Miller's contention that Ulalume is not a "dead wife or love" but rather "Death itself, a personification of a turbulent sexual impulse combined with its eventual destruction," presents other problems as do a number of other assumptions essential to his argument (pp. 204-205). For example, if Ulalume is Death why is she called "thy lost Ulalume" (l. 81). Certainly she is not the narrator's death nor is there any reason to describe Death, itself, as "lost." If, as Miller claimed, the narrator's kiss is an indication that Psyche has been transformed in the mind of the speaker from "insubstantial soul to a separate being capable of physical love" (pp. 203-204), why does the narrator call her "sweet sister" (l. 78)? Miller is correct when he suggests that the physical tomb is a reminder of physical death, but I disagree with his contention that the ghouls created the mystical moon in an attempt to advance this physical love and that, as it brings the speaker to the tomb, their moon "succeeded only in accomplishing the reverse of their purpose" (p. 205). The moon's main functions are to attract the speaker and light his way to Ulalume's tomb. By reminding the bereaved lover that Ulalume's death is real and permanent, the "ghouls" have been merciful exactly as they intended.

The reality of death cuts off the speaker's irrational hope of union with Ulalume, a necessary condition for the hero to go on with his life. In leading the hero and his soul to the tomb, the moon has led them away from the spiritually destructive romanticized dwelling on death and ties or demands which obligate lovers beyond death. Seen in this way, the poem presents a number of possible interpretations of "the secret that lies in these wolds." It may be a secret declaration of fidelity beyond death or an as yet unrealized determination for reunion with his dead beloved through such means as suicide or (as occurs in a number of Poe's tales) the re-animation of a corpse. Each of these possibilities represents a blasphemous challenge to what Poe would have recognized as traditional conceptions of God's power and law, but all are in keeping with the principles of the reunification of scattered elements of the divine which Poe articulated in *Eureka*.

If Poe disagreed with traditional Christianity, he was equally at odds with the view expressed by the early Transcendentalists that "If the single man plant himself indomitably on his instincts and there abide, the huge world will come round to him."[11] Unless one can truly transcend the physical, he has not been fully self-reliant. Death and limitation seem painful for those who assume the possibility of transcendence. Mourning must be done so that we can proceed with life. The tomb makes death real and external. It keeps the corpse outside and bans the corpse within.

In an important sense, the plot in "Ulalume" is the opposite of that in "The Raven." In the latter the bereaved lover abandons his rationality, as is symbolized by the surmounting of the bust of Pallas, goddess of reason, by the symbol of magic and death. Even if believed to be prophetic, the raven's single word "nevermore" is dependent for its meaning on the bereaved lover's questions. A rational individual might have asked the raven if his unhappiness will continue; but, abandoning reason, the lover asks only those questions which will lead to despair. Instead of suggesting, as "The Raven" does, that a treacherous mind can make spiritual despair out of a physical object, "Ulalume" blocks the walk into the dark forest of unlimited despair with the physical tomb. Life ends, and burial, even burial alive, ultimately ends with death. The real danger is to bury within the living that suffering which will then be endured by the living.

Whitman in "When Lilacs Last in the Dooryard Bloomed" reminded his readers that although the living who remain suffer, the dead do not suffer; they are "fully at rest." Poe uses his typical inversion of conventional attitudes to advance the same idea in "For Annie": "living" is the fever and death is the release. Certainly, Poe, who had ample experience with both suffering and mourning, was acutely aware of the truth of this proposition. He knew that the attempt to keep alive the memory of a dead loved one was a source of pain, knew that it was more rational to bury the corpse publicly and get on with life. To suffer was to assume a burden of guilt, not necessarily guilt in the loved one's death (although, as we have seen in "Ligeia," the mourner may assume complicity), but the guilt that comes from the pleasure of suffering. Poe was well aware that one might take perverse, irrational satisfaction in such suffering.

In *The Scarlet Letter* Dimmesdale, Hawthorne's sinful minister, declares his doubt that "a wretched man, guilty, we will say, of murder, [would] prefer to keep the dead corpse buried in his own heart, rather than fling it forth at once and let the universe take care of it" (p. 132). Yet, even as he makes this declaration, he himself is guilty of just such a mistake. Poe's characters do not always try to deny the corpse within, but they almost always try to convince themselves that their past transgressions are safely dead; they pretend to go on with life. Poe's stories are a warning against the irrationality of such an action;

but, of course, they also are part of his argument that man is not completely rational.

NOTES

[1] "Compensation," *Collected Works of Ralph Waldo Emerson*, ed. Alfred R. Ferguson et al. (Cambridge, Mass., 1971), 2: 67.

[2] *Mardi*, ed. Harrison Hayford et al. (Evanston, 1970), pp. 593-594.

[3] *Moby-Dick*, ed. Harrison Hayford and Hershel Parker (New York, 1967), p. 354.

[4] Vincent Buranelli, *Edgar Allan Poe* (New York, 1961), p. 72.

[5] *The Recognition of Edgar Allan Poe*, ed. Eric W. Carlson (Ann Arbor, 1966), p. 261.

[6] *The Scarlet Letter*, ed. William Charvat et al. (Columbus, Oh., 1962), p. 131.

[7] *Collected Works*, 3: 45.

[8] *Studies in Classic American Literature* (1923; rpt. New York, 1961), p. 80.

[9] *Major American Writers*, ed. Perry Miller (New York, 1962), pp. 369-382.

[10] "'Ulalume' Resurrected," *PQ*, 34(1955), 204.

[11] Emerson, *Collected Works*, 1: 69.

POE'S "LIGEIA": DEBTS TO IRVING AND EMERSON

JERRY A. HERNDON

Most critical readings of "Ligeia" concern the narrator's reliability. James Schroeter, John Lauber, and Thomas Ollive Mabbott argue that the story is to be read literally. In their view, "Ligeia" is a story of the supernatural told by a narrator whose word is to be trusted.[1] Others—like Roy P. Basler, James Gargano, Floyd Stovall, and G. R. Thompson—consider the tale a portrayal of the delusion of a madman who murders a second wife in order to secure a new body for the spirit of the first.[2]

I agree with those who read the story as the narrator's mad delusion. Poe himself once hinted at this interpretation. In a letter of 21 September 1839 to Philip Pendleton Cooke, he claimed to accept Cooke's literal reading of the ending of the tale, but he undercut his flattering remarks about Cooke's keenness by suggesting that he *should* have ended with the death of Ligeia and her entombment "*as Rowena*" (italics mine). This remark clearly indicates that the central meaning is the narrator's delusion, and that the story is *not* to be read as a recital of actual supernatural events.[3]

To turn to the story itself, it seems significant that the narrator claims that he was so uncertain of having seen the ruby drops fall into Rowena's wine that he "forebore to speak to her" of it, and thus failed to prevent her from swallowing it. Let us consider how he phrases his next observation, having decided that what he thought he saw was an illusion, prompted by "a vivid imagination" and opium: "Yet I cannot conceal it from my own perception that, immediately subsequent to the fall of the ruby-drops, a rapid change for the worse took place in the disorder of my wife." Does this not suggest that there *were* matters which he was trying to "conceal . . . from [his] own perception" in telling his story? Namely, for instance, the source of the fatal ruby-drops? This source, I propose, was his own hand. Moreover, his claim that he was trying to revive *Rowena*, was, perhaps, a self-deception designed to conceal from himself his efforts to recall *Ligeia* by murdering his second wife and providing the first with a new body.

In reading this story, we should bear in mind that the narrator is apparently telling it long after the events he recounts. For instance, he says that "long years have . . . elapsed" since his first meeting with Ligeia, and it seems clear that sufficient time has passed since the fatal conclusion of his marriage with Rowena to enable him to shake off the effects of opium addiction and express himself calmly, and, to a certain point, with clarity. Clearly, too, for a proper reading, the narrator should be imagined as penning his tale in a madhouse. Like the madman in Dickens's "A Madman's Manuscript" of *The Pickwick Papers*,[4] the narrator is in a lunatic's cell, just as the narrator of "The Tell-Tale Heart" obviously is. Recalling the shattering events of the night of Rowena's death, the narrator records: "I felt that my vision grew dim, that my reason wandered." Commenting on the "regal magnificence" with which he furnished his abbey for Rowena's home, he laments: "Alas, I feel how much even of *incipient madness* might have been discovered in the gorgeous and fantastic draperies, in the solemn carvings of Egypt, in the wild cornices and furniture, in the Bedlam patterns of the carpets of tufted gold!" [italics mine].

This, then, is my view of Poe's intentions in "Ligeia." I wish to go farther, however, to examine the possibility that Poe incorporated into "Ligeia" resonances from works by two of his American contemporaries: Washington Irving and Ralph Waldo Emerson. Specifically, I shall indicate how Poe may have imitated elements in Irving's "Adventure of the German Student" in order to produce a sharply-focused satire of Emerson's Transcendental thought, as formulated in *Nature*, published two years before "Ligeia."

I

Poe's "Ligeia" appeared in the first number of a Baltimore journal, Nathan C. Brooks's *American Museum of Literature and the Arts*, in September, 1838. It is interesting to note that Poe refused Brooks's request for a review article on Washington Irving's writings for that same issue. Poe claimed to be "hardly . . . conversant with Irving's writings, having read nothing of his since I was a boy, save his 'Granada'."[5] He was hardly candid, however, as John Ward Ostrom points out. He had reviewed both *The Crayon Miscellany* and *Astoria* for the *Southern Literary Messenger*, the former for the December, 1835 issue, and the latter for the issue of January, 1837.[6] The review of *The Crayon Miscellany* is a one-paragraph notice, but that of *Astoria* is long, covering approximately nine-and-a-half large double-column pages in the *SLM*, and approximately thirty-seven pages in Harrison (9: 207-243).

Undoubtedly, Poe was more aware of Irving's writings than he revealed in his letter to Brooks. Moreover, in a letter to Irving dated 12 October 1839, he admitted to having based "William Wilson" upon Irving's brief article, "An Unwritten Drama of Lord Byron," which had appeared in *The Gift* for 1836.[7] Even in the letter to Brooks, his comments on Irving's shortcomings and merits as a writer seem to indicate more familiarity than he claimed. He even prompts Brooks (who wrote the review of Irving's works himself) to compare Irving's style with Addison's, and observes that "something [should be] hinted about imitation" (*O*1: 112).

I assume that the "hint" Poe wanted was that Irving might have been too close a borrower. He may, that is, have been *hinting* to Brooks that Irving was a plagiarist. As is well known, Poe *was* a bit careless about such charges. It seems almost as if he were morbidly sensitive on the subject, almost as if he were fearful that his *own* borrowings might be detected and construed as plagiarism. Poe probably turned down Brooks's offer to let him review Irving's works because "Ligeia," which would appear in the same issue of the *American Museum* with the review, did in fact contain borrowings from Irving's "Adventure of the German Student." Perhaps Poe did not want to put on record too close a familiarity with Irving's tales, lest some knowledgeable critic detect shadows of Irving's art in "Ligeia."

Irving's story, published in *Tales of a Traveller* in 1824,[8] seems to be a heavily satirical portrait of the Continental Transcendentalism which was to exert so important an influence on English and American Romanticism. Gottfried Wolfgang is apparently a student of German Idealism: "being of a visionary and enthusiastic character, he had wandered into those wild and speculative doctrines which have so often bewildered German students." Wolfgang's "health was impaired, his imagination diseased" by his "singular . . . studies" and "his intense application . . . . until, like Swedenborg, he had an ideal world of his own around him." The reference to Swedenborg is interesting, inasmuch as that philosopher had an important influence on Emerson. This young man's "unhealthy appetite" and shyness has prevented any familiarity with women, but his ardent imagination soon supplies him with a dream, in which "excited and sublimated state" he beholds "a female face of *transcendent* beauty" [italics mine]. Wolfgang becomes "passionately enamored of this shadow of a dream," so much so that he becomes scarcely distinguishable from a madman.

One dark, stormy night the student encounters a solitary female seated on the steps of the guillotine, and is startled to observe the face of his dreams. He quickly offers her his aid, and, discovering that she has neither home nor friend, he takes her to his quarters, a single apartment in a "great dingy hotel." The apartment has "one chamber, an old-fashioned salon, heavily carved, and *fantastically furnished with the remains of former magnificence*; for it was one of those hotels in the quarter of the Luxembourg Palace which had once belonged to nobility" [italics mine]. Irving's brief description of the fantastic furnishings, I suggest, may have inspired Poe's elaborate portrayal of the décor of the bridal chamber his narrator prepares for Lady Rowena— a décor of "more than regal magnificence."[9]

Irving's ironic view of the Platonic element in Transcendentalism is apparent in the student's inability to tear himself away from his new acquaintance, though his offer to take her to his quarters had been prefaced with the reassuring proviso: "'If a stranger dare make an offer ... without danger of being misunderstood ....'." The flesh is rather hard on Platonic relationships, however, as is indicated when the student declares his passion to the young lady, who responds in kind. They shake hands on their "social compact," and are soon in bed together. As Irving wryly remarks, far from misunderstanding Wolfgang, "[S]he was evidently an enthusiast like himself, and enthusiasts soon understand one another." Perfectly.

Unfortunately, Wolfgang discovers the next day, on returning from a search for "more spacious apartments," that his "wife" is dead. When the police officer summoned appears, he declares that the woman was guillotined the day before, and, as he unclasps the "bride's" collar, her head rolls upon the floor. The student "went distracted, and died in a madhouse"; the storyteller says he got the story direct from the student in the asylum.

The striking parallels to elements of this story in "Ligeia" suggest that Poe may have imitated it to sharpen his own satiric thrust against Emersonian Transcendentalism, a subject I discuss below. Both stories illustrate the dangers of an uncritical idealism, even if its focus is "transcendent beauty"; Poe's conviction, expressed clearly in "The Imp of the Perverse," that Emerson and other optimists were wrong in believing that only good is permanent and real, that there is no positive evil, must have made him note the student's "frightful belief that an evil spirit had reanimated the dead body to insnare him." In "Ligeia," the evil spirit is the narrator's own delusive pride that he can conquer death, the greatest of mortal limitations. This presumption leads him to madness and murder.

Poe's narrator says that he first met Ligeia "in some large, old, decaying city near the Rhine," and Irving's student, of course, is German (though, to be sure, his *femme fatale* is French). Poe's character bears the relationship of "student" to Ligeia, resigning himself "with a child-like confidence, to her guidance through the chaotic world of metaphysical investigation at which [he] was most busily occupied during the earlier years" of the marriage. When she becomes ill and can no longer tutor him, he laments, "I was but as a child groping benighted."

Wolfgang's "transcendent beauty" is described as the "*shadow* of a dream"; Ligeia "came and departed as a *shadow*" [italics mine]. Wolfgang's "ravishingly beautiful" paramour's "face was pale, but of a dazzling fairness, set off by a profusion of raven hair that hung clustering about it. Her *eyes were large and brilliant*, with a singular *expression* approaching almost to wildness" [italics mine]. Ligeia's beauty was also transcendent and unearthly, even a "vision . . . wildly divine": "In beauty of face no maiden ever equalled her." Her forehead was "lofty and pale," possessing a "divine . . . majesty"; her skin rivalled "the purest ivory"; her hair was "raven-black . . . glossy . . . luxuriant and naturally-curling . . . ." Her eyes were incredibly large, their *"expression"* [Poe's italics] their most striking characteristic.

Finally, if Poe's story is to be conceived of as told in a madhouse, the two stories share this significant characteristic, and another as well: a hint of necrophilia. In Irving's it is more than a hint. Did the guillotined corpse ever have a head at all? Was not Wolfgang's imagination primed, via his passionate dream, to supply a corpse with a ready-made head? If so, didn't he bed a corpse? As for Poe's tale, what would the passionate lover's first move have been if he really thought Ligeia had returned to him? He has described himself, in the climactic moment, as "a helpless prey to a whirl of violent emotions, of which extreme awe was perhaps *the least terrible, the least consuming*" [italics mine]. The tale ends on a note of reverence, with him on his knees, but what next? The ebony bed is handy to his delusion, and no servants are within call.

We must note, too, that although the narrator recalls shrieking when he sees her eyes that he could "never be mistaken" in accepting Ligeia's return, he also comments, just prior to this (perhaps indicating a flash of sanity in reflection?), on the "inexpressible madness" that seemed to be seizing him.

II

Poe's distaste for Emerson and for Transcendentalism is well known. For the January, 1842 issue of *Graham's Magazine*, in one of his "Autography" series, Poe seized the opportunity to damn Emerson for his obscurity:

> Mr. Ralph Waldo Emerson belongs to a class of gentlemen with whom we have no patience whatever—the mystics for mysticism's sake. Quintilian mentions a pedant who taught obscurity, and who once said to a pupil "this is excellent, for I do not understand it myself." How the good man would have chuckled over Mr. E.! . . . The best answer to his twaddle is *cui bono*? . . . to whom is it a benefit? If not to Mr. Emerson individually, then surely to no man living. (*H*15: 260)

Earlier, in "Never Bet the Devil Your Head" (1841), Poe had presented a character with a habit of carelessly betting the Devil his head, apparently because he disbelieves in evil and therefore thinks the bet a safe one. No gloom, such as that inside a covered bridge, can dampen his spirits; unfortunately, after he has offered to bet the Devil his head that he can leap such a bridge's turnstile, and "cut a pigeon-wing over it in the air" as he does so, the Devil appears and accepts the bet. Toby Dammit, the protagonist, loses both bet and head. The narrator suggests that Toby's optimism might have its source in a certain "disease," namely, "the transcendentals." Because Toby is a Transcendentalist, and has been taught by his mentors to disbelieve in evil, the Transcendentalists are responsible for his death. The narrator therefore buries Dammit, works "a bar sinister on his family escutcheon," and sends a bill for his funeral expenses to the Transcendentalists. When these "scoundrels" refuse to pay (not believing in the Devil, they are certainly not going to believe the story that Dammit was done in by that personage), the narrator "had Mr. Dammit dug up at once, and sold him for dog's meat" (*M*2: 621-631). Poe's meaning is clear: the Transcendentalists' view of evil is dangerous; they are a lot of bastards (or "scoundrels"), fit only for dog food. In *Eureka* (1848), by suggesting that a progenitor of Transcendentalism, Immanuel Kant, would more correctly spell his name with "C" rather than "K," Poe manages to suggest that what passed for Transcendental profundity was mere "cant." Further, he calls the Transcendentalist "an earthly Bedlamite..." (*H*16: 189, 195).

Emerson believed, at least theoretically, in human perfectibility; Poe plainly stated that he did not, in letters written in July, 1844 to James Russell Lowell and Thomas Holley Chivers (*O*1: 256-260). In the letter to Chivers (10 July 1844), Poe defined "spirit" as simply infinitely refined "matter," thus taking a philosophical position that Emerson ridiculed, though without reference to Poe, of course, in "Experience," published later that same year.[10]

According to Mabbott, "most of Poe's numerous references to Coleridge, Kant, Carlyle, and Emerson make fun of what he considered vagueness, obscurity, or confusion of style" (*M*2: 633, n13). It is necessary to point out, however, that Poe believed in a Transcendentalism of his own,[11] one involving acceptance of the fact of evil as a positive reality. He told Chivers, in the letter previously cited: "You mistake me in supposing I dislike the transcendentalists—it is only the pretenders and sophists among them." In a letter of 17 March 1845, to one J. Hunt, he also referred to "the burlesque philosophy, which the Bostonians have adopted, supposing it to be Transcendentalism" (*O*1: 284). Poe obviously thought that his own cosmology, as expressed in "Mesmeric Revelation" (1844) and *Eureka*, was a model of philosophical precision and clarity, with none of the ambiguity and obscurity he found in "Transcendentalism."

III

I propose that "Ligeia," published in September, 1838, two years to the month after Emerson's *Nature* (1836), can be profitably read as a satirical portrait of Emersonian Transcendentalism, as expressed in that book. Perhaps it would be best to begin with the "Glanvill" epigraph, the source of which, according to Mabbott, "has never been found" (*M*2: 331n) Mabbott suggests that "Poe may have made it up"; Poe himself had written in 1844 that "'misapplication of quotations is clever, and has a capital effect when well done'" (*M*2: 335n)

If the epigraph *is* apocryphal, Poe may have meant to produce a close parallel to certain passages in Emerson, but disguised what he was doing through "misapplication" achieved by attribution to Joseph Glanvill:

> And the will therein lieth, which dieth not. Who knoweth the mysteries of the will, with its vigor? For *God is but a great will pervading all things by nature of its intentness*. Man doth not yield himself to the angels, nor unto death utterly, save only through the weakness of his feeble will. [italics mine]

"'A man,'" Emerson wrote, "'is a god in ruins.... the dwarf of himself'."[12] As he becomes spiritually enlightened, he sees that, although "The world proceeds from the same spirit as the body of man.... it differs from the body in one important respect. It is not, like that, now subjected to the human will" (31). Yet:

> The exercise of the Will or the lesson of power is taught in every event.... he [man] is learning the secret, that *he can reduce under his will*, not only particular events, but great classes, nay *the whole series of events*, and so conform *all facts* to his character.... with every thought, does his kingdom stretch over things, *until the world becomes, at last, only a realized will*,—the double of the man. (20) [italics mine]

Man eventually perceives God in himself, the basis, as Emerson wrote later, of true "self-reliance." As we become more spiritual:

> We learn that the highest is present to the soul of man, that the dread universal essence ... is that for which all things exist ... that spirit creates; that behind nature, throughout nature, spirit is present ... [it] does not act

upon us from without . . . but spiritually, or through ourselves. Therefore, that spirit, that is, the Supreme Being, does not build up nature around us, but puts it forth through us . . . . As a plant upon the earth, so a man rests upon the bosom of God; he is nourished by unfailing fountains, and draws, at his need, inexhaustible power. Who can set bounds to the possibilities of man? Once inspire the infinite, by being admitted to behold the absolute natures of justice and truth, and we learn that man has access to the entire mind of the Creator, is himself the creator in the finite. (30-31)

If my surmise is correct, Poe achieved a double-edged irony by attributing an Emersonian hyperbole to Glanvill, who insisted in his writings on the reality of evil. For Emerson, evil was, philosophically considered, simply the absence of good—the only reality—and therefore nonbeing, "nonentity," as he put it in "The Divinity School Address" (1838; Whicher, p. 103). For Glanvill, however, disbelief in the reality of evil—in witchcraft, ghosts, and evil spirits, for instance—logically demanded a disbelief also in good spirits, including God. For him, disbelief in the reality of evil was a coward's back door to atheism, hidden under the guise of optimism. He details his argument in *A Philosophical Endeavour towards the Defense of the Being of Witches and Apparitions* (1666), best known in the posthumous edition titled *Saducismus Triumphatus* (1681). As the latter title indicates, Glanvill saw "Sadduceeism Triumphant" through disbelief in evil. The Sadducees were important adversaries of Christ who disbelieved, among other doctrines, in the Resurrection and the existence of angels. Thus Poe may have attributed an *Emersonian* doctrine to a man who would have regarded it as a damnable heresy.

Under Ligeia's tutelage, Poe's narrator was studying the "mysteries of . . . transcendentalism." Though Mabbott identifies this as a general reference, meaning merely "belief in intuitive knowledge" (*M*2: 333, n18), the story's parallels with passages in *Nature* may indicate that the term is actually a specific reference to Emersonian Transcendentalism.

In the passage from *Nature* quoted above, Emerson asserts that the spiritual man can "conform *all* facts to his character" [italics mine]. Such a sweeping classification, *all* facts, it might have occurred to Poe, included death. He might have wondered how a Transcendentalist, supported by his reassuring philosophy, would actually confront death, the King of Terrors. Emerson suggests, after all, that as he catches sight of the eternal principles on which the Universe is built:

No man fears age or misfortune or death, in their serene company, for he is transported out of the district of change. Whilst we behold unveiled the nature of Justice and Truth, we learn the difference between the absolute and the conditional or relative. We apprehend the absolute. As it were, for the first time, *we exist.* We become immortal, for we learn that time and space are relations of matter; that, with a perception of truth, or a virtuous will, they have no affinity. (27)

Poe's narrator speaks of his "astonishment" at Ligeia's fierce resistance to death, a resistance which he found a "pitiable spectacle" because "[t]here had been much in her stern nature to impress me with the belief that, to her, death would have come without its terrors;—but not so."

Poe appears deliberately to have taken literally Emerson's metaphorical affirmation of mortal man's superiority to death in order to make Transcendentalism more susceptible to satirical treatment. Thus, the narrator tries to bring Ligeia *literally* back from the dead, in the process betraying his presumptuous desire to arrogate to himself the prerogative of the Almighty. Ligeia herself had shared this desire to conquer death, as indicated by her making the supposed quotation from Glanvill an incantation; as her protegé listened to her whispers on her deathbed, he writes: "My brain reeled as I hearkened, entranced, to a melody more than mortal—to assumptions and aspirations which mortality had never before known."

Ligeia and her lover are guilty of more than presumption. Worship of God in the self (Emerson wrote that "self-reliance" is equivalent to "God-reliance")[13] translates as self-worship, i.e., idolatry. If Ligeia represents Emerson's Spirit, as I suggest, the narrator's reverence and love for her is reverence and love for himself, i.e., self-reliance. Thus Ligeia's love for him may be read as his self-worship. Indeed, he writes, as Ligeia lay dying: "For long hours, detaining my hand, would she pour out before me the overflowing of a heart whose more than passionate devotion amounted to *idolatry*" [italics mine]. Later, after his marriage to Rowena, he recalls with longing Ligeia's "lofty . . . ethereal nature [and] . . . her passionate, her idolatrous love." Moreover, as he looks back over his life, he remarks that his first, "ill-omened" marriage, was, perhaps, presided over by the "spirit . . . entitled *Romance* . . . the wan and . . . misty-winged *Ashtophet* of idolatrous Egypt . . . ." This statement, by the way, seems to be one of the early clues that Poe is presenting a chronicle of a Romantic extremist whose intense emotional makeup (like Ligeia, he was "a prey to the tumultuous vultures of stern passion") destroyed him.

Finally, as he looks back from the perspective of final failure, Poe's narrator says that he and Ligeia sought "a wisdom too divinely precious not to be forbidden!" Apparently, Poe takes a dim view of Transcendental optimism about man's capacity to transcend his limitations.

IV

In *Nature*, images of vision predominate. Emerson argues that man must learn to open "the eye of Reason" (24) so that he can ultimately obtain a spiritual fulfillment—"a dominion . . . beyond his dream of God" (37)—which he characterizes, in the final two words of the essay, as "perfect sight" (37). In perhaps the most famous passage, Emerson describes his mystical sense of union with God in terms of a striking visual image:

> In the woods, we return to reason and faith . . . . Standing on the bare ground,—my head bathed by the blithe air and uplifted into infinite space,—all mean egotism vanishes. I become a transparent eye-ball. I am nothing. I see all. The currents of the Universal Being circulate through me. (8)

And, as an instance of "the sublime" in Nature which ought to awaken "reverence" in man, Emerson suggests the stars:

> [I]f a man would be alone, let him look at the stars. The rays that come from those heavenly worlds, will separate between him and vulgar things. One might think the atmosphere was made transparent with this design, to give man, in the heavenly bodies, the perpetual presence of the sublime . . . . every night come out these preachers of beauty, and light the universe with their admonishing smile. (7)

It is not the stars alone, however, which have a spiritual significance to the spiritual man: ". . . all natural objects make a kindred impression, when the mind is open to their influence" (7). This idea is restated later in the essay: "The invariable mark of wisdom is to see the miraculous in the common" (35).

Now, Ligeia's *eyes* are her most noticeable physical characteristic, and the narrator feels a reverence, an awe, when gazing into them. Their extraordinary size is emphasized, almost to absurdity, as he calls them "large and luminous orbs." Significantly, "those large, those shining, those divine orbs . . . . became to [him] twin *stars* of Leda . . ." [italics mine]. Their indefinable meaning, he says, lies in their inscrutable "*expression*," a word which, he suggests, is the best he can do to convey the true significance of Ligeia's eyes. They represent "the *spiritual*" element in her nature [italics mine]. Furthermore, in terms of the comparison with Emerson, the narrator, in turning from his contemplation of the star-like eyes of Ligeia, finds the sense of reverence they evoke in him aroused also as he gazes "in[to] the commonest objects of the universe,"[14] in which he sees "a circle of analogies to that ["spiritual"] expression." Emerson had insisted that there are "relations in all objects," that "analogies . . . are constant, and pervade nature." Consequently, "man is an analogist" (16).

Emerson also insists that when he speaks of the spiritual significance of Nature, he does not mean any *particular* object, however beautiful, but "the integrity of impression made by *manifold* natural objects" (7) [italics mine]. Individual natural forms may be "agreeable to the eye" (11), but it is the "general grace diffused over nature" as a whole (11) which gives it its impact. If "particular objects are mean and unaffecting, the landscape which they compose, is round and symmetrical" (11). Note, too, that Emerson's paean to the stars does not focus on *a* star, or even a few stars, but on the whole visible panoply of the heavens, which he calls "the city of God" (7). For Emerson, "the standard of beauty is the entire circuit of natural forms,—the totality of nature . . . . Nothing is quite beautiful alone: nothing but is beautiful in the whole. A single object is only so far beautiful as it suggests this universal grace" (14).

Obviously, a satirist could mock Emerson's view of the spiritual significance of Nature by insisting too particularly on a spiritual aura in specifically located aspects of the natural world rather than in "the totality of nature." Poe seems to have used this device, the *reductio ad absurdum*, in "Ligeia." The narrator says:

> I found, in the commonest objects of the universe, a circle of analogies to that expression [in Ligeia's eyes]. I mean to say that . . . I derived, from many existences in the material world, a sentiment such as I felt always aroused within me by her large and luminous orbs . . . . I recognized it . . . sometimes in the survey of a rapidly-growing vine—in the contemplation of a moth, a butterfly, a chrysalis, a stream of running water. I have felt it in the ocean; in the falling of a meteor. I have felt it in the glances of unusually aged people. And there are one or two stars in heaven—(one especially, a star of the sixth magnitude, double and changeable, to be found near the large star in Lyra) in a telescopic scrutiny of which I have been made aware of the feeling.

His list is obviously arbitrary. Why would not a "slowly-growing vine" arouse the sentiment? Why not the glances of infants, as well as those of "unusually aged people"? How can one select "one or two stars in heaven" from Emerson's blazing "city of God" (7) and declare that those stars—and only those—fill one with reverence? It is the multitude of the heavenly lights, as innumerable as the sands on the seashore, which intensifies their beauty and fills the observer with awe.

As I have noted, Poe, with some justice, denounced Emerson for his obscurity. Having essentially arrogated to himself the definition of God, Emerson then insisted that he could not actually verbally define what he meant:

> Of that ineffable essence which we call Spirit, he that thinks most, will say least. We can foresee God in the coarse, and, as it were, distant phenomena of matter; but when we try to define and describe himself, both language and thought desert us, and we are as helpless as fools and savages. That essence refuses to be recorded in propositions, but when man has worshipped him intellectually, the noblest ministry of nature is to stand as the apparition of God. It is the great organ through which the universal spirit speaks to the individual, and strives to lead back the individual to it. (30)

Poe's Transcendentalist narrator admits that, though he felt a sentiment of awe aroused in him by the contemplation of Ligeia's eyes and "the commonest objects of the universe" as well, he could not explain what he meant: "not the more could I define that sentiment, or analyze, or even steadily view it." As Poe later remarked of Emerson, to whom is such an obscure philosophy a benefit?

If Ligeia represents Emerson's "Spirit," the highest essence of "Nature," may not the narrator's list of specific aspects of the natural world that fill him with awe constitute a series of "apparition[s] of God [i.e., Ligeia] . . . . through which the universal spirit speaks to the individual, and strives to lead back the individual to it"?

For Emerson, "Spirit" was the "universal soul within or behind [man's] individual life, wherein, as in a firmament, the natures of Justice, Truth, Love, Freedom, arise and shine. This universal soul, he calls Reason . . ." (15). The "Spirit" is God, and thus the possessor of omniscience. This gives point to the narrator's description of Ligeia's boundless and unequalled knowledge—she had "traversed . . . successfully, *all* the wide areas of moral, physical, and mathematical science" as well as both ancient and modern languages, in which the narrator had never found her at fault. As Emerson suggested that the *true* "lover of nature is he whose inward and outward senses are still truly [correctly]adjusted to each other; who has retained *the spirit of infancy* even into the era of manhood" (7) [italics mine], Poe's narrator indicates that "I was sufficiently aware of her *infinite* supremacy to resign myself, with a *child-like* confidence, to her guidance through the chaotic world of metaphysical investigation at which I was most busily occupied during the earlier years of our marriage" [italics mine]. Without Ligeia, he says, "I was but as a child groping benighted. Her presence, her readings alone, rendered vividly luminous the many mysteries of the transcendentalism in which we were immersed." Ligeia, then, represents not only the Divine Mind, but, as the spiritual aspect of Nature, she is the *expositor* of that mind as well. Emerson, significantly, says that Nature's "serene order is inviolable by us. It is therefore, to us, the present *expositor* of the divine mind. It is a fixed point whereby we may measure our departure" from God (31) [italics mine].

The famous "transparent eye-ball" passage in *Nature*, a key section, is paralleled, in a significant respect, in Ligeia's utterance of the key "Glanvill" passage immediately after the narrator repeats the poem, "The Conqueror Worm," to her. In Emerson's recollection of his divine frenzy, he recalls that he feels "uplifted into infinite space,—all mean egotism vanishes. I become a transparent eye-ball. I am nothing. I see all. The currents of the Universal Being circulate through me; I am *part or particle* of God" (8) [italics mine]. Ligeia shrieks: "'O God! O Divine Father!—shall these things be undeviatingly so?—shall this Conqueror be not once conquered? Are we not *part and parcel* in Thee'?" [italics mine][15] The lady then goes on to repeat the "Glanvill" passage.

It might be appropriate at this point to remember that the narrator in "The Raven," like his counterpart in "Ligeia," has lost a beloved woman, and has sought to recall her from the dead. Just as the story's narrator has "assumptions and aspirations which mortality had never before known," so the poem's persona is "dreaming dreams no mortal ever dared to dream before," as he half-fearfully hopes, before seeing the raven, that the lost Lenore has returned to him (*M*1: 364-369). Poe suggests clearly in "The Philosophy of Composition" that the narrator of "The Raven" became mad through "mournful and never-ending remembrance" of the lost Lenore; i.e., he suggests that it is madness to refuse to accept one's mortal limitations. The narrator of "Ligeia," as noted earlier, admits his own derangement during the events he recalls (*H*14: 193-208).

The emphasis in the story on the narrator's opium addiction may be designed to make it easier to hold him up to ridicule. Poe prided himself on his logical powers, and he no doubt thought that the use of opium to stimulate the imagination (as detailed in DeQuincey's

Confessions of an English Opium Eater, which Poe thought was Coleridge's work) was dangerous nonsense; in a word, just one step short of insanity.

Moreover, I doubt that Poe himself put any stock in the idea of reincarnation or metempsychosis. I therefore believe that they err who read "Ligeia" literally and who see the "recall" of Ligeia's spirit as real—and as a triumph.[16] Poe's inserting the implication of reincarnation into this tale makes the Transcendentalist easier to make a fool of. In "Morella," too, the idea is used, with the narrator suggesting that his deceased wife is reincarnated as his daughter. Poe had a logical mind, and would not such possibilities, perhaps, occur to him as sure to create universal confusion and chaos, and, to borrow a sober comment of Emerson's (in "Experience") on the effect of murder, "a horrible jangle and confounding of all relations" (Whicher, p. 270)? Perhaps Poe's attitude toward reincarnation was like that of Hawthorne toward "spiritualism." Hawthorne believed that such a doctrine, if true, would, so to speak, make scrambled eggs of this world and the next. He writes: "I cannot consent to let Heaven and Earth, this world and the next, be beaten up together like the white and yolk of an egg."[17]

To return to "Ligeia," I conclude by citing another passage as a striking parallel to one in *Nature*, specifically, to the concluding statement of that essay. This resonance, like the one discussed above in connection with Emerson's "transparent eye-ball" passage, seems particularly compelling. Emerson writes:

> As when the summer comes from the south, the snow-banks melt, and the face of the earth becomes green before it, so shall *the advancing spirit* create its ornaments *along its path*,* and *carry with it the beauty* it visits . . . . The kingdom of man over nature . . . a dominion such as now is beyond his dream of God,—he shall enter without more wonder than the blind man feels who is *gradually* restored to *perfect sight*. [italics mine]

While Ligeia lived to aid him in his "metaphysical investigation," the narrator recalls:

> With how vast a triumph—with how vivid a delight—with how much of all that is ethereal in hope—did I *feel*, as she bent over me in studies but little sought—but less known, that *delicious vista* [Emerson: "beauty"] *by slow degrees* [Emerson: "gradually"] expanding before me, *down whose long, gorgeous, and all untrodden path*,* I might *at length* pass onward to the goal of *a wisdom too divinely*

precious [Emerson: "perfect sight"] not to be forbidden! [italics mine]

Thus, I believe that in "Ligeia" Poe focused an attack directly on Emerson's *Nature*, demonstrating his skeptical assessment of Emersonian Transcendentalism. He seems clearly to have regarded Emerson's belief that man could achieve "a dominion . . . beyond his dream of God" as simply a presumptuous reaching for a "forbidden . . . wisdom," which would end in madness and despair.

NOTES

[1] James Schroeter, "A Misreading of Poe's 'Ligeia'," *PMLA*, 76(1961), 397-406; John Lauber, "'Ligeia' and Its Critics: A Plea for Literalism," *SSF*, 4(1966), 28-32; rpt. *Twentieth Century Interpretations of Poe's Tales: A Collection of Critical Essays*, ed. William L. Howarth (Englewood Cliffs, 1971), pp. 73-77. Mabbott's views are expressed as part of his commentary on "Ligeia," *M*2: 307-308, 334. All references to "Ligeia" are based on this edition. I am indebted for several additional insights to one of my recent graduate students, Mrs. Maria Flynn, a resident of Mayfield, Kentucky.

[2] Roy P. Basler, "The Interpretation of 'Ligeia'," *CE*, 5(1944), 363-372; rpt. Robert Regan, ed., *Poe: A Collection of Critical Essays* (Englewood Cliffs, 1967), pp. 51-63; James W. Gargano, "Poe's 'Ligeia': Dream and Destruction," *CE* 23(1962), 337-342; Floyd Stovall, "The Conscious Art of Edgar Allan Poe," *CE* 24(1963), 417-421; rpt. Regan, pp. 172-178; G. R. Thompson, "'Proper Evidences of Madness': American Gothic and the Interpretation of 'Ligeia'," *ESQ*, 18(1972), 30-49.

[3] I had noted this in an unpublished essay completed in 1970, but Thompson works out the implications of this view of the letter to Cooke in detail, in the article cited in the previous note. The exchange of letters with Cooke can be found in *H*17: 49-54. See also *O*1: 117-119; 2: 686-688.

[4] Mabbott makes only a brief notation on Dickens as source (*M*2: 306). The relationship of Dickens's piece to Poe's story is discussed in detail, and convincingly, by Benjamin Franklin Fisher IV, "Dickens and Poe: *Pickwick* and 'Ligeia'," *PoeS* 6(1973), 14-16. Fisher interprets the tale as a madman's delusion, and thus supplements the views of Schroeter, Lauber, Mabbott, and others.

[5] Poe to Brooks, 4 September 1838—*O*1: 111-113, esp. 112.

[6] See Ostrom's note to the letter cited in my previous note: 1: 112-113.

[7]02: 688-690. He was soliciting a "puff" from Irving on "William Wilson," to be used in advertising a forthcoming collection of his *Tales*.

[8]See *Tales of a Traveller* (New York, 1894), pp. 59-66.

[9]Other commentators emphasize Poe's tendency to rework and elaborate for his major stories motifs introduced earlier in his *own* slighter pieces. See Ruth Leigh Hudson, "Poe Recognizes 'Ligeia' as His Masterpiece," *English Studies in Honor of James Southall Wilson*, ed. Fredson Bowers (Charlottesville, 1951), pp. 35-44. See also the editor's introduction to *Poe at Work: Seven Textual Studies*, ed. Benjamin Franklin Fisher IV (Baltimore, 1978), pp. 5, 10.

[10]For Emerson's mockery of this idea, see "Experience," in Stephen E. Whicher, ed., *Selections from Ralph Waldo Emerson: An Organic Anthology* (Boston, 1957), p. 258.

[11]This point is made by Eric W. Carlson in "Poe's Vision of Man," *Papers on Poe: Essays in Honor of John Ward Ostrom*, ed. Richard P. Veler (Springfield, Oh., 1972), pp. 7-8. For an extensive treatment of Poe's views on Transcendentalism, see Ottavio M. Casale, "Poe on Transcendentalism," *ESQ*, 14(1968), 85-97. Two studies of Poe's affinity with Transcendentalism are useful: Arnold Smithline, "*Eureka*: Poe as Transcendentalist," *ESQ*, 11(1965), 25-28; Patrick F. Quinn, "Poe's *Eureka* and Emerson's *Nature*," *ESQ*, 9(1963), 4-7. Quinn also discusses *differences* between Poe's thought and that of Emerson. For a study of Poe's story as a commentary on the "Germanizing" of English Romanticism, see Clark Griffith, "Poe's 'Ligeia' and the English Romantics," first published in *UTQ*, 24(1954), 8-25; rpt. Howarth, pp. 63-72. Full treatment of this subject, including analyses of satire upon human perfectibility in the tales, occurs in Richard A. Fusco, "Poe and the Perfectibility of Man" (Unpublished M.A. Thesis, University of Mississippi, 1982); see also his "Poe and the Perfectibility of Man," *PoeS*, 19(1986), 1-6.

[12]All references to *Nature* are to the 1836 text, the one available to Poe, as reprinted in Merton M. Sealts, Jr., and Alfred R. Ferguson, eds., *Emerson's "Nature"—Origin, Growth, Meaning* (New York and Toronto, 1969), pp. 5-37. This reference is to p. 33. Other references to pagination will be incorporated parenthetically in my text.

[13]He stated this in "The Fugitive Slave Law," a lecture he delivered in New York City on 7 March 1854: *The Complete Writings of Ralph Waldo Emerson* (New York, 1929), p. 1165.

[14]That he does not feel any reverence at all for Rowena—another human being and his wife—indicates the depth of his

depravity and madness. He is willing callously to deprive her of life itself to further his delusion.

[15] Was Poe varying the phrasing slightly for subtlety, to avoid being a bit too close to Emerson's phrasing? In the 1856 edition of *Nature*, the phrase was changed to the more common "part or parcel." Alfred Ferguson thinks this was a printer's error, noting that it was changed back to the original in 1870 (see *Emerson's "Nature"—Origin, Growth, Meaning*, p. 67). But both James E. Cabot and Edward Waldo Emerson adopted the 1856 variant for their editions of Emerson's complete works: respectively, The Riverside Edition (1883-1893), and The Centenary Edition (1903-1904). See *The Collected Works of Ralph Waldo Emerson: Nature, Addresses, and Lectures*, ed. Robert E. Spiller and Alfred R. Ferguson (Cambridge, Mass., 1971), 1: 288. Whicher's widely-used anthology cited in this paper for other essays is based on the Centenary Edition. Most anthologies, in fact, reprint the Centenary Edition text.

[16] Several critics see the ending of the story as an indication that the narrator has achieved the oneness with the divine which Poe posits in *Eureka* as man's ultimate destiny. Carlson, for instance, in the essay cited in n11, thinks that in "Ligeia" and several of Poe's other stories, "the poetic intellect . . . achieve[s] an attunement with the Spirit Divine" (15). Casale (95) says Poe "'immersed' Ligeia in the kind of transcendentalism he approved." My conclusion is precisely the opposite.

[17] See *The English Notebooks by Nathaniel Hawthorne*, ed. Randall Stewart (1941; rpt. New York, 1962), p. 617.

EMERSON, THOREAU, AND POE'S "DOUBLE DUPIN"

STANTON GARNER

Students of Poe's tales have looked at them in divers ways, but not often enough have they thought of them in terms of their intellectual context. Mostly, Poe is seen as the isolated voyager of Walt Whitman's dream, the "slender, slight, beautiful figure" standing alone on the deck of a yacht flying uncontrolled before a storm, "apparently enjoying all the terror, the murk, and the dislocation of which he was the centre and the victim."[1] Yet however dislocated Poe the man may have been, his literary ideas grew from and belong to his age, and they can best be understood as they relate to that age. My purpose, then, is to consider Poe as a contemporary of Ralph Waldo Emerson and Henry David Thoreau: in 1836 Emerson's *Nature* appeared;[2] in 1845 Poe published "The Purloined Letter";[3] and in 1854 Thoreau published *Walden*.[4] However different these three works may appear to be, each is a central statement of its author's ideas at the time when it was written; taken together they exhibit a marked similarity of purpose, as though those who wrote them had departed from a common point and had then journeyed in the same general direction. Seen in this context, Poe's principal tale of ratiocination offers itself for analysis more readily than might otherwise be the case.

Such a proposition is Poe-like in the sense that it shocks by asserting the unexpected and improbable. Although it is possible to discover the transcendental scent in a Poe poem, in one of his heavenly colloquys, or in his *Eureka*, what has one of his tales of ratiocination to do with Emerson and his fellow idealists, or they with it? Is it not true that Poe invented the detective story for the casual amusement of mystery enthusiasts and then bequeathed the genre to Doctor Conan Doyle for exploitation? Is it not also true that Emerson and Thoreau pursued objectives far higher on the Platonic scale than mere amusement when they wrote their philosophical exhortations? If so, can we in good conscience elevate to the same lofty plane a work that is, looked at in the light of common sense, just a detective story?

Just a detective story! The lengths to which we will go to avoid giving Poe and his fiction the serious consideration that they deserve are amazing. The blame for this insistent trivialization falls first on Poe himself, of course, for writing some silly, ranting letters and, perhaps, for publishing his tales in popular magazines rather than through one of the more elegant Boston presses. Second in order of culpability come Rufus Griswold and others of Poe's contemporaries who damned his works by damning the man. For a third villain, there is Henry James, with his prohibition against enthusiasms for Poe. Since then, we have continued to take Poe lightly by refusing to believe that he meant what he said—by attempting to force his critical and fictional statements to mean something other than what they purport to mean, that is[5]—by patronizing him, referring to him by frivolous names such as "Edgar," "Edgarpoe," and "Hoaxiepoe," for example,[6] and by applying to his works such terms of dismissal as "just a detective story," implying that literature that entertains, as the tale in question certainly does, must of necessity be insignificant.[7] With the reader's permission, then—and the reader must join me temporarily as well as giving me his permission—I intend to do the opposite, to take Poe perfectly seriously, whatever critical risk that ingenuous stance may involve. Let us look at his criticism as though he really meant what he said in it, and then read his two principal tales of ratiocination, "The Murders in the Rue Morgue" and "The Purloined Letter," as though he intended them to stand at the highest level of his achievement and as though he meant every word that he wrote in them, too. Then I think that we will see that "The Purloined Letter" occupies a central position in his fiction and that it is, indeed, one document among several of the era that speak of things temporal and eternal.

It would be fruitless to deny that Poe hoped that these tales would achieve popular success. To admit that, however, is to say nothing about them that one would not as readily say of *Oedipus Rex*, *Hamlet*, *Paradise Lost*, or *Moby-Dick*. To put it another way, his hopes for them were probably identical to his hopes for, let us say, "Usher," regardless of the fact that they *were* detective stories. In fact, to use that name at all is to employ an anachronism, for the detective story is not what he created but what others later named his invention after it had been appropriated by a host of popular mystery writers.[8] No, for reasons of his own, Poe simply wrote a rather different and very original pair of Gothic tales, in the process adapting some of Mrs. Radcliffe's devices for mystification to a purpose of his own. That purpose was to present to his reading public his conception of the model human being.

As might be expected, Poe's model man is a man of the mind; thus in order to understand that man we must begin with Poe's statements about the mind, for like Emerson and generations of poets before Emerson, he felt that psychology was a proper subject for critical analysis. "Dividing the world of mind into its three most immediately obvious distinctions," Poe wrote, "we have the Pure Intellect, Taste, and the Moral Sense."[9] This is the starting point of a rather lengthy and rather well-known discussion of the intellect. Had Poe been a Hawthorne or a Melville, he would have interested himself in the contrast between the passionate, moral heart and the cold, amoral head, but, being Poe, he concerned himself almost exclusively with the head.

Each of these subdivisions has its own special concern, he said, the nature of which associates it with a distinct type of literary work—all but the moral sense, that is. The moral sense concerns itself with duty, and Poe could think of no form of literature that is primarily associated with duty. Had he conceived of either the sermon or the moral essay as a legitimate literary type, he would not have found it necessary to dismiss the moral sense so summarily, but dismiss it he did.

Taste concerns itself with beauty, and is the sole arbiter of the poem, which is the rhythmical creation of beauty. Unless incidentally, the poem "has no concern whatever either with Duty or with Truth" (p. 275). Because it enables the sensitive reader to perceive beauty, the effect of the poem is an "intense and pure elevation of *soul*—not of intellect, or of heart" (p. 197). When elevated *through* the poem, the soul attains "brief and indeterminate glimpses" (p. 274)—of what? Not of the beauty before us, of the beauty of this world, that is, but of the "divine and rapturous joys" of the beauty above and beyond this world.

The poem, then, is a unique kind of literature that releases us from our normal imprisonment in earthly existence so that we may look beyond it. It does not allow us to scrutinize in detail and to report about what is beyond the material universe, as does Dante's *Divina Commedia*; instead, it gives us only glimpses that lack duration and specificity. If after these glimpses we cannot describe with clarity and precision what we have seen, we have at least had the ineluctable ecstasy of the experience of the glimpses. Finally, the vision meant here functions through the imagination, since what we perceive is an abstraction, an ideal seen not through mortal eyes but through the mysterious, occult perceptions of the soul itself.

Prose fiction is the opposite of poetry in every way, so much so that Poe's tales and poems should not be thought of as being interdependent or cross-referential—a common critical mistake.[10] The pure intellect has as its province truth, and "the object, Truth or the satisfaction of the intellect, and the object Passion, or the excitement of the heart, are . . . readily attainable in prose" (p. 198) much more than they are in poetry. Dismissing passion from the equation, as in the present context of little interest to Poe, a prose tale, since it does not elevate the soul, must concern itself with the truth of this world. The visions of truth are visions of the material world around us as seen clearly and specifically with our material eyes; thus the best description of the tale, as Poe perceived it, may be precisely what Richard Wilbur has said it is not, "a provisional arrangement of reality." Poe's distinction between the two forms of literature, in the very simplest terms, is this: the prose tale deals factually with the things of this world, the poem imaginatively with the abstractions of the next, though he admitted that the boundary between the two was not really this inflexible.

Not only does Poe warn us of the radical differences between the nature and uses of poetry and of prose fiction, he also defines for us (still ignoring the moral sense) two aspects of mind, and here he looks back toward Emerson—and through Emerson toward Samuel Taylor Coleridge and toward Immanuel Kant.[11] Emerson had written that the mind has two modes of operation, one the lower, the other the higher. The "Understanding" is the ordinary, everyday, worldly function of the intellect that "adds, divides, combines, measures," while the "Reason" is the higher, intuitive function that transfers the lessons of the understanding "into its own world of thought, by perceiving the analogy that marries Matter and Mind" (p. 23). Emerson's understanding, then, is identical to Poe's pure intellect, though Emerson believed that the pursuit of truth was the domain of the philosopher rather than of the writer of fiction; except in the sense of marrying matter and mind, Emerson's reason is Poe's taste as, through beauty, it manifests itself in the poetic imagination, and for both men beauty was the domain of the poet. For Poe, the poet gives us those brief, indeterminate glimpses of the world beyond; for Emerson, he functions more materially: the poet "unfixes the land and the sea, makes them revolve around the axis of his primary thought, and disposes them anew" (p. 31).

The Emerson of *Nature* could not envision glimpses of a separate, perfect world beyond his own, precisely because for him the ideal was to be found not somewhere else but in his usual world. For him nature was perfect; it is our ruined perception that is at fault. It is the duty of the reason to perceive that perfection, even though to the imagination the process might *appear* to be the exact opposite, a ruined nature being renewed or rearranged by thought. In this seeming difference between the ideas of the two authors lies their similarity, as well, since for both men the poetic imagination can, through an exercise in point of view, free itself and escape the ordinary prison of the context-defined mind so that it is able, in the one case, to glimpse another world, and, in the other, to perceive the perfection of this world.

The same similarity of thought brought Poe near to, though not coincident with, Thoreau. Thoreau pictured himself both as the man of understanding living in this temporal world and as the man of reason or poetic imagination able to escape from his own mortality, though the two selves were separate and, it would appear, strangers unable to communicate with one another:

> With thinking we may be beside ourselves in a sane sense. By a conscious effort of the mind we can stand aloof from actions and their consequences; and all things, good and bad, go by us like a torrent. We are not wholly involved in Nature. I may be either the drift-wood in the stream, or Indra in the sky looking down on it. I *may* be affected by a theatrical exhibition; on the other hand, I *may not* be affected by an actual event which appears to concern me much more. I only know myself as a human entity; the scene, so to speak, of thoughts and affections; and am sensible of a certain doubleness by which I can stand as remote from myself as from another. However intense my experience, I am conscious of the presence and criticism of a part of me, which, as it were, is not a part of me, but spectator, sharing no experience, but taking note of it; and that is no more I than it is you. When the play, it may be the tragedy, of life is over, the spectator goes his way. It was a kind of fiction, a work of the imagination only, so far as he was concerned. (pp. 134-135)

Here the self who is Indra in the sky is so through an act of the poetic imagination that, in the case of Emerson, appears to redispose empirical reality, and that, in the case of Poe, glimpses eternity. Thoreau differs from Poe in an Emersonian way. As Indra in the sky, he is not looking away from this world toward another, but is rather looking at this one from a new perspective such that when the driftwood in the currents of the understanding passes down the stream of time the soul views *it* as the imagined self.

It is apparent that Poe's ideas were very close to those of these contemporaries, but it is also apparent that he could not have written a *Nature* or a *Walden*. What he *could* do was to be himself and, through his divisions of the intellect, describe his model man. This man is, as Poe probably imagined himself to be, exceptionally brilliant (and thereby he risks the accusation of madness); he maintains an aristocratic *hauteur* even though he is a bit down on his luck; and he is rewarded, pecuniarily or otherwise, for a dazzling feat of imagination. Poe's first attempt to define him was the creation of C. Auguste Dupin in "Murders." Dupin is not an exact duplicate of Poe, but he is a character whose Poe-like attributes make him an exemplary figure.

Just a detective story! It can be argued by those who do not take the tale seriously that there is a radical difference between using the highest function of the mind to achieve glimpses of eternity, as does the sensitive reader of poetry, and using it to pursue or defeat criminals, as does Dupin, and no doubt Poe would have been the first to agree, though he would hardly have called the difference fatal. But the difference lies only in the circumstances. Poe was not writing poems through which the reader's soul might be elevated; he was, rather writing a prose tale to convey a truth *about* the poetic imagination. For that purpose, he employed a manifestation of that imagination that he knew would be readily understood by readers and that would also have the Gothic entertainment values of horror and mystification.

This tale can be read in two contrasting ways. First, it is a marvelous story of ratiocination about a detective who effortlessly discovers a fact that the Parisian police, acting alone, might never stumble upon, that the murders of the L'Espanaye women were not murders at all, but the motiveless acts of violence of an alternately frightened and enraged orangutan. Understandably, many of its readers love the mystery aspect of the tale, and for that reason Poe was justified in republishing it without major revision. Second, however, it is just what it claims to be, that is, a set of propositions followed by illustrative examples, the subject of which is an analysis of the intellectual faculties that Poe had spoken of in his criticism. As an argument, it is intended to convey the truth that Poe had said is the province of prose fiction. Unfortunately, looked at in this light the mystery portion of the story is a wretched failure; had not that been so, "The Purloined Letter" might never have been written.

It is often maintained that these propositions were prefaced to the tale only for reasons of deceptive playfulness on Poe's part (as seems to have been more or less the case with "The Imp of the Perverse"), but in the present study we have agreed to take the narrator at his word in such matters. Dupin's companion begins his narrative with remarks on the analytical features of the mind—Poe was not yet using the concept of the poetic imagination. These remarks are confusing, so that it is not always certain just what is being equated with what, but it *is* certain that the analytic mind that the narrator proposes is a close kin to Emerson's reason. Its method appears to the casual observer to be intuitive and its acumen supernatural, but in fact its ability to disentangle enigmas, conundrums, and hieroglyphics is rational and natural. The opposite mental faculty, the ordinary understanding or calculating power, is not imaginative but fanciful. It deals with complexities, not profundities, and its achievements result from concentration and a retentive memory rather than from an awareness of what observations are important. It is constructive rather than analytical: it combines. The calculating mind may win at chess, with all of the superficial complexities of that game, but the analytical mind is challenged by the profundity of checkers (draughts in the story). The analyst uses the ability of the imagination to shift its point of view to throw himself into the spirit of his opponent and identify with it; in that way, he discovers means of defeating him. In bridge (whist in the story), he does the same thing by observing everything that might betray his opponent's chain of thought, and thereby infers what cards his opponent holds. This is an employment of the mind even lower than that of criminal detection, but the two are linked: "proficiency in whist implies capacity for success in all these more important undertakings *where mind struggles with mind*" (p. 178, italics mine).

This is why the true expert at bridge can also be an expert detective like Dupin. By throwing himself into the spirit of the criminal and identifying with it, the detective can know everything that the criminal knows and thereby, by winning the struggle between his mind and the mind of the malefactor, solve any crime. This is what the major portion of the narrative that follows the preface, the commentary on the earlier propositions, the narrator calls it, fails to do. Its first part, the slight mystification in which Dupin traces the narrator's associative chain of thought from its origin in a collision with a fruiterer to its end in a reflection on a recent stage play, comes close to an instance of mind struggling with mind, it is true. The narrator is not struggling in return against Dupin, for he is unaware that the game is being played, but in all probability that doesn't matter. As an illustration, then, the episode is generally satisfactory. It is in the so-called murders that the major failure occurs.

What possessed Poe to illustrate the workings of the analytic faculty of mind by pitting Dupin against an orangutan? How could the great detective struggle mind against mind with a mindless beast whose motives were brute rage and alarm and who could not, because of his lack of understanding of the meaning of right and wrong, be accused of committing any crime at all? It seems likely that Poe invented the case of the L'Espanaye women because it defied the normal expectations of police officers: when people are killed, it is the usual practice to search for persons who have killed them, while Poe's plot allowed Dupin to demonstrate that ordinary expectations must be abandoned when they contradict existing circumstances. However, if the plot allowed Dupin to do that, it did not allow him to struggle mind against mind with a criminal: as an illustrative example, then, it illustrated either nothing at all or else something other than what required illustration.

Two clues suggest that Poe understood the corner into which he had painted himself by having Dupin's mind do battle with a broken nail rather than with a suitable opponent, and that he attempted to do something about it. The first attempt to conceal the failure is the deceptive advertisement through which the owner of the ape, a common sailor, is lured to Dupin's quarters. Apparently, it was meant to salvage the illustration of mind struggling with mind, but it fails for two reasons. First, the sailor is not a criminal and is, indeed, so incurably peripheral to the story that he might have been omitted without damage to the plot. Second, the newspaper notice that brings him into the story is not a master stroke of an analytic mind but rather the routine trickery of a confidence man.

Having failed to repair the illustration here, Poe tried again by causing Dupin to declare about the Prefect of the Parisian Police, "I am satisfied with having defeated him in his own castle" (p. 197). But it is again true that the Prefect is not the criminal but, rather, a most unpromising (for the purpose of this case) law enforcement official whose appearance in the tale is limited to one sentence at the end. Mind struggling with mind means a *combat* between two minds, and nothing else; in this instance, it means detective at grips with criminal, whereas Dupin has merely won a footrace against the police official to see which of two persons working on the same side of the law can reach the solution to the puzzle first. It is not even certain that, acting alone, the Prefect could ever have reached the finish line.

Somehow, I cannot say just how, this failure appears to be connected to a large conceptual confusion in the term "analysis" in the initial propositions. Is it one quality of mind or is it a combination of two different ones? For Emerson and Thoreau, the understanding and the reason co-existed, so that one man could utilize both qualities: thus Emerson could be poet and philosopher at the same time and Thoreau could at once be driftwood and Indra. That was because for them the temporal and eternal worlds were coaxial, to use Emerson's idea, and therefore neither was "beyond" the other. But because he was *not* a transcendentalist, and did not think like one, for Poe the temporal world was here and the eternal world was there "beyond." Thus his tendency in the case of his criticism was to assign separate and contrasting elements of the mind to the two and in the case of this ratiocinative tale his tendency was to give the faculty of analysis to his detective and the ordinary understanding to his policeman. The two men are at opposite intellectual poles from one another and therefore, a perfectly comprehensible logic might maintain, they should exhibit opposite aspects of mind. In this opposition, the Prefect's understanding is mundane and Dupin's analytic mind is characterized by the single attribute of unworldliness.

This is why Dupin criticizes Vidocq (a police official through whom Dupin comments on the police in general) for being too worldly, for conducting his investigations in the bottom of the well and in the valleys: that is, for doing police work as it is usually done (p. 186). Vidocq impairs his vision, Dupin says, by holding the object too close, while to see a star one should avoid looking directly at it. In contrast to Vidocq (or the Prefect, we might as well say), Dupin inhabits a world of celestial imagination, which Poe symbolizes by a darkness in which the mortal eyes of the understanding are useless but the metaphorical eyes of the imagination are brought into play. Dupin is "enamored of the Night for her own sake" (p. 179), and after sunrise he shutters out the daylight and uses only the weakest of tapers for reading. Dupin exhibits a "rich ideality" or immateriality (p. 180): so far from inhabiting the usual world of events, the narrator says of both of them, "We existed within ourselves alone" (p. 179). From time to time Dupin's mind actually recedes from this world as much as does the soul of the dead M. Valdemar in the later tale: thus when he retraced his analytic thought processes for his companion, Dupin's manner became frigid and abstract (p. 180) and his "voice, although by no means loud, had that intonation which is commonly employed in speaking to some one at a great distance" (p. 187). At such times, his eyes, vacant in expression, regarded only the wall. Yet a detective cannot be confined to another world and still be successful at his profession, because he must function in terms of crimes committed in the upstairs apartments of this world. This is apparent in the fact that from the description we are given of Dupin's usual habits, his daylight visit to the crowded and gruesome setting of the L'Espanaye tragedy presents itself as a bizarre freak. Indeed, an alternative conception of the analytic faculty is implicit in a much different, bipartite Dupin who is occasionally suggested in the tale. He is a Janus who is both of this world and beyond it, as in the narrator's fancy that there is a "double Dupin—the creative and the resolvent" (p. 180). This would be a man who, although not quite Emersonian, could follow the example of Emerson by simultaneously using both the understanding and the reason, and who would thereby be associated simultaneously with the two separate worlds that Poe envisioned.

This confusion, added to the logical failure of the first tale, made necessary a second attempt to explain the features of mind of the model man. The concept of the analytic mind had been misleading at best and at worst wrong, since for the most part it had been conceived as a single faculty different from and opposed to the calculating or combining mind. In the interval between the composition of the two tales Poe came to understand that his double Dupin was the correct one, that crimes are committed in only one world, our world, and that those persons who would solve them must, in addition to the other-worldliness that gives their minds ascendency over others, have intellectual capabilities that allow them to function in the here and the now. The difference between Dupin and the Prefect would have to be that the detective would have an *additional* capacity of mind that the policeman would not share.

"Analysis" is mentioned only once in "The Purloined Letter," and then only as a faint echo of its centrality to the earlier tale, but the idea of calculation persists as a way of suggesting Emerson's understanding, though the term "mathematics" has been substituted for it. As Dupin puts it, "The mathematics are the science of form and quantity; mathematical reasoning is merely logic applied to observation upon form and quantity" (pp. 232-233). The mind that so reasons deals with relation and with finite truths. Associated with form and quantity, this mind necessarily concerns itself with *things*, that is, whatever has shape and extent or duration, or shape *or* extent or duration. All *things*, including seeming anti-things such as voids, fall by definition within the province of the mathematics, as here defined, and since time is measurable, that too is included. Whatever is in the world or the cosmos, whatever is temporal or mortal, and whatever lies outside of "the abstractly logical," according to Dupin, (p. 232), belongs in the category of things with which this aspect of mind deals: animals, buildings, stars, food, precious stones, light-years, and most of what many people know and *all* that *some* people know, that is. This is the faculty that, like the pure intellect, comprehends all fact, all empirical reality. Because this reality *is* empirical, it is known to the mathematical mind through the senses, and so it is best seen when exhibited in the brightest light. The intellect of the Prefect is exclusively of this kind. Confronted with the problem of a stolen letter, he believes without pondering the matter that it must be hidden from *view* behind, under, or within something, since in the mathematical understanding of things objects can only be concealed where the light reflected by them will not reach the peering eye. Thus his instruments of search are his eyes, aided by microscopes, gimlets, and probes.

The Prefect cannot understand Dupin—or the Minister—because they utilize an aspect of mind that for him has no existence, the poetic imagination that in this tale takes the place of the earlier analytic faculty. "I have been guilty of certain doggerel," Dupin says (p. 228), modestly admitting that he is a poet. As a poet, one of his concerns (though it is hardly relevant to this tale) must be the beauty that elevates the soul, but in the practical profession of criminology the faculty is used for a more utilitarian purpose, that of unfixing his mind from its usual confines so that it can invade the mind of a criminal in order to understand the thought processes of that mind. Such an application of the intellect is *terra incognita* to the prefect, who maintains that poets are very nearly fools and who cannot understand why Dupin would say that matters that require "reflection" (a significant choice of words) are better treated in the dark than in the light (p. 226). Dupin punishes him for his impertinent obtuseness, scorning poets and speaking disrespectfully of Dupin's "oddities," by sending him back to repeat his unsuccessful search of the Minister's hotel, knowing full well that the painfully thorough process will again reveal nothing.

In explaining the poetic imagination as "an identification of the reasoner's intellect with that of his opponent" (p. 231), Dupin makes it sound very much like the whist and draughts winning analytic mind of the earlier tale, but it is significantly different. Poe had come to understand that what he had earlier called the analytic feature was actually a combination of two qualities of mind, the mathematical element that attunes the reasoner to the material world in which crime takes place and the poetical imagination that allows him to unfix his thought from the rigidities that hobble the Prefect.[12] Thus Dupin says of the Minister, "As poet *and* mathematician, he would reason well; as mere mathematician, he could not have reasoned at all . . ." (p. 232).

Retracing the Minister's crime, it can be seen to demonstrate just these qualities. Upon entering the royal lady's boudoir, in which she is present with her husband (or so the man seems to be), the Minister sees a letter to her written in the hand of a lover (or so the tale implies). *At once* he fathoms her secret. Having used his mathematical capability to gather the most relevant observations, he then uses his poetic imagination to read *both* of their minds. When he determines that she cannot risk drawing attention to the letter, he takes it casually, knowing that she will not remonstrate before her husband for fear that such a course of action would awaken his suspicion.

After committing the crime, the Minister uses the same poetical imagination to decide upon a hiding place for the letter. Identifying his mind with that of the royal lady once more, he concludes that she will appeal for help to the prefect, and further identifying his thought process with that of the Prefect, he discovers what methods of search will be used against him. Therefore, though the Prefect will use perfect methods for discovering a letter hidden in the world of *things*, he will be at a loss if the game is played in a world of *ideas*. Having realized this, that is exactly where the Minister plays it. Thus, as in the earlier tale, the plot is constructed around the fact that the method of concealing the letter defies the normal expectations of the police.

Not only is Dupin a poet, but he is also, like the Minister, a mathematician—though the latter quality is implicit in what he says and does rather than explicit in the narrative. To win the victory in the case, he follows precisely the same reasoning processes as does the Minister, except that he is able to carry the mind-readings an extra step. Identifying his own thought processes with those of the Minister, he follows his opponent's imagination from the helplessness of the royal lady and the jealousy of her husband all the way to the Minister's method of hiding the letter.

From the point of this discovery to the point at which the letter is safely in his possession, Dupin maintains a delicate intellectual balance between the mathematics, the material existence of the object, and the poetical, the abstract plane on which the struggle is being waged and he takes steps to upset the Minister's balance. In order to accomplish the first, he wears green (dark) glasses in the presence of his opponent (p. 234). Whatever other purposes these glasses may have been intended to serve, most important is the fact that with them Dupin can see the light of the ordinary world while remaining enough in the dark to enable him to see imaginatively. In order to accomplish the second, he deprives the Minister of his poetic faculty by arranging a disturbance in the street outside of the Minister's window (p. 235). When his opponent throws open the shutters and briefly blinds his poetic imagination in the morning brightness, Dupin takes advantage of the moment to retrieve the lady's letter. By the time the shutter has been closed so that the Minister's imagination can function once more, the contest has been won and lost.

Thus Poe at last created the illustration of mind struggling victoriously against mind that had eluded him earlier. Almost unnoticed in this victory is the perhaps unexpected fact—unexpected because Poe is rarely thought of as a moralist—that it is won on specifically moral grounds. Since the two opponents are exactly matched as poets and mathematicians, a stalemate is threatened in which each man, privy to the other's thought process, can counter whatever measures his opponent adopts. Granted this, Dupin's margin of victory lies in the fact that the Minister is "that *monstrum horrendum*, an unprincipled man of genius" (p. 236). As a blackmailer who is unscrupulous enough to obtain power by exploiting the weakness of another, he finds himself aligned against the accepted principles of decency and standards of conduct that bring society together in defense of the victim. Dupin's advantage is that he is aligned with the side of virtue: while the Minister is excluded from essential information—specifically, that Dupin has joined the ranks of his opponents—Dupin is given all of the information about the case with which society can provide him. Had he not had that advantage, it is doubtful that Dupin could have triumphed over his masterful opponent.

Having made his point, Poe had no need to write another such tale, and he did not. He had discovered that rather than two orientations of mind, the calculating and the analytic, there were three, the mathematical, the poetic, and the combined mathematical and poetic. The first confines a person dismally to the narrowness of the purely material universe, and is, unfortunately, the voluntary intellectual limit of many men. The last liberates the genius that is best suited to our world, genius that can win a game of bridge, solve a seemingly insoluble crime, and formulate a theory of the origin and end of the cosmos (or, in twentieth-century terms a theory of relativity). But what of the poetic faculty in isolation, without, that is, mathematical contact with the universe in which it has its corporeal being?

It is just here that Poe departed, not alone from the loyalties that we might have expected of him as a poet but also from the ideas of his transcendental contemporaries. As we have seen, Poe had appeared to be moving closer to them as his ideas changed. At first thrown off the track by the erroneous assumption that there were two principles of mind that were opposed and immiscible, although Emerson was saying that the understanding and the reason can coexist in the same mind, Poe later agreed with Emerson by allotting both functions simultaneously to Dupin and to the Minister. Not only that, but in "The Purloined Letter" he seemed to be moving even closer by causing Dupin to speak in traditionally Emersonian terms: "The material world . . . abounds with very strict analogies to the immaterial; and thus some color of truth has been given to the rhetorical dogma, that metaphor, or simile, may be made to strengthen an argument as well as to embellish a description" (p. 234). How close this statement comes to endorsing the ideas of *Nature* can be seen by comparing it to Emerson's own words: "Every natural fact is a symbol of some spiritual fact. Every appearance in nature corresponds to some state of the mind . . . . these analogies . . . are constant, and pervade nature" (pp. 19-20). However, one irreconcilable difference kept the two men, if I may be excused for putting it this way, worlds apart.

Despite their seeming agreement, there was always this difference. For Emerson the solipsist, the reason was capable of seeing a perfect world, one without sin or death, restored around him, there, right where he stood in Concord; it was only a trick of the understanding of man, the god in ruins, that betrayed him into seeing it otherwise. The brighter the illumination the better the vision of the reason and the more perfect the world. The eye is the best of artists, he thought, and light is the first of painters. "There is no object so foul that intense light will not make it beautiful," and corpses are included (pp. 12-13). "Disagreeable appearances, swine, spiders, snakes, pests, mad-houses, prisons, enemies," will vanish; "they are temporary and shall be seen no more" (p. 45). The only calamity that nature could not repair, he wrote, would be the loss of his eyes (p. 10). "The ruin or the blank, that we see when we look at nature, is in our own eye. The axis of vision is not coincident with the axis of things, and so they appear not transparent but opaque" (p. 43). "I become a transparent eye-ball. I am nothing. I see all" (p. 10). This extraordinary confidence in the power of illumination and vision co-operating with the reason depends wholly on Emerson's belief that all things are coincident, that the "other" world is really this world seen more perfectly. Thoreau agreed. He allied himself with illumination, presenting himself as a morning Chanticleer crowing to awaken his neighbors to the light of the new day (p. 84).

In contrast, Poe's conception of the worlds here and beyond was without question founded on traditional Judeo-Christian hierarchical patters of thought, however much he may have moved beyond orthodoxy by this point in his life. Wherever the other world might be, the scriptural conception of the disposition of heaven and earth that he had retained from his youth told him that it was not this world, and that one could not find it by using dark-lanterns or microscopes as though it were an object to be seen with mortal eyes. To look at the temporal universe in bright light was to see only the temporal universe.

By respecting the poetic imagination, by remaining in the metaphorical half-light, that is, one could free one half of his "vision" to "see" with the "soul" what otherwise could not be seen, while still keeping a firm hold on the material world in which he lived, and this is the most desirable intellectual state for Poe's Dupin, his model man. For Emerson and Thoreau, it was preferable to trust oneself wholly to the poetic imagination or reason because they believed that in doing so one would find, like Thoreau's Artist of Kouroo, that he and his world had become immortal together (pp. 326-327). But for Poe, to lose contact with this world by relinquishing one's mathematical grasp of it is madness. The mind travels elsewhere while the body remains here, adaptation to the world it inhabits miserably and horrifyingly gone. Like the mast-head lookout in Melville's *Moby-Dick*, one must not lose his grip for fear of falling into Descartian vortices . . . or into Usher's tarn.

At this point, the reader is released from his oath, sworn to willingly or otherwise, to take Poe seriously and to look at his tales in the context of their time. Clearly, Poe cannot *always* be taken seriously because he did write his share of hoaxes, satires, farcical pieces, and ill-disguised journalism. "Marie Rogêt" and "'Thou Art the Man'" have been omitted from this study for precisely that reason. Similarly, it would not do to search too minutely for systematic meaning in the earlier Folio Club era pieces written before Poe had attained artistic maturity. Still, a significant body of fiction that *should* be taken seriously remains.

These are the tales that yield the most to the kind of analysis proposed here. As a writer of the second quarter of the nineteenth century, though admittedly an idiosyncratic one, Poe shared the preoccupations of his contemporaries with psychology, and like them he did not hesitate to wed his ideas about the human mind to ideas about philosophy and religion, nor to attach these ideas in turn to insights about cosmological science. In presenting us with the figure of Dupin, he reminded us that the poet in our world is its unacknowledged legislator; in presenting us with his divisions of the mind, he also reminded us that the poet is the prophet of the world to come.

NOTES

[1] *Specimen Days, Prose Works 1892*, ed. Floyd Stovall (New York, 1963), 1: 232.

[2] Page numbers in the text of this essay refer to *Nature, Addresses, and Lectures, The Collected Works of Ralph Waldo Emerson*, ed. Robert E. Spiller and Alfred R. Ferguson (Cambridge, Mass., 1971), vol. 1.

[3] For convenience, the texts referred to for both this tale and for "The Murders in the Rue Morgue" are those in *The Short Fiction of Edgar Allan Poe*, ed. Stuart and Susan Levine (Indianapolis, 1976).

[4] Page numbers in the text of this essay refer to *Walden*, ed. J. Lyndon Shanley (Princeton, 1971).

[5] In his *Edgar Allan Poe*, 2nd. ed. (Indianapolis, 1977), p. 81, Vincent Buranelli says that Poe came to regard the detective story "as an exception to the rule that truth is not the object of literary art." That conflicts with Poe's own ideas on the subject detailed below.

[6] Daniel Hoffman, *Poe Poe Poe . . .* (Garden City, 1973), *passim*.

[7] This has been a problem both early and late. George E. Woodberry wrote "That the ratiocinative tales are on a lower level than the imaginative ones hardly needs to be said," *Edgar Allan Poe* (Boston, 1885), pp. 150-151. Julian Symons, himself an author of "crime fiction," argues against *all* ingenious analyses that would elevate Poe to a level of seriousness higher than that of the Vincent Price film. Calling him a "fine academic property" for scholars, Symons argues that the popular Poe is, essentially, the only Poe. Almost all criticisms of his works, Symons says, are "in varying degrees nonsensical . . . or trivial . . . ." *The Tell-Tale Heart; The Life and Work of Edgar Allan Poe* (Middlesex, etc., 1981), p. 231. For a view that takes account of Poe combining serious art with fun in the ratiocinative tales, see Benjamin Franklin Fisher IV, "Blackwood Articles á La Poe: How to Make a False Start Pay," *RLV*, 39(1973), 418-432.

[8] Symons agrees: "It was not Poe's purpose to create a new literary form . . . ," p. 221.

[9] Poe's critical statements are taken from "The Philosophy of Composition" and from "The Poetic Principle," both in *H*14: 193-208, 266-292—in the present instance, p. 272.

[10] The later *Eureka*, in which Poe annihilates the distinctions between prose and poetry and between beauty and truth, is another matter that requires separate investigation.

[11] I do not mean to imply here that Poe found Coleridge through reading Emerson, but rather to point out a relationship between Emerson and Poe by noting the common source of some of their ideas.

[12] This idea has been on the tips of the tongues of some critics for years. For instance, David Galloway wrote that "Poe's ideal was a perfect synthesis of the two modes of intelligence. In his fiction the closest he came to this ideal was in the creation of the master detective Dupin, a poet who brings to commonplace reality the discriminating eye of the artist . . . ." "Introduction," *Selected Writings of Edgar Allan Poe* (Harmondsworth, etc., 1967), p. 14. Others who have approached the same conclusion without an adequate understanding of Poe's conception of his term "mathematics" include Hoffman, p. 107, and Buranelli, p. 81. Buranelli said that "What is needed is the imagination of the poet and the reasoning power of the mathematician," while Hoffman said of Dupin that "His mind, working by metaphoric analogies, combines poetic intuition with mathematical exactitude."

USHER'S NERVOUS FEVER: THE MEANING OF MEDICINE IN POE'S "THE FALL OF THE HOUSE OF USHER"

DAVID E. E. SLOANE

Edgar Allan Poe knew and used a variety of items taken from the pseudo-scientific and medical doctrines of the early nineteenth century. In some cases, such as "The System of Dr. Tarr and Professor Fether," his purpose was to burlesque scientific certainty—which he saw in conflict with the infinite capacity for cosmogenic insanity within the human mind. Using Richard Wilbur's "House of Poe" lecture as a reference, it is simple to see medical illness as corresponding both to the inward cosmic journey Wilbur describes as well as to the more conventional motif of fear and descent in the Gothic horror tale. "The Fall of the House of Usher," published in *Burton's Gentleman's Magazine* in 1839, is Poe's most carefully worked development of this same theme in a serious Gothic format. Poe is known to have taken contemporary pseudo-medical artifacts from George Combe's *Phrenology*; a second item of contemporary nosology (diagnostic medical nomenclature), "Nervous Fever," plays an even more important role in the plot and imagery of "Usher." Thus, Poe's Gothic fiction is heavily colored by popular science; it is made more realistic and more terrible as the power of medical "fact" weighs on the poetic temperament of Usher, alters our sense of the narrator and of Madeline's malaise, and brings the house of Usher to destruction.

As early as 1836, Poe published reviews of medical works in the *Southern Literary Messenger*, and his interest in George Combe—a leading British exponent of phrenology and mental and physical hygiene who was lecturing in America in 1838 and 1839—when "Usher" was written—has been documented.[1] Poe's interest in phrenology and mesmerism was also indicated by his review of *Miles's Phrenology* in the *Messenger* in March, 1836 (1: 286-287), and elsewhere. Edward Hungerford has thoroughly examined the texts of Dr. Combe's lectures as delivered in Philadelphia where Poe was resident, and published by the house of Fowler & Wells in New York in 1839 and later editions.[2] Poe's use of phrenology, as Hungerford shows, was extensive and purposeful in "Usher." Combe assumed that four "temperaments" ruled the emotions and exaggerated the influence of brain shape. One of these temperaments was the "nervous," which provides descriptive details for Roderick Usher: the high forehead, pale complexion, wispy hair, bright eyes, and vivacity of intellect are virtually identical in Combe's and Poe's descriptions of trait and character. Poe, of course, goes farther by attaching similar details to the Usher mansion, with its wispy strands of moss and vacant eye-like windows, not to mention the pun of the small crack in the foundation of the skull-like house. Furthermore, Poe adapted the phrenological bump of "Ideality," located in the area of the temple in Usher, who—like Ligeia and other Poe figures—has an unusually large ideality bump. It is Usher's chief character trait. Usher's poetic is consistent with Combe's definitions: Ideality was the organ of poetry and music, both prominent in Usher's life, and was a faculty of the most powerful intellect; linked with other traits it would give facility in language and metaphysics: Combe mentions Swedenborg, who is subsequently cited among Usher's readings. Poe's adaptation of phrenology to Usher and to Usher's mansion is the brilliantly creative act of an author, not a literal or gullible transcription. He extends the literary paradigm so that it becomes a cosmos as well as an item of physical description. The expanded literary image of the house supports the kind of cosmocentric development that Richard Wilbur has found as a unifying pattern in Poe's tales. Poe's use of the descriptive details establishes a context of nervous Ideality that predisposes his hero to impending disaster.

With this pseudo-scientific context apparent, Usher's story takes on extra dimensions. At first, it might be seen as a Gothic exercise only. Lonely and crazed, Roderick and Madeline are trapped by repressed physical desire in a decaying mansion where they come to destruction through the climax of their incestuous relationship in premature burial. Poe's borrowings from the American lectures of Combe, however, elaborate upon this design by adding an overlay of contemporary culture—the phrenological terminology rampant in the late 1830s. The central figure is trapped not only in the Gothic web of sin but also in a net of predetermined mental and physiological characteristics, and his *doppelgänger*, Madeline, is easily imaged and imagined—as in "William Wilson"—as the split side of a deranged personality. When more phenomena from contemporary medical theory are added, Usher's case becomes even more complex in the interweaving of external and internal forces.

Madeline's disease is clearly outlined for the reader as having a "cataleptical character" including a gradual wasting away of th eperson and a settled apathy. Moreover, as she is entombed to protect her corpse from a sinister physician interested in the "unusual" character of her disease, the narrator notes "the mockery of a faint blush upon the bosom and the face, and that suspiciously lingering smile upon the lip which is so terrible in death."[3] The narrator leaps to the conclusion that Madeline is dead, taking the reader with him in what appears to be an obvious Gothic cliché. *The Family Physician*, a popular home medical book published in New York by the firm of Greeley and

Winchester in 1834, offers an alternative view of the case, however, under the heading "Of Hysteric Affections":

> Hysteric affections are generally considered peculiar to females, and are supposed to depend on some influence which is owing to the peculiarity of the sex . . . . Women . . . of a delicate habit, . . . and whose nervous systems are extremely irritable, are most subject to the hysterical affections . . . .
> Sometimes the hysteric fit resembles a swoon or fainting fit, during which the patient lies in a sleep, only the breathing is so low as scarcely to be perceived. At other times the patient is affected with strong convulsions. The symptoms which precede the hysteric fits are likewise various in different persons. Sometimes the fits come on with coldness of the extremeties, yawning and stretching, lowness of spirits, oppression and anxiety. (p. 172)

As he will later do with Usher's malady, Poe picks out detail from the nosology, having the narrator cite Madeline's "settled anxiety" in addition to her gradual wasting away and "transient affections of a partially cataleptical character," by which words Poe disguises the idea of "fits." "Oppression" is distributed broadly, with the word applied to the clouds in the heavens, to Usher, and finally to the narrator, all in the first two pages, rather than to Usher's sister. Thus, Poe translates medical descriptions into Gothic apparatus and establishes a double motif, for the narrator in telling us about these symptoms seems to ascribe them to mind and imagination even while noting the physicality of his surroundings with almost clinical detail.

The case becomes more complex as we encounter Usher, predisposed to nervousness by temperament, and in an environment which leads us to two other items of significance. "Nervous Fever" and "Miasma" were important phenomena in the popular nosology of the period around the 1830s. Medical practitioners were not yet free from rational empiricism, the tendency to blend observed fact with logic to reach conclusions. Medical texts show the terms linked to some extent, with Miasma representing a cause and Nervous Fever, comparable to Yellow Fever, as the effect. Benjamin Rush, the Philadelphia physician—advocate of humane healing for the mentally ill and rational empiricist—had suggested the Miasma-Yellow Fever link by empirical logic as the cause of the great Philadelphia Yellow Fever epidemic of 1793, later fictionalized in Charles Brockden Brown's *Arthur Mervyn*.[4] Rush's suggestion, without any connection discovered between mosquitoes and yellow fever through scientific means, was to eliminate the source of miasmic contagion by draining the swamps surrounding the city. Miasma was considered to be dangerously stagnant air—noxious in only a vaguely defined way, but thought to arise in mines, open cellars, and areas with rotting wood. According to *The Family Physician*, where we have just found a disease so like Madeline's illness, air which stagnated in cellars was "to be avoided as the most deadly poison.—It often kills almost as quickly as lightening" (p. 39). Poe repeated these ideas in an essay noting the danger of rotting wood in street paving in 1844 (*H*14: 167-168), but his detailed description of the setting of Usher's mansion focuses on this pathological detail:

> I had so worked upon my imagination as really to believe that around about the whole mansion and domain there hung an atmosphere peculiar to themselves and their immediate vicinity—an atmosphere that had no affinity with the fair of heaven, but which had reeked up from the decayed trees, and the sluggish tarn, in the form of an inelastic vapor or gas—dull, sluggish, faintly discernible, and leaden-hued . . . . In this there was much that reminded me of the specious totality of old wood-work which has rotted for long years in some neglected vault, with no disturbance from the breath of the external air. (p. 146)

Usher is surrounded by the deadliest possible physical contagion, and even the narrator reports his appropriately responsive oppression. In this early version, several words suggest an almost chemical atmosphere, muted in Poe's later texts where "inelastic vapor or gas" was modified to a "pestilent and mystic vapor," more fictive than technical seeming. The reference to rotten wood was inescapable in its implications to a reader of the period. Thus, Poe combines the contamination of heaven—the domain of the angel Israfel and poetry—with the reeking contagion of the underground, or physical earth. The Gothic and the scientific merge.

The results of exposure to Miasma offer a dramatic consequence for Usher and for the reader of the period in Nervous Fever. Here, Poe uses medical detail most profoundly to reflect the physical determinism of Usher's disaster. The symptoms of Nervous Fever—a malady which disappeared from home medical books after the 1830s—were offered in *The Family Physician* between Bilious Fever and Yellow Fever, and were described as originating in decaying animal and vegetable matter. They could remain in the system for up to ten days before breaking out and would then lead to a rapidly sinking state. Various sources of the period cite the disease. Charles G. Leland, in his *Memoirs* for the 1839-1840 period at Hurlburt's school in Philadelphia, remarks, in almost perfect correspondence with Poe's Usher, "my mind, weakened by long illness, had been strangely stimulated by many disorders, nervous fevers being frequent among them . . . . The result of so much nervousness, excessive stimulating by medicine, and rapid growth was a too great susceptibility to poetry, humour, art, and all that was romantic, quaint, and mysterious, while I found it very hard to master any really dry subject. What would have set me all right would have been careful physical culture . . . *amusement* in a healthy sense, of which I had almost none whatever."[5] Other sources treat the disease similarly.[6]

In fact, Poe's description of Usher's malady is so close to the symptoms cited in the 1834 *Family Physician* as to suggest an item by item borrowing with only the order reversed. *The Family Physician* offers the most striking features of Usher's unknown malady—nervous insomnia, murmuring, and fixed staring:

> Nervous Fever . . . The sleep is very much disturbed and unrefreshing; the countenance sinks or seems to change . . . to a ghastly appearance . . . . The mind broods over the most melancholy of feelings without knowing the cause; the sight of food is very unpleasant . . . . The symptoms considered very dangerous are . . . a changing of the voice from its usual tone; great vigelance or watchfulness . . . a muttering as if speaking to one's self; a wild and fixed look, as if the eyes were riveted on some particular object . . . .
>
> This fever originates from putrid animal and vegetable matter, mixing with the air or atmosphere we breathe, such for instance as the decaying vegetable and animal matter arising from stagnant mill ponds. (pp. 53-54)

Poe in borrowing from these details will establish the basis for a ghastly irony. The narrator continues to focus on the disease of Usher as Usher declines in the face of a greater catastrophe, the fate of his sister. The details of Usher's malady clearly indicate Nervous fever to the narrator:

> It was, he said, a constitutional and family evil . . . a mere nervous affection . . . . It displayed itself in a host of unnatural sensations . . . . He suffered much from a morbid acuteness of the senses; the most insipid food was alone endurable; he could wear only garments of a certain texture . . . . To an anomolous species of terror I found him a bounden slave.

Furthermore, Usher connects his malady with the house, its physique, and the tarn—all of which affect the morale of his existence. Woven into the movement of the plot is the decline, supposed death, and entombment of Madeline. As the climax of the story approaches, Usher reflects the most drastic symptoms of terror, which are synonymous with those of Nervous Fever:

> And now, some days of bitter grief having elapsed, an observable change came over the features of the mental disorder of my friend. His ordinary manner had vanished. His ordinary occupations were neglected or forgotten. He roamed from chamber to chamber with hurried, unequal, and objectless step. The pallor of his countenance had assumed, if possible, a more ghastly hue—but the luminousness of his eye had utterly gone out. The once occasional huskiness of his tone was heard no more; and a tremulous quaver, as if of extreme terror, habitually characterized his utterance. There were times indeed when I thought his unceasingly agitated mind was laboring with an oppressive secret . . . . I beheld him gazing upon vacancy for long hours, in an attitude of profoundest attention. (pp. 146, 150)

Even the narrator feels himself "infected" by the malaise, a calculated effect by Poe. Ironically, he diverts the narrator from the greater psychological horror to come in favor of the mundane horror of the miasmic contagion. Usher's doom is absolute: all levels of the action condemn him, from details in the setting, to historical fact, to contemporary science, and to the highest level of sympathetic and spiritual interaction with his universal soul-mate, Madeline, his other self. Physical and spiritual dissolution are combined; the story's irony is that the narrator fails to grasp the full enormity of the action because of his immersion in worldly detail. Poe makes the larger comic entity of the house crumble as well, completing the metaphoric dissolution.

The significance of Poe's use of medicine in "Usher" lies in its reduplicative effects on the Gothic environment of the story. Not only is Usher condemned by the incestuous ancestral environment and the cosmogenic forces pulling downward upon the spirit and the split psyche of himself and his sister. Science, at a more mundane level in Dr. Combe, Dr. Rush, and the corruptive forces of earthly matter as found in *The Family Physician*, also conspire against the tortured ideality of a soul degraded from pure spirit to corruptible physical mortality.

Poe's practice actually pervades a range of stories from this period. "Berenice," for example, seems to derive much from Benjamin Rush's essay on dentistry to evoke a similar theme.[7] Poe's medicine in this earlier story subjects the hero to a cosmic irony when he pulls the heroine's teeth in an effort to free her from corruption. "Usher" uses medicine somewhat more complexly. For a suitably unimaginative reader, the pathology is sufficient to explain the events of the story until the climax bursts upon him as a surprise. Details are appropriate to this end, and are presented by the narrator in such a way as to show him, too, to be such a person of limited imagination. Thematically, however, the details correspond to Poe's major themes surrounding the fever of life and the inevitable corruption of the physical—its entrapment of the metaphysical and spiritual in a corruptible shell. Thus, the meaning of medicine in "Usher" is that the spirit within the physical form is subject to malaise and death, and the attendant horror of that decline is inescapable at any level of the story. Nervous Fever, the vaguely defined malady of the period, merely provided Poe with another means of expressing this vision.

NOTES

[1]*Southern Literary Messenger*, 2(1836), 785-786, shows Poe's sense of medical writers. See David E. E. Sloane, "Early Nineteenth-Century Medicine in Poe's Short Stories" (Unpublished M.A. Thesis, Duke University, 1966); David E. Whisnant, "Edgar Allan Poe's Study of Science" (Unpublished M.A. Thesis, Duke University, 1962); and Carroll D. Laverty, "Science and Pseudo-Science in the Works of Edgar Allan Poe" (Unpublished Ph.D. Dissertation, Duke University, 1951).

[2]Edward Hungerford, "Poe and Phrenology," *AL*, 4(1930), 209-231. For Mesmerism, see Sydney E. Lind, "Poe and Mesmerism," *PMLA*, 62(1947), 1077-1094.

[3]"The Fall of the House of Usher," *Burton's Gentleman's Magazine*, 5(1839), 145-152; further citations are to this text.

[4]*Medical Inquiries and Observations*, 5th ed. (Philadelphia, 1818), and *Observations Upon the Origin of the Malignant Bilious or Yellow Fever in Philadelphia and Upon the Means of Preventing It: Addresses to the Citizens of Philadelphia by Benjamin Rush* (Philadelphia, 1799).

[5](New York, 1893), 1:81.

[6]"New England Sixty Years Ago," *Parlour Magazine*, 1(1840), 36, describes "a slow nervous fever" running sixty days before reaching a climax, for example. Mrs. M. A. Ford, in "An Essay on American Literature and its Prospects," *Graham's Magazine*, 36(1850), 185, a decade later, comments that in medical learning the American author is the best guide to diseases that differ so much in their nature from those of Europe, so contemporary critics

seem to be aware of the practice of American writers in using local scientific detail.

[7]David E. E. Sloane, "Gothic Romanticism and Rational Empiricism in Poe's 'Berenice'," *ATQ*, 19(1973), 19-25.

POE'S CHAPTERS ON "NATURAL MAGIC"

ROBERTA SHARP

Sir David Brewster's *Letters on Natural Magic* (1831) was popular and influential in Poe's time. A respected scientist and noted writer, Brewster addresses the volume to Sir Walter Scott, who suggested the book as part of the *Family Library Historical Series*. In the introductory letter to Scott, Brewster declares his intention to "imbody the information which history supplies respecting the fables and incantations of the ancient superstitions, and to show how far they can be explained by the scientific knowledge which then prevailed."[1]

The first "letter" discusses the "secret use which was . . . made of scientific discoveries" (p. 17). In later chapters Brewster explains natural phenomena which he calls magic—what could be interpreted as supernatural events by the incredulous or naive—and describes spectral images and other visual and auditory puzzles as "chapter[s] in the history of the marvelous" (p. 34). He insists that they have long been used by rulers in subjugating the citizenry:

> When the tyrants of antiquity were unable or unwilling to found their sovereignty on the affections and interests of their people, they sought to entrench themselves in the strongholds of supernatural influences, and to rule with the delegated authority of Heaven. The prince, the priest, and the sage, were leagued in a dark conspiracy to deceive and enslave their species; and man, who refused his submission to a being like himself, became the obedient slave of a spiritual despotism, and willingly bound himself in chains when they seemed to have been forged by the gods. (p. 14)

. . .

> A national system of deception, intended as an instrument of government, must have brought into requisition not merely the scientific skill of the age, but a variety of subsidiary contrivances calculated to astonish the beholder, to confound his judgment, to dazzle his senses, and to give a predominant influence to the peculiar imposture which it was thought desirable to establish. (p. 70)

Only slight attention has been given the significant use Poe made of Brewster's *Letters*. Recently, Burton Pollin speculates that Poe must have used the "1832 pirated edition of the Harpers, reprinted year after year for decades." He identifies the first trace of Brewster's book in Poe's fiction as the word *DISCOVERY* mysteriously written on a sail in "MS. Found in a Bottle" (1833).[2] Years ago, W. K. Wimsatt, Jr., established Poe's reliance on Brewster for "Maelzel's Chess Player," attributing Poe's "exposure" of the chess machine as a person hiding in it to his writing skill, not to his reasoning ability: "Poe alleges as the foundation of his 'result' seventeen 'observations taken during frequent visits to the exhibition.' Some of them are acute and well applied, but these all tend to establish, not the way the machine worked, but as Poe confesses in a footnote, the fact already amply established, that the machine must be regulated by *mind* . . . . Sir David Brewster had assumed it was obvious and dwelt on it momentarily."[3] Pollin speculates upon Poe's going to such lengths to expose the device which needed no exposing as a hoax: "The ignorance of the public and the failure of anyone to note the pretensions of his claim may then have led him to persist in presenting it as a piece of original ratiocination."[4] Actually Poe concentrates on detailing ways how people can be fooled, a judgment which Wimsatt supports: "Poe emerges from the 'Essay' not as a detective drawing from observed facts a conclusion which squares with other facts. He emerges as an imaginative writer, with a power of making bright and acceptable the drab mechanic guesses of writers with an eye to reality" (p. 151).

Little attention has been given the extensive and imaginative use Poe made of Brewster in his other fiction, however. A reading of *Letters* shows that the book had a significant impact on Poe's thought throughout his career and provided him with ideas for creating numerous fictional effects. Although Brewster strove to divest phenomena of its mystery and magic, Poe used mysterious effects in creating his fiction. As Poe's youthful Pym says, "Schoolboys . . . can accomplish wonders in the way of deception" (*H*3: 16).

Plausibly, the author of *Treatise on Optics* (1831) devotes much of *Letters* to the subject of visual distortion. He discusses at length various ways that visual perception can be confounded—mirrors, haze, smoke, light, and other conditions of nature—and the resulting illusions. Brewster clearly provided material that Poe used in creating effects in his fiction. Brewster details how strategically placed mirrors may trick the eye into seeing an image in an inverted position or in some other strange circumstance; for example, if two concave mirrors are placed opposite each other, an aerial image will be formed which "will exhibit the precise form and colours and movements of the living object," but it will make an image "either suspended in the air or depicted upon a wreath of smoke" (p. 66).

This effect must be what Poe has in mind in *Pym* when the native Too-wit looks into the two large mirrors in the cabin of the *Jane Guy*: "Upon raising his eyes and seeing his reflected self in the glass, I thought the savage would go mad; but, upon turning short round to make a retreat, and beholding himself a second time in the opposite direction, I was afraid he would expire on the spot" (*H*3: 183). Poe does not explain that Too-wit may be seeing himself in some distorted fashion, either upside down or floating in the air. Pym and the crew members see Too-wit's reaction as naivete, but their assumptions about the simple-mindedness of the natives soon prove false, of course, when the savages engineer an earthslide which entombs most of the party.

Poe uses mirrors for psychological effect in "Von Jung" ("Mystification") and "William Wilson." Baron Ritzner Von Jung throws a decanter of wine into the mirrored reflection of Mynheer Herman with the words: "I shall discharge this decanter of wine at your image in yonder mirror, and thus fulfill all the spirit, if not the exact letter, of resentment for your insult, while the necessity of physical violence to your real person will be obviated" (*M*2: 300). As part of an elaborate ruse involving both the provocation and eventual aversion of a duel, the mirror thus facilitates the Baron's practical joke. The narrator in "William Wilson" does resort to physical violence by savagely stabbing his own double. Psychologically, the murder of the *doppelgänger* becomes self-destruction; the narrator perceives this truth only when he confronts his image in an imaginary mirror: "A large mirror,—so at first it seemed to me in my confusion—now stood where none had been perceptible before; and, as I stepped up to it in extremity of terror, mine own image, but with features all pale and dabbled in blood, advanced to meet me with a feeble and tottering gait" (*M*2: 447-448). This scene closely parallels Brewster's explanation that mirrors may create an illusion of a person being stabbed by his own image:

> If a person with a drawn and highly polished dagger, illuminated by a strong light, stands a little farther from a concave mirror than its principal focus, he will perceive in the air between himself and the mirror an inverted and diminished image of his own person with the dagger similarly brandished. If he aims the dagger at the centre of the mirror's concavity, the two daggers will meet point to point, and, by pushing it still farther from him towards the mirror, the imaginary dagger will strike at his heart . . . . By using two mirrors . . . the spectator would witness an exact image of the assassin aiming the dagger at his life. (pp. 66-67)

Poe's fiction abounds with scenes which appear out of a smokey or cloudy atmosphere. These scenes are often beautiful as in the "Domain of Arnheim" or "Landor's Cottage," frequently mysterious as in "The Man of the Crowd" or "A Tale of the Ragged Mountains," but sometimes grotesque as in "King Pest." The last may derive macabre imagery involving skulls and skeletons from an observation of Brewster's about effects of light passing through haze, dust, or smoke:

> It has long been a favourite experiment to place at A a white and strongly illuminated human skull, and to exhibit an image of it amid the smoke of a chafing-dish at B; but a more terrific effect would be produced if a small skeleton suspended by invisible wires were placed as an object at A. Its image suspended in the air at B, or painted upon smoke, could not fail to astonish the spectator. (p. 66)

Perhaps achieving a "more terrific effect" is the object of the sinister assembly described in Poe's "King Pest":

> Before each of the party lay a portion of a skull, which was used as a drinking cup. Overhead was suspended a human skeleton, by means of a rope tied round one of the legs and fastened to a ring in the ceiling. The other limb confined by no such fetter, stuck off from the body at right angles, causing the whole loose and rattling frame to dangle and twirl about at the caprice of every occasional puff of wind which found its way into the apartment. In the cranium of this hideous thing lay a quantity of ignited charcoal, which threw a fitful but vivid light over the entire scene; while coffins, and other wares appertaining to the shop of an undertaker, were piled high up around the room, and against the windows, preventing any ray from escaping into the street. (*M*2: 248)

Scenes in this tale are as gruesome as the death ship described in Ch. 10 of *Pym*. Despite the repulsive imagery and the setting in a wine cellar beneath an undertaker's shop, "King Pest" is "one of the most brilliant pure burlesques in the language."[5]

Brewster's discussion of the magic lantern effect perhaps explains one of Poe's strangest stories, "A Tale of the Ragged Mountains." Brewster describes "mysterious handwriting on the wall of an apartment from which the magician and his apparatus were excluded" (p. 89) as well as the arrangement of a speculum and lens which could project an image at a distance when illuminated by sunlight. He adds: "any word associated with the fate of the individual observer could not fail to produce a singular effect upon his mind" (p. 90). This line might well have prompted Poe to tell the story of Augustus Bedloe, who, as if stepping through a space-time warp amid the mists and fog of Indian Summer, vividly experiences what appears to be his own past death in the midst of an uprising in an Oriental city. After the wind blows away the fog, "as if by the wand of an enchanter," Bedloe sees an "Eastern-looking city" on the banks of the river far below him and witnesses events which, Dr. Templeton later reveals, have basis in historical fact.[6] Whether Bedloe's experience is hallucination, dream, fantasy, remembrance, mirage, delusion or clairvoyance is never made entirely clear. Poe wants us to rule out, I think, the simple explanation that it was all a dream in having Bedloe "test" it by suspecting it to be a dream. The narrator finds significance in the palindrome created by the name *Oldeb* by the typographical misspelling of Bedloe's name as *Bedlo* in his obituary, an error which the narrator claims makes "one truth [that] is stranger than any fiction" (*M*3: 950). Ironically, this conclusion creates even more mystification unless one considers Brewster's sketch showing a word projected in reverse by the magic lantern effect (p. 89, Fig. 9) and that the mirror image of *Oldeb* would be *Bedlo*.

Still another idea about visual phenomena which Poe may have borrowed from Brewster is seeing better by indirect vision. Brewster explains that "all objects seen indirectly are seen indistinctly; but it is a curious circumstance, that when we wish to obtain a sight of a very faint star, such as one of the satellites of Saturn, we can see it most distinctly *by looking away from it*, and when the eye is turned full upon it, it immediately disappears" (p. 15). Poe uses this idea in several tales, notably "Murders," and states it in "A Chapter of Suggestions": "The intuitive and seemingly casual perception by which we often attain knowledge, when reason herself falters and abandons the effort, appears to resemble the sudden glancing at a star by which we see it more clearly than by a direct gaze" (*M*3: 1318, n5). Pym applies the principle to his dilemma in the dark hold of the *Grampus* when he needs to examine a piece of paper: "The white slip of paper could barely be discerned, and not even that when I looked at it directly; by turning the exterior portions of the retina toward it, that is to say, by surveying it slightly askance, I found that it became in some measure perceptible" (*H*3: 37).

Pym's action, as he later realizes, is not so clever as it first sounds because the paper appears blank, and he tears it up and throws it away. Later, realizing his folly in not examining both sides of the paper, he finds the pieces and fits them together. His phosphorous almost gone, he feel what he hopes is the written side for some unevenness on its surface: "I now again carried my forefinger cautiously along when I was aware of an exceedingly slight, but still discernible glow, which followed as it proceeded. This I knew, must arise from some very minute remaining particles of the phosphorus with which I had covered the paper in my previous attempt" (*H*3: 40). Pym continues his efforts until he does indeed discover a note, only part of which he can read because his phosphorous supply burned out. Pym's method must owe something to Brewster on reading coins in the dark: "All *black* or *rough* surfaces radiate light more copiously than *polished* or *smooth* surfaces, and hence the inscription is *luminous* when it is *rough*" (p. 113).

Brewster's discussion of spectre images may explain the much-discussed but still puzzling "shrouded human figure, very far larger in its proportions than any dweller among men. And the hue of the skin of the figure was of the perfect whiteness of the snow" (*H*3: 242). The figure at the end of *Pym* could be a visual fantasy according to Brewster on what can happen to vision in twilight:

> The pupil expands nearly to the whole width of the iris, in order to collect the feeble light which prevails; but it is demonstrable that in this state the eye cannot accommodate itself to see near objects distinctly, so that the forms of persons and things actually become more shadowy and confused when they come within the very distance at which we count upon obtaining the best view of them. . . . The spectres which are conjured up are always *white*, because no other colour can be seen, and they are either formed out of inanimate objects which reflect more light than others around the, or of animals or human beings whose colour or change of place renders them more visible in the dark. When the eye dimly descries an inanimate object whose different parts reflect different degrees of light, its brighter parts may enable the spectator to keep up a continued view of it; but the disappearance and reappearance of its fainter parts, and the change of shape which ensues, will necessarily give it the semblance of a living form, and if it occupies a position which is unapproachable, and where animate objects cannot find their way, the mind will soon transfer to it a supernatural existence. (pp. 25-26)

Poe, of course, leaves the significance of the figure to speculation by readers, but Pym survives to tell the tale even though Poe never explains how he survives. Throughout the journey the pattern involves danger and deceptive appearances with even the circumstances which seem most treacherous or inexplicable yielding to reasonable explanation. Richard Kopley theorizes that the "shrouded human figure" is a reflection of a ship's figurehead in the form of a penguin; a ship, of course, could account for Pym's survival. Although he does not consider Brewster's ideas, Kopley believes that the "essential structure of the book" rests on the idea of double mirrors.[7]

Brewster also analyzes spectre images of ships or land projected onto the horizon when atmospheric conditions are just right. He offers an explanation of spectre ships, which in some instances have been seen in duplicate with one image reversed as with the double mirrors:

> If, in serene weather, the surface of the sea is much colder than the air of the atmosphere, as it frequently is, . . . the air next the sea will gradually become colder and colder, by giving out its heat to the water; and the air immediately above will give out its heat to the cooler air immediately below it, so that the air from the surface of the sea, to a considerable height upwards, will gradually diminish in density, and therefore must produce the very phenomena we have described. (p. 142)

These phenomena are circumstances in which atmospheric and temperature conditions are such that the surface of the water acts either as a concave or convex lens and may produce the image of an object "transferred over the intervening convexity and presented in distinct and magnified outline" (p. 140). Such conditions may explain the false shore line envisioned by Parker when Pym knows that their vessel is far from land ($H$3: 121). Similarly, the ship Pym later spots in the same direction may have been a mirage; such a possibility could account for her apparently erratic behavior in that she at first appears to be heading toward the stranded crew. Suddenly Pym sees the "ship all at once with her stern fully presented towards us, and steering in a direction nearly opposite to that in which I had at first perceived her" ($H$3: 122).

Another particularly fascinating image Brewster cites is the spectre of Mt. Aetna, which may have provided Poe a suggestion for *Eureka*; Brewster quotes a Rev. Mr. Hughes on the following illusion: "'At the extremity of the vast shadow which Aetna projects across the island, appears a perfect and distinct image of the mountain itself elevated above the horizon, and diminished as if viewed in a concave mirror'" (p. 139). The narrator of *Eureka* could literally spin around on a spectral mountain about as well as on the real Mt. Aetna, which is a volcano. This gyration, however, would cause "exclusively terrestrial matters" to vanish and allow the "more conspicuous [to] become blended into one" ($H$16: 187).

Poe may be further indebted to Brewster for the notion of seeing all "blended into one." Brewster explains the pinwheel effect of putting part of a sentence on one side of a card and part on the other and then spinning the card:

> Particular letters may be given on one side, and others upon the other, or even halves or parts of each letter may be put upon each side, or all these contrivances may be combined, so that the sentiment which they express can be understood only when all the scattered parts are united by the revolution of the card.
>
> As the revolving card is virtually transparent, so that bodies beyond it can be seen through it, the power of the illusion might be greatly extended by introducing into the picture other figures either animate or inanimate. The setting sun, for example, might be introduced into a landscape (p. 35).

Surely this image of the setting sun suggests a scene in Poe's "The Island of the Fay":

> As I thus mused, with half-shut eyes, while the sun sank rapidly to rest, and eddying currents careered round and round the island, bearing upon their bosom large, dazzling, white flakes of the bark of the sycamore—flakes which, in their multiform positions upon the water, a quick imagination might have converted into anything it pleased—while I thus mused, it appeared to me that the form of one of those very Fays about whom I had been pondering, made its way slowly into the darkness from out of the light at the western end of the island ($M2$: 604).

Besides the visual manifestations that so readily convince people that they have witnessed the supernatural, Brewster explains several incidents involving ventriloquism which suggest to the listener that the voice came from "a spirit": "though the persons of his [the ventriloquist's] fictitious dialogue are not visible to the eye, yet they are unequivocally present to the imagination of his auditors, as if they had been shadowed forth in the silence of a spectral form" (p. 160). Poe has Peters use a disguised voice in the scene where Pym, masquerading as a corpse, frightens one of his captors to death and stuns the others so much that Pym and his companions escape. The narrator of Poe's "Thou Art the Man"[8] uses his "ventriloquial abilities" to accuse a man of murder ($M3$: 1059). The effect of a corpse making an accusation was so shocking that Mr. Goodfellow confessed to the murder and died on the spot.[9]

Brewster's discussion of cavities in minerals could explain the strange color and texture of the water found by Pym and his companions. Brewster describes "two new fluids different from any hitherto known," which can be seen under microscope in the cavities of gems; these fluids exist "in the same cavity in actual contact, without mixing together in the slightest degree" (p. 298). His detailed explanation of this phenomenon concentrates on properties in the fluids which expand and contract differently in response to heat, but he also remarks on the "singular" nature of the fluids and the resulting "beautiful optical phenomena" (pp. 298-306). Poe's account reads:

> At a small brook . . . Too-wit and his attendants halted to drink. On account of the singular character of the water, we refused to taste it, supposing it to be polluted. . . . Although it flowed with rapidity in all declivities where common water would do so, yet never, except when falling in a cascade, had it the customary appearance of limpidity. It was . . . *not* colorless, nor was it of any one uniform color—presenting to the eye, as it flowed, every possible shade of purple, like the hues of a changeable silk. This variation of shade was produced in a manner which excited as profound astonishment in the minds of our party as the mirror had done in the case of Too-wit. Upon collecting a basinful, and allowing it to settle thoroughly, we perceived that the whole mass of liquid was made up of a number of distinct veins, each of a distinct hue; that these veins did not commingle; and that their cohesion was perfect in regard to their own particles among themselves, and imperfect in regard to neighboring veins. Upon passing the blade of a knife athwart the veins, the water closed over it immediately, and also, in withdrawing it, all traces of the passage of the knife were instantly obliterated. If however the blade was passed down accurately between the two veins, a perfect separation was effected which the power of cohesion did not immediately rectify (*H*3: 186-187).

Brewster recounts also an undivulged chemical process that produced a remarkable color transformation:

> Professor Beyruss, who lived at the court of the Duke of Brunswick, one day pronounced to his highness that the dress which he wore should during dinner become red; and the change actually took place, to the astonishment of the prince and the rest of his guests. M. Vogel, who has recorded this curious fact, has not divulged the secret of the German chemist; but he observes, that if we pour limewater into the juice of beet-root, we shall obtain a colourless liquid; and that a piece of white cloth dipped in this liquid and dried rapidly will in a few hours become red by the

> mere contact of air. M. Vogel is also of opinion that this singular effect would be accelerated in an apartment where champaign or other fluids charged with carbonic acid are poured out in abundance. (p. 307)

One need only recall such transformations as that of Berenice's hair changing from dark to light or Rowena's from light to dark to appreciate Poe's fascination with such possibilities. He was intrigued by transformations. One of the most interesting connections of all between Brewster's book and Poe's fiction concerns one of Poe's last tales, "Von Kempelen and His Discovery." This tale is also linked to "Maelzel's Chess Player" in that, according to Brewster, the inventor of the chess machine was M. Kempelen of Presburg (p. 243). Poe's Von Kempelen discovered how to transform lead into gold.

Although on the surface the tone of "Von Kempelen" resembles that of a fairly serious report, Poe makes some of his funniest jokes in it. The narrator's deadpan reference to "protoxide" of azote, for example, is really a reference to nitrous oxide or laughing gas (Pollin, *Discoveries*, p. 179). He also quibbles over grammar in the sentence supposedly quoted from Sir Humphrey Davy's "Diary," a source still unidentified despite Poe's bracketed editorial comment in response to the narrator's promise of a quotation from the "Diary": "As we have not the algebraic signs necessary, and as the 'Diary' is to be found at the Athenaeum Library, we omit here a small portion of Mr. Poe's manuscript" (*M*3: 1358). Pollin believes that Poe invented the "Diary of Sir Humphrey Davy," even down to its spurious facts of publication and page references (*Discoveries*, p. 170).[10]

Interestingly, near the end of *Letters*, Brewster includes several pages of direct quotation from Davy recounting the effects on himself of laughing gas, taken experimentally on three separate occasions. Although Davy claims no ill effects from the gas, he does experience a euphoria which resembles intoxication and causes him to exclaim on one occasion, "'What an annoying concatenation of ideas!'" (p. 309) and on another, "'Nothing exists but thoughts; the universe is composed of impressions, ideas, pleasures, and pains!'" (p. 310). Perhaps these remarks prompted Poe to mock this respected scientist with a cryptic line: "The fact is, Sir Humphrey Davy was about the last man in the world to *commit himself* on scientific topics. Not only had he a more than ordinary dislike to quackery, but he was morbidly afraid of *appearing* empirical" (*M*3: 1359). Probably, Poe's sly references to Davy's "Diary" were directed at the passages in Brewster's *Letters* as the source of the apocryphal "Diary." In fact, Poe claims that the following line appears near the middle of page thirteen in Davy: "'In less than half a minute the respiration being continued, diminished gradually and *were* succeeded by analogous to gentle pressure on all the muscles'" (*M*3: 1359). A sentence from Brewster must be the source of Poe's garbled version: "'The first feelings were similar to those produced in the last experiment, but in less than half a minute, the respiration being continued, they diminished gradually, and were succeeded by a highly pleasurable thrilling, particularly in the chest and the extremities'" (pp. 308-309).

Despite sounding like a title Poe would invent, "Silliman's Journal" was a popular scientific publication—the *American Journal of Science and Arts*, edited by Benjamin Silliman. Immediately following his quotations from Davy, Brewster quotes Professor Silliman's account of two of his students who took nitrous oxide: one of "sanguine temperament" became so excited that he danced and shouted and "was thrown into a frightful fit of delirium" (p. 311); the other, who had been gloomy and depressed, experienced "'an astonishing invigoration of his whole system, and the most exquisite perceptions of delight,'" but also developed a taste for sugar or molasses on everything he ate as a result of this experiment (p. 312). It is not surprising that Poe took a satiric thrust at "Silliman's Journal" in "Von Kempelen."

Brewster's *Letters* may not only have given Poe these hints for humor in "Von Kempelen," but, in a discussion of alchemy, the suggestion for the tale itself. Brewster claims that at one time "gold and silver were actually produced by chemical processes from the rude ores of lead and copper" (p. 269). His further discussion may have provided Poe with the idea for alchemy as a criminal act which could be used for satire.

> When his [the alchemist's] calling was followed, as it soon was, by men prodigal of fortune and of character, science became an instrument of crime; secrets unattained were bartered for the gold of the credulous and the ignorant, and books innumerable were composed to teach these pretented [sic] secrets to the world. An intellectual reaction, however, soon took place; and those very princes who had sought to fill their exhausted treasuries at the furnace of the chemist, were the first to enact laws against the frauds which they had encouraged, and to dispel the illusions which had so long deceived their subjects.
>
> But even when the moral atmosphere of Europe was thus disinfected, chemistry supplied the magician with his most lucrative wonders, and those who could no longer delude the public with dreams of wealth and longevity, now sought to amuse and astonish them by the exhibition of their skill. (pp. 275-276)

Poe apparently considered "Von Kempelen" a "moral disinfectant" for gold fever: "The announcement of the discovery six months ago would have had material influence in regard to the settlement of California" (*M*3: 1364).

Clearly, Brewster provided Poe with sources for some of his most provocative works. He responded imaginatively to Brewster's charge: "If those who have not hitherto sought for instruction and amusement in the study of the material world, shall have found a portion of either in the preceding pages, they will not fail to extend their inquiries to other popular departments of science, even if they are less marked with the attributes of the marvellous" (p. 313). For Poe, Brewster's book was useful as a source of "instruction and amusement," not in studying the "material world" so much as in creating his fictional world.

NOTES

[1] *Letters on Natural Magic* (New York, 1832), p. 17.

[2] "'MS. Found in a Bottle' and Sir David Brewster's *Letters*: A Source," *PoeS*, 15(1982), 41-42.

[3] "Poe and the Chess Automaton," *AL*, 11(1939), 148-149.

[4] *Discoveries in Poe* (Notre Dame, 1970), p. 171.

[5] Constance Rourke, *American Humor: A Study of the National Character* (New York, 1931), p. 183.

[6] Templeton is right in that at least some of the details of Bedloe's vision refer to "actual events" (*M*3: 949). Warren Hastings was indeed administrator of Benares, but Mabbott says that the date of the insurrection should be 1781 (*M*3: 952, n20). Pollin says that Poe plagiarized from Macaulay in using the name *Bedloe* from an account of an uprising against Hastings and cites an interesting historical precedent for Bedloe in English history: "William Bedloe had confirmed the false testimony of Titus Oates in the false charges against the Catholics in 1678, in consequence of which thirty-five men were judicially murdered" (*Discoveries*, p. 26). The implication is that the name *Bedloe* connotes falsification.

[7] "The Hidden Journey of Arthur Gordon Pym," in *SAR* (1982), p. 30.

[8] Interestingly, the title, "Thou Art the Man," ties this tale even more closely to Sir David Brewster through Richard Adams Locke's *Moon Hoax*. This article, which was taken seriously for a time, describes a discussion between Sir John Hershell and Brewster

about a newly developed telescope: "'. . . the conversation became directed to that all-invincible enemy, the paucity of light in powerful magnifiers. After a few moments' silent thought, Sir John diffidently enquired whether it would not be possible to effect *a transfusion of artificial light through the focal object of vision*! Sir David, somewhat startled at the originality of the idea, paused awhile, and then hesitantly referred to the refrangibility of rays, and the angle of incidence. Sir John, grown more confident adduced the example of the Newtonian Reflector, in which the refrangibility was corrected by the second speculum, and the angle of incidence restored by the third. "And," continued he, "why cannot the illuminated microscope, say the hydro-oxygen, be applied to render distinct and if necessary, even to magnify the focal object?" Sir David sprung from his chair in an ecstasy of conviction, and leaping half-way to the ceiling, exclaimed 'Thou art the man!'" Quoted by Gibson Reaves, "The Great Moon Hoax of 1835," *The Griffith Observer*, 18(1954), 129; for a complete transcript of the *Moon Hoax*, see *Sky*, February, March, April 1937.

[9] Goodfellow's confession and the narrator's "solution" leave problems in addition to that of the circumstantial nature of the "evidence." The narrator's suspicions of Goodfellow are supposedly confirmed by the extraordinarily large bullet, having a flaw which matches a mold and a rifle belonging to Mr. Pennifeather. This bullet was found in the chest of Mr. Shuttleworthy's dead horse and allegedly passed completely through the horse only to have been replaced by the culprit. Earlier it caused the magistrate to indict Pennifeather. Later it caused the narrator to convict Mr. Goodfellow without benefit of trial and execute him by shock. Even though the unusually large bullet did fit Mr. Pennifeather's rifle, Mr. Goodfellow's confession mentions shooting the horse with a pistol, a weapon which surely would have been too small for the large bullet. Another problem with Charley's confession is his claim that he dragged the wounded horse to the pond, a doubtful feat for an old man.

[10] See *M3*: 1365, n2; 1366, n8.

POE'S *PYM*-ESQUE "A TALE OF THE RAGGED MOUNTAINS"

RICHARD KOPLEY

In his imaginary novel, *The Approach to al-Mu'tasim*, Jorge Luis Borges suggestively linked Poe's novel, *The Narrative of Arthur Gordon Pym*, and his short story, "A Tale of the Ragged Mountains." Borges's fictive fiction, which touches on "white-shrouded corpses," and ends with "a shining light" emanating from behind a curtain, begins with a young man becoming involved in a fierce battle in an Indian city.[1] This graceful synthesis of elements in the novel and the story invites a consideration of the actual relationship between the two works. Such a consideration may be encouraged by Poe's own possibly anticipative phrase in *Pym*, "absolute *mountains* of *ragged* ice" (*P*1: 164; emphasis added). Careful study reveals that *Pym* and "Ragged Mountains" significantly resemble one another in theme and form.

Elsewhere I present evidence involving corresponding ages, habits, and relationships, which suggests how Augustus Barnard in *Pym* represents Poe's brother Henry. The common date of death, August 1, which may well have prompted Augustus' name, further links him to Henry. Poe's reliance in *Pym* on Henry Poe's short story concerning two brothers, "Recollections," tends to confirm this connection. I also attempt to demonstrate that Poe in *Pym* expresses his guilt for having survived his brother and a longing to "lie close" to Henry, to be with him after death. In addition, I have highlighted critical textual details that suggest how the death of Augustus/Henry distantly echoes the death of Elizabeth Arnold Poe, and that Poe's longing for his dead brother serves, in part, to represent his longing for his dead mother. Poe comes close to associating Henry Poe explicitly with Elizabeth Arnold Poe in his 1829 letter to John Neal: "there can be no tie more strong than that of brother for brother—it is not so much that they love one another as that they both love the same parent . . ." (*O*1: 32). There is ample reason to believe that "the same parent" was Elizabeth Arnold Poe; evidently, for Edgar Allan Poe, his brother became a double of his mother. These family relationships are intimated in *Pym*. Textual and biographical evidence indicates that the mysterious "shrouded human figure," which the Poe-like Pym encounters at the novel's end, reflects the death of Augustus/Henry even as it implies the presence of the white-gowned Elizabeth Arnold Poe in the play *Tekeli*. The otherworldly apparition simultaneously refers to both brother and mother. According to this view, a highly-personal concealed theme of *Pym* is Poe's fervent wish for reunion with his much longed-for dead brother and dead mother.[2]

This theme is recapitulated in "Ragged Mountains," a work which Poe identified as "among his favorite compositions."[3] Augustus Bedloe and the deceased Oldeb are doubles; their similar appearances and comparable experiences attest to this, as do their singular names. Not only is the name "Bedlo, without the *e*" identical to "Oldeb conversed" (*M*3: 950), as the narrator points out, but "Bedloe, without the *e*" and "Oldeb" are virtual anagrams of the word "double."[4] Furthermore, the name Augustus Bedloe unmistakably suggests Augustus Barnard, and, thus, Henry Poe as well. The connection between Bedloe and Henry has been observed; Marie Bonaparte mentions it, stressing, in particular, the consumptive traits of the two.[5] Noteworthy, too, Poe's description of Bedloe as "singularly tall and thin" (*M*3: 940) corresponds with accounts of Henry Poe as "somewhat taller" than Edgar and "willowy."[6] Bedloe's telling of his remarkable experiences abroad—albeit hypnotically-induced experiences—also parallels Henry Poe's sharing with Edgar his varied foreign adventures.[7] Moreover, Bedloe's melancholy nature, his active imagination, and his morphine addiction need not be considered allusive to Edgar Poe, for these characteristics are evocative of Poe's brother Henry, too. It should be remembered that Poe is said to have described Henry as having "far more of the Poe nature" than he had himself.[8]

The connection between a Poe character and Poe's brother may again be reinforced by Poe's reliance upon Henry Poe's writing. Although, as T. O. Mabbott notes, the two major sources of "Ragged Mountains" are Charles Brockden Brown's novel *Edgar Huntly* and T. B. Macaulay's essay on Warren Hastings (*M*3: 936-38), another prior work possesses similarities with Poe's narrative: Henry Poe's "Letter to the Editor of The North American," entitled "Monte Video."[9] This work, like "Ragged Mountains" and the Macaulay source, concerns, in part, fighting which takes place in a foreign city. Again like "Ragged Mountains," but *unlike* the Macaulay source, Henry's piece presents the conflict from a first-person point of view—that of a young man, newly-arrived in the city. This young man in "Monte Video" takes note of "*parties* of the *contending* armies"; the young man in "Ragged Mountains" speaks of a "small *party* of men" which is involved in "the wildest tumult and *contention*" (*M*3: 946; emphasis added). Also in both "Monte Video" and "Ragged Mountains," this young man is later struck in the head—although in a different manner in each work. Moreover, "Monte Video," like Poe's tale, but unlike Macaulay's essay, features an impetuous young officer who takes part in the city's conflict. Furthermore, and significantly, Poe begins "Ragged Mountains" with the narrator's stating that he became acquainted with Augustus Bedloe "during the fall of the year 1827"

(*M* 3: 939). During the late summer and fall of the year 1827, interestingly enough, Edgar Poe renewed communication with his brother Henry, and during the fall of that year Henry's "Monte Video" first appeared.[10]

Just as Augustus Bedloe suggests Poe's brother Henry, so Bedloe's double, the deceased Oldeb, suggests Poe's mother, Elizabeth Arnold Poe. The name Oldeb, analogous to the names E. Ronald and Ariel and the cry "Tekeli-li!" in *Pym*, intimates this link.[11] Boyd Carter was the first to note that the name Oldeb was taken, like many other details in "Ragged Mountains," from *Edgar Huntly*. In particular, Poe's Oldeb derives from Brown's "Old Deb," the name of an Indian woman who "seemed to contract an affection" for young Edgar.[12] Probably, in reading *Edgar Huntly*, Poe would not have missed the possible association of maternal Old Deb and young Edgar with his own mother and himself; also, when Poe borrowed the name "Old Deb," slightly altered, he probably would not have altered its association.[13]

This view is strengthened by the presence in "Ragged Mountains" of "a water-colour drawing," "a miniature portrait" (*M* 3: 948), which Bedloe's physician, Doctor Templeton, owned, and which he produces as proof of Bedloe's resemblance to Oldeb. Templeton's picture, which seems to be a current likeness of Bedloe, is actually a 1780 depiction of Templeton's "dearest friend" (*M* 3: 949), the deceased Oldeb. Poe, too, owned a water-color drawing, a miniature portrait—a rendering of his much adored mother, Elizabeth Arnold Poe, who had inscribed it to him. To his death Poe treasured this gift.[14] We may reasonably infer that by his pointedly employing so personally meaningful an item as a "water-colour drawing," "a miniature portrait" in "Ragged Mountains," Poe was consciously referring to his lost mother.[15]

Augustus Bedloe's physician, Doctor Templeton, who knew both Bedloe and Oldeb, and who owned the miniature of Oldeb, would, in the context of this interpretation, represent Poe himself. Even as the death of Oldeb suggests the death of Elizabeth Arnold Poe, and the eventual death of Bedloe suggests the eventual death of Henry Poe, the involvement of Templeton in Bedloe's death suggests Edgar Poe's inordinate guilt for having survived his mother and brother. According to this reading, Templeton's longing for his "dearest friend," the deceased Oldeb, and his attachment to Oldeb's double, Bedloe, signifies Poe's longing for his dead mother and his remembered devotion to his sick brother, whom he associated with his mother, and who died a young man. Apparently, Poe's intense desire for reunion with his dead loved ones subtly permeates both *Pym* and "Ragged Mountains."[16]

In terms of form, as well as theme, *Pym* and "Ragged Mountains" significantly resemble one another. Novel and story are symmetrically organized around a richly meaningful midpoint. *Pym* is composed of two distinct halves. Poe seems to hint at this form by using such words and phrases as "half-breed" (*P*1: 55), "half certainty" (*P*1: 80), "half buried" (*P*1: 165), "half whine, half howl" (*P*1: 169), and "half swoon" (*P*1: 197); in fact, Poe uses the word "half," in various ways, over forty times in *Pym*. The two halves of *Pym* have been recognized; Charles O'Donnell argues that the first half comprises the *Ariel* and *Grampus* sections and that the second half comprises the *Jane Guy*, Tsalal, and canoe sections.[17] Although the end of the *Grampus* section actually appears to be part of the second half—each half of this twenty-five chapter novel is twelve-and-one-half chapters long— O'Donnell's view is otherwise a persuasive one.

Poe's novel is elaborately symmetrically patterned. The "Preface" and the closing "Note" frame Pym's *Ariel* adventure and Tsalalian canoe journey south, which, in turn, frame the *Grampus, Jane Guy*, and Tsalal sections. Furthermore, as O'Donnell has noted, the action of the *Ariel* adventure in the first chapter is repeated in the canoe journey of the last chapter (pp. 88-90). Poe may well have been alluding to this resemblance when he described Pym's canoe as "modelled with the bow and stern alike" (*P*1: 200). Elsewhere, presenting evidence that elaborates upon O'Donnell's view, I suggest that both the beginning and end of *Pym* involve Pym's confrontation with the ship the *Penguin*, whose penguin figurehead, possessing a penguin's "spirit of reflection" (*P*1: 153), serves, figuratively, as a mirror. Thus, the novel is balanced by mirrors facing one another at either end of the text.[18]

This symmetry in *Pym* is discreetly reinforced by a finely-wrought pattern of words and phrases. Early in the first half of the novel, Pym states that "a fierce wind and strong ebb tide *were hurrying* us *to* destruction" (*P*1: 60; emphasis added here and in the following quotations), "I found that there yet remained to us a chance *of ultimate escape*" (*P*1: 60), and ". . . a loud and long *scream or yell* . . . seemed to pervade the whole atmosphere" (*P*1: 60). Pym also refers to the sailors' exaggerated stories of "having run down a vessel at sea and *drowned some thirty or forty poor devils*" (*P*1: 64), and he admits to romantic visions "*of death or captivity among barbarian hordes*; *of a lifetime dragged out in sorrow and tears*" (*P*1: 65).

This language is reversed late in the second half of the novel, when Pym admits to his fear "*of being put to death by the savages, or of dragging out a miserable existence in captivity among them*" (*P*1: 185). He observes that the *Jane Guy*'s guns "*killed, perhaps, thirty or forty of the savages*" (*P*1: 187). He also states that the injured natives were "*screaming and yelling for aid*" (*P*1: 187), "the faintest possible idea *of ultimate escape* wandered, like a shadow, through my mind . . ." (*P*1: 198), and "it was evident that we *were* still *hurrying* on *to* the southward" (*P*1: 204). This remarkable reversed repetition of language seems to have been covertly acknowledged by Poe; he writes, in the persona of Pym, that when Wilson Allen was found to be missing, ". . . we [Dirk Peters and Pym] determined at once to retrace our steps . . ." (*P*1: 183). This acknowledgment is reinforced by other appearances of the word "retrace" or its variants in Poe's novel (*P*1: 76, 95, 96, 154, 183, 191).

Like *Pym*, "Ragged Mountains" is composed of two distinct halves. Poe again seems to call attention to this structuring, using such words and phrases as "half explanatory, half apologetic" (*M*3: 940), "half-naked" (*M*3: 943), and "half Indian, half European" (*M*3: 946). The first half, seventeen paragraphs, comprises the narrator's introduction and the beginning of Bedloe's account of his illusory Indian adventure; the second half, also seventeen paragraphs, comprises the continuation of Bedloe's account, Templeton's explanation of it, and the narrator's quoting of, and commenting on, Bedloe's obituary notice.

Again like *Pym*, Poe's tale is elaborately symmetrically patterned. The narrator's comments at the beginning and end frame Bedloe's telling of his ordinary experiences, such as his leaving and returning home, which, in turn, frame Bedloe's telling of his extraordinary experiences, such as his apparent fighting and dying in the sacred city of Benares. As in *Pym*, such evident symmetry is subtly strengthened by Poe's meticulous language. Key words and phrases in the first seventeen paragraphs of "Ragged Mountains" reappear in reverse order in the second seventeen paragraphs of the story. For example, the early mention of Bedloe's "bloodless" complexion (*M*3: 940) and his "neuralgic attacks" (*M*3: 940) echoes in the later citation of Bedloe's obituary notice, which refers to his "neuralgia" and his fatal "topical bleeding" (*M*3: 949-950). Such mirroring of language is developed further in Bedloe's story.

In the first half of "Ragged Mountains," Bedloe says, "*I bent my steps immediately to the mountains*" (*M*3: 942; emphasis added here and in the following quotations), "*the sun could not be seen*" (*M*3: 943), "I now arose hurriedly, and *in* a state of *fearful agitation*" (*M*3: 944), and "*amid the crowd* . . . there roamed a countless multitude of holy filleted bulls . . ." (*M*3: 945). Doctor Templeton soon interrupts, saying, "*You arose and descended into the city*" (*M*3: 946). In the second half, Bedloe says, "*I arose*, as you say, *and descended into the city*" (*M*3: 946), "I shrank from *amid them* [the crowd]" (*M*3: 946), "I perceived a vast crowd, *in furious agitation*" (*M*3: 947), "we were borne" near "houses, into the recesses of which *the sun had never been able to shine*" (*M*3: 947), and "*I* became my original self, and *bent my steps eagerly homewards* . . ." (*M*3: 948). This arresting reversed repetition of language also seems to have been acknowledged by Poe; he writes that the "dead" Bedloe sensed his spirit leave the city of Benares, "retracing the circuitous path by which I had entered it" (*M*3: 948). Likewise, in the novel and in the tale, Poe carefully retraces the path of his language in the first half by means of his language in the second half.

The form of *Pym* and that of "Ragged Mountains" attest Poe's faith in "the power of symmetry." Although such faith may naturally have been suggested by the double motif itself, it may also have been animated by a larger faith in an aesthetic and religious code—that of the Providence Tradition. Literature fashioned in the Providence Tradition has been defined by Douglas Brooks as "writings concerned with pointing to God's manifest intervention in human affairs." Furthermore, Brooks states that the form of a work written in the Providence Tradition is often characterized by "symmetrical structural patterning" which frames a symbolic midpoint.[19]

Pym, a book whose narrator speaks with reverence of "the special interference of Providence" (*P*1: 62),[20] features not only the "symmetrical structural patterning," as already discussed, but also the symbolic midpoint. In the middle of the novel's central Chapter 13, Poe writes, as Pym:

> *August* 1. A continuance of the same calm weather, with an oppressively hot sun . . . . We now saw clearly that Augustus could not be saved; that he was evidently dying. We could do nothing to relieve his sufferings, which appeared to be great. About twelve o'clock he expired in strong convulsions, and without having spoken for several hours. (*P*1: 142)

Here, Poe writes autobiographically; the death of Augustus on August 1 signifies the death of Poe's brother on August 1.[21] But Poe is also writing providentially. The sun which is present as Augustus/Henry dies at midday at the midpoint of the novel signifies, according to convention, "the Sun of Righteousness" (Malachi 4:2), which represents, as Douglas Brooks writes, "Christ come in judgment" (p. 13; see also pp. 21, 37-38). The sun, earlier referred to as "the blessed sun" (*P*1: 117), is "oppressively hot," thus calling to mind the intensity of Christ's judgment.[22] The figurative presence of "Christ come in judgment" at the center of *Pym*, even as Augustus/Henry dies, suggests inevitably the possibility of resurrection, of eventual reunion with dead loved ones, thus reinforcing the thematic concern of Poe's work.

"Ragged Mountains" also has the "symmetrical structural patterning," as already described, and the symbolic midpoint, too. When Bedloe doubts that his experience in the Ragged Mountains was a dream, the following conversation takes place at the midpoint of the story: "'In this I am not sure that you are wrong,' observed Dr. Templeton, 'but proceed. *You arose and descended into the city.*' '*I arose*,' continued Bedloe, regarding the Doctor with an air of profound astonishment, '*I arose*, as you say, *and descended into the city*'" (*M*3: 946; emphasis added). The critical repeated line at the center of the story, "You (or I) arose and descended into the city," echoes two related biblical passages.

A biblical phrase in the first half of "Ragged Mountains" tends to direct attention to one particular corresponding biblical passage. Telling of his amazement at hearing a drum in the Ragged Mountains, Bedloe says, "I could not have been more surprised at the sound of *the trump of the Archangel*" (*M*3: 943; emphasis added). The final words, whose source is 1 Thessalonians 4:16, unobtrusively point to a specific biblical passage concerning rise and descent: "For if we believe that *Jesus* died and *rose* again, even so them also which sleep in Jesus will God bring with him . . . . For *the Lord himself shall descend* from heaven with a shout, with the voice *of the archangel*, and with *the trump* of God: and the dead in Christ shall rise first . . ." (1 Thess. 4:14, 16; emphasis added). The theme of the resurrection of the dead in Christ evident in this passage concerning Christ's resurrection and second coming is reinforced by a second biblical passage on Christ's resurrection, one which had been referred to in the conclusion of Poe's early work, "A Dream" (*M*2: 9),[23] and which here seems to be alluded to in the central repeated lines concerning rising and descending into the sacred city of Benares: "And the graves were opened; and *many bodies of the saints* which slept *arose*, And came out of the graves after his resurrection, *and went into the holy city* . . ." (Matt. 27:52-53; emphasis added). The framed symbolic midpoint of "Ragged Mountains" resonates with both these biblical passages concerning the resurrection of the dead, passages which dramatically help to affirm the thematic concern of the story—Poe's powerful desire for reunion with his much beloved dead mother and dead brother.

Pym and "Ragged Mountains," each of which possesses an elaborate "symmetrical structural patterning" and a symbolic midpoint, are skillfully crafted in the Providence Tradition. Formally, then, as well as thematically, Poe's tale significantly resembles his novel. The formal affinity demonstrated here and the thematic affinity it reinforces may help to place generic distinctions in Poe in proper perspective. For, although *Pym* is a sea novel, and "Ragged Mountains" an Oriental tale, these narratives seem profoundly one in their expression of Poe's deep longing to recover, perhaps providentially, the cherished family he had so sorrowfully lost. In the case of these two works, even as Poe respected the requirements of the genres in which he wrote, he employed these genres as vehicles for mourning and for consecration.[24]

NOTES

[1] *The Aleph and Other Stories 1933-1969* (New York, 1970), pp. 45-52. I am indebted to Kent Ljungquist and Benjamin Franklin Fisher IV for helpful comments on early drafts of this essay. Another Borges story, "The South," has been linked with Poe's "Ragged Mountains": Reinhard H. Friederich, "Necessary Inadequacies: Poe's 'A Tale of the Ragged Mountains' and Borges' 'South'," *JNT*, 12(1982), 155-166. *Pym* is cited from *Collected Writings of Edgar Alllan Poe*, ed. Burton R. Pollin (Boston, 1981), and abbreviated as *P* parenthetically throughout my text.

[2] Richard Kopley, "The Hidden Journey of *Arthur Gordon Pym*," *SAR* (1982), pp. 30-37, 40-44.

[3] Sarah Helen Whitman, Letter to John H. Ingram, 19 February 1874, *Poe's Helen Remembers*, ed. John Carl Miller (Charlottesville, 1979), p. 32. "Ragged Mountains" first appeared in *Godey's,* April 1844, and reappeared, lightly edited, in the *Broadway Journal*, November 1845 (*M*3: 938-939).

[4] Significantly, this double motif is strengthened by Poe's use of implied reflection and shadow (*M*3: 944).

[5] *The Life and Works of Edgar Allan Poe* (London, 1949), pp. 559, 566. Although Bonaparte is convincing when she observes the connection between Bedloe and Henry, she is unpersuasive when she argues that Bedloe also represents Edgar Poe and his mother, that Oldeb represents Henry, too, and that Doctor Templeton symbolizes an evil father figure, presumably John Allan (pp. 566-568).

[6] Hervey Allen and Thomas Ollive Mabbott, *Poe's Brother* (New York, 1926), pp. 24, 28.

[7] In *Poe's Brother* Allen and Mabbott maintain that Henry Poe's foreign adventures were "appropriated and perhaps enlarged upon by his younger brother" (p. 25). Clearly, Edgar Poe would have known of these adventures from Henry's writings; also, he would likely have learned of them during "hours of intimate talk" with Henry (p. 36), especially when they lived together in Baltimore in 1829 and 1831 (pp. 33-35). Allen elsewhere describes Edgar's listening to his brother tell of his adventures: *Israfel* (New York, 1926), 1: 253.

[8]Henry Poe's writing reveals that Henry was "undoubtedly melancholic" (*Poe's Brother*, p. xiv; see also pp. 23, 82) and that he had "a vivid imagination" (p. 26). Henry's addiction was to liquor; in *Poe's Brother* Allen and Mabbott state that Henry "early developed a fondness for drink" (p. 26), and they later cite a passage from Edgar Poe's 10 August 1829 letter to John Allan, which includes the remark, "'Henry entirely given over to drink'" (p. 34). For Poe's telling description of Henry, see *John Henry Ingram's Poe Collection at the University of Virginia*, ed. John Carl Miller (Charlottesville, 1960), p. 90.

[9]Henry Poe, "Monte Video," *Poe's Brother*, pp. 44-46. Other sources for "Ragged Mountains" have been suggested by Mukhtar Ali Isani, "Some Sources for Poe's 'Tale of the Ragged Mountains'," *PoeS*, 5(1972), 38-40.

[10]For the relevant passage of Macaulay, see *Edinburgh Review*, 74(1841), 213. For the date of Poe's renewed communication with his brother and that of the publication of Henry's tale, see *Poe's Brother*, pp. 31, 91. Although the narrator's remark briefly links him with Edgar Poe, evidence to be presented here suggests that another character in this tale represents the author.

[11]The names E. Ronald and Ariel and the cry "Tekeli-li!" in *Pym* intimate a link to Poe's mother in diverse ways. E. Ronald is an anagram for E. Arnold, Ariel is the part Elizabeth Arnold Poe played in *The Tempest*, and "Tekeli-li!" is a reference to another play, Theodore Edward Hook's *Tekeli*, in which Elizabeth Arnold Poe also performed. Cf. Kopley, "Hidden Journey," 43-44.

[12]"Poe's Debt to Charles Brockden Brown," *Prairie Schooner*, 27(1953), 193. For the relevant passages by Brown, see *Edgar Huntly or Memoirs of a Sleep-walker*, ed. Sydney J. Krause and S. W. Reid (Kent, 1984), pp. 206-209. Several scholars have offered alternative views to that presented by Carter. G. R. Thompson acknowledges that Poe's Oldeb parallels Brown's Old Deb, but he considers this parallel to be comic: "Is Poe's 'A Tale of the Ragged Mountains' A Hoax?" *SSF*, 6(1969), 458-460. Burton Pollin contends that the name Bedloe derives from the reference to "Bedloes" in Macaulay's essay on Warren Hastings: *Discoveries in Poe* (Notre Dame, 1970), p. 26.

[13]The link between Old Deb and Elizabeth Arnold Poe would likely have seemed particularly strong to Poe upon consideration of Old Deb's fairy nickname, Queen Mab (Brown, pp. 206, 209), since Mrs. Poe had played the role of the fairy spirit Ariel in *The Tempest*, as mentioned above. Furthermore, the appeal of the name Old Deb to Poe because of its maternal connection would probably have been significantly augmented by the susceptibility of its slightly modified version, Oldeb, to palindrome (Bedlo) and near-anagram (double).

[14] Susan Archer Weiss writes of Elizabeth Arnold Poe giving her son Edgar an inscribed miniature of herself: *The Home Life of Poe* (New York, 1907), p. 6. Marie Louise Shew Houghton states that Poe had his miniature of his mother with him when he died—in letters to John H. Ingram, *Building Poe Biography*, ed. John Carl Miller (Baton Rouge, 1977), pp. 99, 136.

[15] For Poe's particular use of the word "miniature" in "Ragged Mountains," there is no evidence to suggest that he borrowed from any other work; accordingly, the word's autobiographical significance heightens. Granted, for his use of the word "miniature" in "The Spectacles" (*M*3: 903, 909, 912), the only other Poe tale in which that word occurs (Burton Pollin, *Word Index to Poe's Fiction* [New York, 1982], p. 217), Poe did borrow from an anonymous tale titled "The Mysterious Portrait." Consistent with this reading, however, both the tale from which Poe borrowed and his own reworking of that tale prominently feature a maternal—if comic—association with the word "miniature." See "The Mysterious Portrait," *the New Monthly Belle Assemblée* (1836), 76-84; and "The Spectacles" (*M*3: 886-916). Cf. Pollin, "'The Spectacles' of Poe—Sources and Significance," *AL*, 37(1965), 185-190 and *M*3: 883.

[16] In this context, it should be added that consumptive Lady Mary of "Metzengerstein" (*M*2: 20n) has been persuasively linked with Henry Poe and Elizabeth Arnold Poe, both of whose deaths involved consumption, too (Allen 1: 22, 320). Cf. William Bittner, *Poe: A Biography* (Boston, 1962), p. 86; Bonaparte, pp. 274-275. To the degree that Baron Frederick's mother may be related to Poe's mother, one may develop further the correspondence of Templeton, Oldeb, and Bedloe with Edgar Poe, Elizabeth Arnold Poe, and Henry Poe. Because Edgar Poe may well have been writing "Metzengerstein" while he nursed his dying brother in the summer of 1831 (Allen 1: 325-326; cf. *M*1: 543, 2: 17), one may reasonably conjecture that Templeton's writing of Oldeb's death even as Bedloe seemed to die (*M*3: 947-949) is comparable with Edgar Poe's writing of Lady Mary's death even as Henry Poe died. A different opinion, which suggests significance in Poe's revisions, appears in Professor Fisher's "Poe's Metzengerstein': Not a Hoax," *AL*, 42(1971), 487-494.

[17] Charles O'Donnell, "From Earth to Ether: Poe's Flight Into Space," *PMLA*, 77(1962), 89. For affirmation and development of O'Donnell's view, see David Ketterer, *The Rationale of Deception in Poe* (Baton Rouge, 1979), pp. 139-141.

[18] "The Secret of *Arthur Gordon Pym*: The Text and the Source," *SAF*, 8(1980), 203-218; "The Hidden Journey," 29-30.

[19] *Number and Pattern in the Eighteenth-Century Novel* (London, 1973), pp. 18-21.

[20] Providence as a critical theme in *Pym* is discussed by Curtis Fukuchi in "Poe's Providential *Narrative of Arthur Gordon Pym*," *ESQ*, 27(1981), 147-156.

[21] The death of Augustus/Henry at the center of *Pym* is infinitely reflected in the mirrors facing one another at either end of the novel. Thus Poe has brilliantly fashioned an image for what he elsewhere terms *"Mournful and Never-ending Remembrance"* (*H*14: 208). Cf. Kopley, "Hidden Journey," 30-35.

[22] An early example of the characteristically intense Sun of Righteousness is cited by Erwin Panofsky, *Meaning in the Visual Arts* (Garden City, 1955), p. 262:

> Further I say of this Sun that He shall be inflamed when exercising supreme power, that is to say, when He sits in judgment, when he shall be strict and severe... because He shall be all hot and bloody by dint of justice and strictness. For, as the sun, when in the center of his orbit, that is to say, at the midday point, is hottest, so shall Christ be when He shall appear in the center of heaven and earth, that is to say, in Judgment....

See also Alastair Fowler, *Triumphal Forms* (Cambridge, 1970), p. 36.

[23] The validity of Killis Campbell and T. O. Mabbott's attribution of "A Dream" to Poe is discussed in my review of Pollin's *Word Index to Poe's Fiction*, *PoeS*, 15(1982), 24-26; and Professor Fisher's review: *JEGP*, 84(1985), 154.

[24] A final point, a conjecture regarding a possible additional biblical motif in "Ragged Mountains," may be warranted here. Bedloe's imagined death in the holy city of Benares from "a poisoned barb" in his "right temple" (*M*3: 947) may suggest the destruction of the Temple in Jerusalem by God's wrath, represented in the Book of Job as the poisoned "arrows of the Almighty" (Job 6:4). Bedloe's actual death from "one of the venomous vermicular sangsues" applied to his "right temple" by Doctor Templeton (*M*3: 950) would, accordingly, recapitulate the destruction of the Temple in Jerusalem. If this reading is valid, then perhaps the theme of resurrection in "Ragged Mountains" relates not only to Poe's mother and brother, but also to the Temple in Jerusalem itself. A link between this reading of "Ragged Mountains" and *Pym* is plausible—see my essay, "The 'Very Profound Under-current' of *Arthur Gordon Pym*," *SAR* (1987), pp. 143-175.

"ELEONORA": POE AND MADNESS

BENJAMIN FRANKLIN FISHER IV

The topic of madness and Edgar Allan Poe places him rather more within than without mainstreams in nineteenth-century cultural contexts. Some biographers opine that he was bad, mad, and altogether sad. These traditions originated in the author's own hints, furthered by his contemporaries. Henry B. Hirst's mild portrait of weird Poe was made lurid via the Griswold alembic. Poe's supposed personal insanity, direct and sans varnishing, was lampooned by Thomas Dunn English: "[Poe] can do nothing in the common way . . . If we ever caught him doing a thing like anybody else, or found him reading a book any other way than upside down, we would implore his friends to send for a straight jacket, and a Bedlam doctor. He were mad, then, to a certainty."[1] Takeoffs upon Poe the crazed drunkard, debaucher, and dabbler in literary matters have mushroomed over many years. Of course, from my own memories of a graduate school professor's observations that madness dogged certain eighteenth-century British writers, such as Swift, Cowper, Blake, and Chatterton—and, moreover, that it infused their writings with whatever value they possessed—and from our more general recollections of Michel Foucault's theory that during the eighteenth and nineteenth centuries the lazar house was supplanted by the madhouse for purposes of conveying an aura of haunted places, we need not wonder that Poe's own attentiveness to madness was repeatedly stimulated.[2]

We should remember, however, while keeping an eye on such potentially exciting backgrounds, that Poe knew much about scientific exploration of deranged mental states—particularly as they came to him via the medical information disseminated by the renowned Philadelphia doctor, Benjamin Rush.[3] An unmistakable preoccupation with diseased minds pervades Poe's works, and that interest must also influence his readers, if we are to judge, say, by the appearance of "The Tell-Tale Heart," "The Black Cat," "The Masque of the Red Death," "The Raven"—plus a host of other pieces in which distorted or disintegrating psyches tend to surface, whatever additional implications may be at work—as perennial anthology favorites. Tales of, and by, crazed characters were, of course, commonplace in Poe's time.

Poe's more than cursory interest in insanity is evident as well in his critical pronouncements, for example in reviews of Robert Montgomery Bird's *Sheppard Lee* and William Gilmore Simms's *The Partisan* (H9: 126-139; 8: 143-157). Poe levels strictures at Simms's revolting details in describing maniac Frampton's murdering a victim by drowning. Poe's own perception that madness and creative artistry draw near in many cases and his dictum (set forth in "How to Write a Blackwood Article") that "sensations are the great things after all," are consistent—because they emphasize the intangible and the emotional—with his denigration of Simms's horrifics.

I wish to concentrate on "Eleonora," a tale in which madness tantalizes us. We find few extended critiques of this piece, although in its own day it gained attention from piratical editors (*M2*: 638). Resemblances to Saint-Pierre's *Paul et Virginie*, to Walter Scott's *The Betrothed* and to Coleridge's "Kubla Khan" have been cited, as has a likeness to Platonic allegory of the twin Venuses.[4] Not long ago, I. M. Walker was content to observe that it is a "morbidly sentimental" tale (p. 29). Critics have usually centered on the romantic elements in "Eleonora," giving credence to themes of passionate love, albeit with a slant toward the triumph of the spiritual over the fleshly. I would add that the general drift in the tale resembles what we find in one of Shakespeare's comedies. The common theme is that when passionate, sexual relationships (or at least the desire for sexual consummation is strong) lead from fantasies into marriage and its tempering responsibilities, a couple has moved toward genuine, fully developed love. Benton reasonably points out that Ermengarde, the earthly Venus (representing married love) balances the high-flown, unrestrained feelings engendered in the narrator by his love for Eleonora, the heavenly Venus.

"Eleonora" was at the printer of *The Gift* for 1842 (where it first appeared, in late February 1841), so Poe had probably completed it at about the close of 1840. The date might in part place this tale as one more counter to charges of "Germanism" that had piqued him sufficiently to prompt his rejoinder in the "Preface" to *Tales of the Grotesque and Arabesque*, published late in 1839. (For "German," we of a later generation substitute "supernatural" or "Gothic.") Poe's earlier love tales, in which violence and supernaturalism seemed to contribute substantially to tragic outcomes, are reversed in "Eleonora." This tale does more than conclude with the death of a formidable woman that in its turn leaves the lover (who is also the narrator) emotionally overwhelmed. Any terror and passion here are, to be sure, not simple "German" sleaziness. Poe, moreover, possibly enjoyed some fun in publishing "Eleonora." Perhaps it out-romanticizes the romantic fiction of his times, but that feature in no way prevents it from simultaneously yielding soberer import. Poe's notions of literary fun, as we know, were seldom without a serious tinge. He himself reviewed *The Gift* in which "Eleonora" first came out [*Graham's*, 19(November 1841), 249], commenting that the ending was imperfect and that in general he deemed it "a good subject spoiled by hurry in the handling." Therefore my critique must encompass matters related to his revisions. "Eleonora" reappeared, revised, in the *Broadway Journal*, 24 May 1845, and the differences between this and *The Gift* version repay a consideration. Those changes bear out Poe's habit of heightening intangibility within a literary work to enrich emotional or psychological texture. Consistently, he tends to minimize or to eliminate the characters' physical features. These methods, in the end, modify ordinary cardboard Gothic figures and their melodramatic actions and dialogue into more sophisticated art.

I

One of Poe's customary unnamed "I" narrators opens "Eleonora" with information concerning himself, which also offers a spirited, if equivocating, defense of madness, and which hints, probably in irony, that he himself is mad. We might suppose that Poe had been reading Charles Lamb, who could never divorce himself from the insanity in his family, when he came to creating a storyteller for "Eleonora." To his friend Coleridge, Lamb had written a long letter, in June 1796, relating how lunacy had overtaken him, without wholly negative effects: "For while it lasted I had many happy hours of pure happiness. Dream not . . . of having tasted all the grandeur & wildness of **Fancy**, till you have **gone mad**. All now seems to me vapid; comparatively so . . . ." Poe, perhaps, encountered this letter in the Talfourd edition of Lamb's correspondence (1837).[5] Direct influence or no—and Poe knew Lamb's works—such sentiments echo in the words of Poe's character: "Men have called me mad; but the question is not yet settled, whether madness is or is not the loftiest intelligence—whether much that is glorious—whether all that is profound—does not spring from disease of thought—from *moods* of mind exalted at the expense of the general intellect. They who dream by day are cognizant of many things which escape those who dream only by night" (*M*2: 638). The second paragraph begins with the narrator's establishing latitude that enables us to entertain multiple perspectives in interpreting his tale: "We will say, then, that I am mad." Thus he can be held to no strict account for introducing fantastic elements.

In dreamlike manner, and in dense, incantatory prose, he recalls his youthful, innocent, love affair with his cousin Eleonora amidst natural, unrestrained surroundings (which led to their sexual initiation); the circumstances involved with her decline toward death and his vow never to marry "any daughter of Earth"; Eleonora's decease; his eventual infatuation and marriage with Ermengarde; and Eleonora's blessing of their union. Although this chronicle of the passionate young couple's maturing in the fantastic Valley of the Many-Colored Grass and the narrator's later remove into urban environs may indeed seem like so much lunatic gush because of lyrical tone and lush description, a more significant drift seems to underlie "Eleonora." Poe weights the fiction with symbolic suggestion to achieve that "undercurrent of meaning" he championed in his critical pronouncements (and embodied in his imaginative work). The ambiguities enveloping madness in the tale have elicited divergent readings by Richard Wilbur and Joan Dayan. Wilbur sees the narrator as a visionary, one who produces a poetic effect throughout the tale akin to what Poe elsewhere would term the "rhythmical creation of Beauty." We should, thinks Wilbur, respond to "Eleonora" as a work in which we identify with the narrator (who is no mere madman) in a quest after supernal beauty. Dayan, conversely, detects in "Eleonora" a skepticism toward ideas of transcendence into realms of spirit. In the conclusion, the narrator makes us intensely crave matter in any of several meanings of that word.[6] What I provide below is intended as a supplement to their readings. Actual madness in the narrator is not the issue as much as portraiture of a mind extremely sensitive to universal human experiences—a repeated feature in Poe's writings.

In revising "Eleonora" Poe removed the subtitle, "A Fable," possibly calculating on diminishing whatever unrealities or implausibilities such phrasing could imply (and he had previously used that same subtitle for his prose tale "Silence"). Adding a motto in 1845—"Sub conservatione formae specificae salva anima (Under the protection of a specific form, my soul is safe)"—from Raymond Lull, or Lully, Poe centralizes the fine line dividing concrete from abstract. That unstable border permeates "Eleonora." In like fashion, he revised an earlier tale, "The Assignation," so that what might have initially appealed to readers intent on seduction themes now stands as a subtle rendering of the life-art dualism, intensified in symbolism of sexual creativity being mingled with artistic endeavor.[7] The "specific form" in the later tale, which in form and theme seems almost a reworking of "The Assignation," signifies Eleonora herself, and here Poe embodies a deft bit of artistry. The heroine's name derives from Helen (as do others among Poe's gallery of female characters), which means "light." Presumably the narrator-lover—that dreamer by day as well as by night— enters the "Vast ocean of the 'light ineffable'," which is her love, in all its ramifications. Just as important, implicitly, *The Gift* text began: "I am come of a race noted for vigor of fancy and ardor of passion. Pyrros is my name." The second sentence was probably expunged on two grounds. First, Pyrros derives from the Greek words "fire" and "ardent." Maybe a too obvious lighting of his sexual fire is deliberately muted, and we are thus directed to witness the protagonist's ardor elsewise. Second, such a name might bring to mind Pyrrho of Ellis (c. 300 B.C.), whose name became synonymous with universal doubt and unalterable skepticism (*M*2: 645). Surely Poe's protagonist was not intended to evince absolute qualities from either of these choices. Instead of being a nihilist, he becomes an everyman type— one whose experiences make him compelling because of a beguiling ambiguity established via his unspecified identity. The name in the original, however, may have hinted that readers should proceed with decided skepticism through the tale. Richard P. Benton alerts us to ironies pervading this seemingly lush decorative prose. One feels the force of his theory when the narrator remarks: "We will say, then, that I am mad," adding that his psyche contains two "distinct conditions"(*M*2: 638). What an adroit escape clause! A like awareness of audience may occasion changes in the narrator's speech about readers' playing the Sphinx or Oedipus in order to accept part two of the tale. Fear of doubting his words ("dare not"), which would entail acting the Sphinx, or long-time destroyer of humankind, transforms into certainty of not doubting ("cannot") as the hearers assume the role of Oedipus, destroyer of the Sphinx and her savagery.

This lover-narrator, we must also remember, resembles the protagonist in another of Poe's love tales, "Ligeia." Their descent from characters in the works of Ossian and Byron (*M*2: 635) bequeaths them poses of the readily acquired jadedness of youth, insofar as worldly experiences go, along with what appears like the muddle-headedness of senile age. Therefore, crystal-clear recollections of the far-away past merge with an incapacity to respond comprehendingly to recent events. The repetitions throughout "Eleonora" could also mime wandering speech coupled with faulty memory. Several textual changes reinforce my hypothesis. What first read as "And the margin of the river" is abbreviated to "The margin of the river," thus eliminating a run-on construction that might emanate from aged garrulity. The word will not be put out of mind, though; another change, from "brinks" to "margins," maintains repetitiveness as it eliminates imperfect diction. Eleonora's revelation of concerns about her lover's destiny after she dies gains no particular strength from occurring on "one still evening," and Poe, rightly, deleted "still" (*M*2: 639, 642). Insertion of one word alone can intensify meaning, however, instead of suggesting rambling discourse. Commenting how their first sexual experience had left them speechless, the lover in 1842 spoke thus: "We spoke no words during the rest of that sweet day; and our words upon the morrow were tremulous and few" (*M*2: 640). Turning the phrase into "even upon the morrow," Poe impresses us with the impact of the young couple's feelings. Thus, in these workbench tactics, we witness a conscious author taking away here, adding there, as occasion warrants, to produce the best in literary art. As advances beyond his experiments, in the Folio-Club tales, with narrators who speak and act as they do from promptings of drunkenness or extreme gluttony, such storytellers as those in "Ligeia" and "Eleonora" hesitate, doubt, halt, qualify, and restate in their expression—and thus they felicitously mate sound with sense.

The "Eleonora" narrator debates the perimeters of madness and dreaming, concluding that madness constitutes the "loftiest intelligence," which in the original had been a less forcible "loftier." Such occupation with mental planes is strengthened in Poe's recasting a phrase, "the dreamers by night," into "those who dream only by night," thereby instilling dramatic vitality into what we would otherwise read as trite phrasing. Several more revisions reinforce the narrator's fair scope as mental geographer. The Valley of Many-Colored Grass originally "lay singularly far away" from normal habitation. Locating it just "far away"—and thus eliminating one of Poe's favorite words—replaces inessential foreboding with improved diction. Another telling alteration occurs when we read that instead of "a vague shadow" gathering over the lover's brain after Eleonora's death, the "vague" departs and with it go wordiness and redundancy that in so short a tale take away from the narrator's character because of faulty diction—surely not his mode of expression. When, after the shock of Eleonora's death, he comes round in "a strange Eastern city," we find a cliché of literary-annual Orientalism. Revising it as "a strange city," Poe shifts from gift-book toward interior landscape, the primary setting here. Likewise in "Silence—A Fable," he condensed "old tomb at Balbec" into the nonspecific "tomb" ($M2$: 199). The emphasis in both tales goes to psychological effects rather than to geographic places. So strange a city as the one where Eleonora's lover "finds himself" (i. e., matures), appropriately contains "pomps and pageantries of a stately court, and the mad clangor of arms, and the radiant loveliness of woman," which "bewildered and intoxicated my brain." Because of the shock he sustains in consequence of Eleonora's death, his lack of coherence is understandable, and thus such imprecise locale functions more plausibly than any designated spot could. Unlike his contemporary, Tennyson, who generally used character as a vehicle for projecting imagined topography, Poe seems to make description illuminate character in "Eleonora." Like Swinburne, rather, he subsumes sharp details to create heightened moods.[8]

In keeping with these deliberate attempts to maintain in "Eleonora" a genuine mental texture, as opposed to another Gothic outpouring for entertainment's sake alone, Poe pruned two heavy-handed references to the narrator's emotions, thereby making the character's ambiguous craziness less of a vehicle for cheap thrills and more of a means for probing depths in a complex psyche. Left alone upon Eleonora's death, the narrator had "longed—I madly pined for the love which had before filled it [his heart] to overflowing." Removing "I madly pined" obliterates an ungainly give-away (and triteness) while strengthening the speaker's credibility. The 1842 description of the narrator's meeting with Ermengarde involves his "madness, and the glow, and the fervour, and the spirit-stirring ecstasy of adoration"—just the sort of high-flown and overdone verbiage that too often marred Gothic fiction. In the 1845 version, the lover experiences "the fervor, and the delirium, and the spirit-lifting ecstasy of adoration," and we also read what register as understandable, if nonrational, feelings. He thus attains greater spirituality. His comment that, in recounting the second part of his story, "I mistrust the perfect sanity of the record," aligns with these emotions because he may or may not allude to actual madness. That he would be prostrated by Eleonora's death and therefore unreliable in his reportage, we would not question. His feelings of loss and isolation are heightened in another textual change—dropping the specific reference to Eleonora's mother living with him in the valley. Such a change makes us think of him concentrating on his grief, a grief that would perforce make him feel as if nobody else had ever experienced such loss and lonesomeness as his own. We are given dramatic renditions of what might be lunacy, but what with equal force may be universal sentiments connected with stunning bereavement. Emotion at a high, but not therefore absolutely mad, pitch is brought forward. This theme is carried into the second part of the narrative. For what he describes as "the passion I had once felt" for Eleonora, we read, as the final recasting, "my passion." The lover's feeling is not supposed to evince such limits as the 1842 text may impose.

Excising two lengthy passages that describe the physical appearances of Eleonora and Ermengarde—as rather similar versions of the same luscious, auburn-haired charmer—Poe deepens psychological dimension. Thus he removes "Eleonora" from the often near-pornographic entertainment of many other Gothics in his era (and our own). He presents us, finally, with no Liliths or other femmes fatales, whose reddish hair might too readily single them out as creatures of Satan. What he substitutes for visual enticement is a pair of symbolic women as centers of the narrator's affections.

II

Poe's changes in "Eleonora" show his ideas about madness. Brief as the tale is, its intense tone and structure resemble those in lyric poems; therefore any revision accumulates importance. We are left, in the final version, with a careful reworking of what could be another

Gothic story featuring stereotypical, shallow characters in lurid situations. The narrator's initial irony (leaving to us the choice of envisioning him as mad or sane, and, therefore, whether his story reveals credibility or insane hallucination) is constantly buttressed by Poe's conscious art. The shift from pastoral, unsophisticated and unrestrained existence, through sexual awakening (which in itself enforces the maturing process) and death (of youthful inexperience) toward a renewed and more substantial emotional life (in which the city represents experience), is managed through hypnotic, dream-like cadences. The city itself suggests aspects of ordered, solacing containment, in contrast to Poe's more usual imprisoning, negative motifs, .

Structure dovetails with the innocence-experience theme. The tale in final form extends to sixteen paragraphs. Of these, the longer units convey the narrator's good feelings and raptures, and the shorter ones deftly coalesce in form with his emotional turmoil, loss, and doubt. Within the second major section that same form reappears, but with this difference: following the tale-teller's lengthy, and lyrical, paragraph that delineates his fumbles with psychic jolts, come two brief paragraphs of pleasant details that depict his union with Ermengarde. Their brevity itself accelerates the return of his dreaming or hallucinating (as well as our ties to them) once again toward ordered existence. Overall, the experiential journey, regardless of how its hallucinatory elements may promote different views, has proved beneficial. The Victorian poet Coventry Patmore was fascinated by what he called "the point of rest" in art, something to which the eye turns for repose, for restoration of internal and external harmony as a stay against confusion. Patmore illustrated his theory by referring to Shakespeare's plays, especially those in which mad, or near-mad characters sought such repose. It may be "trivial, even comic . . . but it has an importance outside itself."[9] Thus the Valley of Many-Colored Grass in "Eleonora" may function as a symbolic ideal rather than a solely fantastic Oriental setting. The narrator resembles a Poe character of perhaps greater fame who is also thought mad by some onlookers: C. Auguste Dupin. As that worthy's personality mingles the poet, or intuitive being, with the mathematician, or rational, scientific being, so the dreamer in "Eleonora" details vignettes of love-in-the-growing with a methodology that allows him to highlight sexual and emotional suggestions with no offense to censors or other readers. The stories of both men are indeed replete with wonders, and so the presumption that madness may stimulate their weird situations is understandable.

Poe's analogies between the lunatic and the dreamer-artist are effectively demonstrated in "Eleonora." His revisions point consistently to his intentional establishment of ambiguity as regards madness. It may be dangerous, as the general interpretation would have it. It may instead promote genius and artistic creativity. Studied turns to an interior landscape and nonconcrete terminology indicate that we encounter no simple Gothic tale of the otherworldly. The "Eleonora" narrator indeed reveals how his vigorous "fancy" (or emotions) rather than his "ardor of passion" (physical-sexual) girds his narrative. From a writer who has often been labeled mad or weird, such art is "Po-etic" justice. His narrator's expression, in its disjointedness—but a compelling disjointedness—adumbrates that which gives life to the works of Joyce, Faulkner, and other later writers who attempt to concretize emotional upheaval in process through the medium of the printed page. Poe's narrator may indeed be an actor, on stage, as it were, before us. In such context, Foucault notes that the nineteenth-century public often watched madmen as actors, performing for the amusement of the onlookers (pp. 68-70). He who tells the tale of Eleonora may be aware that he is acting. Thus he may supply readers with what they want in the sense of popular entertainment, all the while ironically insinuating a more serious context. A like spectacle informs "The System of Dr. Tarr and Professor Fether," for in engaging that tale, we, like the ingenuous narrator who visits a madhouse, only to have his anticipations turned inside out, are manipulated into pondering distinctions between lunacy and rationality. The dreamer-lover in "The Assignation" also comes to mind in this context. His story allows for many interpretations.

Clever Poe, the attentive literary craftsman, keeps readers alert as he manipulates the narrator's guidance of our journey through the consciously wrought language in "Eleonora." The narrator's expression could indeed be the "eloquent madness" Poe mentions elsewhere.[10] We might term the rhetoric in Poe's tale a prettified Germanism, but this beautification carries with it an artistic freight. Like another ancient mariner, and one who is "neither the nihilist nor the Pollyanna,"[11] Poe's storyteller gives us pause to think. His outspoken direction of our attention to madness is couched in terms that place the burden of deciding for or against his madness with us. Analogous tightrope walking occurs in Number 23 in "Fifty Suggestions," written in 1849, when Poe was still mulling the ramifications of mental abnormality. Joy Wiltenburg's study of ambiguous madness in popular balladry may shed light on Poe's techniques. Long before he probed the ambivalences of sanity and insanity, others had approached those phenomena unsure of which treatment was better, a grave or a comic stance. Convincing presentations of love-madness were the most difficult of all to render. Poe's customary confessional narrator-protagonist in "Eleonora" has obviously been greatly affected by his past. However, his account of that past, as he realizes, is subject to unkind responses. As a result, although he must tell his tale, like Coleridge's ancient mariner, he leaves us with all the truth, but truth that is "slant," as Emily Dickinson had it. Once more, we may appropriately gloss Poe's art by alluding to that of his popular contemporary, Tennyson, who probed connections among "dreams, madness, and the laws of the will [because] he recognized the dangers of such a connection." Poe's "Eleonora" narrator, who might with ease step into "Locksley Hall," "Maud" (very much in the vein of late nineteenth-century Gothicism), or certain of the Arthurian idylls, where he would find company among lover-characters of equally doubtful mental conditions, also registers these ambivalences.[12] These poems, among many others, demonstrate how madness makes for fascinating art that is not exclusively a literature of statement. Little wonder, then, that Poe informs "Eleonora" with equivocations and inconclusiveness.

NOTES

[1] Hirst, "Edgar Allan Poe," *M'Makin's Model American Courier*, 20 October 1849, p. 2; English, "Notes about Men of Note," April 1845 *Aristidean*—1: 153; rpt. *Edgar Allan Poe: The Critical Heritage*, ed. Ian Walker (London and New York, 1986), pp. 168-168.

[2] *Madness & Civilization: A History of Insanity in the Age of Reason*, transl. Richard Howard (New York, 1965), Ch. 1.

[3] David E. E. Sloane, "Gothic Romanticism and Rational Empiricism in Poe's 'Berenice'," *ATQ*, 19(1972), 19-26; Richard P. Benton, "Bedlam Patterns": *Love and the Idea of Madness in Poe's Fiction* (Baltimore, 1979), pp. 3-15.

[4] Sinclair Snow, "The Similarity of Poe's 'Eleonora' to Bernardin de Saint-Pierre's *Paul et Virginie*," *Romance Notes*, 5(1963), 40-44; Burton R. Pollin, "Poe's Use of the Name Ermengarde in 'Eleonora'," *N&Q*, 215(1970), 332-333; Sam S. Baskett, "A Damsel with a Dulcimer: An Interpretation of Poe's 'Eleonora'," *MLN*, 73(1958), 332-338; Richard P. Benton, "Platonic Allegory in Poe's 'Eleonora'," *NCF*, 22(1967), 293-297.

[5] *The Letters of Charles and Mary Anne Lamb*, ed. Edwin W. Marrs, Jr. (Ithaca and London, 1975), 1: 18-19.

[6] Wilbur's "Introduction" to the Print Club of Cleveland edition of "Eleonora" (1979) sets forth his views. Dayan's appear in *Fables of Mind: An Inquiry into Poe's Fiction* (New York, Oxford, 1987), pp. 210-223.

[7] See my "To 'The Assignation' from 'The Visionary' and Poe's Decade of Revising," *LC*, 39(1973), 85-109; 40(1976), 121-151.

[8] See my "The Power of Words in Poe's 'Silence'," *Poe at Work: Seven Textual Studies* (Baltimore, 1978), pp. 56-72; Gerhard J. Joseph, "Poe and Tennyson," *PMLA*, 88(1973), 421. Tennyson did not restrict himself to the technique Joseph mentions, however. Sometimes, particularly in "Maud," he made externals a rallying-point for mad characters They furnished stabilization amidst the "contemplation of unending process," according to Humphrey House, *All in Due Time* (London, 1955), p. 129.

[9] E. J. Oliver, *Coventry Patmore* (New York, 1956), pp. 176-177.

[10] Richard Fusco, "Poe and the Perfectibility of Man," *PoeS*, 19(1986), 1-6, fn14.

[11] Dean R. Koontz, "A Genre in Crisis," *Proteus*, 6(1989), 4.

[12] Wiltenburg, "Madness and Society in the Street Ballads of Early Modern England," *JPC*, 21(1988), 101-127. See also Ann C. Colley, *Tennyson and Madness* (Athens, Ga., 1983), p. 127; and Paull F. Baum, *Tennyson Sixty Years After* (Chapel Hill, 1948), pp. 136-140, 310.

"THE RAVEN" AND "THE BRACELETS"

E. KATE STEWART

Although a fair number of sources for Poe's most famous poem, "The Raven," are cited in *The Collected Works of Edgar Allan Poe*, edited by the late *doyen* to all Poe scholars, Thomas Ollive Mabbott, evidence points to yet another addition to this compedium. I propose that a tale by Samuel Warren, "The Bracelets"—in *Blackwood's* for January 1832—contains parallels to "The Raven" too striking to ignore.[1] Poe's awareness of Warren's writings was acute, and that a good Gothic tale like "The Bracelets" should remain in his mind as he composed "The Raven" is probable. After all, that poem is actually a Gothic tale in verse, and to Poe the name of *Blackwood's* ever called forth implications of the *crème de la crème* of Gothic fiction. Moreover, Warren's writings repeatedly lured Poe's interest, so much so that in "How to Write a Blackwood Article" the Britisher's "Passages from the Diary of a Late Physician," serialized in *Maga* (as *Blackwood's* was nicknamed) from 1830 through 1837, is held up as a model for the writing of excellent terror tales. Poe mentioned that work elsewhere, and he subsequently reviewed Warren's popular *Ten Thousand a Year*, suggesting along the way a more elaborate critique to follow. Such a screed he never produced; his distinguishing the worth from the dross in *Ten Thousand a Year*, however, demonstrates his close comprehension of Warren's methods. Poe must have found more dross than worth in this novel because he censured it for being "written in slipshod English" and as being "tedious."[2]

Other commonalities between "The Raven" and "The Bracelets" make likely Poe's borrowing from Warren. The American's long retention of earlier reading has been established, but it is just as possible that he may have read "The Bracelets" at the very time during which "The Raven" began to take shape in his imagination.[3] Internal resemblances warrant our close attention to Poe's adaptation of "The Bracelets" in composing his eerie verse narrative. Warren begins: "It was late in the evening of a gloomy and bitter day in December about the middle of the seventeenth century . . ." (39). Poe echoes this phraseology in the opening of "The Raven": "Once upon a midnight dreary" (1); he continues: "It was in the bleak December" (7). Corresponding dismal beginnings establish melancholy tones in both works, and such tones exemplify the emotions of the protagonists as they pore over mysterious books.

Psychically, Warren's and Poe's characters are near kinsmen. Carl Koëcker, the central figure in "The Bracelets," reads "various volumes of classic and metaphysic lore" (39), particularly texts in occult sciences—an especially treacherous avocation, we are informed, because of the Inquisition's being at its height. In "The Raven" the speaker peruses "forgotten lore" (2). Readers know nothing about the nature of these compelling volumes because they are given no particulars, but they readily comprehend the effects of such reading. More important, gloom and introspection fall upon Koëcker and Poe's speaker as a result of their abstruse readings.

Both protagonists enter stages of semi-sleep, Carl "almost fancying he had been dreaming" (40), he in "The Raven" repeating that he is "nearly napping" (3). Koëcker attributes his state to his mulling a morning lecture, on "pneumatological speculations," attending a romantic opera, or fearing torture from the Inquisition because of his studying the Black Arts. Altogether, irrationality is common to both protagonists. The half-sleep is interrupted by persistent knockings at their doors. Carl hears "Rap, rap, rap!—Rap, rap, rap!" (40), signaling a late-night caller. "Rap" echoes on two subsequent occasions, repeating the same number of sounds each time. Similarly, Poe's speaker tells us: "While I nodded, nearly napping, suddenly there came a tapping, / As of some one gently rapping, rapping at my chamber door" (3-4). Either tapping or rapping appears again in lines 5, 21, 22, and 32. Both protagonists admit seemingly harmless visitors—Warren's old man and Poe's raven—who become psychic tormentors. Carl's small, but sinewy (40) visitor rather subtly resembles the raven. The elderly "Jew-peddlar" wears drab clothing (40) and has "sparkling black eyes" which "peered on the student with an expression of keen and searching inquisitiveness" (41). Later Warren says that Carl's guest sits "with his eyes fixed on the fire . . ." (41). Correspondingly, the narrator in "The Raven" muses: "Thus I sat engaged in guessing, but no syllable expressing / To the fowl whose fiery eyes now burned into my bosom's / core; . . ." (73-74). The man suggests darkness and age—and so does Poe's mysterious bird. Physical appearances ultimately affect the characters little, however: the act of granting entrance to their respective guests intensifies the mental anguish in the speakers.

The unbidden guests' omniscience, to which both writers allude in describing their weird figures' eyes, accounts for much of the protagonists' anxieties. The old man mentions Carl's presence at the morning lecture and later comments on his interest in a bracelet. Realizing that the "Jew-peddlar" knows so much about him, Carl grows agitated. He reacts violently, shouting: "Devil! devil! devil! What want you with me? Why are you come hither?" (41). The raven's persistent "Nevermore" reveals his all-knowingness as well, especially as he responds to the query: "Tell this soul with sorrow laden if . . . /

It shall clasp a sainted maiden whom the angels name Lenore" (93-95). When Poe's speaker realizes the bird's powers, he bursts out much like Carl: "Prophet! . . . thing of evil—prophet still, if bird or devil!—" (85).

As the narratives advance, the primary characters' mental stability becomes more and more questionable. Significantly, their speeches grow halting and disjointed. Koëcker's articulation weakens from his excitement over the bracelet shown him by the old man. With the departure of his elderly visitor, Carl regains his normal voice. The speaker in "The Raven," however, never resumes control because his guest never leaves. Initially, he speaks calmly to the bird. Increasingly, he repeats words and phrases, grows violent, and, finally, "shrieks" at the raven. The poems closes with the narrator suspended in an unreality heightened by the presence of the ominous bird. The raven symbolizes the man's retreat into a fanciful world, a region of delusive imagination and hallucination resulting from grief over Lenore.

The haunting repetition of "Nevermore" is memorable in "The Raven." Interestingly, the same sound in abbreviated form recurs in "The Bracelets." After Koëcker has enthusiastically admired the jewelry, the demonic visitor slips the band up on Carl's wrist. When he cannot remove it, he asks the old man to do so. The answer is: "Off?—never!" (44). The second request elicits like response. Warren's protagonist shriekingly petitions a third time as the visitor leaves. Carl hears again and again: "Never, Carl; never, never!" (45) until the words fade.

Conversely, Koëcker's mental torment is less profound than the narrator's in "The Raven." Carl's occult studies lead him to fear reprisal from the Inquisition, indeed to fear arrest at every turn. He believes that the old man is an agent of the Inquisition. Poe's speaker connects the eerie bird with Lenore. In both works, therefore, the characters associate their obsessions with their uninvited guests. The difference lies in the degree to which the *idée fixe* carries the protagonists into unreality. Koëcker awakens from his "singular and distressing dream" (53) and reenters the everyday world. Poe's protagonist does not.

Poe undoubtedly drew from Warren's story, yet he surpasses his model in creating setting and characterization. The backdrop in "The Raven" is emblematic; its bleakness mirrors the speaker's distraught mental state. He journeys into an emotional, not physical, world, and we observe him caught in a web of mental frenzy. All these circumstances partake of the greater Romanticism typical of early nineteenth-century literary culture. Because Poe subtly manages setting and characterization, the poem becomes a masterpiece of psychological symbolism—far above that demonstrated in "The Bracelets."

A writer's genius is not diminished by the incorporation of literary borrowings into his own work. In fact Poe emphasizes the value of such inspiration and method. In "Peter Snook," where he notes the importance of magazine fiction, he states: "There is no greater mistake than the supposition that a true originality is a mere matter of impulse or inspiration. To originate is carefully, patiently, and understandingly to combine" (*H*14: 73). To *combine* effectively, though, a writer needs a sharp memory. Poe also recognized this fact, exploring in the November 1844 *Democratic Review* the mind's ability to recall knowledge. He notes that most people remember hardly 1/100th of their reading, but he adds: "There *are* minds which not only retain all receipts, but keep them at compound interest for ever."[4] Based on the evidence presented by Mabbott and others, we realize that Poe was blessed with one of those rare minds that could retain, increase, and combine. Poe himself felt that in "The Raven" he had achieved a masterpiece, and time has affirmed the poet's feeling.[5] In the poem, numerous old bottles (i.e., Poe's sources) are filled with new wine of the author's creative genius.

NOTES

[1] "The Bracelets," *Blackwood's*, 31(1832), 39-52 (cited by page within the text); "The Raven" is cited from the version in *M*1: 350-374 (by line within the text).

[2] *M*2: 340. Cf. Kenneth L. Daughrity, "Notes: Poe and *Blackwood's*," *AL*, 2(1930), 290-291. Poe's review of Warren, from *Graham's Magazine* for November, 1841, appears conveniently in *H*10: 210-212. Howard Paul, "Recollections of Edgar Allen [sic] Poe," *Lambert's Monthly* 1(1890), 23; rpt. *Munsey's* 7(1892), 554-558.

[3] Attempting to pinpoint when Poe began "The Raven," Mabbott weighs evidence from several biographical accounts. Susan Weiss reports that Poe admitted that the poem "had lain for more than ten years . . . unfinished," but that he radically altered it before its 1845 publication, changing words, lines, and even the basic plan of the work. Although some sources suggest an 1843 composition, the most "true" story states that Poe wrote "The Raven" at the farm of Mr. and Mrs. Patrick Henry Brennan in late 1844. Mabbott believes that the "metrical form" we have was written at this time. Given the span between 1832 and 1844, then, Poe would have had opportunity to draw from "The Bracelets." For additional scholarship concerning Poe's use of *Blackwood's*, see the following: Margaret Alterton, *Origins of Poe's Critical Theory* (1925; rpt. New York, 1965); Michael Allen, *Poe and the British Magazine Tradition* (New York, 1969); Benjamin Franklin Fisher IV, "Poe, *Blackwood's*, and 'The Murders

AN&Q, 12(1974), 109-110; Kent P. Ljungquist, "Poe's 'The Island of the Fay'; The Passing of Fairyland," *SSF*, 14(1977), 265-271; Thomas Ollive Mabbott, "Edgar Allan Poe: Source of His Tale, 'X-ing a Paragrab'," *N&Q*, 160(1931), 100.

[4]Poe's comment from the *Democratic Review* is found in John Carl Miller's edition of *Marginalia* (Charlottesville, 1981), pp. 13-14.

[5]Maureen Cobb Mabbott, "Reading The Raven'," *UMSE*, n.s. 3(1982), 96-101.

THE RAVEN AND THE NIGHTINGALE

DAVID H. HIRSCH

T. E. Hulme observes that " . . . the whole of the romantic attitude seems to crystallize in verse round metaphors of flight," and that for the romantic, "man's nature is like a well, . . . a reservoir full of possibilities . . . ."[1] Edgar Allan Poe, generally considered a Romantic, does not fully fit Hulme's description. At his most characteristic, Poe seems to conceive man as a paradoxical well, a "reservoir," not of possibilities but of limitations. Thus we find in Poe myriad images of shrinkage, of infinite narrowing. Sometimes the image of narrowing is subtly displaced, as in "William Wilson" (where the protagonist wanders the world only to return to his mirror image) and "The Man of the Crowd," where the protagonist wanders away the night, only to return to his starting point. More often the image is direct, as in "The Fall of the House of Usher," with Roderick Usher, house and all, sinking into the infinite center represented by the miasmic and presumably bottomless tarn. In "A Descent into the Maelstrom" the protagonist is drawn into, and then ejected out of a bottomless vortex. Or, again, in "The Pit and the Pendulum," the narrator starts out either in a courtroom or in a dream of a courtroom, then loses consciousness, or dreams of losing consciousness, only to awaken in a dungeon in which the closing walls of his cell finally force him toward what he imagines or fears to be a bottomless pit. This Poesque movement from a circumference into a devouring infinite center or vortex is at the antipodes of the pure Romantic vision. In crossing the Atlantic, British Romanticism undergoes a sea change. The change, however, is more noticeable in Poe than in his Transcendentalist contemporary and rival, Emerson. In the opening paragraph of "Circles" Emerson wrote that "The eye is the first circle; the horizon which it forms is the second; and throughout nature this primary figure is repeated without end . . . Around every circle another can be drawn; . . . there is no end in nature, but every end is a beginning . . . ."[2]

Emerson's circle, with its fluid circumference moving endlessly outward from a central Ego, reflects the great sage's confidence (at least in 1839) in man's expansive possibilities. The circle is Emerson's version of the Romantics' metaphor of flight; it is his way of asserting that man is a reservoir full of possibilities. Poe did not share Emerson's confidence in man's expandability, though, and consequently he inverted the outward movement of Emerson's circle image. Retaining the Romantic sense of dynamics, he nevertheless presents a dynamics of contraction instead of expansion. As Poe inverted

Emerson's metaphor of the circle, so he transformed the Romantic metaphor of flight. I suggest below that the true progenitor of Poe's raven is that quintessence of "the metaphor of flight," Keats's nightingale. Before doing so, I should like to point out that the raven as "metaphor" has a history as long as the nightingale's. Perhaps the most widely known early appearance of the raven occurs in the biblical story of Noah. After forty days in the ark, "Noah opened the window of the ark which he had made. And he sent forth a raven, and it went forth to and fro, until the waters were dried up from off the earth" (Genesis 8:6-7).

The significance of the raven in the Noah story had been commented upon by the nineteenth-century Hebraist, George Bush.[3] In his *Notes, Critical and Practical, on the Book of Genesis* (1838), Bush noted that the "raven would have stayed away to feed on dead bodies [cf. Poe's "Take thy beak from out my heart"] according to its natural instincts, Proverbs 30:17." Moreover, "[f]rom the raven's emission and return Noah could of course learn nothing favorable, and from this circumstance, the raven has ever been considered as a bird of ill omen . . . ." Poe's familiarity with this commentary is suggested by the fact that Bush's epithet for the raven is repeated exactly in "The Philosophy of Composition": "I had now gone so far as the conception of the Raven—the bird of ill omen . . . ."[4] Three corvine characteristics stand out in Bush's explication. First, the raven is described as a repulsive scavenger of dead flesh; second, the raven does not bring the desired information ("nothing favorable" is to be learned from a raven); finally, the raven is linked to chthonic forces.

Preceding his announcement in "The Philosophy of Composition" that he had gotten "so far as the conception of a Raven," Poe described the process by which he had arrived at this conception as one of elimination: "Here, then, immediately arose the idea of a *non*-reasoning creature capable of speech: and, very naturally, a parrot, in the first instance, suggested itself, but was superseded forthwith by a Raven, as equally capable of speech, and infinitely more in keeping with the intended tone" (*H*14: 200).

The "idea of a *non*-reasoning creature capable of speech" is in itself absurd, self-contradictory, and abhorrent to reason, since *speech* is by definition an enactment of communication which assumes the participation of reasoning creatures. What H. P. Grice says about "meaning" may well be applied to speech in this context: ". . . For *A* to mean something by *x* . . ., *A* must intend to induce by *x* a belief in an audience, and he must also intend his utterance to be recognized as so intended."[5] Precisely what we cannot know, however, is whether the raven in Poe's poem "intends" to "induce a belief" in the bereaved lover.

In this sense, then, an ordinary raven is not a creature capable of speech at all, but one that may be described more precisely as a creature capable of reproducing speech-like sounds. Speech involves intention. Whether the intention can ever be adequately articulated, or, if articulated, whether it can ever be adequately interpreted or understood by a second party we do not, and probably cannot, know. What is important in Poe's poem is that neither the speaker nor the reader can be certain that the raven *intends* anything. It is the lover's madness or folly that he is determined to discover "intention" in the sounds pronounced by the raven, thereby brilliantly or madly converting noise into speech. Enriching as is Roman Jakobson's analysis of the poem as an experiment in communication, he nevertheless permits himself to be bounded by Poe's presumed psychological limitations. He accepts the "theme of the poem as the 'bereaved lover,'" a theme which he points out "haunts all Poe's poetry and prose. In 'The Raven',", Jakobson continues, "this theme displays a particular 'force of contrast,' expressed in a pointedly romantic oxymoron: the colloquy between the lover and the bird is an anomalous communication about the severance of all communication."[6]

Although Jakobson is accurate in describing the non-communicative nature of a naturalistic zoological raven's speech, he underestimates the raven's communicating power as a symbol. In spite of Poe's later pronouncement in "The Philosophy of Composition," that the theme of his poem is the "bereaved lover," the larger theme is the wanderings of the human soul in search of eternal salvation, and this theme is conveyed, not by what the raven *says* (i.e., "nevermore"), but by the dialectic between the meanings encoded in the raven as symbol by centuries of Western usage, and the sublime message that the speaker tries to extract from the bird's utterance. The encoded meanings are elucidated by Bush in his commentary on Genesis 8:9:

> *Found no rest for the sole of her foot.* For though some of the mountain tops were bare, yet they were either at so great a distance, or so far out of the course she took, that she did not now alight upon them. Besides, it is well known that in general doves fly low and are perhaps on that account called Ezek. 7.16. 'doves of the valleys,' as ravens also are called 'ravens of the valleys,' Prov. 30.17, from their usually finding their prey on the low grounds. The vain and weary wanderings of the soul in quest of rest are strikingly shadowed forth in the disappointment of the dove. No solid peace or satisfaction can it find in this deluged, defiling world, till it returns to Christ as to its ark, its Noah. The carnal heart, like the raven, takes up with the world, and feeds on the carrion it finds there, but

the gracious soul still sighs out its 'Oh, that I had wings like a dove,' that I might fly to him and be at rest; and, as Trapp remarks, 'if that 'Oh' will not set her at liberty, then she takes up that 'Wo' to express her misery; 'Wo is me, that I sojourn in Meshech, and dwell in the tents of Kedar.' Let our language then ever be, 'Return thou to thy rest (Heb. *limnuah*, to thy Noah, as it were), O my soul!' Ps. 116.7.[7]

It seems that Bush's commentary may have activated not only the image of the raven, but also the larger theme of the poem. The raven does not represent the "severence of all communication"; his message of "nevermore" in answer to all the speaker's questions about the immortality of the soul are negative because the raven has been coded by Western symbol-making as the symbol of "the carnal heart." The grotesqueness of the poem lies in the speaker's asking of a raven questions that are inappropriate to its encoded symbolic meaning. It is as if the speaker is the dove seeking "solid peace and satisfaction . . . in this deluged, defiling world . . . ."

If the situation of a bird bearing messages were unique to Poe, then the psychological inferences might be sufficient in themselves. Poe's talking bird, however, invokes echoes not only of the biblical raven; it suggests further associations with two other widespread figures: the caged bird as a metaphor for the soul entrapped in the body, and the nightingale, Keats's bird "most musical, most melancholy." Among the British Romantic poets the soul-bird was most often a nightingale, stripped of its melancholy and represented "as a happy bird singing of summer in full-throated ease."[8] Instead of calling on the singer out of Greek mythology, melancholy or happy, Poe turns, rather, to the biblical scavenger bird symbolizing the "carnal heart." Poe's disjunctive imagination exchanged the Romantic metaphors of flight and Dionysian song for metaphors of stasis and monotony. Poe converted the traditional symbol of the flesh into a wished-for harbinger of immortality. The innovativeness of these exchanges is in no way diminished by the many possible sources of the poem that have been documented by Poe scholars. The full richness of Poe's poem, however, does not lie merely in his disjunctive and unsettling adaptation of the repulsive and unclean raven as a "love messenger" taking precedence over both the dove and the nightingale. Poe reverses the panting vision of the Romantic poets by converting what Leo Spitzer, in his explication of Whitman's "Out of the Cradle Endlessly Rocking," calls the "age-old theme of world harmony"[9] into a theme of world silence.

Poe's "The Raven" is a rejection of this age-old theme of world harmony, and specifically it is a direct reaction against the Romantic metaphorical structures set in motion by Wordsworth, Coleridge, Keats, and Shelley, and a reversal of the time honored uplifting meaning of the image of the soul-bird in Western poetry.[10] Instead of using this powerful long-lived metaphor of the singing bird to convey the idea of "world harmony," Poe uses a chthonic talking bird to convey the idea of world silence. Whereas Matthew Arnold, three years after the publication of "The Raven," still refers to the nightingale as a "wanderer from a Grecian shore," singing a song of "eternal passion, eternal pain," Poe arranges for his ancient raven to come "wandering from . . . Night's Plutonian shore . . . ." And whereas Shelley's skylark (1820) is addressed as "bird or sprite," Poe's raven is addressed as "Prophet, . . . thing of evil." Whereas the speaker in Keats's ode apostrophizes the nightingale as a symbol of positive immortality, "Thou wert not born for death, immortal bird," Poe's speaker apostrophizes the raven as a symbol of negative immortality: "And my soul from out that shadow that lies floating on the floor / Shall be lifted—nevermore!" Poe's speaker experiences immortality as agony.

We may, in fact, think of "The Raven" as a poem of reversals. For example, Poe reverses the raven imagery of the Noah narrative by having a raven fly into the window, rather than having his narrator, like Noah, send forth a raven *from* his window. There is also a similar reversal of the situation in Keats's poem. If we agree with Brooks and Warren that the speaker attempts to enter the world of the nightingale unsuccessfully,[11] then it is clear that Poe reverses this procedure by having the raven attempt to enter, and succeed in entering, the world of the speaker. Also, Keats's speaker finds himself outdoors, surrounded by lush Nature, while Poe's speaker is enclosed in a chamber, which itself seems to enclosed in a vacuous wasteland.

Keats's lushly singing nightingale remains invisible; its ecstatic song ravages the listener, transports him (if only momentarily) to the realm of the transcendent, but to a realm of the transcendent that he later comes to realize can be reached only through death: "Now more than ever seems it rich to die, / To cease upon the midnight with no pain, / While thou art pouring forth thy soul abroad / In such an ecstasy." The listener yearns to follow that ecstatic song to its mysterious source. His soul tallies (as Whitman was to put it) the song of the bird. The speaker's gaze is fixed upward. The only movement the nightingale makes (and we can only infer this from the description given by the speaker) is upward and outward (like Noah's raven).

Here we have the paradigm of Hulme's description of the Romantic attitude that "seems to crystallize in verse around metaphors of flight." In Keats's ode, the speaker himself longs to move upward and outward to join the soul-singing bird, but he is weighted down by his mortal clay. Like Hamlet at his most melancholy, Keats's speaker would like his "too too sullied flesh . . . to melt, thaw, and resolve itself into a dew," to "Fade far away, dissolve, and quite forget / What thou amongst the leaves hast never known . . . ." Instead of soaring, he starts by sinking into death-like sleep: "My heart aches, and a drowsy numbness pains / My sense, as though of hemlock I had drunk . . . ." In "The Raven" this melancholy extravagance is also reversed. In place of a lushly singing ethereal bird there is a croaking, fluttering, black raven that is all too physically present. Instead of a speaker who wants to dissolve himself so that he can fuse with the song of the bird, we have a speaker who is possessed by the bird which will not release him: ("And my soul from out that shadow that lies floating on the floor / Shall be lifted—nevermore!").

It may also be observed that although Keats's speaker opens his statement with an emotional outburst, "My heart aches," Poe's speaker chants in a disaffected monotone: "Once upon a midnight dreary, while I pondered weak and weary, / Over many a quaint and curious volume of forgotten lore—." Poe also makes it clear that his narrator's experience is nocturnal, whereas Keats, as critics have pointed out, seems unable to decide between a summer day with "shadows numberless" or a "midnight" in which "darkling" the speaker listens.

Although Keats's speaker sinks into his deathlike sleep as a result of what seems to be an excess of pleasure, an overdose of concentrated joy in the face of beauty (" 'Tis not through envy of thy happy lot / But being too happy in thine happiness . . ."), Poe's narrator is being lulled to sleep by his excessive study of forgotten lore: "While I nodded, nearly napping, suddenly there came a tapping, / As of someone gently rapping, rapping at my chamber door." We may say that the raven's first venture into communication occurs in this tapping and rapping rather than in his initial utterance of the word "Nevermore." This tapping prevents the narrator from nodding off and represents an indication of either a real or imagined force outside the narrator's chamber seeking to enter.

Unlike Keats's speaker, Poe's bereaved lover does not start by responding directly to the Beautiful (the song of the bird) with emotions of joyful pain. Rather, the first quotation that the narrator attributes to himself ("'Tis some visitor," I muttered, "tapping at my chamber door— / Only this and nothing more."), suggests the reverse. That is, instead of responding emotionally to a stimulus that can be linked to the Beautiful, he responds analytically to a stimulus that is qualitatively neutral. Moreover, the speaker's ratiocination must give the reader pause. The speaker does not do what someone in his position might normally be expected to do: get up and see who, if anyone, is tapping at his door. Instead, he continues absurdly to ponder the imponderable.

When "The Raven" appeared in the *American Review* it was prefaced with a short prose explanation, probably written by Poe himself, which spoke of "the curious introduction of some ludicrous touches" into the poem. That this mention of "ludicrous touches" was not a momentary aberration is confirmed by Poe's assertion, in his later analytic and highly calculated essay, "The Philosophy of Composition," that ". . . an air of the fantastic—approaching as nearly to the ludicrous as was admissible—is given to the raven's entrance. He comes in 'with many a flirt and flutter'" (*H*14: 205).

Poe justified this flirtation with the ludicrous in a poem whose dominant tone was to be "Melancholy, . . . the most legitimate of all the poetical tones," by appeal to the need for "force of contrast, with a view of deepening the ultimate impression." I would argue, however, that the ludicrous enters the poem, not as Poe suggests, in the middle, but is there throughout, except that I would add that we should translate the concept of the ludicrous into its twentieth-century incarnation, the Absurd. In fact, Poe has been quoted as saying that "he wrote his poem 'to see how near the absurd I could come without overstepping the dividing line'" (*M*1: 369).

The root of the absurd in "The Raven" lies not only in Poe's inversion of the bird-flight imagery but also in his parody of the Romantic meditative poem. In Poe's poem, the speaker's imagination focuses with fierce and unwavering intensity on one object and on that alone. Neither a vision of glory nor of the ordinary world does this imagination grasp. It is that inability to bring anything else within the compass of his imagination that results in the touches of the ludicrous that Poe talks about: Keats's speaker starts from a presumed physical location and then proceeds to launch out into the poetic-mythic world of Provencal song, the world of Greek mythology, the physical world of decay and death. But the imagination of Poe's bereaved lover remains fixed always on the raven.

The meditation on a fixed object in the hope of forcing the object to yield its meaning is a common Romantic obsession. Keats's urn, that "still unravished bride," is such an object; so is his nightingale, Blake's Tiger, Coleridge's frost, and so are the ruins at Tintern Abbey. Among the British Romantics, though, a dominant element in the poems is what may be called a rich language of reference-to-nature, or a language of reference to strongly positive human feelings. It may be, as Keats's friend Charles Brown asserted, that Keats wrote the "Ode to a Nightingale" after hearing an actual nightingale sing, while the poet rested under an actual plum tree. Yet were it not for Brown's intrusion, the actual nightingale and plum tree would be lost, for it is not as description that we value the poem. We value it because Keats fuses nature-referential words and feeling-referential words and myth-referential words in such a way as to create a symbolic structure so powerful that it ultimately overshadows the descriptive structure. What Poe does is similar except that the feeling-referential words are words of disharmony and terror instead of harmony and joy, while the nature-referential words are replaced by language that can only be described as non-referential or pseudo-referential.[12]

In fact, Keats's speaker does not describe the bird or its song, but rather his reaction to the latter. He tells us that his "heart aches," and describes his own "drowsy numbness," yet he avers that these are not symptoms of "envy of thy happy lot, / But being too happy in thine happiness . . . ." And again, he avers: "Now more than ever seems it rich to die, / To cease upon the midnight with no pain, / While thou art pouring forth thy soul abroad / In such an ecstasy!" By mixing the diction of death and ecstasy with the diction of nature-description, the speaker moves toward a discovery of vision. The imagination seems to be expanding into an "intimation of immortality" ("Thou wast not born for death, immortal Bird!"). As so often happens in British Romantic poems, however, at the very moment of rapturous discovery the "imagination" fails, the vision dims, the world of uncertainty, death, and physical decay eclipses the world of visionary joy and beauty ("Was it a vision, or a waking dream?").

Poe moved beyond this poetics of alternating vision and failure to an uncannily twentieth-century poetics of immediate failure. The major British Romantics soared Icarus-like before they fell to earth. They kept probing the limits of imagination by soaring upward on a language of muted (as in Wordsworth) or ecstatic joy and then plummeting downward on the language of sorrow and despair ("Forlorn! the very word is like a bell / To toll me back from thee to my sole self!"). The speaker in the "Ode" descends from ecstasy to that "Forlorn!" Poe's bereaved lover starts with the "Forlorn" in its phonemic and semantic variant of "Nevermore." (It is instructive, too, to consider the aptness with which the "forlorn" fits Poe's description of the ideal sound of a single-word refrain: "That such a close, to have force, must be sonorous and susceptible of protracted emphasis, admitted of no doubt: and these considerations led me to the long o as the most sonorous vowel, in connection with r as the most producible consonant" [$H$14: 20].) If we can take Poe at his word when he describes the writing of the poem, then his two starting points were the melancholy tone, and the word "nevermore" as the ideal refrain. In other words, he started with the imagination confronting a blank wall.

In addition to his reversal of the Romantic evaluation of imagination, Poe also renders another noteworthy inversion of symbols. Whereas Keats's nightingale, singing in "full-throated ease," is associated with Dionysian ecstasy, Poe's raven, with its one-word croak of "Nevermore," is linked, rather, with what can only be called a parody of Apollonian decorum. Poe's is an Apollonianism gone sour. Ordinarily, Apollo and the Apollonian are associated not only with control and form but with a world of sunlight, moderation, and sweet reason. "The Raven," however, presents us with the paradox of Apollonian darkness. Although it is a cliché of literary criticism to say that art redeems by bringing order out of chaos, for Poe, at least, order was not in itself redemptive.

One final reversal I would like to underscore. The British Romantics shifted the burden of Transcendence from God to Nature and then to Imagination, which eventually became synonymous with God. If there was a "beyond" that could give meaning to man's life on earth, the imagination either was that "beyond" or could discover it. Joseph Warren Beach, in his now much neglected study, *The Concept of Nature in Nineteenth-Century English Poetry*, points out that "a growing dualism shows itself in Wordsworth's emphasis on imagination as a spiritual faculty necessary to the reading of nature, and he ended by virtually giving up nature and deriving man's spirit directly 'from God, who is our home'."[13] Coleridge made a similar derivation in his famous definition of the primary imagination as "a repetition in the finite mind of the eternal act of creation in the infinite I AM."[14]

Keats did not make this derivation. He tried to retain faith in the ability of the expansive imagination to negate the limiting fact of human mortality. So his greatest ode, perhaps his greatest poem, is centered not only on the metamorphic myth of the nightingale but also on the myth of Orpheus. In the speaker's effort to conquer death (escape from it according to Morris Dickstein) he is re-enacting the archetypal quest of Orpheus, who, through the power of song, won the privilege of descending to the underworld to bring back his beloved Eurydice. Keats, too, would conquer Death through song. He projects the power of orphic song into the bird and in a sense assigns to himself the role of Eurydice, so that he is almost saved from death by the bird's ecstatic outburst. Poe, too, renders a displacement of the orphic myth. As in the traditional story, we have in Poe's poem an earthly lover who seeks to be rejoined to a loved one now dead. But instead of winning his way to the underworld on the wings of song, he finds that an apparent messenger from the underworld breaks in on his consciousness. From Ovid to Keats to Poe the orphic power of song declines. Orpheus, charming his way into the underworld, almost overcomes death. Keats's nightingale chants a powerful music that almost charms his speaker into immortality. But Poe exchanges nightingale for raven, real or illusory song for real or illusory croak.

Neither Nature nor song, not vision nor myth nor imagination will suffice. The beauty of song is transmuted into the croaking "nevermore!" of the raven. Nature, with its "soft incense" hanging "upon the boughs," its "fruit tree wild," its "white hawthorn, and the pastoral eglantine," its "fading violets" and "musk-rose," and "murmurous haunt of flies," has given way to a darkened room decorated with Gothic trappings and enveloped in a lightless vacuum. Imagination yields only emptiness, silence, and a mocking message.

Two parallel, yet contrasting, passages may help to focus the thoroughness and deliberateness of Poe's reversal of Keats's poem and of the orphic motif. Listening to the nightingale's song, the Keats speaker feels, "Now more than ever seems it rich to die / To cease upon the midnight with no pain / While thou art *pouring forth thy soul abroad / In such an ecstasy!*" [my italics]. The bereaved lover, describing the raven to his audience, at once borrows and reverses this image of the bird pouring forth its soul in ecstatic song: "But the Raven, sitting lonely on the placid bust, spoke only / That one word, as if *his soul* in that one word *he did outpour*" [my italics]. Thomas Weiskel has recently remarked that "the essential claim of the sublime is that man can, in feeling and in speech, transcend the human."[15] Whether the nightingale's song is a vision or a waking dream, there can be no doubt that in describing his moment of overflow the poet is reaching for a description of the experience of the sublime in Weiskel's sense. The nightingale is "transported" and the speaker yearns to be "transported" too.

Poe, however, converts the exploding ecstasy of nightingale and speaker into a collapsing despair. He even reverses the verbal construction "pouring forth" to "outpour." Moreover, the word "outpour" itself is excessive in relation to the events that are being described. The automaton-like raven can hardly be said to overflow with emotion. Parodying the Romantic metaphors of flight and the Romantic predilection for the language of "overflow," Poe undermines the Romantic sublime and replaces it with the Existential absurd.

This undermining of the Romantic sublime is achieved in part by a disjunction between form, sound, and semantics in the poem. W. H. Auden takes note of this disjunction when he comments that "the trouble with 'The Raven' is that the thematic interest and the prosodic interest, both of which are considerable, do not combine and are even often at odds."[16] While the form is strictly contained (Hulme's bucket), the sound constantly pushes toward overflow. At the same time, the meaning belies both the contained form and the lushness of sound. Clearly, the containing form is one source of the poem's power—a pounding sound pattern of trochees and dactyls intensified by multiple internal vowel and consonantal, full and slant rhymes. Poe himself describes the tightness of the form rather elaborately in "The Philosophy of Composition":

> Of course, I pretend to no originality in either the rhythm or metre of the "Raven." The former is trochaic—the latter is octameter acatalectic, alternating with heptameter catalectic repeated in the refrain of the fifth verse, and terminating with tetrameter catalectic. Less pedantically—the feet employed throughout (trochees) consist of a long syllable followed by a short: the first line of the stanza consists of eight of these feet—the second of seven and a half (in effect two-thirds)—the third of eight—the fourth of seven and a half—the fifth the same—the sixth three and a half. (*H*14: 203-204)

Out of this strictly controlled form emerge verbal alignments that in the context of the rhyme and meter are semantically absurd. Consider, for example: " 'Though thy crest be shorn and shaven, thou," I said, "art sure no craven, / Ghastly grim and ancient Raven wandering from the Nightly shore—'[.]" The interweaving of sounds is rich: the consonants "*th*ough" "*th*y," "*th*ou"; "*c*rest," "*c*raven," "*g*rim"; "*sh*orn," "*sh*aven," "*sh*ore," "*s*ure,"; "*g*hastly," "*g*rim"; vowel rhymes "sh*o*rn," "sh*o*re"; "sh*a*ven," "cr*a*ven," "R*a*ven," "*a*ncient."

But given the richness of sound there is what can only be called a hollowness of meaning. I should emphasize that I am not repeating the oft-leveled charge of meaninglessness. Rather, Poe deliberately creates a gap that underlines the absurdity of man's dual nature—physical and spiritual—and of his aspiration to transcendence. This hollowness is carried by the narrative and imagery which contend against the sonic richness. Consider stanza four:

> Presently my soul grew stronger; hesitating then no longer,
> "Sir," said I, "or Madam, truly your forgiveness I implore;
> But the fact is I was napping, and so gently you came rapping,
> And so faintly you came tapping, tapping at my chamber door,
> That I scarce was sure I heard you"—here I opened wide the door;—
>   Darkness there and nothing more.

We cannot apprehend Poe's sense of the comic Absurd unless we bear in mind that the student is addressing this highly formal apology, with its attendant pedantic explanation, to a closed door with nothing and no one, it turns out, on the other side. He makes his courtly and elaborate explanation to a blank wall. This ludicrous (Poe's word) action presents a most shattering image of the human form. The bereaved lover offers his courtly and servile gesture to a wholly uncaring, absolutely indifferent universe: "Darkness there and nothing more."[17] The next stanza is in the same vein:

> Deep into that darkness peering, long I stood there wondering, fearing,
> Doubting, dreaming dreams no mortal ever dared to dream before;
> But the silence was unbroken, and the stillness gave no token,
> And the only word there spoken was the whispered work, "Lenore!"
> This I whispered, and an echo murmured back the word, "Lenore!"
> Merely this and nothing more.

Again we have the absurd image of man peering out into the darkness—looking for what? Encountering no "objects" for his mind to meditate over (no urns, no ruins, no wintry scenes), his mind performs its operations upon nothing, simply doubting and dreaming. Only a whispered word, the name Lenore, is spoken, and that, we learn from an afterthought, is spoken by the lover himself. What he projects out into the blank universe comes right back to him in an echo. The eleventh stanza continues the bitter, mocking humor:

> But the Raven still beguiling my sad fancy into smiling,
> Straight I wheeled a cushioned seat in front of bird, and bust and door;
> Then, upon the velvet sinking, I betook myself to linking
> Fancy unto fancy, thinking what this ominous bird of yore—
> What this grim, ungainly, ghastly, gaunt, and ominous bird of yore
> Meant in croaking "Nevermore".

Did Poe intend the reader to react to this description with total solemnity? This student who is so overwhelmed by sorrow has to do his suffering in the luxurious confines of a cushioned velvet sofa. Again, we might compare him with the agitated listener in Keats's "Ode to a Nightingale." Instead of responding with an overflow of emotion to the rapturous song of an invisible ecstatic singer flying freely through the natural air, Poe's student sinks himself into a cushioned seat and tries to back-construct an intention into the sounds generated by a non-reasoning creature in order to coerce a sublime message out of the croaking bird. Here again we can perceive Poe's fascination with cryptography. The lover is determined to break the code, decipher the message. In this instance, however, there is no message, and the thing to be decoded is not just the word "nevermore," but the raven itself.

Poe, if he is not signalling the death of the poetic imagination as a source of cognition, is anticipating, at least, its eclipse by the scientific mode of inquiry. Thomas S. Kuhn, in *The Structure of Scientific Revolutions*, comments that "Effective research scarcely begins before a community thinks it has acquired firm answers to questions like the following: What are the fundamental entities of which the universe is composed? How do these interact with each other and the senses? What questions may legitimately be asked about such entities and what techniques employed in seeking solutions?"[18] The British Romantics and their American counterparts (Emerson, Thoreau, and Whitman) still wished to believe that poetic inspiration could provide answers to those questions; they asked, and all of them were eventually frustrated. They believed that somehow the poet could use metaphor to wrench out of nature a design that would give meaning to human existence, whether that design were benevolent or, as Frost was later to put it, a "design of darkness to apall." By 1845, though, Poe had already discarded a belief in any design at all. Poe perceived that the new science would relegate the poetic imagination to the status of the decorative. So instead of having language and poetic imagination provide a springboard to ecstasy, as Keats had apparently hoped they would in his "Ode to a Nightingale," Poe makes language and the poetic imagination become the blank wall itself. Absurdly pressing the bird for a language message from "the beyond," the bereaved lover can manage to extract only the repeated utterance, "Nevermore!"

NOTES

[1]"Romanticism and Classicism," *Speculations* (London, 1924), pp. 117, 120.

[2]"Circles," *Selections From Ralph Waldo Emerson*, ed. Stephen E. Whicher (Cambridge, Mass., 1957), p. 168.

[3]Poe had written about Bush in the "Literati" papers in 1846.

[4]Bush, *Notes* (New York, 1859), p. 144.

[5]"Meaning," Zabeeh, Klemke, Jacobson, eds., *Readings in Semantics* (Urbana, 1974), p. 507.

[6]"Language in Operation," *Mélanges Alexandre Koyre* (Paris, 1964), pp. 276-277.

[7]*Notes*, pp. 144-145.

[8]See C. L. Finney, *The Evolution of Keats's Poetry* (1936; rpt. New York, 1963), p. 622. Finney gives a useful survey of the changes in the nightingale image in English poetry.

[9]*Essays on English and American Literature*, ed. Anna Hatcher (Princeton, 1962), p. 14. Spitzer also surveys the changing image of the nightingale in linking it to the Western concept of world harmony.

[10]Poe's awareness of the British Romantics may be inferred from an assertion uttered by the speaker of the story "The Landscape Garden," (1842): "We may be instructed to build an Odyssey, but it is in vain that we are told *how* to conceive a 'Tempest,' an 'Inferno,' a 'Prometheus Bound,' a 'Nightingale,' such as that of Keats, or the 'Sensitive Plant' of Shelley" (*M* 4: 269). What does this assertion tell us about "The Philosophy of Composition," in which Poe claims to be instructing us "to build" a "Raven"? Moreover, Thomas Holley Chivers reports the following conversation with Poe: "'What do you think of Keats,' asked I. 'He was the greatest of any of the English poets of the same age, if not at any age,' answered he, with the air of a man who was not only conscious of his own consummate ability, but who had long before deliberately formed his opinion. 'He was far in advance of the best of them, with the exception of Shelley, in the study of his themes. His principal fault is the grotesqueness of his abandon'" [Richard Beal Davis, ed., *Chivers's "Life of Poe"* (New York 1952), p. 48].

[11]*Understanding Poetry*, 3rd ed. (New York, 1960), pp. 426-431.

[12]Although it is customary to think of Poe as a monolithic writer, the poetic imagery of the 1845 poems is quite different from the imagery of the poems published in 1827 and 1829. Certainly, the rich floral imagery of ll. 41-82 of "Al Aaraaf," whatever its meaning, is nowhere to be found in "The Raven."

[13]New York, 1956, p. 13.

[14]*Biographia Literaria*, ed. J. Shawcross, 2 vols. (1907; rpt. London, 1965), 2: 202.

[15]*The Romantic Sublime: Studies in the Structure and Psychology of Transcendence* (Baltimore and London, 1976), p. 3.

[16] *The Recognition of Edgar Allan Poe*, ed. Eric W. Carlson (Ann Arbor, 1966), p. 225 [orig. 1950].

[17] See Edward H. Davidson's observation on "the pompous and inflated rhetoric of (the student's) query . . . ," *Poe: A Critical Study* (Cambridge, Mass., 1957), p. 87.

[18] *The Structure of Scientific Revolutions* (Chicago and London, 1974), pp. 4-5.

THEME AND PARODY IN "THE RAVEN"

DENNIS W. EDDINGS

"The Raven" is undoubtedly Poe's most famous poem, although its defects have not gone unnoticed. The impossibility of footfalls tinkling on a tufted floor is a commonplace, and the detailed remarks of Clement Mansfield Ingleby, Howard Mumford Jones, and Jesse Bier, among others, show that despite its hypnotic effectiveness, "The Raven" abounds in absurdities of situation and poetics.[1] These deficiencies pose a problem in light of Poe's critical standards and his incisive application of them in dissecting bad verse. He insists, for example, that the passion so prevalent in "The Raven" is "absolutely antagonistic to that Beauty" that is "the province of the poem . . ." (*H*14: 198). Furthermore, implausibilities and infelicities of phrasing in the poem are of a kind with the excrescences Poe frequently remarked in his criticism.[2]

How, one wonders, can we reconcile obvious flaws in "The Raven" with Poe's critical dictates? Perhaps the lapses are deliberate, but, if so, to what end? Parody is an evident possibility, but of what and of whom? The answer to this last question, I suggest, enables us to reconcile Poe's critical standards with the poetic absurdities in "The Raven." Although the narrative progression of the poem depicts the dead end of the uncontrolled Romantic imagination, the flaws are Poe's means of ridiculing the bad verse produced by that imagination. Thus what appears to be an aberrant element in "The Raven" is actually integral to its strategy, the vehicle by which form and language satirically reinforce the poem's theme.

This reading requires us to see "The Raven," from one perspective, as a product of its narrator. True, the overall poem is obviously Poe's, for he created its form, setting, and language. We have learned, however, thanks largely to the studies of James W. Gargano, that the cock-eyed perceptions and purpled rhetoric in many of Poe's tales emanate from their narrators and not from Poe's daily life.[3] As a dramatic monologue, "The Raven" is a kissing cousin to the tales, and a similar principle applies in all: the narrator tells us what has occurred and he does so in his own language and form. What is overwrought in language results from his overwrought state of mind; what is incongruous results from his inability to think congruently; what is flawed in form results from his failure to control the mode of his expression. "The Raven," like many other satires, masquerades as a product of its narrator and its absurdities are the means of revealing the error of the narrator's ways. Seeing "The Raven" as a product of the student, we can appreciate fully the relationship between its serious narrative theme and reinforcing parody.

The narrative progression of "The Raven" graphically depicts the dead end of the uncontrolled Romantic imagination. The student who recounts his fate is a stereotype of the dark brooding Romantic youth Howard Mumford Jones identifies as the nineteenth-century hero-figure of the Anonymous Young Man (p. 133). We see his Romantic proclivities in the gloomy, Gothic decor of his room, in his reliance upon obscure lore as a means of escaping reality, and in his self-indulgent anguish over the lost Lenore. Most typically Romantic, however, aside from using himself as the subject of his poetry, is his insistence upon seeing everything in terms of his own *angst*, the external world being nothing more than a projection of his psyche. The three six-stanza sections of "The Raven" delineate that projection and, in the student's fate, its inherent insanity.

Preceding the raven's melodramatic entrance, the first section introduces us to the narrator's Romantic posturing and his insistence upon reading external phenomena as reflections of his own being. Seeking "surcease of sorrow" by poring over "many a quaint and curious volume of forgotten lore," he nonetheless reads in terms that enhance that sorrow, indicative of the self-indulgent nature of his grief. Thus the "dying ember" casts its "ghost upon the floor"—not its gleam or reflection (and let us not ask how a "tufted floor" can reflect). The "uncertain rustling of each purple curtain" is "sad" (nor let us ask how rustling can be uncertain—a curtain either rustles or it remains still; the uncertainty is in the mind of the student). Furthermore, that rustling, innocent enough in its own right, thrills the narrator "with fantastic terrors never felt before." This deliberate cultivation of terrifying sensation for its own sake is repeated when, looking into the darkness outside his room after the gentle tapping has broken through his ponderings, he dreams "dreams no mortal ever dared to dream before." There is more involved here than the perfervid lamentations of a sorrow-laden soul. Such overstatement and indulgence in sensation for its own sake point to the student's incipient madness and suggest it is grounded in his Romantic posturing.[4]

The next six stanzas bring out the narrator's progression from bemused witness to devout believer. When the raven enters, the student smiles at its "grim and stern decorum," but when the bird responds "Nevermore" to the query as to its name, new possibilities arise. The student initially notes that the response "little meaning—little relevancy bore," and then promptly proceeds to try to find that relevancy. Once again projecting his grief upon the world, he asserts that the raven speaks "That one word, as if his soul in that one word he did outpour." The narrator thus imaginatively links his *angst* with the raven's utterance, making it relevant to his own predicament. Consequently, he ceases to be amused by the raven and returns to his ponderings by linking the raven with Lenore. Thus he finds what he enjoys far more than the heretofore comic raven provides—he finds a means of indulging in his anguish. He then murmurs in self-pity: "Other friends have flown before— / On the morrow *he* will leave me, as my Hopes have flown before." The raven responds "Nevermore." Immediately struck by the appropriateness of this remark, the student at first accounts for it by noting "what it utters is its only stock and store." This, of course, is the rational explanation: "Nevermore" *is* the only word the raven can utter. The student, however, dismisses reason as quickly as it surfaces. Beguiled by linking his fate with the raven and enthralled with the imaginative vistas that link opens before him, he rushes forward to account for the *reason* "Nevermore" is all the raven can utter. That word, he speculates, has been "Caught from some unhappy master whom unmerciful Disaster / Followed fast and followed faster till his songs one burden bore / Of 'Never—nevermore.'" At this point the student pulls together bird, former master and himself in a melancholy lament that simply flies in the face of reason. The pivotal point in "The Raven" occurs at this moment when rational explanation of the bird's "Nevermore" runs head-on into the student's insistence upon interpreting the external world as an extension of his own sorrowful being. Rejecting reason, ignoring the obvious fact that the raven's "Nevermore" is merely a conditioned response to any verbal stimulus, the student wheels his chair before the bird to discover what it *meant* in "croaking" that word. Linking his *angst* to the raven leads the student into an insane insistence that the bird's conditioned reflex has existential import.

The final six stanzas follow with inexorable logic. Committed to finding a meaning in the raven's "Nevermore," the student does so in terms calculated to exacerbate his sorrow and the resulting sensations. He begins by perceiving the raven as a means of gaining "respite and nepenthe" from his memories of Lenore. The two questions he asks to gain that respite, however, are perversely couched in terms that will produce the opposite effect, given the predictability of the raven's "Nevermore." Furthermore, those questions simultaneously confirm his imaginative view of the hopelessness of the human condition, thus intensifying his anguish.

His first question confirms his idea that existence is "Desolate," a "desert land" that is a "home by Horror haunted." Having described life in these words, he then asks, "Is there—*is* there balm in Gilead?" Is there some hope for human happiness beyond this life? The raven's response confirms his view by denying that hope, as the student knew it would. Now that the prophetic raven has established the validity of the student's negative perspective, the next question can settle his desire to maintain his anguish: "Tell this soul with sorrow laden if, within the distant Aidenn, / It shall clasp a sainted maiden whom the angels name Lenore— / Clasp a rare and radiant maiden whom the angels name Lenore." Again, the raven's predictable response allows the student to see life as hopeless, but it also lets him dismiss all thoughts of ever being reunited with Lenore. As a result, his deliberately cultivated anguish is all but complete. What remains is for him to transfer the focal point of his suffering from Lenore so he can concentrate it totally upon himself. He accomplishes this by imaginatively seeing himself as being cast into the abyss of despair. The raven's "Nevermore"—so predictable—has pierced him to the heart. The student is now so overwhelmed by the nightmare he has created that he surrenders to it:

> "And the Raven, never flitting, still is sitting, *still* is sitting
> On the pallid bust of Pallas just above my chamber door;
> And his eyes have all the seeming of a demon's that is dreaming,
> And the lamp-light o'er him streaming throws his shadow on the floor;
> And my soul from out that shadow that lies floating on the floor
>   Shall be lifted—nevermore!"

The image of this final stanza is significant. The raven dominates Pallas, reason, and throws its shadow over the student, symbolic of the student's abdication of reason and immersion in the black shade of the imagination. The student, a Romantic posturer to begin with, has opted to ignore the voice of rationality so he can pursue his imaginative perceptions and cultivate the delicious, horrifying sensations they arouse. Madness results. Intent upon exploring his sensations, the student subverts reason in order to allow his imagination full sway in that exploration. The consequence is his entrapment of self. Like many another Poe narrator, this one is a victim of his own imagination;[5] despite the evidence to the contrary, he has insanely come to accept as gospel the croakings of a bird with dubious credentials.

The student's failure to control his Romantic imagination through the balancing power of reason leads him into chaos. He has fallen prey to the force Poe warns of in "Marginalia": "The Imagination of Man is no Carathis, to explore with impunity its every cavern. Alas! the grim legion of sepulchral terrors cannot be regarded as altogether fanciful; but like the Demons in whose company Afrasiab made his voyage down the Oxus, they must sleep, or they will devour us—they must be suffered to slumber, or we perish" (*H*16: 167). Following in the footsteps of Roderick Usher and the narrators of "Ligeia," "The Black Cat" and "The Tell-Tale Heart," to name a few examples where Poe reveals the destructive potential of the uncontrolled imagination, the narrator of "The Raven" has allowed his imaginative speculation to get the better of him, and has perished. The shadow that overwhelms him at the end of the poem is not, finally, the shadow of the raven, but the shade of his own destructive, uncontrolled Romantic imagination.

The narrative progression of "The Raven" thus treats a theme frequently advanced by Poe. Imagination, unchecked by reason, leads to a dead end. It also has another result—it leads to bad poetry. The student's rejection of reason so he can indulge his imagination and the resulting sensations represents a type of Romantic posturing Poe found abhorrent. He had little use for self-indulgent Romanticism that exalted the inner light of the imagination over reason. He frequently attacked or satirized it in his tales and criticism.[6] The motive for these attacks is in part esthetic—a self-indulgent, uncontrolled imagination leads to a self-indulgent, uncontrolled art. Robert Jacobs demonstrates how, during the 1840s, Poe had come to deplore "the aesthetic of the romantic period and the expressionistic purpose of much romantic art."[7] Poe's attitude toward the poetry produced by such an "inspirational aesthetic" enables him to make "The Raven" more than a depiction of the dead end of the uncontrolled Romantic imagination. By identifying the student with that diseased Romantic temperament, he can not only reveal its dead end; having the poem masquerade as a product of its narrator allows him to parody the bad poetry that such a temperament produces. The deliberate badness in "The Raven" thus becomes a means for ridiculing the verse of those who see art as all inspiration without recognizing the necessity of applying reason to that inspiration.[8] Interpreting "The Raven" as a parody of the verse produced by the diseased Romanticism the student represents, we can recognize that the parody is not an aberrant element but an integral part of the poem.

We need not go far to find evidence that "The Raven" is indeed such a parody. In January of 1845, the same month in which "The Raven" first appeared in print in the New York *Evening Mirror* (*M*1: 363), Poe reviewed Elizabeth Barrett's *The Drama of Exile, and Other Poems*, describing those poets later known as the Spasmodics:[9]

> From the ruins of Shelley there sprang into existence, affronting the Heavens, a tottering and fantastic pagoda, in which the salient angles, tipped with mad jangling bells, were the idiosyncratic faults of the great original....
> Young men innumerable, dazzled with the glare and bewildered with the *bizarrerie* of the divine lightning that

flickered through the clouds of the Prometheus, had no trouble whatever in heaping up imitative vapors, but for the lightning, were content, perforce, with its *spectrum*, in which the *bizarrerie* appeared without the fire. (*H*12: 33)

I do not believe we stray in identifying the student with this school, "The Raven" exemplifying its defects. If Poe does not specifically identify Barrett with those "young men innumerable," the link is still evident. As Jacobs indicates: "It was the school of the Spasmodics that Poe rightly condemned as licentious, and in spite of his admiration for Tennyson and Miss Barrett, he regretted that some of their verse belonged to what he had earlier called the 'school of all Lawlessness' that had magnified the errors of the great romantic poets" (p. 390). What is most interesting about this review in relation to "The Raven" is that Poe's analysis of Barrett's poetic faults is carried out in terms that reverberate with haunting familiarity in his own poem.

There is, for instance, Poe's catalog of Barrett's "multiplicity of inadmissable rhymes," including "glory and doorway," "taming and overcame him," and "Eden and succeeding" (*H*12: 27). Do we not detect echoes here of some of the more notorious rhymes in "The Raven," including the progression of "lattice," "that is," and "thereat is," or "evil" and "devil" and "undaunted" and "enchanted"? Poe also speaks of Barrett's being "not infrequently guilty of repeating herself," citing as her "chief favorites" the repetition of "down" and "leaning" (*H*12: 24-25). "The Raven" also abounds in repetition. Not counting the legitimate refrain, "Nevermore," we must still contend with the recurring "door" (fourteen times) and the "nameless" Lenore (eight times). There is also repetition of phrases in the fourth and fifth lines of each stanza, as in "Let me see, then, what thereat is, and this mystery explore— / Let my heart be still a moment and this mystery explore." In addition, there is substitution of repetition for rhyme, as in "'Wretch,' I cried, 'thy God hath lent thee—by these angels he hath sent thee . . .'."

Perhaps even more revealing are Poe's remarks about Barrett's "deficiencies of rhythm," for they are directed toward "Lady Geraldine's Courtship," the very poem from which Poe took the form of "The Raven" (*M*1: 356). Speaking of Barrett's trochees, he notes that "the natural rhythmical division, occurring at the close of the fourth trochee, should never be forced to occur, as Miss Barrett constantly forces it, in the middle of a word, or of an indivisible phrase" (*H*12: 28). "The Raven," however, contains many examples of such forcing, as in "So that now to still the beating of my heart, I stood repeating" and "Much I marvelled this ungainly fowl to hear discourse so plainly." As Poe notes, in such an occurrence "we must sacrifice, in perusal, either the sense or the rhythm" (*H*12: 28). Are we not justified in applying Poe's comment in this regard, "Inefficient rhythm is inefficient poetical expression" (*H*12: 29), to "The Raven"? Furthermore, the resonances of "Lady Geraldine's Courtship" found in "The Raven"—purple chamber, crimson carpet, perfumed air, window casement, "silken stirring," "With a murmurous air uncertain, in the air the purple curtain," and "Ever, evermore"—suggest Poe's sly pointing to Barrett's poem and his treatment of it as a clue to his parody. The process is identical with that Robert Regan delineates in his demonstrating how "The Masque of the Red Death" is a duplicitous plundering of Hawthorne, with the clue to that hoax being contained in Poe's second review of *Twice-Told Tales*.[10]

The Barrett review does draw our attention to many of the deficiencies in "The Raven," suggesting Poe's awareness of those flaws and his deliberate incorporation of them into the poem to parody the bad poetry he describes elsewhere. Surely the parallels in terms of time of composition of the poem and the review and the congruence of technical concerns point in this direction. We should also remember that Poe dedicated the 1845 volume, *The Raven and Other Poems*, to Barrett, for that dedication calls our attention to the review and its applicability to "The Raven." Although Poe calls Barrett "the noblest of her sex," he also specifically refers to "The Drama of Exile." Such direct reference to the poem appearing in the title of his review helps to steer readers to link it with "The Raven."

Evidence, then, points strongly to "The Raven" as parody. Seeing it as such, we recognize that it is as much about art as about psychological disintegration. The student's fate reveals the dead end of the uncontrolled Romantic imagination, while the poem reflects the bad art that imagination creates. In the narrative of the poem and in the parody that reinforces that narrative, Poe insists that reason must prevail. Reason would have saved the student. The same reason would have allowed him to write a better poem. Poe's success in incorporating the parody in a meaningful relation with the narrative is a tribute to his poetic theory and practice. "The Raven," in its unity of theme and supporting parodic structure, is an example of the proper poetics the student violates, for it reflects the application of reason to imaginative insight the student fails to achieve. Construing "The Raven" as parody does not oversimplify Poe's art. Rather, it helps us to comprehend how Poe's penchant for satire works hand in hand with his serious presentation of theme. Only when we recognize the interrelationship of the two do we appreciate the totality of Poe's work.

NOTES

[1] For Ingleby, see Francis F. Burch, "Clement Mansfield Ingleby on Poe's 'The Raven': An Unpublished British Criticism," *AL*, 35(1963), 81-83. Among other absurdities, Ingleby points out that "A man who is 'nodding' and 'nearly napping' can scarcely be engaged in 'pondering'" and that "The phrase 'hesitating then no longer' is clearly contradicted by what follows; for he does not go directly to the door . . . ." Howard Mumford Jones, "Poe, 'The Raven,' and the Anonymous Young Man," *WHR*, 9(1955), 127-138, takes exception to W. H. Auden's negative comments on "The Raven," arguing that its hypnotic effectiveness overrides its obvious absurdities, including meter and setting. Jesse Bier, *The Rise and Fall of American Humor* (New York, 1968), points to other problems, including anti-climax, in "The Raven" (p. 68).

[2] In addition to his review of Barrett, discussed at some length in my argument, see also, among many that could be mentioned, Poe's comments on Brainard (*H*11: 15-24), Dawes (*H*11: 131-147), Flaccus (*H*11: 160-174), Channing (*H*11: 174-190), and Amelia Welby (*H*11: 275-281). This last, published in December 1844, also condemns passion in poetry and points to lapses that are suspiciously present in "The Raven," such as the overuse of "o'er." I point to comments made between 1840 and 1845, these being representative of Poe's views at the time of writing "The Raven."

[3] See "'The Black Cat': Perverseness Reconsidered," *TSLL*, 2(1960), 172-178; "The Question of Poe's Narrators," *CE*, 25(1963), 177-181; "Poe's 'Ligeia': Dream and Destruction," *CE*, 23(1962), 337-342. G. R. Thompson, in "Poe's 'Flawed' Gothic: Absurdist Techniques in 'Metzengerstein' and the *Courier* Satires," *New Approaches to Poe: A Symposium*, ed. Richard P. Benton (Hartford, 1970), pp. 38-58, argues that "The first-person narrators of 'MS. Found in a Bottle,' 'Berenice,' 'The Fall of the House of Usher,' 'Morella,' 'Ligeia,' 'The Man of the Crowd,' and 'The Oval Portrait' . . . are involved participants in the action; and their bizarre mental states are integral to the deceptively ironic, serio-comic, and satiric perspectives of the tales" (p. 54). So it is, I believe, with "The Raven."

[4] The indulgence in sensation and the necessity of "getting it all down" is the focal point in Poe's satiric "How to Write a Blackwood Article." The narrator of "The Raven" can be seen as Psyche Zenobia's brother, for he too revels in his sensations. Benjamin Franklin Fisher IV argues the same for the narrator of "The Fall of the House of Usher": "Playful 'Germanism' in 'The Fall of the House of Usher'," *Ruined Eden of the Present: Hawthorne, Melville, and Poe*, ed. G. R. Thompson and Virgil L. Lokke (West Lafayette, 1981), pp. 355-374.

[5] An obvious parallel is the narrator of "Ms. Found in a Bottle." See the cogent remarks of Clark Griffith, "Caves and Cave

Dwellers: The Study of a Romantic Image," *JEGP*, 62(1963), 551-568.

[6] See, for instance, Clark Griffith, "Poe's 'Ligeia' and the English Romantics," *UTQ*, 24(1954), 8-25; and Kent Ljungquist, "Poe's 'The Island of the Fay': The Passing of Fairyland," *SSF*, 14(1977), 265-271. For Poe's criticism, see n3.

[7] *Poe: Journalist & Critic* (Baton Rouge, 1969), p. 382.

[8] Such, of course, is the thrust of "The Philosophy of Composition," which shows the application of reason to the imagination in operation.

[9] Jacobs makes the connection clear on pp. 339-340 and 361-363.

[10] "Hawthorne's 'Plagiary': Poe's Duplicity," *NCF*, 25(1970), 281-298.

EDGAR ALLAN POE IN FRANCE: BAUDELAIRE'S LABOR OF LOVE

GARY WAYNE HARNER

In *Fleurs du mal* Charles Baudelaire often writes about the same themes and subjects as Edgar Allan Poe, no mere coincidence since Baudelaire saw in Poe a kindred spirit. Indeed, the Frenchman spent some seventeen years translating the works of the American, often neglecting his own writing to do so. In 1852 he had written in a letter to Sainte-Beuve: *"Il faut, c'est-à-dire je désire, qu'Edgar Poe, qui n'est pas grand-chose en Amérique, devienne un grand homme pour la France."*[1] Baudelaire more than fulfilled this task and his obsession was important in furthering the popularity of Poe in Europe—his translations were read throughout the continent as the definitive renditions of Poe's work.

Some critics even claim that Baudelaire's translations enhance the originals.[2] His translations are surely excellent, but one would be hard pressed to prove that they are actually "better" than the originals. The possibilities of a translation are numerous: in its rawest form it is merely a reproduction, an attempt to convey the sense or give the equivalent of a word or entire work in another language. It can also be much more. Although rules in a given language often govern the choice, order and structure of the words in a translation, the translation, at its best, turns a foreign composition into the new vernacular so as to capture the spirit of the original, both in meaning and connotation.

To examine the quality of Baudelaire's translations, one may compare a representative segment from Poe with Baudelaire's corresponding translation. Such a comparison reveals that the Frenchman's translation, rather than enhancing the originals, in general, faithfully duplicates them. Comparing the climactic moment in "The Tell-Tale Heart" with the rendition from *Le coeur révélateur* will illustrate Baudelaire's methods of translation. Following are the English and French versions of the last paragraph, with corresponding lines numbered to facilitate reference.

> No doubt I now grew *very* pale;—but I talked more fluently, and with a heightened voice. Yet the sound increased—and what could I do? It was *a low, dull, quick sound—much such a sound as a watch makes when enveloped in cotton.* I gasped for breath—and 1
> yet the officers heard it not. I talked more quickly—more vehemently; but the noise steadily increased. I

arose and argued about trifles, in a high key and with
violent gesticulations, but the noise steadily increased.
Why *would* they not be gone? I paced the floor to and
fro with heavy strides, as if excited to fury by the
observation of the men—but the noise steadily
increased. Oh God! what *could* I do? I foamed—I
raved—I swore! I swung the chair upon which I had
been sitting, and grated it upon the boards, but the
noise arose over all and continually increased. It grew
louder—louder—*louder!* And still the men chatted
pleasantly, and smiled. Was it possible they heard
not? Almighty God!—no, no! They heard!—they
suspected!—they *knew!*—they were making a mockery
of my horror!—this I thought, and this I think. But
anything was better than this agony! Anything was
more tolerable than this derision! I could bear those
hypocritical smiles no longer! I felt that I must
scream or die!—and now—again!—hark! louder!
louder! louder! *louder!*—

"Villains!" I shrieked, "dissemble no more! I
admit the deed!—tear up the planks!—here, here!—it is
the beating of his hideous heart!" (*M*3: 797)

*Sans doute je devins alors très pâle;—mais je
bavardais encore plus couramment et en haussant la
voix. Le son augmentait toujours,—et que pouvais-je
faire?* C'était *un bruit sourd, étouffé, fréquent,
ressemblant beaucoup à celui que ferait une montre
enveloppée dans du coton. Je respirai laborieusement.—Les officiers n'entendaient pas encore. Je
causai plus vite,—avec plus de véhémence; mais le
bruit croissait incessamment.—Je me levai, je disputai
sur des niaiseries, dans un diapason très élevé et avec
une violente gesticulation; mais le bruit montait,
montait toujours.—Pourquoi ne voulaient-ils pas s'en
aller?—J'arpentai çà et là le plancher lourdement et à
grands pas, comme exaspéré par les observations de
mes contradicteurs;—mais le bruit croissait régulière-
ment. O Dieu! que pouvais-je faire? J'écumais,—je
battais la campagne,—je jurais! j'agitais la chaise sur
laquelle j'étais assis, et je la faisais crier sur le parquet,
mais le bruit dominait toujours, et croissait
indéfiniment. Il devenait plus fort,—plus fort!—
toujours plus fort! Et toujours les hommes causaient,
plaisantaient et souriaient. Etait-il possible qu'ils
n'entendissent pas? Dieu tout-puissant!—Non, non!
Ils entendaient!—ils soupçonnaient!—ils savaient,—
ils se faisaient un amusement de mon effroi!—je le*

> crus, et je le crois encore. Mais n'importe! quoi était 8
> plus intolérable que cette dérision? Je ne pouvais pas
> supporter plus longtemps ces hypocrites sourires! Je
> sentis qu'il fallait crier ou mourir!—et maintenant
> encore, l'entendez-vous?—écoutez! plus haut!—plus 9
> haut!—toujours plus haut!—toujours plus haut.
> —Misérables!—m'écriai-je,—ne dissimulez pas
> plus longtemps! J'avoue la chose!—arrachez ces
> planches! c'est là! c'est là!—c'est le battement de
> son affreux coeur![3]

Some passages are closely equivalent translations; some may be considered embellishments or improvements; and others represent losses or inadequacies. The bulk of Baudelaire's translations closely resemble Poe's version; therefore, let us first examine this group. In line (1) one easily sees the difficulties standing in the way of an absolutely literal translation. Since it is impossible to translate "I gasped for breath" word for word or in the same word order, the French translation must make a transposition. Baudelaire represents the verb of "I gasped" with a verb and an adverb. The prepositional phrase "for breath" disappears, but this slight loss is offset by the combination of the verb and adverb. Thus Baudelaire's translation, "*Je respirai laborieusement,*" literally re-rendered, would be something like *I breathed laboriously* or *with difficulty*. This close equivalent is neither an embellishment nor a loss.

Line (3) illustrates even closer transfers. Baudelaire translates "I paced the floor to and fro" as "*j'arpentai çà et là le plancher.*" The French do not usually say "*arpenter le plancher*" (to pace the floor) but simply "*arpenter*" (to pace or stride along). To achieve as accurate a translation as possible, Baudelaire employs a direct transfer by borrowing a foreign syntax with a close translation of its elements. He uses "*çà et là*" (here and there) to express the idea of "to and fro." This stylistic choice gives an effective equivalent.

Baudelaire's translation of "It grew louder—louder—louder!" (line 6) maintains Poe's tonality: "*Il devenait plus fort,—plus fort!—toujours plus fort!*" There would have been an obligatory dilution in the French because the language does not have a single word to express "louder." To counter this dilution and effect a close rendition, Baudelaire uses the word "*toujours*" (still, yet) to elevate "*plus fort*" to the equivalent strength of "louder." Thus the extra word, used to achieve the emphasis, as well as the two needed to express "louder," results in this excellent equivalent translation, although it is longer than the original.

These closely equivalent translations represent the bulk of Baudelaire's renditions of Poe, and they achieved his aim, for in explaining the character of his translation of another Poe tale,

"Mesmeric Revelation," he maintained that he tried to be as literal as possible: "It is necessary to follow the text literally. Certain things would have become otherwise obscure if I had paraphrased my author, rather than sticking strictly to the letter. I have preferred a rather painful and sometimes baroque kind of French so as best to bring out the philosophical mode of Edgar Poe."[4]

Having made this decision, Baudelaire gives a solid rendition of Poe's work. His translations are, for the most part, on the same level of meaning and competence as the originals. Among all the French translations of Poe, "Baudelaire's version," says Curtis Hidden Page, "has remained the standard. He has followed Poe . . . line by line, and almost word by word . . . and yet has made of his translation a living work. That it possesses all the qualities of an original is sufficiently proved by the influence it has exerted."[5]

Indeed, there are passages that "possess all the qualities of an original," for Baudelaire's translations, in some instances, actually enhance Poe's texts. There are instances where Baudelaire employs a word or words that clarify an idea generalized in the original version; that is, he enriches the phrases in that the translation expresses a precision merely implied in Poe's version. These "improvements" usually come when Baudelaire employs a word other than the obvious synonym or literal translation. The word *"niaiseries"* in line (2) exemplifies a word well chosen. It means "nonsense" or "foolishness," and it evokes the meaning of "trifles" much better than the other possibility, *"vétilles"* ("mere nothings"). This is an excellent embellishment.

Line (5) is an interesting translation because the particularization is not necessary, but rather stylistic. Poe's "of the men" becomes Baudelaire's *"de mes contradicteurs"* ("of my contradictors" or "opponents"). Baudelaire conveys the idea that the narrator of the text believes the officers to be not mere "men" but truly his "opponents" or "interrogators." It is a compensation that effectively emphasizes the increasing paranoia and desperation of the narrator. By line (9) the tension and despair have become quite unbearable for the narrator: *"l'entendez-vous?—écoutez!"* The English version, "hark," may be economical, but there is a significant gain in the French translation. Through his considerable amplification through two verbs, Baudelaire strengthens the impact of Poe's lone expression "hark."

Obviously, Baudelaire embellished Poe's original text. He enriches phrases from time to time by expressing a precision merely implied in the Poe text. Patrick Quinn writes: "One of Baudelaire's modern editors, Yves Le Dantec, after a careful study of the poet's methods as translator, sums up his procedure as follows: first, a literal translation, sometimes quite feeble; then, careful and sensitive retouchings; and, finally, a masterly transposition onto his own keyboard."[6] Baudelaire's changes are striking and generally ameliorate the original text. Before anyone else proclaims Baudelaire's translations superior to the originals, however, one must note instances where the translations do not effectively express the full idea or feeling of the original. Furthermore, in some rare cases the sense of Poe's text is even absent in the translation.

To put these "inadequacies" into perspective, one should first be aware of Baudelaire's command of English. Although Baudelaire learned that language early in life from his mother, he never became fully bi-lingual: "When he realized the extent of the work cut out for him by his desire to make Poe a great name in France, he regretted that his abilities in English were not much better than they were" (Quinn, p. 97). He greatly improved his English for and through his translations, but he never developed complete fluency in it.

Baudelaire used a bi-lingual dictionary for translating. For a while he was forced to work with editions of Poe's works containing misprints, sometimes leading him to make some incorrect translations. He finally acquired the definitive edition of his day: *The Works of the Late Edgar Allan Poe*, published by J. S. Redfield.[7] With this excellent text Baudelaire prepared the bulk of his translations.

To complicate Baudelaire's dilemma, there was the immense diversity of Poe's writing. For example, in "The Gold-Bug" Poe displays his knowledge of the dialect of the Black slaves of the nineteenth century. Not understanding some words and unable to find them in his dictionary, Baudelaire assumed that they were typographical errors and would sometimes translate them incorrectly. In his introduction to *Seven Tales*, W. T. Bandy illustrates Baudelaire's difficulty.

> A typical example is found in "Le Scarabée d'or" (*The Gold-Bug*) where the Negro servant, Jupiter, is asked about his master's health and replies, in Poe's text, "Him pale as a gose." Not finding "gose" in his English-French dictionary, which he kept ever at hand, Baudelaire assumed he was faced with a typographical error and came up with "pâle comme une oie [or *pale as a goose*]."[8]

Poe's prose and poetry abounds with modifications of American syntax and vocabulary, plus imitations of dialect. Such language doubtlessly fascinated Baudelaire; it also caused him problems.

Some of the difficulties appear in "The Tell-Tale Heart." Line (4) in the last paragraph is significant because Baudelaire chooses to translate "as if excited to fury" by "*comme exaspéré*" ("as if exasperated"). *Exasperated* may be synonymous with *furious*, but it fails to express the idea of being <u>excited</u> *to fury*. Thus the loss of the original meaning is not sufficiently compensated. The translation does not succeed in faithfully recreating the original.

Line 7 is another case in point: "And still the men chatted pleasantly, and smiled" (*"Et toujours les hommes causaient, plaisantaient et souriaient"*). Most of the sentence is translated literally. The exception is "pleasantly," which Baudelaire renders as *"plaisantaient"* ("joked"). Is this a change of meaning by Baudelaire and a bad translation? Possibly not; it could be a stylistic choice, a substitution of verb for adverb. More probably, Baudelaire simply is mistaken, fooled by the misleading similarity of *"plaisanter"* and "pleasant." Thus, the translation would literally mean: "And still the men chatted, joked and smiled."

The most striking example of a translation that fails to express the idea of the original is line (8). Poe writes two phrases that have the same meaning and that convey the same idea: "But anything was better than this agony! Anything was more tolerable than this derision!" Baudelaire omits an entire sentence in this case and creates a substantial loss because he omits the idea of "anything was better than this agony." He employs a negative question to try to capture the gist of the original: *"Mais n'importe! quoi était plus intolérable que cette dérision?"* ("But no matter! what could be more intolerable than this derision?"). This remains a weak translation, probably because Baudelaire ran into trouble with "agony." It is one of the rare instances where the sense of Poe's text is missing from the translation. Some, however, feel that this translation may not necessarily be the fault of Baudelaire. In his notes commenting on Baudelaire's translations of Poe, Jacques Crépet suggests that Baudelaire's posthumous editors made a mistake in judgment:

> *"Supposons maintenant que Baudelaire, qui revisait ses textes, même après qu'ils avaient paru en librairie,—se soit aperçu de son omission et en vue de la réparer quelque jour, en ait marqué l'endroit sur son exemplaire,—celui-là même qui dut venir aux mains de ses éditeurs posthumes,—au moyen du signe conventionnel d'intercalation. En quoi consiste ce signe? Essentiellement en un trait vertical. Et où devait-il être porté pour répondre au but envisagé? Exactement après 'n'import,' c'est-à-dire à l'endroit précis où le texte de 1869 montre un point d'exclamation. Voilà l'origine de celui-ci, selon toute vraisemblance."*[9]

It seems that Baudelaire's original translation was *"Mais n'importe quoi était plus tolérable que cette dérision!"* ("But anything was more tolerable than this derision!"). Crépet argues that the editors never took the trouble to check the English text. If so, they were not aware of the confusion they had committed. Believing that Baudelaire's mark to spot the place for correction was intended to be an exclamation point, they placed the exclamation point after *"n'importe."*

Crépet concludes that the editors were now faced with another problem: what to do with the rest of the phrase, *"quoi était plus tolérable que cette dérision"* ("what was more tolerable than this derision"), a translation *"qui présentait un sens exactement contraire à celui qu'exigeait le context?—Ils se tirèrent de la difficulté par l'adjonction du préfixe négatif in (intolérable) et du point d'interrogation final"* (p. 376). Thus a phrase which Baudelaire had possibly wanted to correct himself was botched up by his editors after his death. Theoretical as to the poor translation given by Baudelaire, it is plausible when one considers the care with which Baudelaire translated and revised these texts.

In the final analysis, Baudelaire's translations attain a healthy balance: the majority of the passages in Poe are literal or equivalent translations, although the remainder are a mixture of slight improvements and losses (it must be noted that the former outnumber the latter). Thus, in their entirety, Baudelaire's translations are not so much an embellishment of Poe as a faithful homage to him and an effort to recreate him in French with as little interference as possible.

Baudelaire's obsession with Edgar Allan Poe paid off. He successfully brought the spirit of Poe to France through his translations. One of the most original writers of his time, Poe continuously fascinated the French. The power of his imagination, his command of a rich and fluid language, and his tendency to dwell on the macabre captivated his European audience. Metaphysical in thought and often using symbolism to intensify his stories, Poe, though distinctly American, became cosmopolitan in reputation and influence.

Baudelaire, as translator, had license to enhance, undermine or merely reproduce the text. Indeed, the contribution of any translator is generally so significant that it might be difficult to determine whether a final translation should be considered the work of the translator or the originator. For Baudelaire, it is one and the same. Baudelaire himself was not able to make the distinction because he saw Poe as a double of himself, a kindred spirit: *"Savez-vous pourquoi j'ai si patiemment traduit Poe?"* he wrote to a friend. *"Parce qu'il me ressemblait. La première fois que j'ai ouvert un livre de lui, j'ai vu avec épouvante et ravissement non seulement des sujets rêvés par moi, mais des phrases pensées par moi et imitées par lui, vingt ans auparavant."*[10] The popularity of Poe in France suggests that the French appreciated his subjects, his obsessions, his style—in essence, his art. In translating

Poe's work so well, Baudelaire has forever blended the style, form and spirit of Poe with the literature of France.

NOTES

[1] Jacques Cabau, *Edgar Poe par lui-même* (Paris, 1960) p. 40.

[2] See, for example, Thomas Stearns Eliot's comments, Library of Congress Lecture, 19 November 1948; published in *HudR*, 2(1949), 327-342.

[3] Edgar Allan Poe, *Nouvelles histoires extraordinaires*, transl. Charles Baudelaire (Paris, 1965), pp. 112-113.

[4] Pierre Cambiaire, *The Influence of Edgar Allan Poe in France* (New York, 1927) p. 96.

[5] As quoted by Cambiaire, pp. 36-37.

[6] *The French Face of Edgar Poe* (Carbondale, 1957) p. 128.

[7] 3 vols. (New York, 1850).

[8] (New York, 1971) p. 8.

[9] *Oeuvres complètes de Charles Baudelaire*, translations, *Nouvelles histoires extraordinaires par Edgar Poe*, notes and remarks by J. Crépet (Paris, 1933) p. 376.

[10] *Op. cit*, p.17.

ELEGY FOR A "REBEL SOUL": HENRY CLAY PREUSS AND THE POE DEBATE

J. GERALD KENNEDY

In the decade following Poe's death, periodical writers on both sides of the Atlantic disputed his place in American letters. From the outset, "practically all criticism began, and as a rule ended, with a consideration of the life and character of the man."[1] Griswold's notorious "Ludwig" article was largely responsible for this preoccupation, as its moralistic half-truths prompted a flurry of attacks and defenses, all concerned as much with Poe's social conduct as his literary accomplishments. Before the Civil War, the Poe controversy had generated more than a dozen extended essays and the first book-length study, Sarah Helen Whitman's *Edgar Poe and his Critics* (1860).[2] Although these biographical wrangles impeded understanding of Poe's writing, they now reveal much about the literary sensibility of that period dubbed by F. L. Pattee "the feminine fifties." Behind the Poe quarrel lies a broader, more significant disagreement about the duty of the artist to his culture and specifically to prevailing moral and religious attitudes. This problem had been posed initially by the Romantic poets—mainly Byron and Shelley—whose private affairs had scandalized (and intrigued) respectable middle-class readers of the early nineteenth century. Poe was virtually the first writer of note in America to shock the popular audience; the rumor of his dissolution did nearly as much to make him known as his fifteen years in the magazine world. Quite undeservedly, he achieved notoriety as our first literary Bohemian, and his death triggered a debate, the implications of which would not become clear until the advent of twentieth-century literary modernism. For what Poe's case dramatized for Victorian critics was the potentially subversive autonomy of art from the value code of bourgeois society.

Students of Poe have long been familiar with the major documents in this war of words, but one suggestive item has escaped scholarly notice: the essay and elegiac poem by Henry Clay Preuss, published in the Washington *National Intelligencer* on 19 May 1853. At times betraying his own ambivalence about Poe's alleged frailties, Preuss nevertheless felt compelled to defend the dead author from the denunciations of certain literary pundits. In the process, he framed a resonant tribute to Poe's genius, appealed for an end of moral judgments, and helped to mythologize Poe as a fated poet. Little is known of Preuss's own career, but the meager available details suggest that his defense of Poe was occasioned not by friendship or personal loyalty—there is no evidence that the two ever met—but by Preuss's own youthful identification with the emerging image of Poe, the literary martyr. Born in Maryland about 1825 and named for the great Kentucky statesman, Preuss later moved to Washington, where in 1847 he attempted to launch a career as a poet by publishing, at his own expense, a slender volume, *The Artist and Other Poems*. The title poem sheds some light on Preuss's creative sympathies, for it commemorates the death of a young poet named Albion Floyd, who apparently languished in poverty and succumbed to tuberculosis, thus epitomizing the destiny of the artist victimized by the "cold neglect and baseness of a sordid world." Unhappily, *The Artist* also met with cold neglect, and Preuss, perhaps conceding the impossibility of supporting himself as a writer, accepted a position on 23 July 1852, as a clerk in the office of the Chief Engineer of the War Department at a mere $800 per year.[3] In such circumstances he penned the *Intelligencer* piece the following year, voicing both a specific admiration for Poe and a general regret about public disregard for the man of letters.

The tenor and timing of Preuss's tribute suggest that he was in all likelihood responding obliquely to Griswold and more directly to Richard H. Stoddard, whose censorious essay, "Edgar Allan Poe," had appeared in the March 1853 *National Magazine*. Stoddard's sketch, like the earlier portrait by Griswold, displays precisely the malice and self-righteousness against which Preuss sought to defend Poe. We know from Stoddard's *Recollections Personal and Literary* (1903) that the New-England poet and critic had a long standing enmity for Poe, dating back at least to 1845, when Poe (then editing the *Broadway Journal*) rejected Stoddard's "Ode on a Grecian Flute," accused him of plagiarism, and forced him to leave the *Journal*'s editorial office.[4] In October 1852, Stoddard published a fictionalized narrative in the *National Magazine* that presented Poe as "A Great Man Self-Wrecked," a "confirmed drunkard." With his March 1853 essay he took up the cudgel once again: "To write a satisfactory paper on Poe is no easy task, there is so much that is unsatisfactory in Poe himself." Grudgingly, Stoddard admitted that Poe was "not a confirmed drunkard" but rather a man who became intoxicated with a single drink. The truly monstrous aspect of Poe was his analytical mind, which, according to Stoddard, "seems to have utterly lacked the moral sense." He claimed that all of the author's work was darkened by "the radical depravity of a simply analytical mind"; over his writing hung "a starless night of desolation, the shadow of insanity." In Stoddard's judgment, Poe belonged to the "dyspeptic" school of Goethe and Schiller, a mode of literature corrupted by "melancholy and misanthropy" and dedicated to making its readers "unhealthy and unhappy" by laying bare "the black gulfs and chasms of our spiritual nature." Expressing the quintessence of mid-century moral sentimentalism, Stoddard concluded: "What we want is not darkness, but light; not thorns in our path, but roses, and everywhere dew and freshness."

When Preuss shortly thereafter published his appreciation of Poe in the *Intelligencer* (then perhaps the most widely-read newspaper in America), he pitted himself against vengeful critics like Griswold and Stoddard rather than the "dewy-roses" philosophy *per se*. Nevertheless he understood the relationship between the two: Poe's "onslaught upon the 'literary lights' of the day," his attack upon dullness and preciosity, had alienated him from many of his contemporaries. And these were the very purveyors of froth who, after his death, found retribution in calumny. Preuss wrote of Poe: "He had no mercy on a certain class of writers in his life; and they, in their turn, had no mercy on him after his death. Scarcely were his ashes cold in the ground when the whole pack was let loose, 'Tray, Blanch, Sweetheart, and all'." Preuss saw Poe as a "reformer," whose "searching criticisms" sometimes created "the sensation of cold steel searching through the warm flesh," but whose "cathartics" helped to impart a "healthy tone" to "our national literature." Those who had felt the "scorching effects" of his criticism included, of course, Griswold and Stoddard; the latter's essay, decrying the lack of "moral sense" in Poe, seems the implicit point of reference for subsequent remarks by Preuss: "Among other things, it was charged that his nature was a 'moral vacuum'; that he had the most obscure conceptions, if any, of moral rectitude, the holiness of virtue, the sanctity of the affections, even the common proprieties of life, etc."

Preuss answered such accusations in three ways: he first reminded readers of Poe's domestic side, portraying him as "a most loving husband," whose "heart was alive to the most genial impulses of our nature."[5] Preuss then implied that Poe's critics were too crass to appreciate his work; he recalled Fanny Osgood's contention that "'none but a woman could judge of Edgar A. Poe'," and made the patently ironic argument that "none but a woman, with her refined and holy sympathies, could catch, with artistic skill, the delicate shades, the ever-varying lights, the 'lines within lines' of such an exquisitely-wrought piece of God's workmanship." Finally, he insisted that Poe's loneliness and suffering entitled him to a freedom from moral condemnation. Poe experienced alienation because he saw more, felt more than other men; he lived his life on a visionary plane with which conventional morality had nothing to do:

> There is a class of minds so isolated from their kind— so far removed beyond the sphere of our own thoughts, feeling, and existence—that it would be cruel injustice to submit them to the Protean standard of our common humanity. Poor Ishmaelites in the desert of this life, the

very loneliness of their fate should dispose us to suspend our final judgment, and leave them to the Great Master who said "judge not lest ye shall be judged."

Here is the principal thrust of Preuss's defense. The radically different sensibility of the poet entitles him to immunity from censure, for the "Protean standard" of genteel conduct has no applicability to the realm of his imagination. Such "Ishmaelites" as Poe must be judged only by the products of their genius, not by the vagaries of their private lives. In the rhetoric of Christian charity, Preuss thus argued for the primacy of aesthetic values in literary criticism and the right of the artist to pursue a defiant course.

As if in response to the poem "Miserrimus," which closed the March 1853 diatribe by Stoddard, Preuss appended to his seven-hundred-word appreciation a poem of seven stanzas, which merits reprinting as an addition to the corpus of poems about Poe and as an amplification of the image of Poe limned in the prefatory comments:

> Thine was a mind of most unearthly cast,
> Which held no kindred with its fellow-kind;
> But, soaring on the pinions of the blast,
> It towered 'mid the clouds, while far behind
> Earth's humbler millions, wond'ring, shrunk aghast
> From sights which strike the weaker vision blind,
> While thou, like eagle soaring to the sun,
> Hadst deemed thy giant race but scarce begun!
>
> And hadst thou still maintained such dizzy height,
> And dreamt thy dreamings out amid the skies,
> Thou mightst have shone a bright unfading light;
> But, like the setting sun, thou didst but rise
> To lose thy peerless splendor in the night,
> Which set its seal of darkness on thine eyes,
> And, blind and tott'ring in its moral gloom,
> Thy traitor-genius shaped its master's tomb.
>
> Life is a cup, its *surface* sweet to taste;
> And he who would enjoy must learn to *sip*,
> For, quaffing it with much-too-eager haste,
> Its dregs soon turn to ashes on his lip,
> And leave his soul a bleached and ruined waste,
> With all the visions of his fancy nipp'd
> E'en in their bud. And thus it was with thee,
> O, POE! poor fallen child of Poesy!
>
> With bold and fearful power thou didst tear
> The mystic veil from all life's hidden things,

And then thy rebel soul was doomed to bear
The penalty which too much knowledge brings:
Life's brighter lights to thee grew dark and drear—
The mortal drooped though perched on angels' wings!
And now, with all the gifts of genius blest,
Thou didst but ask of Death the boon of rest!

A child of frailty, as an heir of fame,
Men judged thee only in thy darker mood—
Stamped their cold unfeeling verdict on thy name,
Nor paused to sift the evil from the good.
Yet were there moments when the *liquid flame*
Had ceased with mad'ning heat to fire thy blood,
Oh! then thy better nature proved its worth
And wore a hue of Heaven more than earth.

Ah! little reck we of the fearful throes
Which scorched and agonized thy struggling soul
When moved by war between those deadliest foes,
The demon Vice and godlike Self-control!
How oft thy crushed, defeated spirit rose
To dare the fight again—*this* is not told;
We only know, now thou art 'neath the sod,
The *brute* at last has triumphed o'er the God!

Sleep, minstrel, sleep! Oh, life e'en at its best
Was but as some dark fev'rish dream to thee;
'Tis not for us to mar thy "long last rest"
With cold upbraidings on thy memory.
As sunset glories in the fading west
Proclaim the day-god's fallen majesty,
So genius shines about the gifted dead
To tell mankind how great a soul has fled!

Surely we understand better from this elegy Preuss's own limitations as a poet, yet beyond the fustian and trite phrases, the poem expresses a more interesting idea of Poe than we find in the prose defense. That the details of the poet's struggle bear little resemblance to biographical fact is beside the point: what we see here is the myth-making process at work, the construction of an image that presumably answers a personal and cultural need. We watch Preuss endeavoring to create, out of the rumor of inebriation, an heroic Poe capable of withstanding condemnation, a Poe whose personal torment stemmed from a clash between "the demon Vice and godlike Self-control." If Preuss concedes the issue of intemperance, he does so to dramatize Poe's agony with his "traitor-genius." The poem thus interweaves two main themes: the poet's lonely quest for dangerous knowledge, suggested through images of flight, and his battle with drink, portrayed in terms of fire and combat. Perhaps controverting Stoddard's claim (in "Miserrimus") that Poe had failed to reach "the gates of light," Preuss depicts him "soaring to the sun." Reaching the "dizzy height" of supernal revelation carries its inevitable "penalty," however; "too much knowledge" blasts his vision and thrusts him into "moral gloom." By the very nature of such Promethean defiance, his "rebel soul" must endure despair ("Life's brighter lights to thee grew dark and drear"), and this doom leads to the desire for death. Although Preuss acknowledges the self-destructive aspect of Poe's flight toward illumination, he also depicts its godlike boldness; the poet's "power" to "tear / The mystic veil from all life's hidden things" separates him from common humanity and reveals his greatness.

Seen as a reply to Griswold, Stoddard, and critics of that ilk, Preuss's defense undercuts attacks based upon narrowly moralistic grounds. Exponents of the chaste, middle-class ethos of feminized Protestantism regarded Poe as the prototypical lost soul, destroyed by his presumed faithlessness, intemperance, and morbidity. Griswold had pictured Poe in 1849 as one who "walked the streets, in madness or melancholy, with lips moving in indistinct curses"; Stoddard placed him in 1853 among those writers who confused "the boundaries of right and wrong," ignored "the ancient landmarks of faith and morality," leagued themselves "with darkness," and perverted "the very life and mission of all art, viz.: the promotion of joy and gladness, and undying faith in the good and the beautiful."[6] Poe thus represented to the conservative literati of the fifties a subversive force threatening the status quo: the dominance of the "dewy-roses" school. To defend the values of religion, temperance, optimism, and pleasantness required the vilification of Poe—a task taken up readily by those whose mediocrity Poe had exposed.

For Willis, Graham, Preuss, and other admirers, the dark episodes of Poe's life seemed more the result of misfortune than iniquity. They acknowledged the strangeness of his intellect and his tendency to alienate himself from certain arbiters of literary taste. But if his writing did not embody the sentiment and didacticism demanded in the ladies' magazines, it was because his "teeming brain" drew its inspiration from other sources. Absorbed by the problem of disorientation—the unstrung mind and the orphaned soul—Poe largely ignored conventional notions of gentility and rectitude; this indifference (which made him Baudelaire's patron saint) probably disconcerted even some of his American defenders, but they recognized his originality and appreciated, as his hostile critics could not, the agony of genius in an anti-intellectual culture. Like Preuss's friend, Albion Floyd, Poe fell victim to the "cold neglect and baseness of a sordid world." If the genteel literati stereotyped Poe as an unprincipled inebriate, Preuss and others resisted such moralizing and praised his "rebel soul." Although we cannot be sure that Preuss grasped all of the dark implications of Poe's writing, he at least perceived that work in terms of a conflict between the desire for ideality and the disillusionment of forbidden knowledge. In resisting the cultural anaesthesia of pleasantness as he probed "all life's hidden things," Poe gave literary expression to the phenomenology of dread, the existential dilemma, which has afflicted Western thought from Poe's day down to our own. Six years after Preuss's defense, Sarah Helen Whitman shrewdly remarked, "Edgar Poe came to sound the very depths of the abyss. The unrest and faithlessness of the age culminated in him."[7] This quality of rebellious despair, the element which so repulsed moralistic critics, seemed to Poe's early defenders the very essence of his genius and the basis of his legacy.

As for Preuss, the ensuing years brought notoriety rather than fame. A few months after his defense of Poe, he submitted a long historical poem, "A Vision of Freedom," to a local literary competition; when the selection committee, disappointed with all entries, decided not to award "Mr. Latham's prize" of $500, a resentful Preuss published the work at his own expense in early 1854. He then began to compose lyrics for patriotic songs, and in 1854 he also published, with Stewart Macaulay, a rousing popular tune called "The Star-Spangled Home of the Free." His most ambitious literary endeavor appeared in 1857: a five-act farce entitled *Fashions and Follies of Washington Life*, which in all likelihood never saw a public performance. The Civil War years brought controversy for Preuss when his loyalty to the Union cause came into question. In an 1861 newspaper essay, he questioned the use of military force to deal with the secession of South Carolina, and he forgave the insurgent troops, believing them to be simply misled by their commanders. In August 1861 Preuss came under the scrutiny of a congressional committee and was listed among government employees "against whom the evidence furnished a well-grounded suspicion of their loyalty." The evidence against Preuss was slight—the testimony of a fellow-boarder who "came to the conclusion, from frequent conversations with him, that his sympathies were with the south in this movement."[8] Through public displays of patriotism, such as the publication in 1862 of *God Save Our Noble Union and Other Poems of the Times*, Preuss managed to exonerate himself and to retain his position in the War Department, where he held forth as a clerk until the mid-1870s. His literary productions remained sporadic, patriotic, and undistinguished: in 1873 he published a light eight-page poem, "From Columbus Crocket to General Grant on the Indian Policy," and nine years later he brought forth a final collection of seven lyrics, *Songs of National Harmony, Peace and Brotherhood*. The date of his death remains to be established, for unlike the poet whom he had celebrated in 1853, Preuss achieved final and complete obscurity. No traces of his life remain, excepting a handful of chapbooks and his early, fervent defense of Edgar Poe. Even in its outlines, however, the abortive literary career of Henry Clay Preuss suggests something of the difficulties of authorship in nineteenth-century America and something of the process by which Poe became a symbol of the artistic struggle against Philistine convention. For writers from Baudelaire to Hart Crane, his life came to epitomize the persecution of the poet in a basely materialistic culture. In large measure the apotheosis of Poe came about through the effort to counter the slander of his enemies, and in lending his pen to the honorable cause, Preuss participated in the making of an influential myth.

NOTES

[1] Alice L. Cooke, "The Popular Conception of Poe from 1850 to 1890," *UTSE*, 22(1942), 146. The same pattern is noted in Dudley R. Hutcherson, "Poe's Reputation in England and America, 1850-1909," *AL*, 14(1942), 211-233.

[2] Some of the more substantial articles are: C. Chauncey Burr, "The Character of Edgar Allan Poe," *Nineteenth Century*, 5(1852), 19-33; John M. Daniel, "Eulogium," *Southern Literary Messenger*, 16(1850), 172-187; George R. Graham, "The Late Edgar Allan Poe," *Graham's Magazine*, 36(1850), 224-226; and "The Genius and Characteristics of the Late Edgar Allan Poe," *Graham's Magazine*, 44(1854), 216-225; G. W. Peck, "The Works of Edgar Allan Poe," *American Whig Review*, 11(1850), 301-315; John Savage, [untitled], *Democratic Review*, 27(1850), 542-544; 28(Jan. 1851), 66-69; (Feb. 1851), 162-172; John R. Thompson, "The Late Edgar Allan Poe," *Southern Literary Messenger*, 15(1849), 694-696. Mrs. Whitman's book, not published until after the death of Griswold, aimed to contradict innuendo circulated by Poe's enemies.

[3] U.S. Cong., House, *Executive Documents*, 32nd Cong., 2nd sess. (Washington, D.C., 1853), 4: Rpt. 33, 11.

[4] See Stoddard's chapter, "Meetings with Poe," in *Recollections* (New York, 1903), pp. 145-160. See also Burton R. Pollin's chapter on Stoddard, *Discoveries in Poe* (South Bend, Ind., 1970), pp. 189-204.

[5] Preuss drew his information, one suspects, from the 1850 essay by Graham and the 1852 essay by Burr, cited in n2.

[6] The "Ludwig" memoir of Griswold, from which the former passage is taken, is reprinted in *The Recognition of Edgar Allan Poe*, ed. Eric W. Carlson (Ann Arbor, 1966), p. 32; the latter quotations from Stoddard come from the essay on Poe in the *National Magazine*, 2(1853), 200.

[7] *Edgar Poe and his Critics*, p. 65.

[8] U.S. Congress, House, *Reports of Committees of the House of Representatives*, 37th Cong., 2nd sess. (Washington, D.C., 1862), 3: Rpt. 16, 8.

ELIZABETH OAKES SMITH ON POE: A CHAPTER IN THE RECOVERY OF HIS NINETEENTH-CENTURY REPUTATION

KENT LJUNGQUIST AND CAMERON NICKELS

New York literary society of the 1840s enjoyed soirées at which those in attendance listened to occasional poetic recitations, exchanged polite valentines, and heard the most recent gossip. These gatherings provided not only a convenient forum for literary small-talk but also a foundation for subsequent reminiscences about the major and minor *literati* of the time. A frequenter of these affairs was Elizabeth Oakes Smith, wife of the new England humorist Seba Smith, author of *The Jack Downing Letters*. This period in New York furthered her literary career as she was gaining a wider poetic reputation and solidifying her feminist principles, which would reach full expression in *Woman and Her Needs* (1852). Smith also recorded impressions of the famous *literati* with whom she came into personal contact, absorbing anecdotal material that would become part of personal reminiscences and a full autobiographical memoir. Among such literary figures was Rufus Griswold, who basked in the attention of women writers as he edited their works. Smith also became acquainted with Sarah Helen Whitman, Frances Sargent Osgood, and Anne Lynch; moreover, her contacts reached outside the realm of women's poetry and New York society in general to include Ralph Waldo Emerson and Charles Fenno Hoffman. Another entrant to this literary *mise en scène* was Edgar Allan Poe, whose critical reputation was later almost permanently damaged because of Griswold's stinging memoir. A tradition in defense of Poe also emerged at this time, partially because of women who knew him in the 1840s and who felt compelled to answer Griswold's careless rebuke. Beginning in 1858, Elizabeth Oakes Smith launched an opening salvo in what would be a sustained campaign to counter Griswold's attack. Focussing more on the person than the writer, she made one of the earliest attempts to disentangle the legend created by Griswold from Poe's career.

Smith's earliest published commentary on Poe anticipated by two years Sarah Helen Whitman's *Edgar Poe and His Critics* (1860), which stimulated a wholesale revaluation of his critical reputation. As the correspondence between Whitman and Poe's British biographer John Henry Ingram indicates,[1] a painstaking attempt to correct Griswold's gross inaccuracies proceeded while vilifications like those of R. H. Stoddard continued. Smith's unique perspective on Poe has received scant attention, perhaps because her even-handed comments echo neither his most famous champions nor his most infamous detractors.

Nevertheless, her series of periodical articles between 1858 and 1876 provides some of the amplest portraiture of Poe by any of his contemporaries: "Mrs. Oakes Smith's articles on Poe are illuminating productions and perhaps the most unprejudiced of descriptions by his contemporaries. She is alone in preserving C. F. Hoffman's remarks on 'The Raven,' the finest I have met in reading about Poe."[2] Rivaling neither Ingram's pioneering contributions for biographical accuracy nor Whitman's important volume for penetrating insight,[3] her comments will interest students of Poe and his times on several scores. These articles mark a sometimes critical, generally balanced evaluation of Poe, explicitly counter to Griswold's baneful legacy. Unpublished comments in Smith's "Autobiography," moreover, enhance her sympathetic portrait of Poe in the light of tensions in her life and career. Finally and most interestingly for students of the nineteenth-century literary subculture dubbed the Poe Cult, Smith illuminates her contentious relationships with Whitman and Ingram, each vying for attention in efforts to remove the stain from Poe's reputation. In sum, if we connect Smith's articles, unpublished reminiscences, and letters on Poe with the Ingram-Whitman relationship, we can learn more about the respective motives of Ingram, the antiquarian scholar of Poe, and Whitman, the poet's most ardent nineteenth-century defender.

Poe's exposure to the poetry of Elizabeth Oakes Smith, known initially to him only as the wife of Jack Downing's creator, preceded their meeting. He reviewed differing editions of *The Poetical Writings of Elizabeth Oakes Smith*, his first essay appearing in the 23 August 1845 *Broadway Journal* and the second in the December 1845 *Godey's Lady's Book* (*H*12: 228-233); 13: 78-93). His initial response was lukewarm. The first review denigrates the "somewhat forced conception" of Smith's most famous poem "The Sinless Child," a piece she would perceive as having affinities with Poe's *Eureka*.[4] Poe turns the remainder of the review to charging Longfellow with plagiarism from Smith's poem "The Water." A similar skepticism appears in *Godey's*. Citing "The Sinless Child" as "one of the most original of American poems" (*H*13: 79), Poe claimed that its "conception is much better than its execution"; it possesses an "indeterminate air" with only "traces of high poetic capacity."

The first meeting of Smith and Poe thus took place in an atmosphere of tension and defensiveness, since she may have felt compelled to defend her husband's writings against Poe's animadversions.[5] Poe's comments about her poetry,[6] harsher than his somewhat uncritical response to that of other female authors, also may have made her ill-disposed to meet him. Nevertheless, as reported in her first memoir, "Edgar A. Poe," in the *United States Magazine* in

1858 (1: 262-268), she tried to show no malice when they met at the literary soirées of Anne Lynch sometime in 1845. Largely on the basis of these conversations at the homes of Lynch and other New York *literati*, Smith drafted her memoirs of Poe. These meetings occurred when both were on cordial terms with Griswold, whom Smith continued grudgingly to respect despite what she regarded as his inhuman treatment of Poe.[7] Without naming Griswold in the first installment of her developing portrait, Smith charges that Poe was victimized by "great injustice . . . both to the character and the man." In sum, her initial essay marks an attempt to correct biographical inaccuracies, to give a moral estimation, and to comment on his literary output. Acknowledging that Poe was given to excesses, especially from an infirm moral education during his youth, she claims that he "had no appetite for the life of the debauchee." She balances censorious comments, altogether excised from subsequent essays, with corrections of Griswold's charges: "That Edgar A. Poe has been sinned against by the press at large and biographers in particular, is not a subject of doubt . . . ." Charging Poe with a "profound selfism, and reckless disregard for all interests," she nonetheless says: "His character and genius are, perhaps, more remarkable than any which have appeared among us for the same opportunity afforded for analytical investigation." Opposing the slander of Griswold to the claims of those who would prefer to canonize Poe, Smith's comments on "character" mark the first step in what she would later see as a "mental analysis"[8] of Poe, a phrase suggesting phrenological claptrap but indicating Smith's dedicated concern to uncover Poe's idiosyncrasies.

Having developed an estimation of Poe the man, Smith devotes the remainder of her essay to a knowledgeable, if somewhat idiosyncratic, assessment of his writings. Unwilling to place Poe "in the higher ranks" of the poets, she grasps his rejection of passion as an unsuitable subject for poetry and his poetic thrust for high, unearthly beauty. She acknowledges his "weird startling vocabulary," which alerts the reader "to the high, cold realms of the imagination, where we yield instinctively as to a wizard spell." According to Smith, Poe's verse is replete with images of sleep, mystery, and dreams. Subsequently, she would impute Poe's fascination with a transcendent world to his temperamental desire to be "living in dreams" and to be "bedeviled by the real."[9] For the purposes of her 1858 essay she quickly designates the quintessence of his poetic output as "The Raven," then just as abruptly dismisses its explained origin. Not naming Charles Fenno Hoffman, she quotes his penetrating summation of the meaning in that poem: "It is the image of despair brooding above all earthly wisdom." Endorsing neither Poe's poetic subject matter nor his versification,

Smith acknowledges their seductive appeal, the expressive, "dirge-like quality of his muse."

Just as Smith tempers her enthusiasm for Poe's poetry, she admits reservations about his fiction. As in her response to his verse, though, she acknowledges the visceral attraction of the tales: "We have no sympathy with his characters or their surroundings, but he holds us, nevertheless, as the ancient mariner held his victim; we read on with ghastly interest, we hurry on to the close, we cannot escape; we are not pleased but fascinated, and that is his power, a sort of serpent-holding that we cannot resist. He was a truly demonized man—a man possessed—in other words a man of genius." In this tribute to Poe's genius, Smith harks back to the ancient concept of the "daemon," the classical connotations of which linked possession with skill, knowledge, and artistic inspiration.[10]

Smith's initial responses to Poe's critical powers are ambivalent. Calling him "bold, startling, pretentious, but utterly unreliable," she adds: "He was totally dishonest as a critic, not always knowingly so, it may be not at all knowingly." She subsequently laments that no contemporary critic musters comparable trenchancy or courage— echoing the nineteenth-century sentiments about Poe's "tomahawking" style as a critic, a characterization that had wide distribution during the "Longfellow War."

Despite effusive praise for Poe's genius and an attempt at "mental analysis" of "character," the 1858 memoir contains several inaccuracies. Smith announces Poe's birth date as 1811, also mistakenly identifying the location as Baltimore. She alludes to the legend that Elizabeth Arnold Poe was somehow related to the traitor Benedict Arnold. Such errors are ironic because her expressed desire in writing to Ingram in the 1870s was to provide accurate information for the biography that would lay to rest erroneous legends. Though Ingram desired information about his subject from any source, he suspected biographical speculations provided by Smith, who overemphasized the alleged amorous connection between Poe and Lizzie White, daughter of the proprietor of the *Southern Literary Messenger*. All the more ironic are Smith's explicit wishes for biographical accuracy about her own life, a concern for truth that would approach personal obsession when she drafted her own autobiography.[11] Her most egregious factual error, one that she would unfortunately repeat, concerns an assault by a stranger before Poe's death in Baltimore. The discussion stimulating the greatest controversy, one that raised the ire of Whitman and Ingram, focussed on Poe's notorious relationships with women. Springing to his defense, Smith contends that Poe was never treacherous to women. She cites his attraction to a "lady of rare genius and deep spiritualism," without mentioning Whitman by name. She quotes Poe to the effect that a woman of pure spirit would have helped him surmount his personal problems after the death of Virginia. Smith may have intended here a fairly innocuous comment on the "angel-mission of woman," a hallmark of her brand of nineteenth-century feminism; her mentioning the "myriad little loves which make up the experience of the world," however, minimized the importance of Whitman in Poe's life when Smith was publicly revealing Poe's late *amour*, which the knowledgeable *literati* immediately recognized as his attachment to Whitman.[12] Thus, while supporting a poet who had been traduced by Griswold, "Edgar A. Poe" also brought Smith center stage in the cause for biographical accuracy, soon to become a bitter fray involving Whitman and Ingram.

Whitman's response to Smith, which contributed to her ultimate rift with Ingram, appeared in a subsequent issue of the *United States Magazine*.[13] Calling Smith's estimate of Poe "most kind and tolerant," one serving to remove "some undeserved imputations," Whitman questioned the allegation about Poe's dishonesty. In private dealings and in literary expression, Whitman found Poe thoroughly genuine, but she tendered a comment that she would regret when correspondence with Ingram began. She called Poe "vindictive, revengeful, and unscrupulous in the use of expedients to attain his ends."

Much of the material in Smith's "Edgar A. Poe" was reprinted in a subsequent paper retitled "Autobiographic Notes," published in 1867.[14] The differences between Smith's "Edgar A. Poe" and "Autobiographic Notes" lie less in their respective commentaries on Poe than in their relationship to divergent genres. "Edgar A. Poe" is a character sketch *cum* literary analysis, combining factual data and conventional interpretation. In contrast "Autobiographic Notes" constitutes one of the set-pieces that Smith envisioned for her "Autobiography." As such, her piece on Poe, one of a series of autobiographical memoirs prepared for *Beadle's Monthly* in the 1860s, is uncharacteristic of the "Autobiography" overall, most of which she composed in the 1880s. Large portions of the "Autobiography" deal with personal traumas and tensions, reflecting her incapacity to reconcile the puritanical and free-thinking strains in her family heritage.[15] Her 1867 piece on Poe, one of the more public sections of the "Autobiography," represents her desire to play personal problems against public personae. Nevertheless, Smith filters her impressions of the "public Poe" through the consciousness of an autobiographical narrator.

Smith's revisions give a clearer chronological overview of Poe's career than her treatment in the *United States Magazine*. She excises mention of Griswold's charges, largely because she casts herself in the role of a more exacting autobiographical and biographical reporter. She expands her literary analysis, comparing Poe favorably with Byron and Shelley. Perhaps heeding the criticism she received from Whitman, she deletes the section on Poe's dishonesty as a critic. More appropriate in an autobiographical memoir, her treatment becomes anecdotal with personal matters intruding upon public pronouncements: she alludes to her husband's sensitivity about Poe's criticism of the *Downing Letters*, to Emerson's indifference to "The Raven," and to Hoffman's (identified by name) praise for the same poem. Discussion of the salutary contributions of women to society increases. Smith asks: "'Will not women be thus installed as teachers—ay, even as protectors, in the true, ideal development of society?'" Such comments bear relevance to her discussion because Maria Clemm in particular assumed a stabilizing role in Poe's life. As Smith notes, adopting a personal perspective: "I do not know how it would have fared with him had he not found one true, patient, devoted friend in the person of his wife's mother, Mrs. Clem [sic]. She never wearied in her love and thoughtfulness for him." Such comments reflect Smith's growing feminism in the 1850s and 1860s, a cause which would invite controversy as many of the contemporary *literati*, including Poe's British biographer Ingram, would ultimately turn against her. No less significant than the support of Maria Clemm was that of Sarah Helen Whitman; Smith quotes Poe as follows: "a true woman, with superior intellect and deep spiritualism . . . would have transformed my life into something better." Smith completes her 1867 reminiscence by dubbing Poe a "Hamlet-like man," a brooding dreamer of high genius.

For all the differences between "Edgar A. Poe" and "Autobiographic Notes," Smith intended these pieces as progressive contributions to the recovery of Poe's reputation. In the second, she acknowledged the intrinsic value of autobiography in correcting errors of malicious biographers. Just as she hoped her own "Autobiography" would provide a personal, but truthful portrait of an aspiring woman writer in an unsympathetic milieu, she strove to portray Poe in the manner in which he might have presented himself:

> I must and will speak of this man, not as he manifested himself to the world, but by the measure of his intimations, by his own estimate of himself, which is a truer mode of judgment than the world knows. Yes, this man knew what was in himself, and this it was that sustained him through all the perplexities and disheartments of poverty, and all the abuse heaped upon him by the cruelty and malice of his enemies; and it is this faith in himself which enabled him to command the respect even of those critical in judgment and austere in practice,

and which sustained him to the last, and is now fast redeeming his memory.

Her defense of the autobiographical mode could as easily derive from concern about her own diminished reputation in the 1860s as from her support of Poe. Ironically, Poe's most relentless nineteenth-century biographer, Ingram—a man who perhaps earned the characterization "critical in judgment and austere in practice"—heaped abuse on Smith's well-intentioned ventures for their common subject. She sent a copy of her *United States Magazine* memoir to him, already progressing on his life-consuming labors to establish Poe's rightful place in the literary pantheon and eager to receive information from any source. Ingram's response lacked warmth, however, as reflected in correspondence of the 1870s when Smith circulated her essays to what she hoped would be a sympathetic audience.

Ingram's devotion to a more respectable image for Poe is overshadowed by a clear pattern of ambitious competitiveness evident in his correspondence with Whitman and in his responses to Smith's well-meaning contributions. Having found Whitman a better source of information because of her more intimate connections with Poe, he played one woman against another in his attempt to build a storehouse of knowledge. Whitman anguished over Smith's reproduction of "apocryphal conversations which Poe is said to have held" (*PHR*, p. 234) concerning the influence of women on his career. By the 1870s, the cause of recovering Poe's reputation was subsumed in squabbling over which surviving woman most or least influenced Poe. The relationship among Smith, Whitman, and Ingram became a triangular battle of wits: Whitman assumed the role of the wronged woman of probity and gentility whose discrete *amour* with Poe, she felt, had been tastelessly revealed; Smith was seen by Whitman, and by Ingram in particular, as a bumbling culprit who spread misinformation about Poe; and Ingram, adopting the pose of a self-satisfied voyeur, received letters from both and sorted the wealth of data that entered his 1880 biography. He scorned the inaccuracy of Smith's biographical information, but he maintained her as a steady correspondent despite his revelation to Whitman: "Mrs. E. O. Smith is no good & I am in hope that I shall be free from her in a friendly manner" (*PHR*, p. 306). Moreover, he used Whitman's words against her in 1875 by quoting her characterization of Poe as "vindictive, revengeful, and unscrupulous," adjectives she used to reply to Smith's 1858 paper in the *United States Magazine* and reprinted in *Beadle's* in 1867. Ingram's upbraiding of Whitman for Smith's article, which he must have known about for some time—for he had written to Smith before Whitman had recommended her to him—seems disingenuous at best. The tension between Ingram and Whitman intensified because of this characterization, one he advanced judgmentally in an 1876 letter to test Whitman's devotion to Poe. He challenged Whitman to reproduce the letter to Smith in which she purportedly used the words "vindictive, revengeful, and unscrupulous":

> You did not enclose the letter of Mrs. Oakes Smith as stated as, I dare say, you have since discovered. What makes you say about her *not* thinking ill of him [Poe]? She always writes as if a great admirer of him; her most unpleasant allusions were those purporting to be an extract from a letter of yours—by the way, you never denied authorship of that letter. (*PHR*, p. 386)

Whitman attempted to defend herself, acknowledging that she had no copy of the *Beadle* paper before her (*PHR*, p. 391). If she had not portrayed Poe as a paragon, if he were indeed "revengeful," this trait, in her view, recalled Hamlet's righteous indignation. Ironically her defense echoes Smith's characterization of Poe as a "Hamlet-like man."

Despite John C. Miller's glorification of him as Poe's nineteenth-century champion, Ingram's response to Whitman and Smith suggests calculation and duplicity. He perhaps tipped his hand about his attitude toward "literary ladies" in an 1875 letter to Whitman, during a more amicable period in their relationship: "Were it not so terrible I should often laugh at my American lady correspondents. Half their time & space is devoted to *slandering each other*—swearing that Poe cared only for them, & that everybody else who lays claim to his friendship is an imposter! . . . In fact they all look upon Poe's fame as a convenient peg upon which to hang their mediocrities where the world may see!" (*PHR*, p. 306) By 15 April 1876, he could comment about Smith to Whitman: "We can drop her; she is played out" (*PHR*, p. 411). Smith had by this time published two additional articles on Poe—one in *Baldwin's Monthly* in 1874[16] and another in *The Home Journal* in 1876[17]—but these pieces essentially rehashed her previous reminiscences, and as such, were less useful to Ingram. As Smith had "played herself out" in Ingram's eyes, Whitman, too, would eventually fall from his graces, as John Carl Miller's edition of their correspondence indicates.

Nevertheless, in the 1870s Smith continued to expound upon Poe's virtues and explicitly called Griswold's "Life" a "libel, as are many other sketches of him." Her composite portrait of Poe—derived from essays, letters, and her "Autobiography"—underestimated his concrete involvement in the literary matters of his time: his satirical attacks, his deductive *tours de force*, and his editorial achievements. To her Poe remained "more spectral than human. Impassioned was he in a high, weird sense, an unearthly Promethean sense, in a tragic, Shelley-like sense that suggested awe and mystery, if not dread." If she overemphasized the Romantic visionary, she respected his uncompromising dedication to artistic and intellectual pursuits, calling him one of America's foremost writers. An indicated by such comments, her reminiscences fulfill Mabbott's characterization of them as impartial and substantial contributions from a knowledgeable contemporary. Within the context of Ingram's and Whitman's audacious, sometimes strident, attempts to portray Poe definitively, Smith's memoirs provide convenient introduction to the cult of Poe's supporters that constitutes a part of the century's literary subculture.

If some of her comments overemphasize Poe the dreamer, a man who could "be judged from the standpoint of the Ideal alone,"[18] she also contributes to the myth of Poe, the literary bohemian. But as with her comments on the problems of biography and autobiography, her analysis contains self-revelation. Poe symbolizes a side of the obsessive Puritan-bohemian tension in her own life, a conflict arising from memories of her free thinking Universalist grandfather on one side of the family and the traditional piety of her grandfather on the other. Toward the end of the "Autobiography" (AMS, p. 549), as she pondered her influence in the struggle for women's rights—specifically some "poetic tributes" she received for it—she wrote: "I was reaping the benefit of stepping outside of my Puritanic bondage. Brought up as I had been, I had so much to renounce, and so much to do, that I almost danced over my freedom." Suggesting a daughter of the Puritans dancing on the graves of her forefathers, this passage parallels another in which Poe emerges as a figure of "bohemian" artistic freedom in a world of puritanical constraints. In a section, entitled "Myself," she comments, "It may be that the Puritanic mind is not well adapted to purely artistic pursuits." In contrast to puerile obligations imposed by stern, puritan disciplines, "Poe instinctively accepted progressive ideas, and had admiration for those that labor in their behalf, but he would not have toiled, denied himself, and suffered martyrdom for them. His intensity, and he had it greatly, expended itself in a dreamy, beautiful idealism, half sensuous, half intellectual . . . . Poe was Bohemian in every fiber of his body . . ." (AMS, pp. 579-580). Smith advanced the myth of Poe the dreamy-eyed bohemian, but she thereby committed the simple offense of seeing through the lens of her unique vision, a temptation tellingly acknowledged: "There must have been in him a chamelion-like temperament, by which he assimilated to those with whom he associated, and thus each analyzer of Poe gives us a glimpse of his own idiosyncrasies rather than a revelation of this unique, wonderful creation."[19]

NOTES

[1] *Poe's Helen Remembers*, ed. John Carl Miller (Charlottesville, 1980). Subsequent quotation from this volume will be noted in the text by *PHR* and page number. Although the correspondence is meticulously edited, Miller's reticence prevents him from commenting on friction and competitiveness among Ingram, Whitman, and others like Smith who tried to set the record straight about Poe. For the possibility that the "facts" of the Ingram-Whitman relationship may match the fiction of James's *The Aspern Papers*, see Joel Porte's review of *Poe's Helen Remembers*, *AL*, 53(1980), 124-127. Porte's hypothesis was foreshadowed by J. Gerald Kennedy, "Jeffrey Aspern and Edgar Allan Poe: A Speculation," *PoeS*, 6(1973), 17-18. For a brief comment on Smith in regard to Ingram and Whitman, see Kent Ljungquist's review, "J. H. Ingram and Mrs. Whitman," *The Poe Messenger*, 10(1980), 2-3.

[2] The remarks are those of the late *doyen* of Poe scholars, Thomas Ollive Mabbott, as cited in Mary Alice Wyman, ed., *Selections from the Autobiography of Elizabeth Oakes Smith* (Lewiston, Me., 1924), p. 116.

[3] *Edgar Poe and His Critics*, Introduction by Oral S. Coad (1949; rpr. Staten Island, 1980).

[4] Wyman, ed., *Selections*, p. 124 and "Autobiography," AMS, p. 540. Smith's autobiography is a 600-page manuscript in the New York Public Library. She wrote most of it in the 1880s, but many set pieces in it—reminiscences for the most part, such as some of those of Poe—appeared in periodicals in the 1860s and '70s. In *Beadle's Monthly* in the 1860s these pieces appeared as a series titled "Autobiographic Notes." The complete manuscript she prepared was not published in her lifetime, but about half of it appeared as *Selections*, edited by Wyman. Wyman also wrote a biography of Elizabeth and Seba Smith—*Two American Pioneers* (New York, 1927)—and the entries about them in the *Dictionary of American Biography*. Wyman's works have been the standard source of information about Oakes Smith, although the entry about her written by Alice Felt Tyler for *Notable American Women, 1607-1950* is an informative one based upon a fresh assessment of the manuscript autobiography and other sources. Information about Oakes Smith also appears in Patricia and Milton Rickels *Seba Smith* (Boston, 1977). Further references to the autobiography here will be taken from consecutively numbered leaves of the manuscript version and are used with the permission of the New York Public Library.

[5] Poe launched his admittedly "scurrilous" attack on Seba Smith's poem, *Powhatan: A Metrical Romance*, in *Graham's*

Magazine (1841) [*H*10:160-165]. For Poe's possible borrowing from Smith's poem "The Life-Preserving Coffin," see William T. Bandy, "A Source of Poe's 'The Premature Burial,'" *AL*, 19(1947), 167-168. Bandy refers to Mrs. Seba Smith.

[6] An informative general discussion of Smith's poetry appears in Emily Stipes Watts, *The Poetry of American Women from 1632 to 1945* (Austin, Tx., 1977), pp. 97-105.

[7] In her memoir "Autobiographic Notes" on Griswold, *Beadle's Monthly*, 3(1867), 438, Smith ironically connects Poe and Griswold as "exceptional men," "Demonized creations of the laws of whose being the Procrustean outside world knows but little, and upon whom the cacklings and parrot-talk of society are all lost."

[8] In a June 1875 letter to J. H. Ingram, Smith announces that her written impressions of Poe constitute a "mental analysis," a task she sees fit to undertake since she understood Poe's "idiosyncrasies"—Item 196, John Henry Ingram's Poe Collection at the University of Virginia, Microfilm complied by John Carl Miller (Charlottesville, 1960), p. 77.

[9] The quotation is from an April 1875 letter to Ingram, Item 214 Ingram Collection, Microfilm, p. 89.

[10] For a discussion of the classical daemon and its appeal to American Romantics and to Poe in particular, see Ljungquist, "Uses of the Daemon in Selected Works of Edgar Allan Poe," *Interpretations*, 12(1980), 31-39.

[11] In a 17 April 1875 letter to Ingram, she writes of how posterity might treat her: "Indeed when I shake off this mortal coil, I should be glad to find as disinterested, independent, and sturdy a biographer, capable of seeing *within* the *laws* of *my own being*," Item 214 Ingram Collection, Microfilm, p. 89. In an 8 June 1875 letter to Ingram, she laments: "How like a tragedy life becomes when we have looked behind the scenes! How few can ever be written! I am filled with joy over your labor of love for the unhappy poet, and already I think it begins to tell upon the public mind."—Item 233 Ingram Collection, Microfilm, p. 100.

[12] Whitman's early exposure to the *United States Magazine* piece is insured by her quotation from it (p. 264) in *Edgar Poe and His Critics*. She quotes loosely from a woman of the "finest genius" (pp. 39-40) and adds a sentence, not Smith's, about Poe's delighting in the society of "superior women."

[13] Also entitled "Edgar A. Poe," *United States Magazine*, 1(1858), 633-734.

[14] *Beadle's Monthly*, 3(1867), 147-156. Quotations in the next paragraph are from this essay.

[15] Concerning the Puritan-bohemian tension in her own life, there is surely something akin to it in her own family, her grandparents. In a chapter titled "Household of the Liberal Thinker," she describes her maternal grandfather, a Universalist, "at a time when to be one was to be ostracised by his pious neighbors," AMS, p. 18. The following chapter describes the paternal grandfather or Pilgrim side of the family, the Princes. "There had been a feud of several years standing between these Yankee Capulets and Montagues," a feud that the marriage of EOS's mother and father did nothing to end. "As a child," she writes, "I was sorely puzzled between these two Grandparents, and could not fail to hear critiques upon them, which often distressed me, but my immature judgement inclined to the Pilgrim side of the family, as more in accordance with my turn of mind, though certainly the smart, handsome tone about the Huguenot ancestor quite captivated my taste," AMS, p. 18.

[16] "Reminiscences," *Baldwin's Monthly*, 9(1874), 1.

[17] "Recollections of Poe," *The Home Journal*, 15 May 1876, pp. 1-2. Other materials by Smith touch on Poe: her "Autobiographic Notes" on Griswold, *Beadle's Monthly*, 3(1867), 437-441 in which she opines that Griswold had not "felt him human," referring to Poe; her "Sarah Helen Whitman," *Baldwin's Monthly*, 19(1879), 2-3; comments in AMS, pp. 540, 579-580; and her "Reply to Mrs. Whitman" in the John Hay Collection at Brown University.

[18] April 7, 1875 letter to Ingram, Ingram Collection, Item 214, p. 89.

[19] Quoted from "Poe and Rachel," *Phrenological Journal* (1879), in the Elizabeth Oakes Smith Collection at the University of Virginia. In this piece, Smith refers to Poe's "chamelion-like temperament," a phrase foreshadowed in a February 1875 letter to Ingram, Item 203, Ingram Collection, Microfilm, p. 83. The "Rachel" referred to is a contemporary actress eulogized in "The Death of Rachel," *Baldwin's Monthly*, 21(1880), 2-3.

HENRY JAMES AND THE QUESTION OF POE'S MATURITY

JAMES W. GARGANO

Many admirers of Edgar Allan Poe have bristled at young Henry James's pronouncement that "An enthusiasm for Poe is the mark of a decidedly primitive stage of reflection."[1] Indeed, James may be among the first of those critics who, like Paul Elmer More and T. S. Eliot, stigmatize Poe enthusiasts as chronically immature. From his high humanist perch, Paul Elmer More looks down on Poe as "the poet of unripe boys and unsound men."[2] Eliot's point in "From Poe to Valéry" differs from James's but it certainly springs from a Jamesian sensibility.[3] Eliot contends that Poe had "the intellect of a highly gifted young person before puberty. The forms which his lively curiosity takes are those in which a pre-adolescent mentality delights." Granted—something often forgotten—that James concedes a "very original genius [to] the author of the 'Tales of Mystery'" just as Eliot credits him with a "powerful intellect." Yet, when the final word is spoken and the greatest are separated from the merely original, James debunks Poe as a charlatan who never outgrew an immature addiction to flashy effects. As will be shown at some length, he also provoked a mild international incident which vividly illustrates how, even from the beginning, James's observations were lifted from an interesting context, garbled, or completely misunderstood.

For all the debate they have generated, James's strictures on Poe are almost parenthetical remarks contained in an essay on Charles Baudelaire, originally published in the *Nation* (2 April 1876, pp. 279ff). In that early essay, James takes a line entirely different from that of Eugene Benson who, in 1869, described Baudelaire for the readers of the *Atlantic Monthly* (22: 171-179) as the "Poet of the Malign" and as a writer "remarkable for his pitiless logic and lyric fury of expression." In contrast, James belittles the French poet as focusing on the picturesque elements of the sordid rather than on "human life at large" and accuses him of a "permanent immaturity of vision." Essentially, James disparages Baudelaire's treatment of evil as something which "begins outside and not inside, and consists primarily of a great deal of lurid landscape and unclean furniture" (p. 77). Unlike Hawthorne, who "felt the thing at its source," the author of *Les Fleurs du Mal* is condemned as a shallow connoisseur of filth wishing to shock and disgust: in other words, Hawthorne treats the confrontation with evil as a psychologically crucial experience, while Baudelaire quite consciously utilizes it as a perverse adornment for his verses. James can find no justification for Baudelaire in the argument that literature must be judged in terms of art rather than subject matter. For him, art is riches and most mature when it springs from the inner compulsion of a unified sensibility that embraces the whole gamut of experience; thus, a literature, which like Baudelaire's, exempts itself from the moral sense—and James is not thinking about restrictive religious or ethical codes—proceeds from a limited consciousness and is necessarily puerile.

Despite his seemingly inexhaustible inventiveness, then, Poe is like Baudelaire obsessed by adventitious effects rather than the large central concerns of man. His works do not appeal to the serious mind because he disdains to incorporate into them the multiple aspects of reality. He prefers the thin fringe to the core, the *outré* and unnatural to the natural. In short, he refuses to put his whole self and life into the creative act. In words that might not be out of place in an Eliot essay, James asserts, "People of a large taste prefer rich works to poor ones" (p. 82). From this we can infer that Poe and Baudelaire are not quite adult writers because they childishly conceive of literature as splendid exhibitionism.

When he wrote this essay on Baudelaire, James's career as a novelist had just begun and his critical views had less catholicity than they would acquire. That his opinions could change may be observed by his later admiration for Walt Whitman, another poet he had once refused to take seriously. The influence of Poe that Burton Pollin and other critics discover in James's fiction may appear to suggest an alteration in James's perception of Poe's worth.[4] After all, in *The Golden Bowl*, James's last novel, the Italian Prince cites a "wonderful tale by Allan Poe" that illustrates the far reaches of the American imagination in its evocation of a "thickness of white air that was a dazzling curtain of light, concealing as darkness conceals."[5] If the Prince could read into *The Narrative of Arthur Gordon Pym* an instance of the American imagination at its most "impenetrable," it may be deduced that James belatedly arrived at a more favorable appraisal of Poe than he had expressed in 1876.

Yet, James saw fit to include his essay on Baudelaire in *French Poets and Novelists* in 1878 without modifying his condescension to Poe. In addition, he was only slightly kinder when in 1879 he pronounced Poe "a man of genius" whose "intelligence was frequently great," only to castigate his critical judgments as "pretentious, spiteful, and vulgar."[6] Moreover, as Adeline Tintner points out, James's very use of *Pym* in *The Golden Bowl* did not deter him from depreciating the material he borrowed and, he thought, improved upon;[7] he could still say in 1909 that the "would-be portentous climax of Edgar Poe's '*Arthur Gordon Pym*'" relies excessively on "the horrific in itself" and thus is so much "imagination wasted."[8] Once again, Poe is blamed for expending precious genius on anomalies and wonders without human import; he figures as the manipulative artist who produces sensations to stimulate readers seeking thrills (perhaps, he has some affinity to the early version of the clever and cynical sculptor, Gloriani, in *Roderick Hudson*, a novel roughly contemporaneous with the essay on Baudelaire). Finally, in 1913, with the publication of *A Small Boy and Others*, the aging James relegates his enthusiasm for Poe to his own extreme youth when he and his brother William "communed to satiety, even for boyish appetites, over the thrill of Poe's choicest pages.[9]

Even without prevision, any unbiased reader should have found the argument of James's early criticism of Poe in *French Poets and Novelists* unmistakable. In comparing Baudelaire with an American fiction writer and in referring indiscriminately to Poe's tales, verse, and even *Eureka*, James concerned himself primarily, not with individual works, but with the quality of the authors' sensibilities. If James's logic had been addressed, it might have been questioned and a heady critical debate might have ensued. Instead, most American reviews of *French Poets and Novelists* paid little attention to James's animadversions on Poe, although the *Atlantic Monthly* (42[1878], 119) approved of the praise accorded Hawthorne at the expense of the French poet in the "shrewd and trenchant essay on Baudelaire." The *New York Times* (13 May 1878, p. 3) declared the essay on Baudelaire among the best things in the book, but it seemed to worry about the reception of James's critical views in England. It concluded with the conviction, however, that "whether England likes these reviews or not, Americans may be sure that from no one else will they get criticism of finer flavor and sounder quality than from Mr. James."

The English reviewers were far from sympathetic to James's facile dismissal of Poe as poet. In the *Academy*, for example, George Saintsbury noted as a strange phenomenon "the incomprehensible fancy of American critics for depreciating Poe" and ruled James "out of court" for categorically referring to Poe's "very valueless verses" (20 April 1878, p. 337). The *British Quarterly Review* did not agree with the critical sentiments in "the short paper upon Baudelaire" but refrained from concrete objections (1 January 1878, p. 575). The *Athenaeum* registered dismay at James's wholesale indictment of Poe's poetry. Conceding that Poe sometimes wrote badly and ultimately lacked the "deep vision of Vishnu," the *Athenaeum* critic ranked "Ulalume" as "the greatest *tour de force* in English literature, perhaps the greatest in its line in any literature." Although he hedged his praise of Poe with minor reservations, the reviewer affirms that if James "means to characterize as valueless the body of Poe's poetry we ... decidedly dissent from the criticism" (16 March 1878, p. 339). It appears that

English periodical writers took Poe more seriously in the 1870s and 1880s than did their American confreres. Indeed, in an 1879 review of William Gill's *The Life of Edgar Allan Poe*, the lordly *Westminster Review* concludes (n.s. 55: 224): "It is in his Poems and Tales that Poe is to be studied. In them, he was certainly great; and we predict for them a vigorous life when many productions which have succeeded better are dead."

To examine the little international episode already mentioned is interesting as a manifestation, if not an outburst, of an ongoing English-American controversy about Poe. As the *New York Times* admitted in 1878, "What England thinks is still a matter of no little concern to a large majority of Americans," Undoubtedly, the *Nation's* hostility in 1875 (25 March, p. 209) to John H. Ingram's *Works of Edgar Allan Poe* can be partly attributed to Yankee pique. Rebuking him for his account of Poe's dismissal from West Point, the reviewer charges Ingram "with a total misapprehension . . . of the case (pardonable, perhaps, in an Englishman who dislikes America, and rather prefers to show that he does)." The *Nation* injects more nationalistic peeve into its rejection of Ingram's survey of Poe's life: "The picture which we must draw even from the conflict of testimonies does not justify Poe's English biographer in inveighing against the Americans for not doing for him what it was quite impossible for any one to do." Overly sensitive or not, at least some Americans resented British superiority to their putative attitude toward Poe as man and poet.

The actors in the international drama I wish to consider were an anonymous reviewer in the London *Pall Mall Gazette* and the once reputable poet-novelist-critic Edgar Fawcett. One can imagine a detached Henry James, like one of his cool, spectatorial characters, enjoying the critical skirmish from the sidelines and marveling at how totally the combatants missed the point of his essay on Baudelaire and his comments on Poe.

The controversy was occasioned by the publication in 1882 of *The Poems of Edgar Allan Poe*, with an appreciative essay by Andrew Lang. In his notice of the book, 14 January 1882, the reviewer for the *Gazette* (p. 5) concedes Poe's faults as a man and poet but praises his "extraordinary gift of style." First, the reviewer, like Saintsbury before him, impugns those Americans who will not admit that "the poetry of Edgar Poe still remains the most individual poetic product to which the United States have given birth." Henry James is then singled out as the typical American disparager of Poe, but his main charge—that Poe is an immature and undeveloped genius—is completely ignored. With less good nature than Saintsbury, the English reviewer airs his general annoyance with American critics, but he seems particularly upset by

James for "venturing to speak of Poe's 'very valueless verses'." With the heavy hand of many reviewers past and present, the anonymous Englishman lumps James with other Americans who "ask if critics can be 'sincere' in preferring Poe's light tones of music to the intellectual severity of Bryant, the humanity of Longfellow . . . the wit of Holmes." Of course, James never asked such a preposterous question, and his argument is passed over in favor of journalistic commonplaces.

Once he has denounced James as a "typical American" to whom he attributes judgments not expressed in the Baudelaire essay, the English reviewer further narrows the argument and delivers himself of a lecture on why Poe will outlast Bryant, Longfellow, and Holmes, who are not even mentioned in James's work. He instructs his readers that intellectual force, love, pity, and the refinements of wit cannot insure the survival of poetry: only those poets endure who achieve "a certain indefinable felicity of style, a power of saying things as they never were said before." With a strong whiff of chauvinism, the reviewer asserts that, since all objective critics acknowledge the superiority of English poetry to American, the English verdict that Poe "has taken his place as one of the fashioners of style" must be accepted. After all, doesn't Poe's influence on Tennyson, Arnold, Rossetti, and Swinburne certify the enduring qualities of his poetry? Poe was surely blessed with an "extraordinary gift of style" which "will preserve his verse, like a rose petal in a drop of glycerine."

Two months after the *Gazette's* defense of Poe, Edgar Fawcett entered the lists in support of James. His essay, "Poe As A Poet," appeared on 25 March 1882 in *The Literary World* (pp. 96-97). Announcing himself a partisan of James and no friend of Poe, Fawcett recalls that upon reading "the American critic's rather laconic condemnation," he was impressed by his "daring posture toward a clique who have for years rhapsodized over the poetry of Poe." Extolling James as a balanced and brilliant critic without belligerency, Fawcett applauds him for exposing an "empty poetic method and over-praised literary artificiality."

The reference to artificiality encourages the hope that Fawcett will face up to James's major thesis. Yet, after an angry prelude, Fawcett limits himself to contesting the *Gazette's* three main points: that Poe's gift of style makes him superior to Bryant, Longfellow, and Holmes; that Poe had the ability to say things that were never said before; and that his uniqueness of expression will insure imperishability to Poe's verses. In presenting his counter-arguments, Fawcett disregards the larger theme of the essay on Baudelaire and never even broaches the question of Poe's appeal to those readers arrested at a "decidedly primitive stage of reflection." Indeed, his response to the *Gazette* has, strictly speaking, little to do with James, who serves as a pretext for an attack on British opinion and Poe.

Fawcett confronts the *Gazette's* first argument with the unJamesian remark that such "pure and noble writers" as Bryant, Longfellow, Holmes, and Lowell—the last of whom is mysteriously smuggled into the polemic—"are not to be named in the same year as Poe." Such an assertion apparently calls for no proof, its truth being manifest to all readers who prefer "sincerity" to "attitudinizing." Here Fawcett misses the opportunity to relate Poe's imputed lack of sincerity to James's belief in his fixation on effects for their own sake. Instead, he pursues his headlong course, making a lukewarm concession to Poe's prose, as James had done, but still devaluing it as "not great in the first degree": in order to see its weakness, we are advised to measure it by Hawthorne's more imaginative works. Even "The Fall of the House of Usher" merits attention only as an arresting example of the second-rate.

Fawcett satirically agrees with the *Gazette's* second claim, that Poe said things as they were never said before: "Ulalume" is charged with being about as "ludicrous" as Bret Harte's parody of it (a far cry from the *Athenaeum*'s early praise of it as the greatest *tour de force* in English literature); melancholy in "The Raven" does not disguise its banality, and its rhythm seduces the ear and "almost insults the intelligence"; and "Annabel Lee" is so wretched a piece of melodic inanity that its very "name ought to be a warning to unborn poetasters." Clearly, Fawcett echoes the sense of Emerson's dismissal of Poe as the "jingle man" who concocted mindless verses. Instead of being a master of style, Poe replaces style with a multitude of febrile mannerisms.

In concluding his diatribe, Fawcett does not bother to rebut the contention that Poe's poetry will last like a "rose-petal in a drop of glycerine." Instead, he explodes into a series of invectives: among the terms used to characterize Poe's poetry we find "senseless," "tiresomely vulgar"—an anticipation of Aldous Huxley's broadside against Poe?— "silly artifice," "vapid inanity," and "incontinent epithets." Fawcett impatiently denies that Tennyson owes any debt to Poe, though he says nothing about Poe's possible influence on Arnold and the others. With a sort of summary justice, Fawcett then exults that it is about time that Poe should be unmasked for the benefit of "those who blindly adopt the shiboleths of certain prejudiced spokesmen." One can only suppose that Poe's devotees were a formidable and intimidating lot in 1882 and that James went directly against received opinion.

"Poe As A Poet" ends with a vindication of James and a panegyric on his style. Blaming the literary climate in the 1880s for the undervaluation of James, Fawcett assails the times for ignoring "good sense" and preferring "gushing sentimentality in place of honest feeling." After predicting that the future will celebrate James for the "native grandeur of his great style," Fawcett concludes by seeing an appositeness in the true stylist's unmasking of the false and pretentious one: "It appears quite in the logical way of things that he who wrote *The American*, *Roderick Hudson*, and *The Portrait of a Lady*, should waken us to a recognition of how tame and meretricious are *Annabel Lee*, *The Bells*, and *Ulalume*."

So, an intemperate critical debate about James's essay says nothing about his judgment that Poe's sensibility never expanded beyond the passions and preoccupations of a precocious boy. The Jamesian bias that Poe and Baudelaire are crafty merchandisers of artistic effects designed for show rather than psychological revelation is never faced.

For what it is worth, I should like to speculate on why James perpetually downgraded Poe's artistry. First, in spite of subterranean similarities, the two writers seem to be concerned with basically different concepts of reality. Unlike James who imported terror and evil into drawing rooms and well-mannered country gardens, Poe seeks to know the self through its relation to—perhaps confrontation with—what he regarded as elemental and universal forces. He wanted to know God and man's place in the eternal scheme and lacked James's almost wholly secular concern with the minutiae of contemporary social relations. Poe's purpose requires the invention of a fictional world reflecting in its enigmatic manifestations the ultimate mystery of transcendent reality; he revels in singularly dreary tracts of no-man's land that arouse inexplicable and other-worldly sensations, castellated abbeys fortified to shut out Death himself, pentagonal rooms that contain the history of sorrow, maelstroms and pits that conceal infernal depths, and Pym's haunted ocean leading to quintessential blackness. To realize his fictional world, Poe refines away domestic manners and social nuance, blurs the line between the natural and the supernatural, and, in general, dissolves the delicate traceries of the actual. To James, all this was not only highly colored Gothicism but it had no structure of thought or deep feeling behind it. It is an instructive literary irony that the author of "The Jolly Corner," the touching story of Spencer Brydon's search for and flight from his *alter ego*, could not be moved by the mixed emotions of attraction and repulsion that William Wilson experiences toward his double. It is positively mystifying that the late-nineteenth-century master who narrated some of his best tales from the first-person point of view could not see his debt to Poe's anguished and probing centers of consciousness in such masterpieces as "The Cask of Amontillado" and "Ligeia."

I believe that James was wrong about Poe and that his blind spot was his failure to recognize what Poe was doing; he could not accept the landscapes of the famous tales and poems as emblematic of inner, spiritual states and real torment. Finding the horror gratuitous, he could sense no humane truth in the disorders that Poe's narrators find echoed, mirrored, and implied in natural and cosmic phenomena. I suspect that James did not grasp the fundamental fact that Poe's visions had a stark, personal basis. Perhaps he was partly misled by Poe's description of the calculation with which he wrote "The Raven" and the strong emphasis on deliberate effect in his famous definition of the short story. Perhaps, too, he too glibly subscribed to his friend James Russell Lowell's superficial view that in Poe the heart was all squeezed out by the mind. In any case, James conceived Poe's scenic horrors to be ends in themselves, cerebral tricks that aim at the purely childish excitation of sensation. Poe, then, was a clever juvenile who became adept at playing bogey man and never developed an adult involvement in the intricate web of human intercourse. For all his critical perspicacity, James saw Poe's works as hocus-pocus and mere scenery, and he missed the inner drama, the irony, and quest for meaning behind the painted device and the stagy foreground.

As early as 1872, four years before the Baudelaire essay appeared, James had already—and I am afraid permanently—categorized Poe as an ingenious showman. Reviewing an exhibition of French art in Boston, in the *Atlantic Monthly* (29: 116), he describes Alexandre Decamps, a painter of the exotic and melodramatic, as an artist "whose mission is the pursuit of effect, without direct reference to truth." He then goes on to belittle Decamps, whom he contrasts to the more serious Delacroix, by comparing the details of one of Decamps's pictures to "some first-rate titbit of Edgar Poe or Charles Baudelaire." Already in 1872, James had made up his mind about the nature of Poe's talent. More than thirty-five years later, in his Preface to *The Beast in the Jungle* volume of the New York Edition, James still thought of Poe as the marvelous boy who never put his heart or conscience into his deliberately sensational art.[10]

Yet—and it is a big "yet"—Poe was a part of James's literary consciousness, a part of the native American tradition in which he had his roots. Poe's works entered his literary bloodstream and became endemic to him. In tracing the development of his own social and aesthetic sensibility in *A Small Boy and Others*, James could recall that, in their earliest youth, he and his brother William recognized with their "small opening minds" the "predominant lustre" of Poe's genius in such tales as "The Gold-Bug," "The Pit and the Pendulum," and "The Murders in the Rue Morgue." He remembers "forever mounting on little platforms at our infant schools to 'speak' The Raven and Lenore and Annabel Lee," and he maintains that "far from misprizing our ill-starred magician we acclaimed him surely at every turn; he lay upon our tables and resounded in our mouths, while we communed to satiety, even for boyish appetites, over the thrill of his choicest pages."[11] In his later, conscious literary career, James could feel free to borrow, revise, and, as he imagined, improve upon his fictional ancestor, but he could do so only after he had established that in Poe there was a fatal disjunction between manner and content—that in the truest sense there was only manner and no content at all.

NOTES

[1] *French Poets and Novelists* (1878; rpt. Freeport, N.Y., 1972), p. 76.

[2] "A Note on Poe's Method," *SP*, 20(1923), 309.

[3] *HudR*, 2(1949), 335.

[4] Burton R. Pollin, "Poe and Henry James: A Changing Relationship," *YES*, 3(1973), 232-242.

[5] *The Novels and Tales of Henry James* (New York, 1909), 23: xix.

[6] *Hawthorne* (1879; rpt. Garden City, n. d.), p. 58.

[7] "James Corrects Poe: The Appropriation of *Pym* in *The Golden Bowl*," *ATQ*, 37(1978), 91.

[8] *The Novels and Tales of Henry James*, 17: xix.

[9] Frederick W. Dupee, ed. *Henry James: An Autobiography* (Princeton, 1983), p. 36.

[10] See n. 8.

[11] Dupee, p. 36.

IN DEFENSE OF BEAUTY: STEDMAN AND THE RECOGNITION OF POE IN AMERICA, 1880-1910

ROBERT J. SCHOLNICK

In November 1878 Dr. Josiah Gilbert Holland, the powerful editor of *Scribner's Monthly*, devoted the first portion of his "Topics of the Time" column to a proud analysis of the several factors that had contributed to the extraordinary success of the magazine that he had founded only eight years ago. In revealing that circulation was "crowding closely upon a hundred thousand," Holland gave factual basis for the growing realization that *Scribner's* was now pressing *Harper's* for preeminence among American middle-class monthlies. Far and away the most important factor in the magazine's popularity, Holland observed, was the unrivalled excellence of its pictorial department. After also crediting the magazine's preference for serializing novels by American writers, which contrasted with *Harper's* policy of relying on English imports, he boasted of the great popularity of its editorial section, which included columns on "Home and Society," "Culture and Progress," "The World's Work," and "Bric-a-Brac." "Of a carefully prepared editorial department, treating political, social, and household matters, giving literary and art criticism, and detailing the progress of invention and discovery," he asserted, "the characteristic popular magazine of Great Britain knows nothing."[1] Through his own column he instructed his fellow Americans on these and many other subjects, becoming, as Edward Eggleston wrote after his death in 1881, "the most popular and effective preacher of social and domestic moralities in his age; the oracle of the active and ambitious young man; of the susceptible and enthusiastic young woman; the guide, philosopher and school-master of humanity at large, touching all questions of life and character."[2]

Also a best-selling poet and novelist and—as "Timothy Titcomb"—the author of such books of instruction as *Titcomb's Letters to Young People, Single and Married* (1858), Holland well understood the power of literature to shape the character of a people. He demanded that all art serve an explicitly moral, even didactic purpose: "Art is not a master, but a minister," he insisted in an 1872 column, and he forthrightly condemned the art-for-art's sake movement: "All that is written about beauty being its own apology and art for its own justification—about 'truth to art for art's sake'—is the baldest nonsense. Art has no 'sake' . . . . All art that has its end in itself or in its author is a monstrosity." The only creative expression worth attending to according to *Scribner's* editor was that solidly based "on the revelations of The Great Book."[3]

For the most part, the American literary tradition as he knew it, New England in origin and continuing inspiration, was consistent with those expectations. In his column for October 1878, "Our Garnered Names," which had been occasioned by Bryant's death, he celebrated the moral purity of the national literature as a fitting expression of its lofty civilization. But in concluding, he launched a furious attack against three American writers who represented a challenge to the values of the tradition: Whitman, Poe, and Thoreau. Of Poe he fulminated, "Why an age which can produce such a poet as Bryant, who is as healthy and health-giving in every line as the winds that soar over his native hills, can be interested in the crazy products of a crazy mind, so far as to suppose that they have any poetry in them, or any value whatever, except as studies in mental pathology, we cannot imagine."[4] The intensity of Holland's anger provides one indication of the growing popularity of Poe and Whitman. He had refused to allow any mention of Whitman in *Scribner's*, and within the previous three years had published three major articles by other writers warning that, entrancing as Poe's art might appear at first, in truth it was vitiated by the same immorality that had ruined its author's disgraceful life.

The first, Francis Gerry Fairfield's notorious "A Mad Man of Letters," published in October 1875, is devoted to proving that Poe "was the victim of cerebral epilepsy, and that the majority of his later tales are based upon the hallucinations incident to that malady; furthermore, that he was always aware, in his later years, of impending dementia." Making a show of enlightened generosity, Fairfield remarked that, since Poe's incurable condition was responsible for a "perversion of the moral nature" which "fatally perverts our perception of reality," he should not be held responsible either for the moral failures so evident in his life or the "deficiency in ethical emotion of his works." Fairfield drew from Poe's works to construct what he called "a kind of psychological biography" to trace the progressive degeneration of "his brain until sanity was only a recollection, and in the gutter he fell and died."[5]

The next April *Scribner's* published "Poe, Irving, Hawthorne," by George Parsons Lathrop, husband of Hawthorne's daughter Rose. Lathrop conceded the magnetic force of Poe's art: "As a mere potency, dissociated from qualities of beauty or truth, Poe must be rated almost highest among American poets; and high among prosaists; no one else offers so much pungency, such impetus and frightful energy crowded into such small space." But Lathrop's essential point was that art cannot be considered apart from moral categories, as Poe's case demonstrated so well: Poe's "passionate search for the beautiful, unhelmed, erring, guided by no North Star of faith . . . is the very thing which drove him into such whirlpools of physical horror and ignoble wallowings in decay; because it issued from interior discord,and was not a normal, deep-seated desire."[6] Lathrop then contrasted Poe's lack of moral purpose with the sane, healthy moral vision of Hawthorne—a familiar point of comparison during this period. Lathrop seems to be responding to one of the few articles sympathetic to Poe to appear in a major American magazine in the post-Civil War years, Eugene Benson's "Poe and Hawthorne," published in the *Galaxy*, December 1868. This neglected, penetrating essay, mistakenly characterized in one bibliography as "unsympathetic to Poe,"[7] forcefully argued that Poe and Hawthorne were "the only two American literary men who have had the sense of beauty and the artist's conscience in a supreme degree."[8]

Finally, in "Last Days of Edgar A. Poe," published in *Scribner's* for March 1877, Susan Archer Talley Weiss provided a pleasant report of Poe's gracious behavior during his final visit to Richmond, where, as a young girl interested in poetry, she had come to know him. She admiringly recounted Poe's gentlemanly manners and polite interest in her verse. But such was the censorious climate of the 1870s that Mrs. Weiss felt compelled to separate herself from his immorality. To do this, she resorted to the pseudo-science of phrenology:

> The shape of his head struck me, even on first sight, as peculiar. There was a massive projection of the broad brow and temples, with the organ of casualty very conspicuously developed, a marked flatness of the top of the head, and an unusual fullness at the back. I had at this time no knowledge of phrenology; but now, in recalling this peculiar shape, I cannot deny that in Poe what are called the intellectual and animal portions of the head were remarkably developed, while in the moral regions there was as marked a deficiency. Especially there was a slight depression instead of fullness of outline where the organs of veneration and firmness are located by phrenologists. This peculiarity detracted so much from the symmetrical proportions of the head that he sought to remedy the defect by wearing his hair tossed back, thus producing more apparent height of the cranium. (15: 711-712)

Perhaps Holland, a medical not a theological doctor, felt the observations of Fairfield and Weiss on Poe's neurological condition provided sufficient evidence for him to brand Poe's work "the crazy product of a crazy mind."

The *Scribner's* essays, if perhaps extreme, reflect an attribute of much post-Civil War criticism of Poe: an inability to separate the work from the alleged failings of the man.[9] As Lathrop asserted: "The life and writings stand intimately connected, almost inseparable, in Poe" (p. 803). Certainly, this is evident in Richard Henry Stoddard's mean-spirited biographical sketch for *Harper's*, published in September 1872.[10] The smug dismissal of Poe by most of the leading American men of letters is reflected in the comments of Henry James in an essay on Baudelaire published in the *Nation* in 1876. James, who would later modify his opinion, observed that

> For American readers, . . . Baudelaire is compromised by his having made himself the apostle of our own Edgar Poe. He translated, very carefully and exactly, all of Poe's prose writings, and, we believe, some of his very valueless verses. With all due respect to the very original genius of the author of the 'Tales of Mystery,' it seems to us that to take him with more than a certain degree of seriousness is to lack seriousness one's self. An enthusiasm for Poe is the mark of a decidedly primitive stage of reflection. Baudelaire thought him a profound philosopher, the neglect of whose golden utterances stamped his native land with infamy. Nevertheless, Poe was vastly the grater charlatan of the two, as well as the greater genius.[11]

The critical situation was complicated by the appearance in the late 1870s of works by such English champions as John H. Ingram and William F. Gill which sought primarily to vindicate Poe's behavior. The *International Review* published Ingram's error-filled "Edgar Allan Poe" in March 1875 (pp. 145-173). The *Atlantic* recognized that Gill's biography, published in 1877 by C. T. Dillingham, had set out to uphold the familiar position of Poe's partisans, that he must "be regarded as a remarkably praiseworthy being, with slight faults, who has been the victim of wholly unaccountable criticism."[12] A way had to be found to put aside the problem of Poe's life—however fascinating—if American readers were to be able to appreciate his art.

The article that did precisely this—first demonstrate the irrelevance of biographical considerations to literary evaluation and then undertake an appreciative but critical analysis of the work—Edmund Clarence Stedman's "Edgar Allan Poe"—appeared in May 1880, ironically in the magazine that had been most hostile to Poe, Holland's *Scribner's*. Born in 1833, Stedman was a member in good standing of the New York Stock Exchange and as both poet and critic he had been from the first a valued contributor to *Scribner's*.[13] His series in the magazine on the *Victorian Poets*, published in 1875 by Houghton, Mifflin, had been both a critical and popular success. Holland included Stedman on his list of "Garnered Names" of American poets, and he was anxious to have him begin a series on American poets similar to that on the Victorians. "You will do it for the literary class as well as Lowell, and for the popular reader a great deal better."[14] Such was Stedman's standing that he was able to insist—over Holland's strenuous objections—on publishing in *Scribner's* favorable essays on the two American poets the doctor had attacked most vehemently; his "Walt Whitman" appeared in November 1880, just six months after the essay on Poe. Appearing in Holland's citadel of middle-class piety, these essays were responsible for a dramatic change in the reputations of both writers and so contributed to the evolution of a more cosmopolitan literary environment in America. We can be sure that Stedman's essay on Poe was for Holland, as he conceded of the Whitman, "a bitter pill" (p. 228).

Stedman recognized that he could not simply ignore the subject that had absorbed so much attention, Poe's life. But in briefly reviewing the biographical facts, he charted a middle course. He freely admitted that Poe's behavior was by no means blameless, that he did suffer from an "inherent *lack of will*."[15] On the other hand, Stedman reminded his readers that as "poet and man of letters," Poe faced extraordinary difficulties in attempting to earn his living by his pen in a "new country" where conditions were decidedly unfavorable to the professional writer (p. 111). Stedman's essential purpose, however, was not to judge the man but to demystify the writer; Poe, he asserted, was "a man of like passions with ourselves,—one who, if weaker in his weaknesses than many, and stronger in his strength, may not have been so bad, nor yet so good, as one and another have painted him" (p. 107). Asserting that "the essential part of an artist's life is that of his inspired moments," Stedman sensibly argued that "from first to last he was simply a poet and man of letters, who rightly might claim to be judged by the literary product of his life" (p. 111).

Stedman's purpose in analyzing Poe's poetry was to draw attention away from such familiar works as "The Raven" and "To Helen" so as to demonstrate that the essential Poe is to be found elsewhere, in such poems as "The Sleeper," "The Conqueror Worm," "The Haunted Palace," and "The City in the Sea," its pictorial qualities suggestively compared to the paintings of Turner and "that sublime madman, John Martin." In describing these as poems of loss, of the "Irreparable," works in which "the tomb, the end of mortality, is voiceless still," Stedman explicitly recognized that they do not offer the expected consolation of Christian theology, that they are not based on the revelations, as Holland would have it, of "The Great Book." "If you would find the beginning of immortality," he asserted, "seek some other oracle" (pp. 113-115).

Stedman regrets that the literary marketplace did not allow Poe to devote himself more consistently and purposefully to poetry. Rather, Poe's "intellectual strength and rarest imagination are to be found in his '*Tales*'" to which, along with "literary criticism, his main labors were devoted" (p. 117). Although primarily concerned as a critic with poetry, here Stedman wrote appreciatively and suggestively of Poe's fiction. In making the obligatory comparison, he does judge Hawthorne both the more "spiritual" and the more "masculine" of the two writers. However, in analyzing the great power of Poe's fiction, he found a serious purpose,

> a feeling that in the realms of psychology we are dealing with something ethereal, which is none the less substance if we might but capture it. They are his resolute attempts to find a clue to the invisible world. Were he living now, how much he would make of our discoveries in light and sound, of the correlation of forces! He strove by a kind of divination to put his hand upon the links of mind and matter, and reach the hiding places of the soul. (p. 117)

As in his treatment of the poetry, Stedman argued that Poe's fiction embodies a vital imaginative quest for understanding of man's place in the universe, one which should be appreciated even though it could not be placed within the context of traditional religion.

Stedman based his primary argument for Poe's importance in American literature on the aesthetic power of his work in both prose and verse. Responding directly to Dr. Holland's Christian didacticism, he urged his readers to "accept him, then, whether as poet or romancer, as a pioneer of the art of feeling in American literature. So far as he was devoted to art for art's sake, it was for her sake as the exponent of beauty. No man ever lived in whom the passion for loveliness so governed the emotions and convictions . . . . This consecration to absolute beauty made him abhor the mixture of sentimentalism, metaphysics, and morals, in its presentation [of the New England writers]" (p. 121). Although Stedman argued that Poe's excessive concern with beauty at the expense of truth limited the scope of his achievement, his essay is a remarkably compressed and lucid exposition of the great power of Poe's art.

Stedman well understood the broader cultural significance of his battle for public acceptance of both Poe and Whitman. Poe, he wrote in *Scribner's*, "represents, or was one of the first to lead, a rebellion against formalism, commonplace, the spirit of the bourgeois. In this movement Whitman is his countertype at the pole opposite from that of art; and hence they justly are picked out from the rest of us and associated in foreign minds" (p. 121). Stedman was attempting to change America's familiar conception of itself, especially as that image had been formulated by the great high priest of the middle class, Dr. Holland. Stedman's most basic message was directed to those who may have been intimidated by the condemnatory attacks on Poe's character: "After every allowance, it seems difficult for one not utterly jaded to read his poetry and tales without yielding to their original and haunting spell" (p. 108).

With the publication of the essay in *Scribner's*, Stedman felt, as he explained to John H. Ingram, that he had "done with Poe."[16] "I cannot, and will not, figure as a *Poe specialist*," he wrote to William Winter in 1883 (*LL* 2: 219). As it turned out, of course, his "Edgar Allan Poe," which has been called "probably the most comprehensive essay on Poe before 1900" (Hyneman, p. 51), marked the beginning of an involvement with Poe as critic, editor and advocate that would last until Stedman's death in 1908. Whatever his intentions, Stedman became the best-known and most effective American Poe "specialist" of this period.

The response to the *Scribner's* essay astonished Stedman. He "received over a score of letters about it," as he wrote on 13 May 1880 to Thomas Wentworth Higginson, and it was favorably reviewed in such periodicals as the *Nation*, on April 29, and the *New York Times*, April 19th (*LL* 2: 212). So great was the interest in the essay that Houghton, Mifflin published it as a monograph the next year. In England it was released in this form by Sampson, Low.

Next, Stedman contributed an introductory "Comment on the Poem" to the deluxe edition of *The Raven* published by Harper and Brothers in 1884. This edition features twenty-six illustrations by the French artist, Gustave Doré. Sadly, Doré's rather affected drawings reflect the well-known decline in artistic power of that prolific illustrator, who died before the publication of the book. Perhaps the best comment is to be found in the *Atlantic*:

> The figure which stalks, or stiffens, or writhes, through the varying scenes is the melodramatic Poe as he has been too often conceived,—a man of shattered nerves, haunted by phantasms of fear, half crazed . . . . Such a preconception of Poe, such romancing about his sorrows, probably underlie the misrepresentations of which the illustrations are guilty . . . . In opposition, however, to the impression of Poe given by the cuts stands Mr. Stedman's remarkably just criticism and estimate of this particular poem among Poe's other verse. As he says, it is not the poet's best in

imagination, in passion, or in the lift of its melodies; it is nevertheless his greatest because of the wide reach of its power. The comment makes a complete monograph on the subject.[17]

The first critical history of American poetry, Stedman's *Poets of America* (1885) became, like the earlier volume on the Victorian poets, the standard text. Placed between the chapters on Longfellow and Holmes, "Edgar Allan Poe," a reprinting of the *Scribner's* essay with slight revisions, clearly proclaimed the importance of its subject. Four years later, Stedman again gave public recognition to Poe's status as a major American writer by featuring him prominently in volume six of the *Library of American Literature*, which Samuel Clemens's publishing firm, Charles L. Webster, brought out in eleven volumes (1889-90).[18]

Poe figures centrally in Stedman's next major publication, the *Nature and Elements of Poetry* (1891), a series of lectures which he delivered at Johns Hopkins and which were published in the *Century* before Houghton, Mifflin brought them together in book form. His purpose here is to mediate between two contrasting native traditions, the aesthetic, as represented best by Poe's insistence that beauty is the sole aim of art, and the moral, as represented by Emerson's emphasis on the spiritual or truth content of poetry. Stedman's formal definition of poetry as *"rhythmical, imaginative language, expressing the invention, taste, thought, passion, and insight, of the human soul"* is confessedly based on Poe's succinct statement that poetry is "the *Rhythmical* Creation of Beauty" (*Nature and Elements*, p. 44).

On 29 December 1893, Herbert Stuart Stone, one of the principals in the new publishing firm of Stone and Kimball, wrote to Stedman urging that he undertake the editorship of a new edition of Poe. Since in the course of outlining his expectations for the edition he also defines the publishing philosophy of this remarkable firm, the letter is given in full (and with Stone's spellings allowed to stand):[19]

Cambridge, The 29th day.

Edmund Clarence Stedman, Esq.

New York City

Dear Sir:—We have in contemplation—almost in preparation a rather large undertaking in which we should like to have your aid. Taking a suggestion from the pretty little edition of Jane Austen's novels which J. M. Dent & Co. of London, brought out last year: we have thought of publishing an edition of the writings of Edgar Allan Poe. If you will stop to think a moment, we believe you will realize that there is not a decent edition of Poe's works in existence. The best is probably that edited by R. H. Stoddard which came out in 1883. At best that was no more than ordinary. It was gotten up with an absence of taste in manufacture quite usual and was far from adequate. We are trying to make good books—beautiful books:—we are trying first of all to publish poetry in suitable form and it seems really very appropriate that we should attempt primarily to set off Poe's writings as well as possible. It has occured to us that you might consent to undertake the editorship of the edition. As far as we had planned there would probably be eight volumes containing the writings as follows:—

Volumes I and II	Tales of the Grotesque and Arabesque
Volumes III	Humorous Tales
" IV	Narrative of Arthur Gordon Pym
" V	Poems
" VI, VII	The Literati
" VIII	Miscellanies.

We are in hopes of having Volumes I and II illustrated by photogravures from sketches by that clever young English decorator, Mr. Aubrey Beardsley. We have also written to Mr. Elihu Vedder, regarding the illustrations for the poems. It seems to us that he is the most *thoughtful*—perhaps the most intellectual of our American illustrators. Mr. Howard Pyle might be able to do the work if Mr. Vedder did not care to. The books would be printed either at the DeVinne Press in New York or the University Press here in Cambridge. The paper used would be some rough laid paper and the edges would be deckled. In fact we should use all our endeavors to make the books beautiful—worthy first of memory of Edgar Allan Poe and secondly of the name and reputation of the Editor. We trust you may see your way clear to undertake this task, which ought, we think, to be rather a pleasant one. That we may not appear to be presumptuous in writing you thus—as strangers:—we beg to introduce ourselves by saying that we have in press books by Maurice Thompson, Eugene Field, Joaquin Miller, Grant Allen, Louise Chandler Moulton, Gilbert Parker, Hamlin Garland, and Stuart Merrill—all—with two or three exceptions—books of poetry. So far we have done nothing well—we have made several attempts and learned much. Before long we expect to make one book—at least—which will be—not bad. At present we send you a copy of Mr. Joaquin Miller's latest book which will—in a measure—show what we are trying to do.

Awaiting your reply, we are, Sir,

Very truly yours

Stone and Kimball

Herbert Stuart Stone

Worn out by the unexpectedly great effort required to bring out the *Library of American Literature*, Stedman had determined never to undertake demanding editorial projects again. But he had broken his resolve and agreed to edit, as a companion to his *Victorian Poets*, a major collection for Houghton, Mifflin, *A Victorian Anthology*. He was at work on this project when Stone's letter came. We must remember that since he spent his days on Wall Street, he was forced to find time for literary work during the evenings and weekends. But he simply could not reject this proposal. Long a lover of beautiful books, he no doubt was moved by the efforts of Herbert Stone and Ingalls Kimball, both still Harvard undergraduates, to bring to America a dedication to printing as an art similar to that which had been inspired by William Morris's work with the Kelmscott Press in England. And of course Stedman would have been taken immediately by the appropriateness of this firm's selection of Poe as the American author whom it would honor by publishing a complete illustrated edition in the new style. He did, however, set two conditions before accepting the project: that George Edward Woodberry, author of a cold but scholarly biography of Poe published in 1885, be hired as co-editor and that the edition be a complete re-editing of the text (*LL* 2: 225). In a letter of 10 January 1894 Stone agreed to Stedman's stipulations, and expressed the hope that "finally ... the 'ideal edition of Poe' is a possibility—we trust a probability. We are quite ready to do anything in our power to bring it to a successful event."[20]

Working closely and harmoniously with Stone, Stedman and Woodberry were able to bring out all ten volumes of *The Works of Edgar Allan Poe* within two years of undertaking the project, 1894-95. Woodberry served as the primary "text expert" and supplied the biographical "Memoir," published in the first volume (pp. 3-87). Expanding his compressed essay for *Scribner's*, Stedman wrote introductory essays on the tales (1: 91-121), the literary criticism (6: xi-xxvi), and the poetry (10: xiii-xxxv). A reprint of *The Works* is available today from Arno at $250.00.

In addition to the regular trade edition, Stone and Kimball published a large paper edition limited to two hundred and fifty copies. Four drawings by Aubrey Beardsley, commissioned by the publisher, appeared in this edition only: "The Murders in the Rue Morgue," "The Black Cat," "The Masque of the Red Death," and "The Fall of the House of Usher." Since these drawings are not widely known, they have been reproduced here.[21]

Elihu Vedder, the publisher's first choice for general illustrator, had created the frontispiece for Harper's deluxe *The Raven*, which was illustrated by Doré. He had scored a great success with his illustrations for an edition of *The Rubaiyat of Omar Khayyam*, published in 1884. Regretfully, he declined the project. Stone explained his position in the letter to Stedman of 10 January 1894: "It is a question whether he can ever get the "Rubaiyat" out of his mind, sufficiently, to create a comparatively new style for himself." The selection of the popular Albert Edward Sterner came about as a result of a suggestion of Richard Watson Gilder, who had succeeded Holland as editor of *Scribner's* (now the *Century*). Stone explained to Stedman in a letter of 12 March 1894: "Did you know that the *Century* Company had thought of doing a Poe—and that Sterner would have been its illustrator? I am anxious to know what you think of him for he is enthusiastic over Poe and wants to do the work."[22] Evidently Stedman consented, and Sterner was hired. The *New York Times* in its enthusiastic review of the edition observed that "Mr. Sterner's pictures show that he worked himself thoroughly into the Poe mood when he made them."[23] D. L. Maulsby, in an extended review for the *Dial*, "The Renascence of Poe," called Sterner's illustrations "a distinct addition," showing "great sympathy with the weirdness and beauty that gave tone to the tales."[24] Much closer to the truth, however, is the understated comment of the *Atlantic*, that "the imaginative illustrations have scarcely the quality of Poe's own creative genius."[25]

From the first Stedman recognized that Griswold's text was inadequate, and he accepted the responsibility of attempting to perfect it. He and Woodberry wrote in the "General Preface" for the edition (1: xvii), dated 28 October 1894, that

> after the lapse of nearly half a century, something more may be exacted from those who have had the custody of a great writer's works, and something more is due from those who care for the literature of the country. Poe's fame has spread as widely through the world as that of any imaginative author of America; and longer neglect of the state of his text would be discreditable to men of letters

among us, now that his works have passed by law into the common property of mankind.

The editors accepted the responsibility of explaining their editorial procedures fully, and they did so both in the "General Preface" and in notes to individual works. They adopted the sound editorial principle of printing as the "authentic text" the "last form having Poe's authority." They were able to make use of Poe's textual notes in the margins of his own copies of three works: the *Tales, The Raven and other Poems*, and *Eureka*. Wherever possible, they consulted his manuscripts, and collated works published by Poe in more than one place during his lifetime. Volume ten is a variorum edition of the poetry. In these matters it would be hard to fault the editors' principles, and one must admire their dedication and diligence in attempting to discover and reproduce Poe's final intention.

Strictly committed to honoring Poe's intentions in substantives, the editors nevertheless confess to what is, from the perspective of modern editorial practice, an unacceptable freedom in dealing with accidentals. They report that "the punctuation, and all that concerns typographical style, has been modified to accord with later usage and taste, and generally the editors have exercised free judgment in all matters not affecting the integrity of the text" (1: x). In 1903 Stedman reported to one correspondent that "I *repunctuated the entire writings*" (his emphasis; *LL* 2: 230). Similarly, the editors adopted the scheme of rearranging the tales and presenting them under headings of their own devising. Although Stedman and Woodberry deserve credit for producing "the first American collected edition having any serviceable notes and critical apparatus," they generously left a good deal of work for later textual scholars to do and—to undo.[26]

The true significance of the edition, however, lies elsewhere, in what it accomplished for Poe's reputation. The reviewer in the *Athenaeum*, after pointedly identifying a number of representative textual errors—primarily mistakes of omission—concludes: "Take it for all in all, however, this is the best edition of Poe's works which has yet been published, and as regards typography and general 'get-up' it is in every way a desirable acquisition."[27] The *New York Times* used the occasion of its review of an edition which promised to be "final" and which seemed to carry "the stamp of authority," to certify Poe's status as a major American writer: "The time of conflict over the poet and his poetry has passed, and his fame and influence are living."[28] Similarly, in her "Chicago Letter" for the *Critic* Harriet Monroe asserted that it would be

> difficult to exaggerate the importance of this edition to our conception of Poe. For the first time his work has careful editing, all irregularities of the text and eccentricities of punctuation being removed. And what is more important, Mr. Stedman gives the tales a symphonic unity by his orderly arrangement.... A great writer is at last sympathetically presented, so that the phases of his mind develop harmoniously in the reader's imagination. The gain to Poe's reputation will be incalculable. His biography is, perhaps, yet to be written; but this edition of his works will probably establish its claim to be definitive. No more sympathetic interpreter of the mystic harmonies of this man of genius will ever appear to challenge Mr. Stedman's masterly presentation of his work.[29]

Monroe's review suggests that in judging this edition we should keep in mind at least two criteria: its success in meeting the most exacting standards of modern textual scholarship and its ability to meet the needs of its own time for an edition which would make Poe's work accessible. Clearly, it met the second requirement, if not the first.

A number of reviewers expressed dismay over what Monroe termed the "iciest New England formalism" of Woodberry's "Memoir." The great warmth of Stedman's essays, however, struck a responsive chord with these and other reviewers. As the *Athenaeum* predicted in its review of the first four volumes, "A revulsion of feeling will be created in the minds of those who have hitherto regarded Poe as some monstrosity of nature. Such words as these, coming from a man of Mr. Stedman's eminence, cannot miss their aim."[30]

As the leading critic and historian of American poetry, Stedman edited a major anthology to mark the turn of the century. In the introduction to *An American Anthology, 1787-1899*, published by Houghton, Mifflin in 1900, he insisted even more strongly than before on Poe's centrality: "Has any singer of our time more demonstrably affected the rhythmical methods of various lands than Poe with his few but haunting paradigms? ... It is now pretty clear, notwithstanding the popularity of Longfellow in his day, that Emerson, Poe, and Whitman were those of our poets from whom the old world had most to learn.... Years from now, it will be a matter of fact that their influences were as lasting as those of any poets of this century" (xxiv).

Evidently, Stedman's words in praise of Poe had not been universally convincing. In 1900 and again in 1905 he was not chosen by the select group of one hundred electors to join the newly-established Hall of Fame for Great Americans in New York City. President Hadley of Yale, one of the electors, explained why Poe had been kept out:

"Poe wrote like a drunkard and a man who is not accustomed to pay his debts."[31] There is evidence, however, to suggest that the opinion of the people at large at this time was far more favorable than that of the distinguished electors. In an article published in the *Independent* on 16 August 1900, "Guesses at Fame," Thomas Wentworth Higginson reported on two newspaper polls requesting readers to name the best American writer. Poe topped the ballot in the survey of the *Brooklyn Eagle* and came in a close second (behind Jonathan Edwards) in the poll of the *Minneapolis Times* (Hubbell, p. 94). After Poe failed of election the second time, Stedman, who normally avoided such controversies, went public. In "Poe, Cooper and the Hall of Fame," published in the *North American Review*, 16 August 1907, he chastised his fellow electors in an impassioned tribute to Poe's genius:

> On your conscience, fellow judges, whether you are realists or dreamers, jurists, scholars or divines, pay some slight regard to that voice of the outer world, which one of our own writers termed the verdict of 'a kind of contemporaneous posterity'; note that there is scarcely an enlightened tongue into which Poe's lyrics and tales have not been rendered.... That he was poor and headstrong is true; that he was the congenital victim of an abnormal craving for stimulants, now accounted a disease, is true; but what of all this beside the gift that made its shining way against such odds—beside one's gratitude for his crystalization of our inchoate taste and for the recognition which his poetry and romance did so much to gain for the literary product of his native land. (pp. 805-806)

Perhaps—at last—this appeal succeeded; Poe was elected to the Hall of Fame on the next ballot in 1910 (Hubbell, p. 94). But that honor came after Stedman's death on 18 January 1908. Stedman's thirty-year campaign for Poe had—at last—achieved its goal. He had explained the motive for his life-long advocacy of Poe in a letter to John H. Ingram written after the publication of his essay in *Scribner's*: "Poe exercised a great fascination over me, in my youth. I knew his works by heart, and as you see, have analyzed them closely and with more than ordinary critical *reverence*" (*LL* 2: 216-217).

NOTES

[1]"The Magazine," *Scribner's* 17(1878), 146-147.

[2]*Century Magazine*, 23[n.s. 1](1881), 164.

[3]"A Heresy of Art," *Scribner's*, 3(1872), 744-745.

[4]"Our Garnered Names," *Scribner's*, 16(1878), 896.

[5]*Scribner's*, 10(1875), 692, 696, 699.

[6]*Scribner's*, 11(1876), 802, 803.

[7]Esther F. Hyneman, *Edgar Allan Poe: An Annotated Bibliography* (Boston, 1974), p. 33.

[8]*Galaxy*, 6(1868), 741. For an analysis of Benson's short career as a magazinist, see my "Between Realism and Romanticism: The Curious Career of Eugene Benson," *ALR*, 14(1981), 242-261.

[9]See Alice L. Cooke, "The Popular conception of Edgar Allan Poe from 1850 to 1890," *UTSE*, 22(1942), 145-170; and Dudley R. Hutcherson, "Poe's Reputation in England and American, 1850-1909," *AL*, 14(1942), 211-233.

[10]"Edgar Allan Poe," *Harper's Monthly*, 45(1872), 557-568.

[11]"Charles Baudelaire," *Nation*, 27 April 1876, p. 280. James's concluding phrase about Poe's "genius" should not be disregarded. For evidence of what James may have learned from Poe, see Christopher Brown, "Poe's 'Masque' and *The Portrait of a Lady*," *PoeS*, 14(1981), 6-8. In "Poe and James on the Art of Fiction," *PoeS*, 13(1980), 4-8, Elsa Nettels explores "the number of points at which the critical principles of Poe and James coincide." See also James W. Gargano's essay on Poe and James elsewhere in this book.

[12]"Recent Literature," 40(1877), 373. See also the angry notice of Gill's book in the *Nation*, 11 April 1878, p. 248.

[13]For an analysis of Stedman's literary career, see my *Edmund Clarence Stedman* (Boston, 1977).

[14]This letter is reproduced in full in my "Whitman and the Magazines: Some Documentary Evidence," *AL*, 44(1972), 228.

[15]*Scribner's* 20(1880), 124. Stedman modified the essay slightly for its appearance in his *Poets of America* (Boston, 1885), pp. 225-272. My quotations are taken from *Scribner's* and page references are given in the text.

[16]Letter of 30 June 1880. Quoted in Laura Stedman and George M. Gould, M.D., *Life and Letters of Edmund Clarence Stedman* (New York, 1910), 3: 216 (Hereafter cited in the text as *LL*).

[17]"Illustrated Books," *Atlantic Monthly* (1884), 132. For a favorable treatment of Doré's work, see the *Academy* 3 November 1883, pp. 296-297.

[18]*Library of American Literature* (New York, 1890), 6: 429-469. Stedman used: "To Helen," "The Raven," "The Fall of the House of Usher," "To One in Paradise," "Israfel," "The Cask of Amontillado," "The City in the Sea," "Ulalume," "The Poetic Principle," "The Tale-Writer and His Art," selections from *Marginalia*, and "Annabel Lee." In this volume Stedman included as well Sarah Helen Whitman's "The Portrait" and excerpts from her *Edgar Poe and His Critics*, 215-217. A brief biography appears in 11: 570-571. To represent the opposition to Poe, Stedman included excerpts from Griswold's "Memoir," 7: 285-288. Similarly, in 8: 228, he published Richard H. Stoddard's "Miserrimus," from which I take the following:

> His faults were many, his virtues few.
>
> . . .
>
> He glimmered apart
> In solemn gloom,
> like a dying lamp in a haunted tomb.
> He touched his lute with a magic spell,
> But all his melodies breathed of hell,
> Raising Afrits and the Gouls,
> And the polled ghosts
> of the damnèd souls.

[19]This letter is owned by Columbia University and is quoted with the permission of the University.

[20]This letter is owned by Columbia University and is printed by permission of the University.

[21]A. E. Gallatin, *Aubrey Beardsley: Catalogue of Drawings & Bibliography*, (New York, 1945), pp. 57-58. The Beardsley illustrations that appear at the end of this study are reproduced, courtesy of Brian Reade, who holds copyright, from his *Aubrey Beardsley* (New York and London, 1967)—plate numbers as in Reade.

[22]These letters are owned by Columbia University and are printed by permission of the University.

[23]"The New Edition of Poe," *New York Times*, 9 February 1895, pp. 2-3.

[24]"The Renascence of Poe," *Dial*, 1 March 1895, p. 139.

[25]"The New Poe," *Atlantic Monthly*, 77(1896), 552.

[26] Burton R. Pollin, "The Text," *Collected Writings of Edgar Allan Poe* (Boston, 1981), 1: 42.

[27] Untitled review, 28 March 1896, p. 407.

[28] "The New Poe," p. 3.

[29] *Critic*, 5 January 1895, pp. 15-16.

[30] Untitled review, 21 December 1895, p. 86.

[31] Quoted in J. B. Hubbell, *Who Are the Major American Writers?* (Durham, N.C., 1972), pp. 94-95.

The Murders in the Rue Morgue (Plate 337)

The Black Cat (Plate 338)

The Fall of the House of Usher (Plate 339)

The Mask of the Red Death (Plate 340)

CONTRIBUTORS

Maurice J. Bennett, University of Maryland, is author of several studies of Poe. His most recent—on Poe and Borges—appeared in *Poe and Our Times: Influences and Affinities* (1986).

Joan Dayan, Associate Professor of Comparative Literature at Queens College and of Comparative Literature and French at CUNY Graduate Center, is author of *Fables of Mind: An Inquiry into Poe's Fiction* (1987). She is working on a book, "History and Poetic Language."

Dennis W. Eddings, Professor of English at Western Oregon State College and Secretary-Treasurer of the Poe Studies Association, has published studies of Poe's "Dream-Land" and the Dupin tales, and edited *The Naiad Voice: Essays on Poe's Satiric Hoaxing* (1983).

Benjamin Franklin Fisher IV, Professor of English, editor of *The University of Mississippi Studies in English,* specialist in American and Victorian literature, former Secretary-Treasurer for the American Literature Section in MLA and an officer in many more professional organizations, has published and edited many works on Poe, Southern literature, and on other Americans and Victorian-Edwardians. His latest books are *Frederick Irving Anderson* (1987) and *The Gothic's Gothic* (1988).

James W. Gargano, Professor Emeritus of English and former chairman of the Department of English, Washington and Jefferson College, has edited *Critical Essays on John W. De Forest* (1981) and *Critical Essays on Henry James* (2 vols., 1987). His studies of American literary figures have appeared in *NCF, SR, JEGP, TSLL, AL, CE, SAQ, AzQ, WHR, HJR,* and *Novel.*

Stanton Garner, independent scholar, has taught at public and private institutions in the U.S.A., Brazil, and Portugal. For many years he was General Editor for the Harold Frederic Edition. He has edited *The Captain's Best Mate* (1966), the journal of a captain's wife aboard a whaleship, written extensively on Herman Melville and Harold Frederic, and published articles on O. W. Holmes, T. B. Thorpe, Stephen Crane, Theodore Dreiser, and Lord Byron. He is currently at work on the life of Melville during the Civil War and the making of *Battle-Pieces.*

Gary Wayne Harner works in the administration at Towson State University and teaches courses in History of Film and writing. He is a Life Member of the Poe Society.

Jerry A. Herndon, Professor of English, Murray State University, has published many studies of American literary figures. An authority on Kentucky writers, he is particularly interested in Jesse Stuart.

David H. Hirsch, Professor of English, Brown University, is author of a book on American fiction and of many studies, including such subjects as Poe, Mary Wilkins Freeman, and issues in criticism. He is editor of *Modern Language Studies*.

David K. Jackson, a Duke University alumnus, is author of *Poe and The Southern Literary messenger* (1934) and co-author with Dwight Thomas of *The Poe Log: A Documentary Life of Edgar Allan Poe* (1987). In 1986 the Poe Studies Association awarded him its highest tribute, Honorary Membership.

Steven E. Kagle, Professor of English, Illinois State University, has published and presented studies of Poe, Hawthorne, Melville, and Whitman, among others. he is probably best known for his work on American Diary literature, including this series: *American Diary Literature 1607-1800* (1979), *Early Nineteenth Century American Diary Literature* (1986), and *Late Nineteenth Century American Diary Literature* (1988). For ten years he served as editor of *Exploration*, a journal on literature of travel and exploration; recently he has been helping to edit a book of essays on Phillis Wheatley and finishing a novel.

J. Gerald Kennedy, Professor of English at Louisiana State University, has recently published *Poe, Death, and the Life of Writing* (1987). He is working on a book about the image of Paris in American expatriate writing.

Richard Kopley, Associate Professor of English, Pennsylvania State University, DuBois Campus, is editor of the *Poe Studies Association Newsletter*, former compiler of "International Poe Bibliography," and organizer of the conference, "*Arthur Gordon Pym* and Contemporary Criticism" (1988). His series of articles on *Pym* appeared in *SAF* and *SAR*. He has published a study of "Bartleby, the Scrivener" in *ATQ* and prepared a study of four hitherto unknown sources for "The Murders in the Rue Morgue."

Kent Ljungquist, Professor of English, Worcester Polytechnic Institute, is the author of *The Grand and the Fair: Poe's Landscape Aesthetics and Pictorial Techniques*, co-editor of Cooper's *The Deerslayer*, and author of articles on Poe, Thoreau, Melville, and

Cooper. He is also a past Vice President and President of the Poe Studies Association.

Cameron Nickels, Professor of English, James Madison University, is author of studies on American humor and American periodicals. He is currently engaged on a book about American humor.

Glen A. Omans, Professor of English and former chairman of the Department of English, Temple University, is a specialist in Poe and in Victorian literature. His articles have appeared in several periodicals. His book, *Passion and Poe*, appeared in 1986.

Robert J. Scholnick, Dean of Graduate Studies, Arts and Sciences, and Professor of English, the College of William and Mary, is author of many articles on nineteenth-century American literature and culture. The essay included in this collection is an outgrowth of his *Edmund Clarence Stedman* (1977). He is completing a full-scale study of Walt Whitman and science.

April Selley, Assistant Professor of English, College of Saint Rose, Albany, New York, has published poetry, as well as articles on Emily Dickinson, H. P. Lovecraft, and J. F. Cooper. She has also delivered several papers about film. Her current project is a book-length study of posthumous narrators in the works of seven American authors, including Poe.

Roberta Sharp teaches English at California State Polytechnic University, Pomona. Her dissertation treated Poe's attitude toward science. She is author of articles and reviews on American authors.

David E. E. Sloane studied Poe with Richard Wilbur and Arlin Turner. Professor of English, University of New Haven, he is author of *Mark Twain as a Literary Comedian*, editor of *The Literary Humor of the Urban Northeast, 1830-1890*, and *American Humor Magazines and Comic Periodicals*, and author of articles on Poe in *ATQ*.

E. Kate Stewart teaches English at University of Arkansas, Monticello. Author of *Arthur Sherburne Hardy: American Man of Letters* (1986), she has also published articles on Poe, in *UMSE* and *PoeS*, as well as essays on American periodicals and American humor.

Bruce I. Weiner, Associate Professor of English and currently chairman of the Department of English, St. Lawrence University, is author of several studies of Poe, including *The Most Noble of*

Professions: Poe and the Poverty of Authorship (1987), and of American magazines. He is at work on a study of early American magazines and the growth of American culture.

Liliane Weissberg teaches in the Department of German, University of Pennsylvania. She has published articles on American and German literature and literary theory, edited a German anthology of Poe's writings on women, *Ligeia und andere Erzählungen*, and has forthcoming a monograph on Poe. She is completing a study, "*Geistersprache*: Philosophical and Literary Discourse in the Late Eighteenth Century."

INDEX

Academy 249
Addison, Joseph 115
Aderman, Ralph M. 93
Alcott, Bronson 1
Allan, Frances 8
Allan, John 174
Allen, Hervey 174, 175
Allen, Michael 46, 47, 51, 61, 192
Allston, Washington
  WORKS: "Address to Great Britain" 1, 24; "Amy Robsart" 9, 12, 22; "Art" 6; "Beatrice" 9, 10, 11, 12, 14, 22, 23; "Belshazzar's Feast" 23; "Composition" 12; "Contemplation" 9, 10, 11, 15, 22; "The Dead Man Restored to Life by Touching the Bones of the Prophet Elisha" 23; "Evening Hymn" 10, 11, 12, 13, 14, 22, 23; "Form" 15; "Introductory Discourse" 6; "Italian Shepherd Boy" 10, 22; "Jacob's Dream" 13; *Lectures on Art* 2, 3, 5, 10, 24, 25, 26; "Life Study of Ann Channing" 13, 14; *Monaldi* 2, 15, 21, 24, 26; "Moonlit Landscape" 13; "On the Statue of an Angel, by Bienaimé, in the Possession of J. S. Copley Greene, Esq." 6; "A Roman Lady Reading" 9, 10, 11, 12, 22, 23; "Rosalie" 9, 11, 12, 13, 14, 16, 17, 18, 20, 21, 22, 23, 24; "Samuel Taylor Coleridge" 11; "Self-Portrait" 12; "Song" 20, 21; "Sonnet on the Group of the Three Angels before the Tent of Abraham, by Raffaelle, in the Vatican" 6; "The Spanish Girl in Reverie" 10, 11, 12, 13, 14, 16, 17, 23; "The Spanish Maid" 1, 16, 24; *The Sylphs of the Seasons, and Other Poems* 24; "A Tuscan Girl" 10, 12, 16; "The Tuscan Girl" 16, 17, 24; "Una in a Wood" 10, 11; "The Valentine" 9, 10, 11, 12, 13, 14, 22, 23
Alterton, Margaret 48, 50, 51, 61, 62, 64, 75, 87, 192
American Journal of Science and Arts 164
American Museum of Literature and the Arts 114, 115
American Review 200
Anthon, Charles 88
Apollo Belvedere 7, 9, 13
Arnold, Benedict 238
Arnold, Matthew 198, 251, 252
Athenaeum 249, 252, 267, 268
Atlantic Monthly 247, 249, 254, 259, 262, 266
Auden, W. H. 203, 216
Bailey, J. O. 87
Baldwin' Monthly 242, 246
Bandy, W. T. 222, 245
Barbour, Brian 94, 100
Barrett, Elizabeth B. 213, 214, 215, 216
Baskett, Sam S. 187
Basler, Roy P. 113, 127
Baudelaire, Charles 12, 218-225, 231, 233, 247, 248, 249, 251, 253, 254, 259, 270
Baum, Paull F. 188
Beach, Joseph Warren 202
Beadle's Monthly 239-246
Beardsley, Aubrey 264, 266, 271

Bell, Michael Davitt 85, 87
Benson, Eugene 258, 270
Benton, Richard P. 182, 187
Bible (biblical) 1, 23, 173, 195, 196, 197
Bier, Jesse 209, 216
Bird, Robert Montgomery 17
 WORKS: *Sheppard Lee* 178
Bittner, William 176
Blackwood's Edinburgh Magazine 45-65, 189, 192
Blair Hugh 74
Blake, William 200
Bloom, Harold 77, 80, 87
Bonaparte, Marie 73, 75, 168, 174, 176
Borges, Jorge Luis 167, 174
 WORKS: *The Aleph and Other Stories* 174
Brewster, Sir David 154-166
 WORKS: *Letters on Natural Magic* 154, 155, 163, 164, 165; *Treatise on Optics* 155
Bristol Journal 2
British Quarterly Review 249
Broadway Journal 174, 180, 227, 236
Brooks, Cleanth 198
Brooks, Douglas 172
Brooks, Nathan C. 114, 127
Brown, Charles 200
Brown, Charles Brockden 147, 168, 175
 WORKS: *Edgar Huntly* 168, 169
Brown, Christopher 270
Brown, Thomas 50
Brownson, Orestes 61
Bryant, William Cullen 103-104, 251, 252, 257
Buranelli, Vincent 112, 144, 145
Burch, Frances F. 216
"The Buried Alive" 54
Burke, Edmund 62, 65

Burr, C. Chauncey 233
Burton's Gentleman's Magazine 146, 152
Bush, George 195, 197, 206
Byron, George G. N., Lord 182, 226, 240
Cabau, Jacques 225
Campbell, Killis 61, 177
Carlson, Eric W. 128, 129
Carlyle, Thomas 10, 118
Carter, Boyd 169, 175
Casale, Ottavio M. 128, 129
Century 263, 266
Channing, Ann 13, 14
Channing, William Ellery 1, 10
Charvat, William 61, 66, 74
Chivers, Thomas Holley 118, 207
Chorley, Henry F. 79
Clemm, Maria 240
Coleridge, Samuel Taylor 2, 3, 4, 10, 15, 23, 26, 27, 50, 56, 64, 65, 80, 99, 118, 126, 133, 145, 179, 180, 187, 198, 200, 202, 207
 WORKS: *Biographia Literaria* 10, 50, 207; "On the Principles of Genial Criticism" 2
Colley, Ann C. 188
Collins, William 14
Columbian Lady's and Gentleman's Magazine 75
Combe, George 146, 147, 151
Cooke, Alice L. 233, 270
Cooke, Philip Pendleton 48, 113, 127
Cousin, Victor 3, 10, 50
Craig, Hardin 75
Crane, Hart 233
Crane, Stephen 103
Crépet, Jacques 223, 224, 225
Critic 267
Curti, Merle 61

INDEX

Dana, Richard Henry 1
Dana, Richard H., Jr. 8
Daniel, John M. 233
Dante 14, 132
Daughrity, K. L. 192
Dauber, Kenneth 87
Davidson, Abraham A. 7
Davidson, Edward H. 102, 208
Davy, Sir Humphrey 163
Dayan, Joan 43, 181, 187
de Bergerac, Cyrano 87
Decamps, Alexandre 254
Delacroix, Eugene 254
Democratic Review 192, 193
DeQuincey, Thomas 47, 50, 63, 64, 125
de Sallé, Marie 70, 72
Dial 23, 266
"Diary of Sir Humphrey Davy" 163, 164
Dickens, Charles 48, 114, 127
Dickinson, Emily 187
Dickstein, Morris 202
Dillingham, C. T. 259
Doré, Gustave 262, 266, 271
Downing, Andrew 75
Downing Letters 240
Doyle, Arthur Conan 130
Drake, Nathan 62
Edinburgh Review 46
Edwards, Jonathan 269
Eggelston, Edward 256
Eliot, T. S. 45, 59, 96, 225, 247
Emerson, Ralph Waldo 1, 10, 32, 43, 94, 103, 106, 112, 113-129, 130-145, 194, 195, 206, 235, 240, 263, 268
English, Thomas Dunn 178, 187
Fairfield, Francis Gerry 257, 258
    WORKS: "A Mad Man of Letters" 257
The Family Physician 147, 148, 149, 150, 151

Family Library Historical Series 154
Faulkner, William 186
Fawcett, Edgar 250-253
    WORKS: "Poe As a Poet" 252, 253
Felton, C. C. 1, 24
Fichte, J. G. 56
Finney, C. L. 207
Fisher, Benjamin Franklin IV 62, 64, 75, 101, 127, 128, 144, 176, 177, 192, 216
Flagg, Jared B. 7, 14, 26
Fletcher, Giles 7
Floyd, Albion 227, 231
Ford, Mrs. M. A. 152
Foucault, Michel 178, 186
Fouqué, F. H. K. 66, 67
Foust, R. E. 87
Fowler, Alastair 177
Friederick, Reinhard H. 174
Fukuchi, Curtis 177
Fuller, Margaret 1, 7, 10, 14, 22, 23, 25
Fusco, Richard A. 128, 188
Galaxy 258
Galloway, David 145
Gargano, James W. 113, 127, 209, 270
Gerdts, William H. 13, 16, 22
The Gift 114, 179, 180, 181
Gilder, Richard Watson 266
Gill, William F. 250, 259, 270
Glanville, Joseph 44, 108, 119, 120, 121, 125
Godey's Lady's Book 23, 174, 236
Godwin, William 56, 57
Goethe, J. W. 227
Goncourt, Jules and Edmond 86
Graham, George R. 231, 233
Graham's Magazine 1, 23, 24, 25, 61, 117, 152, 179, 233, 244, 245

284   INDEX

Grave, S. A. 61, 62
Greenough, Horatio 7
Grice, H. P. 195
Griffith, Clark 64, 65, 128, 216, 217
Griswold, Rufus 24, 130, 226-234, 235-246, 266, 271
    WORKS: *The Poets and Poetry of America* 24
Halleck, Fitz-Greene 88
Hammond, Alexander 101
Harpers' 47
Harper's Monthly 256, 259
Harte, Bret 252
Hastings, Warren 165, 168, 175
Hawks, Francis Lister 92
Hawthorne, Nathaniel 1, 10, 24, 39, 45, 60, 74, 94, 100-106, 111, 131, 215, 217, 247, 249, 252, 257, 261
    WORKS: "The Artist of the Beautiful" 1; *Twice-Told Tales* 24, 215
Heath, James E. 48
Heine, Heinrich 78, 87
Hershell, Sir John 165, 166
Higginson, Thomas Wentworth 262, 269
Hirsch, David H. 64
Hirst, Henry B. 178, 187
Hoffman, Charles Fenno 235, 236, 237, 238, 240
Hoffman, Daniel 144, 145
Hoffmann, E. T. A. 45, 50, 54, 56, 59, 62
Holland, Josiah Gilbert 256, 257, 258, 260, 261
Holmes, Oliver Wendell 1, 22, 23, 29, 251, 252, 263
The Home Journal 242, 246
Hook, Theodore Edward 175
Houghton, Marie Louise Shew 176
House, Humphrey 188

Hubbell, J. B. 269, 272
Hudson, Ruth Leigh 128
Hulme, T. E. 194, 198
Hume, David 49, 50
Hungerford, Edward 146, 152
Hutcherson, Dudley R. 233, 270
Huxley, Aldous 252
Hyneman, Esther F. 270
Independent 269
Ingleby, Clement Mansfield 209, 216
Ingram, John Henry 176, 235-245, 250, 259, 262, 269
International Review 259
Ireland, William Henry 64
Irving, Washington 93, 113-129, 257
Irwin, John 74
Isani, Mukhtar Ali 175
Jackson, David K. 93
Jacobs, Robert D. 63, 66, 74, 213, 214, 217
Jakobson, Roman 196
James, Henry 45, 85, 130, 244, 247-255, 259, 270
    WORKS: *The American* 253; "The Beast in the Jungle" 254; *French Poets and Novelists* 248, 249; *The Golden Bowl* 248; "The Jolly Corner" 253; *The Portrait of a Lady* 253, 270; *Roderick Hudson* 249, 253; *A Small Boy and Others* 249, 254
James, William 249, 254
Jameson, Anna 16
Jannaccone, Pasquale 74
Johns, Elizabeth 15, 16, 24, 25
Jones, Howard Mumford 209, 210, 216
Joseph, Gerhard J. 188
Joyce, James 12, 186
Kames, H. H., Lord 74

INDEX

Kant, Immanuel 2, 3, 30, 43, 50, 56, 64, 118, 133
Keats, John 194-208
   WORKS: "Ode to a Nightingale" 194-208
Kennedy, J. Gerald 101, 102, 244
Ketterer, David 45, 86, 87, 176
Knickerbocker Magazine 60, 61
Koontz, Dean R. 188
Kopley, Richard A. 159, 160, 174
Kuhn, Thomas S. 206
Lamb, Charles 180, 187
Lang, Andrew 250
Lathrop, George Parsons 257, 258, 259
Lauber, John 113, 127
Laverty, Carroll D. 152
Lawes, Rochie W. 102
Lawrence, D. H. 86, 106
Leland, Charles G. 149, 150
"Le Revenant" 52
Lessing, G. 64
Levine, Stuart and Susan 101
Lewis, Matthew G. 62
Lind, Sydney E. 152
Link, Franz H. 75
The Literary World 251
Ljungquist, Kent 102, 193, 217, 244, 245
Locke, John 30-44, 48-53, 56, 61, 64, 65, 103
Locke, Richard Adams 80, 165
   WORKS: "The Great Moon Hoax" 165, 166
London Magazine 47
Longfellow, Henry Wadsworth 1, 24, 33, 236, 238, 251, 252, 263, 268
   WORKS: *Ballads and Other Poems* 24
Lowell, James Russell 86, 118, 252, 254, 260
Lull, Raymond 181

Lynch, Anne B. 235, 237
Mabbott, Maureen Cobb 193
Mabbott, Thomas Ollive 44, 46, 57, 93, 113, 118, 119, 120, 127, 165, 168, 174, 175, 177, 189, 192, 193, 243, 244
Macaulay, Stewart 232
Macaulay, T. B. 66, 165, 168, 175
Mackenzie, Alexander Slidell 88, 92
Maginn, William 53
   WORKS: "The Man in the Bell" 53
Mandeles, Chad 17, 22, 28
Martin, John 260
Martin, Terence 63
Maulsby, D. L. 266
Mayo, Robert D. 62
Melville, Herman 30, 31, 45, 94, 100, 104, 131, 143
Michelangelo 6, 21
Miles's Phrenology 146
Miller, James E. 110
Miller, John Carl 242, 244
Miller, Stephen F. 92
Milton, John 107, 131
Moldenhauer, Joseph J. 76, 86, 87
Monroe, Harriet 267, 268
Mooney, Stephen L. 98, 102
Moore, Robert G. 88, 92, 93
More, Paul Elmer 247
Moss, Sidney P. 25, 64, 93
Mott, Frank L. 60
"The Mysterious Portrait" 176
Nation 247, 250, 259, 262
Washington *National Intelligencer* 226, 227, 228, 234
National Magazine 227
Neal, John 167
Nettels, Elsa 270
The New-England Magazine 61
New York Mirror 44

New York Evening Mirror 213
New York Sun 80
New York Times 249, 250, 262, 266, 267
Newbern Spectator 88, 92, 93
North American Review 1, 16, 61, 269
Novak, Barbara 13, 14, 26, 27
O'Donnell, Charles 86, 87, 170, 176
"Oenone" 6
Oliver, E. J. 188
Olney, Clark 86
Omans, Glen A. 26, 28
Osgood, Fanny 228, 235
Ossian 182
Ostrom, John Ward 114, 127
Page, Curtis Hidden 221
Pall Mall Gazette 250, 251, 252
Panofsky, Erwin 177
Parkes, Henry Bamford 94, 100
Parlour Magazine 152
The Partisan 178
Pasteur, John I. 88, 92
Patmore, Coventry 185, 188
Pattee, F. L. 226
Paul, Howard 192
Paulding, James Kirke 47, 88, 93
Peck, G. W. 233
Philadelphia Gazette 44
Phrenological Journal 246
Poe, Edgar Allan
  WORKS: "Al Aaraaf" 36, 80, 107, 207; *Al Aaraaf, Tamerlane, and Minor Poems* 24; "Annabel Lee" 252, 253, 254, 271; "The Assignation" 181, 186, 188; "Autography" 1, 22, 92, 117; "The Bells" 253; "Berenice" 34, 37, 38, 41, 42, 43, 47, 66-75, 151, 152, 153, 163, 187, 216; "The Black Cat" 100, 106, 178, 213, 216, 266; "The Cask of Amontillado" 101, 106, 253, 271; "A Chapter of Suggestions" 158; "The City in the Sea" 260, 271; "The Coliseum" 24; "The Colloquy of Monos and Una" 78, 99, 102; "The Conqueror Worm" 260; "The Conversation of Eiros and Charmion" 96, 98, 99; "A Descent into the Maelstrom" 74, 98, 100, 194; "The Domain of Arnheim" 66-75, 157; Drake/Halleck review 74; "Dream-Land" 80; "Eleonora" 82, 178-188; *Eureka* 32, 42, 43, 67, 75, 76-77, 80, 83, 85, 102, 110, 118, 129, 130, 145, 160, 236, 249, 267; "The Facts in the Case of M. Valdemar" 97, 98, 100, 101, 138; "The Fall of the House of Usher" 48, 58, 59, 64, 65, 95, 100, 105-106, 131, 143, 146-153, 194, 213, 216, 252, 266, 271; "Fifty Suggestions" 186; "For Annie" 111; "The Gold-Bug" 74, 222, 254; "Hans Pfaall" 76-87; "The Haunted Palace" 24, 260; "How to Write a Blackwood Article" 30, 34, 42, 46, 50, 51, 63, 96, 179, 189, 216; "The Imp of the Perverse" 106, 116, 135; "The Island of the Fay" 161, 217; "Israfel" 2, 5, 17, 18, 20, 271; "King Pest" 157; "Landor's Cottage" 157; "The Landscape Garden" 70, 75; "Ligeia" 34, 36, 37, 39, 40, 41, 42, 43, 44, 59, 64, 95, 100, 106-109, 111, 113-129, 182, 183, 213, 216, 217, 253; "Loss of Breath" 46, 56,

63, 96; "Maelzel's Chess Player" 155, 163; "The Man of the Crowd" 157, 194, 216; "The Man That Was Used Up" 64; "Marginalia" 104, 212, 213, 271; "The Masque of the Red Death" 109, 178, 215, 266, 270; "Mellonta Tauta" 79; "Mesmeric Revelation" 98, 118, 221; "Metzengerstein" 176, 216; "Morella" 34-38, 43, 126, 216; "MS. Found in a Bottle" 84, 87, 155, 165, 216; "The Murders in the Rue Morgue" 62, 81, 130-145, 158, 254, 266; "The Mystery of Marie Rôget" 143; "Mystification" 156; *The Narrative of Arthur Gordon Pym* 84, 87, 155-162, 165, 167-177, 248, 249, 253; "Never Bet the Devil Your Head" 57, 117; "The Oval Portrait" 216; "Peter Snook" 192; "The Philosophy of Composition" 6, 25, 66, 74, 94, 125, 145, 195, 196, 200, 202, 207, 217; "The Pit and the Pendulum" 35, 46, 57, 96, 100, 101, 102, 104, 194, 254; *Poems* (1831) 17, 24, 80; "The Poetic Principle" 6, 25, 81, 82, 84, 94, 104, 145, 271; *Politian* 88-93; "The Power of Words" 81, 99; "A Predicament" 46, 52, 96; "The Premature Burial" 57, 65, 96, 100, 101; "The Purloined Letter" 101, 130-145; "The Raven" 67, 111, 125, 178, 189-193, 194-208, 209-217, 236, 237, 240, 252, 254, 260, 262, 266, 271; *The Raven and Other Poems* 215, 267; "Shadow—A Parable" 96, 97, 100; "Silence—A Fable" 97, 100, 188; "The Sleeper" 24, 260; "Some Words With a Mummy" 57, 96; "The Spectacles" 41, 176; "The Sphinx" 58; "The System of Dr. Tarr and Professor Fether" 57, 64, 146, 186; "A Tale of the Ragged Mountains" 42, 97, 98, 100, 157, 158, 167-177; "The Tale-Writer and His Art" 171; *Tales* 267; *Tales of the Grotesque and Arabesque* 179; "Tales of the Folio Club" 143, 183; *Tales of Mystery and Imagination* 247; *Tamerlane and Other Poems* 24; "The Tell-Tale Heart" 38, 100, 106, 113, 178, 213, 218, 219, 220, 221, 222, 223, 224; "'Thou Art the Man'" 143, 161, 165, 166; "To Helen" (1831) 2, 8, 9, 11, 12, 260, 271; "To One in Paradise" 271; "Ulalume" 109-111, 249, 252, 253, 271; "Von Kempelen and His Discovery" 163, 164, 165; "William Wilson" 35, 100, 114, 128, 147, 156, 194, 253; *The Works of Edgar Allan Poe* 265

Poe, Elizabeth Arnold 167, 169, 175, 176, 238

Poe, Henry 167, 168, 169, 172, 174, 175, 176, 177
  WORKS: "Monte Video" 168, 169, 175

Pollin, Burton R. 154, 155, 163, 165, 174, 175, 176, 177, 187, 233, 248, 255, 272

Pope, Alexander 37

Porte, Joel 244
Preuss, Henry Clay 226-234
　WORKS: *The Artist and Other Poems* 227; *Fashions and Follies of Washington Life* 232; "From Columbus Crocket to General Grant on the Indian Policy" 232; *God Save Our Noble Union and Other Poems of the Times* 232; "Ode on a Grecian Flute" 227; *Songs of National Harmony, Peace and Brotherhood* 233; (with Stewart Macaulay) "The Star-Spangled Home of the Free" 232; "A Vision of Freedom" 232
Price, Vincent 144
Pyle, Howard 264
Quarterly Review 46
Quinn, Patrick F. 128, 221, 222
Quintilian 66, 74, 117
Radcliffe, Ann 45, 54, 62, 131
Mrs. Radcliffe 54, 131
Reaves, Gibson 166
Redfield, J. S. 222
Rees, J. K. 67, 74
Regan, Robert 215
Reid, Thomas 48, 49, 50, 61
Richard, Claude 74
Richardson, Edgar Preston 1, 10, 24, 25, 26
Rickels, Patricia and Milton 244
Riley, I. Woodbridge 61
Rossetti, Dante Gabriel 16, 251
Rourke, Constance 165
Rousseau, J. J. 50
Rush, Benjamin 147, 151, 152, 178
　WORKS: *Medical Inquiries and Observations* 152
Rutledge, Anna Wells 29
Saint-Pierre, B. 179, 187

Sainte-Beuve, C. A. 218
Saintsbury, George 249, 250
Satan 184
Savage, John 233
Schelling, F. W. J. 2, 50, 56
Schiller, F. 227
Schlegel, A. W. 2
Schroeter, James 113, 127
Scott, Sir Walter 22, 60, 62, 75, 154, 179
　WORKS: *Kenilworth* 22
Scribner's Monthly 256, 257, 258, 259, 260, 261, 262, 263, 265, 266, 269
Shakespeare, William 109, 131
Shaw, George Bernard 76, 86
Shelley, Percy Bysshe 67, 74, 85, 198, 207, 226, 240, 243
Sigourney, Lydia Huntley 88
Silliman, Benjamin 164
Simms, William Gilmore 178, 179
"Singular Recovery from Death" 54, 57
Sloane, David E. E. 75, 152, 153, 187
Smith, Elizabeth Oakes 235-246
　WORKS: "Autobiographical Notes" 239, 240, 244, 245 246; "Autobiography" 236, 239, 240, 241, 242, 243; "Edgar A. Poe" 236, 237, 239, 240; "The Life-Preserving Coffin" 245; *The Poetical Writings of Elizabeth Oakes Smith* 236; "The Sinless Child" 236; "The Water" 236; *Woman and Her Needs* 235
Smith, Seba 235, 244, 245
　WORKS: *Powhatan: A Metrical Romance* 244, 245
Smithline, Arnold 128
Snow, Sinclair 187

INDEX

Snowden's Ladies' Companion 75
Sophocles
 WORKS: *Oedipus Rex* 131, 182
Southern Literary Messenger 47, 75, 79, 88, 92, 93, 114, 146
"The Sphinx. An Extravaganza Sketched in the Manner of Callot" 54, 55, 57
Spitzer, Leo 197
Stanard, Jane Stith 8, 13
Stebbins, Theodore E., Jr. 26
Stedman, Edmund Clarence 256-272
 WORKS: *Nature and Elements of Poetry* 263; "Poe, Cooper, and the Hall of Fame" 269; *Poets of America* 263
Steele, Richard 36, 44
Sterner, Albert Edward 266
Stewart, Dugald 50
Stoddard, Richard H. 227, 228, 229, 231, 233, 234, 235, 259, 264, 265, 271
 WORKS: "Miserrimus" 229, 231, 271; *Recollections Personal and Literary* 227
Stone, Herbert Stuart 263, 264, 266
Stovall, Floyd 113, 127
Swedenborg, Emanuel 115
Swift, Jonathan 34, 35, 38, 44
Swinburne, A. C. 183, 251
Symbolist writers 12, 16, 56
Symons, Julian 144
Tate, Allen 45, 86
Tennyson, Alfred, Lord 6, 39, 187, 188, 214, 251, 252
Thomas, Dwight R. 92, 93
Thompson, G. R. 45, 46, 58, 101, 113, 127, 175
Thompson, John R. 233

Thoreau, Henry David 105, 130-145, 206, 257
Tieck, Ludwig 45, 54, 59
Tintner, Adeline 248
Tintoretto 7
Titcomb's Letters to Young People, Single and Married 256
Titian 7
Transcendentalist Club 1
Tucker, George 87
Turner, J. W. M. 260
Tuveson, Ernest Lee 49, 61, 62, 63
Tyler, Alice Felt 244
The United States Magazine and Democratic Review 61, 236, 237, 239, 241, 245
"Uriel in the Sun" 11, 13
Vedder, Elihu 264, 266
Veronese 7
Walker, I. M. 179
Warren, Robert Penn 198
Warren, Samuel 47, 63, 189, 190, 191, 192, 198, 199
 WORKS: "The Bracelets" 189-193; "Passages from the Diary of a Late Physician" 189; *Ten Thousand a Year* 189
Watts, Emily Stipes 245
Weiner, Bruce Ira 101
Weiss, Susan Archer Talley 176, 192, 258
Westminster Review 250
Whisnant, David E. 152
White, Lizzie 238
White, Thomas W. 47, 48, 75
Whitman, Sarah Helen 75, 174, 226, 232, 233, 235, 236, 238, 239, 240, 241, 242, 243, 244, 245, 246, 271

Whitman, Walt 111, 130, 197, 198, 206, 248, 257, 260, 261, 262, 268, 270
Wilbur, Richard 102, 105, 107, 132, 146, 147, 181, 187
Williams, William Carlos 76, 86
Willis, N. P. 231
Wilson, John 47
Wiltenburg, Joy 186
Wimsatt, W. K., Jr. 155
Winter, William 262
Woodberry, George Edward 144, 265-268
Wordsworth, William 10, 15, 26, 78, 87, 198, 200, 201, 20
   WORKS: "She Dwelt Among the Untrodden Ways" 15; "She Was a Phantom of Delight" 15; "The Solitary Reaper" 15; "Strange Fits of Passion Have I Known" 15; "Three Years She Grew" 15; "To a Highland Girl" 15; "To My Sister" 15
Wright, Nathalia 7, 24, 25, 27
Wylie, Clarence R., Jr. 101
Yeats, William Butler 12

WITHDRAWN